ALSO BY MICHAEL A. McDONNELL

The Politics of War: Race, Class, and Conflict
in Revolutionary Virginia

MASTERS OF EMPIRE

MASTERS OF EMPIRE

GREAT LAKES INDIANS AND THE MAKING OF AMERICA

MICHAEL A. McDONNELL

HILL and WANG

A DIVISION OF FARRAR, STRAUS AND GIROUX

NEW YORK

Hill and Wang
A division of Farrar, Straus and Giroux
18 West 18th Street, New York 10011

Library of Congress Cataloging-in-Publication Data
Names: McDonnell, Michael A.
Title: Masters of Empire : Great Lakes Indians and the Making of
  America / Michael McDonnell.
Description: New York : Hill and Wang, 2015. | Includes index.
Identifiers: LCCN 2015022331 | ISBN 9780809029532 (hardback) |
  ISBN 9780374714185 (e-book)
Subjects: LCSH: Ottawa Indians—Huron, Lake, Region (Mich. and
  Ont.)—History. | Indians of North America—First contact with
  Europeans. | Huron, Lake, Region (Mich. and Ont.)—History. |
  Great Lakes Region (North America)—History. | United States—
  History—Colonial period, ca. 1600–1775. | BISAC: HISTORY /
  Native American.
Classification: LCC E99.O9 M36 2015 | DDC 977.4/01—dc23
LC record available at http://lccn.loc.gov/201502233

Designed by Jonathan D. Lippincott

3   5   7   9   10   8   6   4   2

In memory of Bob, Yvonne, and Robbie Thomas

CONTENTS

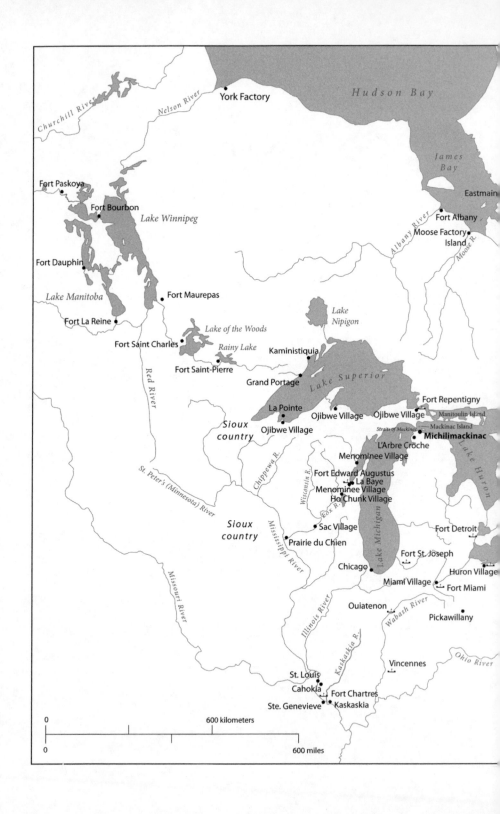

Hudson Bay

James Bay

Churchill River

Nelson River

York Factory

Eastmain

Fort Paskoya

Fort Bourbon

Lake Winnipeg

Albany River

Fort Albany

Moose Factory
Island

Moose R.

Fort Dauphin

Lake Manitoba

Fort Maurepas

Lake Nipigon

Fort La Reine

Lake of the Woods

Fort Saint Charles

Rainy Lake

Kaministiquia

Fort Saint-Pierre

Grand Portage

Lake Superior

Red River

La Pointe

Ojibwe Village

Ojibwe Village

Fort Repentigny

Manitoulin Island

*Sioux
country*

Ojibwe Village

Mackinac Island

Straits of Mackinac

Michilimackinac

L'Arbre Croche

Lake Huron

Menominee Village

Chippewa R.

Fort Edward Augustus

La Baye

Wisconsin R.

Menominee Village

Ho-Chunk Village

St. Peter's (Minnesota) River

Fox R.

Lake Michigan

Fort Detroit

*Sioux
country*

Sac Village

Prairie du Chien

Mississippi River

Fort St. Joseph

Huron Village

Chicago

Miami Village

Fort Miami

Missouri River

Ouiatenon

Wabash River

Pickawillany

Illinois River

Kaskaskia R.

Vincennes

Ohio River

St. Louis

Cahokia

Fort Chartres

Ste. Genevieve

Kaskaskia

0		600 kilometers	

0		600 miles	

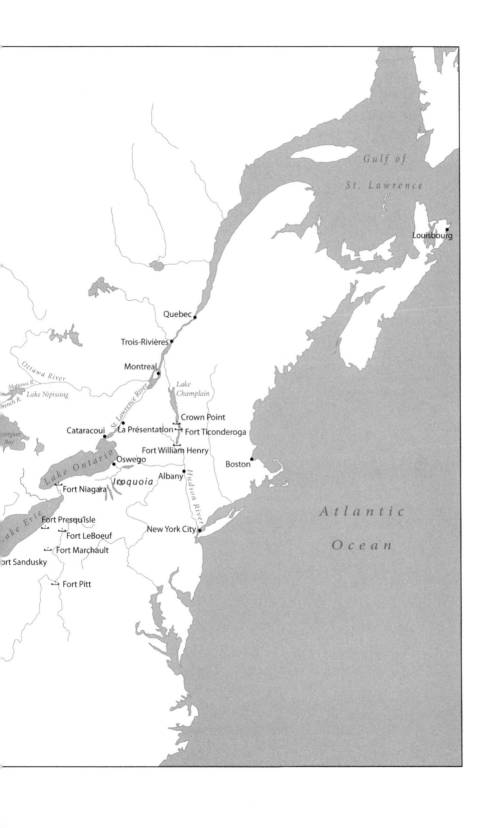

Lake *Superior*

Whitefish Point

N

50 miles

Fort de Repentigny (1750–51)
St. Marys River
Ojibwe Village

St. Joseph
Island

Drummond
Island

Odawa Village (1670s)
Huron Village (1670s)
Mission of St. Ignace (1670–71)
Fort de Buade (1687) †

Mission (1670)
Ojibwe Village
Mackinac Island

Straits of Mackinac

Lake Huron

Odawa Village and Fields (early 1700s)
Fort Michilimackinac (1715)
Mission of St. Ignace (early 1700s)

Bois Blanc
Island

Ojibwe Village

† Mission of St. Ignace (1742)
Waganawkezee
(L'Arbre Croche (1742))

Cheboygan R.

*Lake
Michigan*

Burt Lake

Mullett
Lake

Black Lake

MASTERS
OF EMPIRE

INTRODUCTION:
OLD STORIES AND NEW

THE VIEW FROM MICHILIMACKINAC

In the early hours of a June morning in 1752, the Ohio Valley erupted in violence. At Pickawillany—a Miami Indian village and fortified trading post located at the confluence of several rivers—250 Odawa and Ojibwe warriors burst from the edge of the woods and attacked. In the initial skirmish, they killed 13 of the defenders and captured several more, along with a number of British traders who were residing with the Miami. The remainder of the villagers found refuge in a stockade. They had to watch in horror as the attackers seized one of their captives, a British blacksmith, and stabbed him. As he lay dying, his assailants ripped his heart out and ate it. Next, the raiders killed, boiled, and ate the village chief, Memeskia, in front of his own family. Hurling insults and taunting the defenders, the enemy warriors then melted back into the forest in the direction of a French post at Detroit with at least four English traders in tow.

This attack, far from an insignificant skirmish in the woods, set off a chain reaction of events that culminated in George Washington's attack on French forces at the Battle of Jumonville Glen in the Ohio Valley in May 1754. Pickawillany was thus arguably the opening salvo in the Seven Years' War in America between the two great imperial powers of the eighteenth century, England and France. The war quickly spread to Europe and Asia and ultimately transformed the imperial and global landscape of the early modern world.[1]

The reputed leader of this deadly raid was Charles-Michel Mouet de Langlade. Langlade was what we have come to call *métis*—the son of an Indian woman and a French man. He was baptized in 1729 at Michilimackinac (now Mackinaw City, Michigan), a small but thriving Algonquian-French fur-trading community located at the straits that connected Lake Huron to Lake Michigan. Stories about the part played by Langlade in the violence at Pickawillany are relatively well known. But his exploits did not end there. Indeed, Langlade seems to have participated in most of the imperial conflicts of the latter half of the eighteenth century in North America. He was, for example, alleged to be the leader of the ambush that cut down British general Edward Braddock's expedition against Fort Duquesne in 1755—an event depicted in a celebrated 1903 painting by Edwin Willard Deming that now graces the corridors of the Wisconsin Historical Society (see illustration on page 168). Langlade almost certainly also led the largest contingent of Indian warriors at the so-called "massacre" of Fort William Henry in 1757, the infamous event forever immortalized by James Fenimore Cooper, and later Daniel Day-Lewis, in *The Last of the Mohicans*. And Langlade fought in the Battle of the Plains of Abraham at Quebec in 1759, where he was rumored to be among the sharpshooters who brought down British general James Wolfe.[2]

Surprisingly, given this history of fighting for the French, when New France fell to the British, Langlade forged relations with the incoming conquerors. When a group of hostile Indians seized the newly arrived British garrison at Michilimackinac, during Pontiac's War in 1763 (one of the greatest pan-Indian uprisings in North American history), Langlade and his kin rescued the soldiers and officers and returned them safely to Montreal. Later, during the American Revolution, Langlade joined General Burgoyne on his ill-fated campaign that ended with the Battle of Saratoga, mobilized warriors to fight George Rogers Clark and the Continental Army in the Mississippi Valley, and raised Indian allies against the American general Anthony Wayne in 1794 during the Northwest Indian War. But perhaps most surprising, Langlade, who also had extensive trading interests throughout the Great Lakes, eventually settled in Green Bay, Wisconsin, where he and his father, the first permanent "white" settlers in the state, became known as the "Fathers of Wisconsin."[3]

•

In our era of best-selling biographies of founding fathers, telling Langlade's story was an attractive proposition. But as I began to piece together Langlade's complex biography in more detail, a different story emerged. It quickly became apparent that Langlade's Indian family from the Great Lakes was crucial in facilitating and enabling his movements. Almost everywhere Langlade went, including Pickawillany, warriors from among his Indian kin accompanied him. Indeed, Langlade's actions were explicable only in light of a complex set of Indian politics that lay behind attacks such as that at Pickawillany. Moreover, there were also events—such as Braddock's defeat—at which Langlade was almost certainly *not* present, regardless of what he and his descendants later claimed. But warriors from Michilimackinac *were* there, and their involvement in these early battles had a significant impact on the course of the Seven Years' War in America. As I traced Langlade and his family's story back in time across the seventeenth and eighteenth centuries, I realized, too, that the Indian community from which he emerged was crucial to the region for centuries. When Europeans arrived on the scene, Langlade's kin continued to play a powerful part. They were the Anishinaabe Odawa of Michilimackinac—and Langlade's story quickly became their story.[4]

For too long now, the history of the Anishinaabeg of the Great Lakes has been largely hidden behind Euro-American stories—perhaps typified by the image of Langlade himself as a "white" settler. Even the name Anishinaabeg—the term that these Native peoples use to refer to themselves, meaning the real, or original, peoples—is unfamiliar to most modern readers. Instead, we know them only, if at all, through the names Europeans began to call them in the seventeenth and eighteenth centuries: the Ottawa, Potawatomi, Chippewa, Algonquin, Nipissing, and Mississauga. We have often lumped them under the more general category of Algonquian speakers, and not recognized that they all spoke Anishinaabemowin—a distinct subset of Algonquian. And we have failed to appreciate their significance in the history of the continent. Despite their central location in what the French called the *pays d'en haut*—literally, the high country, or the vast territory stretching west from Montreal to the Mississippi River and encompassing most of the Great Lakes and their tributary rivers—the Anishinaabeg have appeared only at the edges of European and American histories, shadowy figures on the frontier, as it were. They have remained largely invisible to Euro-American observers.[5]

In this reading, the communities in which Langlade moved come to attention only when Europeans noticed them and wrote about them. Yet while many newcomers passed through the Great Lakes in the seventeenth and eighteenth centuries, few stayed and settled. The resulting snippets of correspondence and reports from transient Euro-American visitors have given us a fragmented history of the place, the era, and the peoples who lived there. And while historians have of late begun to take more note of the importance of some Indian groups at particular moments in time, Native Americans—especially in the *pays d'en haut*—have almost invariably appeared and disappeared at a correspondent's whim, apparently a volatile, fleeting, and ephemeral presence throughout the colonial period. They have been noticed by historians only when called onstage by imperial officials and scribes. They are often described as being led, and led astray, by Europeans or go-betweens such as Langlade. They have been effectively dependent on early Europeans for their history. And we share the legacy of these Europeans, struggling to comprehend a people with an autonomous history because we rely on fragmented accounts. When we look at the Anishinaabeg from the perspective of successive waves of newly arrived Europeans, little makes sense.[6]

But tracing Langlade's story to his origins in this Anishinaabe world at Michilimackinac, and particularly amid the thriving Odawa (or Ottawa) settlements at the straits, made me pause long enough to try to make sense of this history. His story compelled me to stay focused on one people and one place over the longue durée. It forced me to comprehend a tale that situated the Odawa at the center of their own history. In doing so, I was surprised to find that few people had taken this story seriously, despite the profound strategic and commercial importance of the straits of Michilimackinac for most of the seventeenth and eighteenth centuries and despite the unique and powerful role the Odawa played in the region. Significantly, the region was never invaded or settled during the colonial period—at least not by Europeans. This fact alone gave the Odawa a history that differs sharply from that of the better-known stories of the Iroquois, Shawnee, Cherokee, Creek, and others whom we now know a great deal about. Their story also differed from that of many of their own kin living farther south at Detroit and in the Ohio Valley. Indeed, the Odawa's long history of mastering empires and keeping them at bay ultimately helped them to evade the Indian removals of the nineteenth century and remain where they were into the twentieth. Many remain there still. Yet, more than that, the history of the Odawa at Michilimackinac revealed just how much the Anishinaabeg of the Great Lakes had shaped early America.[7]

•

The warriors who attacked Pickawillany in 1752 were Odawa and their close kin, the Ojibwe. They had traveled more than 450 miles to face off against Memeskia. Most of them came from a cluster of small but important villages nestled around the straits of Michilimackinac, at the far north end of Michigan's Lower Peninsula, where visitors today can take a ferry to Mackinac Island or stay in one of the many hotels in the tiny tourist town rather grandly named Mackinaw City. In the mid-eighteenth century, this was Indian country. More specifically, it was one of the most important sites in the expansive and still-expanding Anishinaabe world. Thousands of Native families called the straits home and lived in dozens of towns and villages along the coastlines and islands of Lakes Huron and Michigan and up into Lake Superior. While these settlements were sometimes multiethnic, they were primarily communities of the peoples we now call Ojibwe (or Chippewa) and Odawa (or Ottawa). The Ojibwe were more often associated with the falls at St. Mary's (Sault Ste. Marie) that drained Lake Superior into Lake Huron, but by 1752, Ojibwe villages could be found throughout the region and as far south as Mackinac Island and the northeast coast of the Lower Peninsula, near Cheboygan. Likewise, the Odawa were primarily associated with the straits at Michilimackinac that separate Lakes Michigan and Huron. Yet Odawa settlements could be found across the islands in the region and all along the east and west coasts of Lake Michigan.[8]

Among the most important of these towns in 1752 was Waga-nawkezee (the French called it L'Arbre Croche, or Crooked Tree). Waganawkezee had been recently settled by Odawa who had lived for many years at the straits of Michilimackinac. In the early 1740s, they moved to more fertile lands about twenty miles southwest of the straits, along the eastern shore of Lake Michigan between present-day Cross Village and Harbor Springs. There, in a warm microclimate behind the dunes and below the colder central plateau, the Odawa thrived. They had long mastered the teeming fisheries of the Lakes, and they grew enough corn and other vegetables to trade with other nations and sell provisions to the small nearby French garrison and canoe-loads of fur traders who had to stop at the straits. They also made a decent profit from building, selling, and repairing the canoes of sojourning Europeans and Indians alike. In the winter, they traveled south in smaller family groups to do some fur trapping themselves. But always they returned in the spring. The straits had been home for many years. Waganawkezee would continue to be home for many more.[9]

Among the thousands of Odawa who lived at Waganawkezee was Langlade's own Indian family. Born around 1729, either at the Odawa village at the straits or at their winter camp farther south at Grand River, Langlade had the advantage of an important Anishinaabe lineage. His mother, Domitilde, was the sister of one of the most influential *ogimaag* (chiefs) of the settlement. Nissowaquet, or, as the French called him, La Fourche (the Fork), headed up a powerful family line, or *doodem* (pronounced "doh-dem"), that was based at the straits but had tendrils all across the Lakes. While perhaps dozens of Anishinaabe *doodemag* (the plural form of doodem) made their home at Michilimackinac, and later Waganawkezee, several stood out over time and collectively helped make the settlement at the straits an Odawa stronghold. Together with the ogimaag and the people of the Sinago and Kiskakon doodemag, Nissowaquet and the "nation de la Fourche"—as they were often called by the French—created an important nucleus of Odawa families at the straits.[10]

In turn, from this base at Waganawkezee, the Odawa were at the center of an expansive weave of relations that helped them dominate the central and upper Great Lakes. Yet they did not dominate it in a way that made immediate sense to newly arriving Europeans. While the Odawa were scattered in towns and villages of varying sizes, most often at strategic or resource-rich lakeshore locations such as La Pointe, Sault Ste. Marie, Manitoulin Island, or Michilimackinac,

Europeans struggled to find permanent villages. Most Anishinaabeg spent winters away from their summer settlements. Sometimes in parallel with this seasonal mobility there existed a longer-term mobility as small groups joined larger communities for a year or two or more, to trade or for safety. Adding to the confusion of Europeans, the particular groupings at summer villages and winter camps did not make for easy identification. Villages were often multiethnic, and sometimes even multilingual, with Siouan and Iroquoian speakers mixed with Anishinaabemowin speakers.[11]

From the start, newly arrived European visitors were quick to believe these mobile multiethnic villages must have been communities of refugees who'd been brought together under pressure of attacks by other Indians—most notably the Haudenosaunee, or Iroquois. Not finding the kind of dense and permanently settled villages and towns they were familiar with in Europe, early French commentators believed they were seeing a world that had collapsed. But as historians have recently uncovered, these were stable and coherent communities to the peoples who lived in them. As Michael Witgen has written, they were held together by "strands of real and fictive kinship" that had been established through trade, language, and intermarriage. These strands intersected and crisscrossed over a vast space, knitting together disparate peoples and places across the *pays d'en haut*. They connected winter bands and village communities in far-flung places. And they shifted across time, as trading and kinship relations changed.[12]

Perhaps the most important glue holding these communities together was the doodem. The historian Heidi Bohaker's pathbreaking work on eastern Algonquian-speaking Anishinaabe peoples suggests that the patrilineal kinship networks called doodemag were fundamental to "Anishinaabe collective identities" during and likely prior to the early period of contact with Europeans. Doodemag identities, usually but not always identified by pictographs based on some kind of other-than-human progenitor such as a squirrel or beaver, were inherited from fathers and implied an obligation toward those with the same lineage. The nuclear family was only one unit, and the smallest, in a series of often overlapping kinship groupings, because membership in a patrilineage automatically bestowed inclusion in a larger kinship unit that cut across band and village lines: the patri-clan, or doodem.

These extended families were "linked by the rights and obligations of kinship to form larger groups to cooperate in production, trade, and warfare."[13]

These kinship ties shaped the political landscape of the Great Lakes region because the Anishinaabeg created new alliances through marriage. Most Algonquian nations practiced some form of exogamy. It was taboo for a man to marry any female—cousin, aunt, niece, and siblings—who belonged to his clan. Among the Anishinaabeg, daughters and sisters generally married outside their doodem, often men from different communities. Though the precise details of these practices varied from nation to nation, and across time, it seems most likely that throughout the upper Lakes, newly married men lived among their wife's kin for a short while before husband and wife returned to the husband's doodem. While a wife would retain her father's doodem for life, her children would take her husband's doodem. Thus, all communities of families invariably contained multiple doodemag and kinship relations.[14]

The doodemag that made up the Odawa communities at Waganaw-kezee used these relations to forge an important place for themselves in the *pays d'en haut*. In his study of the Odawa, the historian James McClurken has shown a relationship between the doodemag at Michilimackinac and trading relations. Noting that the Anishinaabe word *ota'wa'* means "to trade," the French initially called many of the Anishinaabeg with whom they traded Odawa or, as they often wrote it, "Ouatouais." Yet a cluster of families emerged at Michilimackinac who, over time, became dominant figures in this trade and whom the French more commonly called the Odawa. McClurken maintains that this was because these families were originally middlemen for the Huron-Ojibwe trade and each Odawa family "owned" different routes. These routes were geographical paths, but also a set of trading and kinship relations along the way. Marriages were often arranged to turn potential trading partners into family members and so extend kinship ties. Trade rights and routes could be used only by the families who pioneered them and who maintained the gift exchange and kinship ties that assured safe passage.[15]

Yet kinship politics meant that decision making was highly decentralized (to the perennial frustration of European colonial officials).

Each doodem was generally represented by a single leader, an ogimaa, who was chosen by consent of the family based on his war exploits and/or ability to provide for and share goods with friends and family alike. Yet ogimaag had little coercive power. They could only persuade. As Chingouabé, an Ojibwe ogimaa at Michilimackinac, told the French governor in 1695, "It is not the same with us as with you. When you command all the French obey and go to war. But I shall not be heeded and obeyed by my nation in like manner. Therefore I cannot answer except for myself and those immediately allied or related to me." The decentralized nature of authority and decision making was the reason the French had so much trouble understanding Anishinaabe policy toward them. While officials may have been able to extract offers or promises from one or more ogimaag, there was no guarantee that their kin, let alone their villages, would agree.[16]

While this kinship system often confused Europeans, its inherent flexibility was the great genius of Anishinaabe social organization and expansion. Indeed, while this decentralized system led to disagreements among the Anishinaabeg, it almost never led to outright conflict. As one ogimaa told British officials in 1760, "All the Indians in this Country are Allies to each other and as one People." Marriages outside the community allowed for an ever-thickening network of relations across great spaces. They also facilitated the establishment of new villages and communities and the peaceful sharing of resources across the region. Families might use their kin relations to join a different village, or establish a new one. Leaders changed, and doodemag rose and fell in importance. And villages, in turn, waxed and waned in terms of importance to the larger network of Anishinaabe relations depending on the vitality of the relationships created and maintained. Yet because of kinship obligations, these new communities ensured an expansive and powerful network of alliances throughout the Great Lakes. This network helped the Anishinaabeg consolidate their hold on the Great Lakes and underpinned their expansion during this tumultuous period. Ultimately, these relations defined Anishinaabewaki—their territory, or homeland.[17]

European officials struggled to understand how this world worked. They wanted to know where the borders of Anishinaabewaki were, who were its leaders, and how it was governed. When they could not find easy answers to these questions, they often dismissed the Anishi-naabeg as a political force. Yet while many Europeans struggled to understand the kinship-based political-social geography of the *pays d'en haut*, Native peoples themselves did not. The Odawa at the straits of Michilimackinac saw themselves simultaneously as members of par-ticular lineages, doodemag, towns, and a greater Anishinaabe world. They shared close relations with the other Anishinaabe doodemag nearest to them, including those who made up the Ojibwe and the Potawatomi. Together, these three groups would come to be known as the Three Fires Confederacy. But the Odawa also had relations with other Anishinaabe nations farther afield, including the Nipiss-ing, Algonquin, and Mississauga on their eastern and southeastern flanks. Indeed, by the time Europeans arrived on the scene, Anishi-naabemowin speakers could be found from the gulf of the St. Law-rence River as far west as the Mississippi River. Across this great territory, the Anishinaabeg shared a mutually intelligible language, many cultural characteristics, and kinship relations. And while Anishi-naabewaki was not as clearly defined as the French or English colo-nies, or even some of the larger confederacies of Indian nations farther to the south, it was no less powerful (see map on pages 120–21).[18]

Situated at the heart of Anishinaabewaki, the Odawa families at Waganawkezee were well positioned to benefit from this formidable array of relationships. They enjoyed extensive trade relations with thousands of kin across the Lakes. Kinship obligations might mean they were expected to help defend their kin elsewhere—against their Siouian-speaking rivals to their west, for example—but by 1752 at least, the Odawa at Michilimackinac were insulated from direct at-tack; other Anishinaabe communities stood between them and their enemies. Because of their connections with peoples all across the Lakes, they were also well respected for their mediation skills. Many European officials came to realize that if a peace treaty was to last, the Odawa had to broker it.

But the Odawa at the straits also came to play a central part in the history of colonial America because they stood at the heart of the continent, too. For centuries, Michilimackinac was one of the few strategic entry points into and out of continental North America. Any nation, European or Native, wishing to pass back and forth from east to west, or indeed even from north to south, would have to come through either Michilimackinac or the Sault sixty miles to the north. If Michilimackinac was the door to North America, the Odawa, backed up by a powerful array of relations across the Lakes, held the key.[19]

•

Putting the Odawa at Michilimackinac at the center of their own world in turn allows us to think of their history in a very different way from the story that is usually told. As Europeans vied with one another for claims to North America, the familiar tale goes, they destabilized and enmeshed Native groups in an ongoing cycle of trade, dependence, and warfare. While the French focused their efforts on the St. Lawrence Valley and the extraction of beaver pelts from the continental interior, the English and Dutch vied for territory to the south and fought with each other and different Native Americans over both land and trade. Though historians have made much of the creation of "middle grounds" between some Native groups and European powers—places and processes that neither Natives nor newcomers could dominate completely and where new worlds were created—the end result was often the same in the eastern half of North America: Native Americans were eventually defeated, dispossessed, and usually removed from the line of European settlement. In this tale, Europeans drive the story of early America.[20]

But if we face east from Michilimackinac instead of west from Montreal, or Jamestown, the Odawa can tell us a very different story. We might take our cue from some of the earliest Anishinaabe chroniclers themselves. Some time ago now, the historian D. Peter MacLeod noted the similarities across separate Anishinaabe-authored histories written in the nineteenth century. In at least three of these histories, including one by Andrew J. Blackbird of the Michilimackinac Odawa, the coming of Europeans is only a minor part of the story. More important were the numerous and long-standing rivalries and relationships with nations and communities east, west, north, and south of them, especially warfare with the Iroquois. And in all of these Native-authored histories, the Anishinaabeg—not Europeans—stand in the middle of a complex web of social relations, all of which had to be constantly negotiated and renegotiated. Village life at places such as Michilimackinac remained a constant—evolving and adapting to be sure, but present and vital nonetheless. In all of these stories, continuities are emphasized over decline, and Europeans stand at the periphery.[21]

These nineteenth-century Anishinaabe historians—along with many of the new Indian histories that are emerging—have also made clear the need to study European-Indian relations over the longue durée. Often our accounts have relied on a cultural analysis of particular moments—thick descriptions of key events that seem to illuminate or characterize relations between Europeans and Indians. But focusing on these moments alone tends to overprivilege the voice of Europeans. Sojourning Europeans often had little idea of the longer-term context in which they interacted with their Native counterparts. Snapshots of words exchanged over a newly kindled council fire have to be put into the context of Indian history over many years. We need to rely less on European words and more on Native actions over time. In the long run, those actions are usually a more reliable source of meaning.[22]

A tentative "middle ground" might have been established between Europeans and Indians at forts such as the one the French established at Michilimackinac. That middle ground sometimes acted as a bridge between two cultures, or even among many diverse peoples. But for Indians, European posts were only one among many sites of meeting, encounter, and community. Forts and posts such as the one at Michilimackinac were the center of European worlds in the *pays d'en haut*. But they were often only at the edge, or at the margins, of a vast Indian country that surrounded these posts.[23]

We have also misinterpreted the role, and sometimes overestimated the importance, of cultural brokers—men such as Langlade who could seemingly move between two worlds. Imperial officials privileged such men in their orders and correspondence because they were often so dependent on them—as interpreters, mediators, and go-betweens. They were among the few who had access to Indian communities and knowledge about the politics of the *pays d'en haut*. For incoming post commanders, lost missionaries, intrepid new traders in the region—and subsequent historians—men and women who had connections in Indian country were an invaluable resource.[24]

Nonetheless, these go-betweens play a secondary, supporting role.

Though we have for a long time privileged the stories of a handful of European missionaries, traders, explorers, troops, and settlers who seemingly foreshadowed the world to come, for much of the seventeenth, eighteenth, and into the nineteenth century, the straits of Michilimackinac remained Indian country. Even the history of men such as Langlade cannot stand apart—it has to be woven into that rich and compelling world. The primary story of this era and this region has to be a Native-driven story.[25]

•

Viewed in this way, we can move on from an older story of dependence, and further on even from an idea of mutual dependence between natives and newcomers, and begin to think about a history of the Anishinaabe Odawa at Michilimackinac that emphasizes strength and expansion in the midst of empire. Significantly, there is no real evidence throughout this long era to suggest that the Odawa viewed either the French or the English, or even the late-arriving Americans, as a threat to their existence. Instead, they created alliances or provoked wars with others that often conflicted with European interests. They threatened Europeans themselves and at several critical moments did not hesitate to turn on them when it was in their interests to do so, paying little regard to the possible consequences. The Odawa were able to exploit European imperialism when it came, and they did so mostly for their own purposes. The collective strength of the Anishinaabeg across the *pays d'en haut* meant they were too important to be ignored, and too powerful to be cowed.

The hold that different Anishinaabe communities had on key strategic and resource-rich points throughout the Lakes meant that they dominated the newcomers at the local level, too. At Michilimackinac, the Odawa allowed the French and later the English to maintain a post at the straits in return for generous provisions, presents, and offers of alliance. Yet European posts did not mean European dominance. Quite the contrary. For most of the colonial period, Europeans at Michilimackinac were dependent on the Odawa and other Algonquian nations for their very subsistence. They could maintain a tiny post at the strategic crossroads of Michilimackinac only at the invitation of—and as a result of the encouragement of—thousands of Anishinaabeg who lived along the shores of the Lakes nearby. For this reason, the Odawa were able to hold their own and insist on their own terms when it came to dealing with French missionaries, traders, and colonial officials.

With a European post in their midst, the Odawa in particular positioned themselves as key players in what was ostensibly an expanding nation. At Michilimackinac, they exploited the commercially strategic importance of the site and took advantage of the thousands of summer visitors who flocked to their shores to create a reliable subsistence. The prosperity this trade created at the straits contributed to population growth and almost constant expansion outward across the Lakes. While the population at Michilimackinac stayed relatively stable, the extended families who made the straits their home could count on an ever-growing number of kin with whom they could trade, share resources, and rely on as war allies.

As we know from the story of Charles Langlade, this expanding network of relations eventually came to incorporate Europeans, too. French traders along the St. Lawrence who wanted furs quickly came to realize that they needed the patronage of their Anishinaabe counterparts to survive in the turbulent world of the *pays d'en haut*. Fortunately for them, well-connected Odawa women such as Charles Langlade's mother, Domitilde, actively sought out fur trade husbands who would be of benefit to their kin relations. And in marrying French traders, Anishinaabe women created expansive kinship networks that stretched east as well as west and eventually came to encompass peoples and communities that ranged from the Mississippi River to Montreal.[26]

This extensive kinship network, together with the prestige and influence that close relations with French traders brought to the Michilimackinac Odawa offered benefits beyond material goods. Their access to French trade goods enhanced their status in the region and among their own kin. This influence, along with their location at the strategic straits and their mastery of the waters in the region, meant that they were integral to Indian regional diplomacy. Time and again the Odawa brokered peace in the region. Though the French liked to claim the role of peacemakers and mediators among the Indians, the most astute officials realized there could be no lasting peace unless it was first made among Native Americans themselves. And most acknowledged there were no more capable people of bringing peace to the *pays d'en haut* than the Odawa.[27]

Yet the Odawa held the key to war in the region, too. While outsiders had trouble discerning the contours of Anishinaabewaki, the Odawa at Michilimackinac were at the center of a powerful network that expanded over the colonial period. They and their kin dominated the Lakes in the seventeenth and eighteenth centuries and were able to manipulate relations with newcomers, including Europeans, to their advantage. The Odawa at Michilimackinac cleared the region of enemies and rivals and created a secure place for themselves in the heart of the Great Lakes. They also made the straits central to the French and then the British empires in North America, and made themselves indispensable within them. When Europeans tried to sideline the Anishinaabe Odawa at Michilimackinac, as they did in 1700 and 1760, for example, those at the straits showed they could mobilize powerful alliances and orchestrate deadly demonstrations of their power.

•

Such moments also made clear that the Anishinaabe Odawa at Michilimackinac profoundly shaped European imperialism in North America. While Europeans for a long time took a subordinate role in the *pays d'en haut*, the Odawa at the straits and other Anishinaabe and Algonquian peoples across the region together played a critical part in the making of early America. Not one canoe would have survived the trip up to the *pays d'en haut* without the help of Indian guides and translators. Not one fur would have made it to Europe without the intervention of Native trappers and the consensual trade of Indians. Little westward exploration would have taken place without the consent of the people of the straits, and almost certainly no posts would have been built in the heart of Indian country that could provision or protect unwelcome travelers. The French were there because the Anishinaabeg wanted them there. In turn, without the fur trade from the interior, it is unclear how long the French would have stayed in the St. Lawrence Valley. Without Indian alliances and the threat they could pose to powerful rivals such as the Iroquois and English, the French might have survived for considerably less time on the continent than they did. Only their Indian alliances saved them. But those alliances came at a high cost to the progress of European empire.[28]

Subsequently, the French struggled to maintain harmonious relations with nations such as the Anishinaabe Odawa at Michilimackinac. For many years, historians—following in the footsteps of English colonial commentators—have believed that the French somehow better managed their relations with neighboring Native nations. Yet French colonial officials never enjoyed the kind of harmonious relations with the Indians that their English counterparts dreamed they did. While some French traders managed to insinuate themselves seamlessly into Anishinaabe families, French imperial officials, including Jesuit missionaries, rarely did. From the start, French agents of empire were buffeted by the politics of the *pays d'en haut*—a politics over which they had very little control.

The rocky relationship with the Anishinaabeg had serious consequences for French imperial ambitions, as officials were dragged into one war after another between the founding of Quebec in 1608 and the middle of the eighteenth century. As English influence on the continent grew, too, the Anishinaabe Odawa, like others in the region, played the French and English against each other and often embroiled them in new conflicts. Seen in this light, the attack at Pickawillany was not, as often interpreted, a symbol of the strength of French-Indian alliances, but testimony to its weaknesses. When looked at carefully, the raid exposed the limits of French power in an Indian country that was less and less inclined to ignite inter-Indian wars for the sake of European imperialism. Yet, as the result of the attack at Pickawillany also showed, skirmishes in Indian country could still have a significant impact in Europe—and beyond.

In the aftermath of the Seven Years' War—the conflict that the Anishinaabeg had helped trigger—the British inherited French claims to the *pays d'en haut*. But they also fell heir to these uncertain relations. The British learned this when they were suddenly confronted with the conflagration now known as Pontiac's War—a remarkably successful pan-Indian war against the new British regime. Amid the turbulence of war, the Odawa exploited the situation, mediating between different Indian groups and ultimately acting as saviors to the British. Again, though, their actions—along with those of other native groups in the *pays d'en haut*—cost Europeans dearly. Coming on the heels of the end of the Seven Years' War, the British spent thousands of pounds fighting another conflict, and thousands more on councils, provisions, and presents to Indians to bring it to an end. Subsequently, many British officials came to the conclusion that their colonists in America ought to bear some of the expenses of placating Native Americans, and thus they introduced new taxes. In this way the Odawa helped set the fuse that would ultimately ignite the American Revolution.

As tensions between Britain and the colonies exploded into warfare, the British grew more and more dependent on their Native neighbors for help. The Odawa, using their French connections and the presence of the Spanish along the Mississippi, continued to play off European powers during the Revolutionary era and well into the nineteenth century. They promised much but gave little. They were happy to take advantage of British dependence on them even while they disappointed British strategists time and again—often much to the peril of empire. They helped shape the conflict that engulfed the British and the contours of the new international boundaries that resulted. Eventually, as the balance of power shifted toward the growing numbers of American settlers on their southern flank, the Anishinaabe Odawa drew on longer-term strategies to secure a place for themselves in the new American republic. Their struggle to maintain that place is ongoing.

What this long history reveals most, then, is that we cannot understand the history of early America without comprehending Indian country on its own terms. At the very least, a more complete history of this critical period has to take into account a diverse range of viewpoints and perspectives that together shaped European empires and the looming new nations of North America. From offering furs and allowing trade to goading imperial schemers and sparking wars, the Anishinaabe Odawa at Michilimackinac helped precipitate critical turning points in this history. Both French and British dreams of expansive colonies and imperial dominance grew, and foundered—at least in part—in Indian country. Certainly the history of North America would look very different had the nations of the *pays d'en haut* made different choices about their relationships with Europeans. What happened at Michilimackinac mattered. It shaped early America—and the world in which we now live.

1

RECENTERING MICHILIMACKINAC

Standing on the shores of the straits of Michilimackinac or atop the bluffs of Mackinac Island, it is easy to understand why many believed this region to be the birthplace and center of the world. The teeming blue waters of Lakes Huron and Michigan bending away from the narrows both east and westward give an impression that one is standing on a peak of sorts, at the top of the world. Knowledge of where those waters lead only reinforces the idea that Michilimackinac is central. A vast interconnected system of waterways could take a savvy paddler just about anywhere on the continent and beyond. From here, one could travel southwest to Green Bay, St. Joseph's, or Chicago. Short and manageable portages would take you to either the Wisconsin or Illinois River, which in turn empty into the Mississippi. From there, the rest of the continent east of the Rocky Mountains along with the Gulf of Mexico are accessible. Likewise, traveling north from Michilimackinac would take you through Sault Ste. Marie into Lake Superior. From there, the many rivers and lakes that drain into Lake Superior also give access to the north country and even Hudson's Bay. Finally, south and east of Michilimackinac lie Lakes Huron, Erie, and Ontario and Georgian Bay. Skilled canoeists could take one of many routes across these lakes and quickly find themselves heading down the mighty St. Lawrence River toward the open seas of the Atlantic Ocean. From Michilimackinac, anything is possible.

For the Anishinaabeg of the upper country, the land and vital surrounding waters of Michilimackinac were not only geographically central but also the key to their cosmology. In numerous sacred stories, called *aadizookaanag*, or grandfathers, Michilimackinac is literally the birthplace and center of the world. Several important doodemag claimed their origins from the region. Mackinac Island was also the native country of Michabous, the Great Hare. Various stories note that Michabous began rebuilding the world with the island of Michilimackinac. And it is at Michilimackinac that Michabous placed the most fish, and taught people how to catch them. But Michilimackinac was also a place of origin in another sense. While Anishinaabe stories emphasize migration from the east, most commentators agree it was at the straits that the split between the nations of what we now know as the Three Fires Confederacy took place. Here, the groups of families, or doodemag, that would become known as Odawa, Ojibwe, and Potawatomi diverged. As William Warren wrote in the early nineteenth century, when the Anishinaabeg reached Michilimackinac, they separated into three distinct nations "from natural causes." The Odawa, he wrote, "remained about the spot of their final separation." The Potawatomi moved south, and the Ojibwe headed north and west of the straits. Each saw Michilimackinac as a kind of birthplace. So while they divided at the straits, Michilimackinac remained a central, and sacred, place for all Anishinaabeg across the region.[1]

Though it is now little more than a backwater border town between Canada and the United States, Michilimackinac also rapidly became central to European empires in the seventeenth and eighteenth centuries. It was in the first instance a critical node in an extended and expansive French fur trade that sustained empire in the New World. In hindsight, European posts such as the one established at Michilimackinac in the 1680s seem to symbolize the inevitable expansion of European imperialism. From a tiny and struggling settlement along the banks of the St. Lawrence River, the French quickly used bases like Michilimackinac to explore, trade, and claim the entire *pays d'en haut* and beyond, stretching west to Lake Winnipeg and including the Mississippi Valley down to the Gulf of Mexico. In this story, the post at Michilimackinac was an important site—but only one of a string of holdings that suggested French dominance over this region. These posts were the basis upon which the French claimed much of inland North America by the end of the seventeenth century.

Yet a closer look at this story from Anishinaabe perspectives reveals a different tale. For the importance of Michilimackinac to the Anishinaabeg would have far-reaching consequences for European imperialism. From the start of the French venture in North America, events at the straits helped shape developments along the St. Lawrence River and beyond. Native groups, including the Anishinaabeg, quickly enmeshed the arriving French in a world of Indian warfare that almost consumed them. Yet even in the midst of the destructive wars with the Iroquois in the seventeenth century, the Anishinaabeg—and especially the Odawa—created an important link between the French to the east and thousands of Indians to their west. That crucial role helped save the struggling French colony. Subsequently, the Odawa effectively forced the French to build an empire to protect the trade they coveted while they maintained their own key position in the expanding trade. As much as Michilimackinac was central to their world, by the end of the century the Odawa also made it essential to the French. Yet, as important as it became to Europeans, Michilimackinac was, and would remain, Indian country. Never in a position to coerce the Anishinaabeg, the French were dependent on the hospitality and goodwill of their more numerous neighbors and hosts.

•

Along with its geographic centrality and its historic and cultural importance, there were other good reasons why many Anishinaabeg chose to make Michilimackinac home. Foremost among these were its hospitable climate and rich natural resources. The Lakes moderated the temperatures along the shores around Michilimackinac, leading to shorter winters and milder temperatures than points farther north and even in central Michigan to the south. That climate fostered a broader base of natural vegetation, with a mix of coniferous and deciduous forests in the region. Maple, beech, birch, hemlock, and fir could be found near black spruce, tamarack, and cedar stands. It also made the straits one of the more northerly points with a potential to grow corn, since on average there were up to 140 frost-free days at Michilimackinac.[2]

The transitional climate at Michilimackinac induced the Anishinaabeg who stayed at the straits to practice a mixed form of subsistence based on and around this important location. The Lake effect helped moderate the temperature enough to plant corn in the summers, but it was not quite warm enough to rely on corn all year round, or sometimes even from year to year. Thus the Odawa had to supplement their subsistence activities. They did this by moving in smaller family groups during the winter, mainly south toward the Muskegon and Grand Rivers, where they could find a wide variety of game, including black bear, raccoon, squirrel, deer, and moose. But they could also source rich stocks of mink, otter, marten, muskrat, and beaver, all valued for their fur and their flesh. In the spring, the leanest time of the year, Odawa families would begin to regather to collect the sap from maple trees for sugaring and to make and repair canoes from birch bark. Moving back to their permanent villages a little later in the spring, most of the community was involved in preparations for the spawning season of the lake sturgeon, which lasted for approximately two months until the warmer weather of the summer. This was followed by the planting season, supplemented with the gathering and drying of berries, which intensified as the autumn approached.[3]

For the last couple of crucial weeks before the winter, usually about late November, different doodemag, such as the Kiskakon and Sinago, worked together to catch and dry as much lake trout, herring, and especially whitefish as would sustain them in the coming months, before dispersing again in smaller family groups for the winter hunt. Fishing was thus one of the most important economic activities of the Odawa. While they were at the edge of the practicable growing season for corn, the Odawa had access to one of the richest fisheries in the Lakes. Several Frenchmen claimed that the waters around the straits alone could support ten thousand people at Michilimackinac. It was the spot "most noted in all these regions for its abundance of fish." So much so, one priest noted, that the Indians call this place its "native country." The Jesuits believed that fishing was the main reason the Odawa stayed at the straits.[4]

The significance of fishing was also reflected in the importance of the canoe to the Odawa in the upper Lakes. They were renowned for their skills on the water. Using the abundant birch and cedar trees in the transitional zone of the northern Great Lakes, the Odawa had long mastered the art of making hardy canoes that could handle the often turbulent waters of the larger lakes. These craft were essential not just for fishing but also to facilitate Anishinaabe seasonal mobility around the Lakes. The Odawa in particular were well known and admired for their ability to travel across the Lakes. While others undertook canoe travel along the rivers and edges of lakes, few dared venture across the open waters out of sight of land as did the Odawa. They were one of the few groups in the region who did not fear the vast open waters of the Great Lakes. This mastery of the canoe thus put the Odawa in a good position to dominate the Lakes. It would be a key element in their future success.[5]

Certainly, their canoe skills combined with the rich natural resources of Michilimackinac meant that many of the Anishinaabeg became adept traders over time. Usually well provisioned, and often bearing their own surpluses, they were able to exchange goods over long distances across the Lakes. The Anishinaabeg had long acted in this role. Before 1600, they were eager to trade small surpluses—which included beaver skins, fish, and manufactured reed mats, baskets, and tobacco pouches—both to their more mobile neighbors to the north and to the thickly populated agriculturally based Huron peoples to the south. Taking advantage of their neighbors' needs and their own mastery of the Lakes' waters, Anishinaabeg in the central region, and particularly the families that would become known as the Odawa, served as middlemen between different nations.[6]

•

It was only natural, then, that with the arrival of the French in the St. Lawrence Valley, the Anishinaabeg were eager to extend their trade relations for the new goods on offer from Europe. Eyeing the success of the Spanish in Central and South America, the French dreamed of a new world empire of their own. Beginning as early as 1534, the French explored the Grand Banks of Newfoundland and the St. Lawrence River, even planting a colony at Cap-Rouge (Quebec) in 1541. France wanted to set up new colonies and find a direct route to the riches of the East Indies via the ever-elusive Northwest Passage. The French also sought to protect their homeland by extending their borders and enriching their war chest through overseas exploration. But bitter cold, few enticements, and conflict with the local Indians ended these early efforts, and the crown was soon distracted by devastating religious wars that tore the country apart in the latter half of the sixteenth century.[7]

During this period, it was French fishermen who continued quietly to expand the frontiers of France's overseas claims. Norman and Breton fishermen who had long exploited the teeming cod stocks off the Grand Banks of Newfoundland began pushing farther westward into the Gulf of St. Lawrence in search of less crowded waters. As they did so, the Indians they met while drying or salting their fish on Canadian shores plied them with furs in return for the iron knives, axes, kettles, and pots and beads and cloths that the French offered. Eventually, the furs themselves became the basis for trading expeditions farther up the St. Lawrence, as merchants sought out Indians before other ships could compete. Over time a village called Tadoussac, located where the Saguenay River flows into the St. Lawrence, became a customary spring meeting place for thousands of Algonquin, Etchemin, Montagnais, and French traders. When the broad-brimmed beaver felt hat became fashionable in Europe in the latter part of the sixteenth century, it was only a matter of time before the French began again to lay more formal claim to North America.[8]

After the French planted a fur trading post at Tadoussac in 1600, the explorer Samuel de Champlain—the so-called Father of New France—pushed upriver and landed at Quebec in 1608. By establishing a permanent base there, Champlain hoped to forestall the summer traders who plied the shores of the lower St. Lawrence. The "colony" was, in some sense, merely a trading factory and warehouse for storing furs and trade goods. But it was nevertheless in the middle of Indian country. He was there at the sufferance of numerous and powerful groups that ringed the tiny French outpost.[9]

A year after Champlain established the post, delegates from the even more numerous Huron Confederacy also visited him. Living between the north shore of Lake Ontario and the southern shores of Georgian Bay, the Huron (or, as they are also known today, the Wendat, or Wyandot) numbered as many as twenty to forty thousand in densely settled permanent villages. Prolific horticulturalists, the Huron thrived in what is now southern Ontario. They had plenty of surplus corn and additional food to trade with other Indian nations and the struggling

French, but they were more sedentary than their northerly neighbors, the Anishinaabeg, and so lacked easy access to the furs the French craved. Fortunately, although the Huron were Iroquoian speakers, they enjoyed good relations with the Anishinaabeg. This was in part because at least some Odawa doodemag, including most notably the Kiskakon, lived near and intermarried with the Tionnontaté (Petun, or Tobacco, nation, a people closely related to the Huron confederacy).[10]

Drawing on these relations, the Anishinaabeg from farther north were eager to take advantage. As one early French account noted, the Odawa would intercept Huron trading parties returning home from the St. Lawrence. They did so expressly for the "purpose of bartering with the Hurons," with whom they spent a few days "trading and doing business." In turn, the Odawa traded away some of these goods with Indians "of different regions who came to their village." The Odawa simply took advantage of their location and waterborne mobility to become middlemen in a sprawling but indigenous trading system across the Lakes.[11]

•

The ability and initial willingness of the Anishinaabeg to act as intermediates in early French-Indian trading ventures had far-reaching and devastating consequences for both their neighbors and the fledgling colony along the St. Lawrence. Quickly recognizing the French lust for fur, the Anishinaabeg were in a good position to satiate it by bringing the thick northern beaver pelts down from the colder regions of the *pays d'en haut*. Initially trading furs via their more numerous neighbors, the Huron, and relations among the Algonquins and Montagnais farther to the southeast, the Anishinaabeg helped Samuel de Champlain dream that his efforts to establish a colony at Quebec in 1608 to monopolize the inland fur trade were not in vain. To keep the settlement alive, and to make the vulnerable commercial outpost work, Champlain eagerly sought out the friendship and trade of these and other Indian nations. In turn, they were happy to exchange their pelts for the valuable goods and arms the French offered.[12]

But there was a catch. The Huron and allied Algonquian nations, including the Anishinaabeg, all made it clear the French would have to prove they were worthy trading partners. Even before the French arrived, they were locked in a deadly conflict with the powerful Iroquois League—the Haudenosaunee—who dominated the region southwest of the French settlement on the St. Lawrence. Perhaps as many as twenty thousand people from five separate nations (the Mohawk, Oneida, Onondaga, Cayuga, and Seneca) had created a League of Peace and Power that rapidly expanded their hunting territory on the eve of the arrival of Europeans and claimed the region upstream from Quebec. The Huron and their Algonquian allies risked the wrath of the Iroquois when journeying to Quebec to trade. They soon made it clear to Champlain that he was precariously positioned between them and their longtime rivals in the Iroquois League. In return for their trade, Champlain would have to demonstrate his worth.[13]

Thus within a year of his arrival at Quebec, Champlain was, unwittingly or not, drawn in to this long-standing Native conflict. In the summer of 1609, he and two other Frenchmen armed with arquebuses—the forerunner of the musket—accompanied some sixty Montagnais, Algonquin, and Huron warriors southward to what we now call Lake Champlain, where they surprised and intercepted a raiding party of two hundred Mohawk warriors. The following year, enjoying the shock value of his steel weapons and firearms, Champlain again joined the Algonquians and Huron in a bloody attack on a Mohawk fort on the River of the Iroquois (now Richelieu River). Nearly all of the hundred Mohawk warriors there were slaughtered. A few years later, after meeting an Anishinaabe party at the mouth of the French River in 1615—Champlain called them "Cheveux-Relevés," or High Hairs—they and the Huron again pressed him to war on the Iroquois. Within a month or so, Champlain again found himself with about a dozen French arquebusiers accompanying a large expedition of at least five hundred Algonquian and Huron warriors south of Lake Ontario, deep into the heart of Iroquoia.[14]

While the shock of these initial attacks using European firearms led to a temporary détente between many of the Iroquois and the French, the damage was done. The Algonquians and Huron had secured a valuable ally by making the French implacable enemies of the Iroquois. They had embroiled the French in a world of Indian warfare. These early joint attacks on the Iroquois renewed an almost century-long war, marked by ferocious attacks, temporary truces, and diplomatic intrigues among all parties concerned. The French little understood this long history, but they soon realized their early choice to war against the Iroquois would come at a tremendous cost.[15]

At first, small-scale raiding and pirating marked the new round of conflict. To counter the Algonquian-Huron threat from the north, the Iroquois began to seek out access to vital trade goods and firearms from new Dutch trading posts. The Dutch, formidable Protestant rivals of the French, had begun exploring the region around New York as early as 1609, also seeking the fabled Northwest Passage across America. But they quickly realized there were riches enough to be had through the emerging and increasingly lucrative fur trade. They hastily moved up what we now call the Hudson River to establish a trading post at Fort Orange (Albany, New York), where they came into contact with the Iroquois. The Iroquois knew the Dutch were after the highly marketable beaver pelts that came from the colder regions far to the north of Iroquoia. Unable to trade for furs themselves because of their long-standing conflict with the nations to the north (one early French colonist said that they "never go to trade with the other Indian nations, because they are detested by all"), the Iroquois hijacked convoys of fur-laden canoes traveling down the St. Lawrence to Quebec. But as the Iroquois responded to Dutch trade overtures by mounting increasingly devastating attacks on the Huron and their Algonquian allies, the Huron in turn kept up the pressure on the French to aid and supply them. Small-scale raids quickly turned to full-scale warfare. For most of this initial phase of the conflict, the French were merely of peripheral interest to the Iroquois. Yet from the French perspective, the wars seemed a direct result of their intervention, and the fury of the conflict shocked them.[16]

The intensifying scale of the warfare on the St. Lawrence was exacerbated by several cycles of devastating epidemics among the Indians of the eastern seaboard and Great Lakes. As Europeans introduced new diseases for which most Indian communities had little immunity, population losses were dramatic. One of the first recorded episodes took place in 1633–1634 when colonists in New England infected local Indians, who then spread the disease among their trading partners and allies. Within a few years, a "sort of measles"—some called it smallpox—accompanied by stomach pains had spread through Iroquoia, south to the Delaware, and up into Huron country. In 1636–1637, an epidemic of scarlet fever or perhaps typhus racked both Europeans and Indians alike, but it caused many more deaths among the latter, especially among the densely settled Huron of southern Georgian Bay. Finally, in 1639–1640, a major smallpox epidemic spread from coastal Abenaki to inland Allumette on their island in the Ottawa River, and possibly reached the Anishinaabeg on Manitoulin Island.[17]

While such epidemics weakened the ability of many groups to withstand Iroquois attacks, they also contributed to the intensification of inter-Indian conflicts. With their own population cut perhaps in half in a few short years, the Iroquois launched an increasingly devastating series of traditional "mourning wars." The Iroquois saw population losses as a decrease in their individual and collective spiritual power. The death of someone in the community left a vacant social position that required filling by a process of "requickening." Captives taken in war and adopted into the community were one way these losses could be mitigated. The Anishinaabeg also saw death in a similar light, as a loss of spiritual collective power. But they had a different solution to replace that loss. They demanded compensation to "cover the dead." If the loss was a result of an accident or the fault of an individual or group with whom the Odawa were not at war, the offending party could offer compensation in the form of valuable goods, or even a war captive who could serve as a slave. In rare circumstances, the Odawa might demand the death of the individual who killed their own. But if a rival group killed a warrior or ogimaa in battle, the Odawa would almost certainly demand "flesh for flesh" and set out to avenge the death by killing their rivals. Either way, they "covered" the death and regained the power they lost either through material goods or through the energy drawn from the vengeance killing.[18]

While the Anishinaabeg were possibly insulated from the worst effects of the devastating new diseases because they lived in more dispersed and less densely settled villages, the Iroquois and Huron suffered badly. In response to the dramatic population loses from diseases, they stepped up their attacks. Whereas previously, Iroquois raiding parties might have taken one or two captives to replace their dead, by the 1640s, these raids reached new heights as the Iroquois and Huron systematically organized summer-long campaigns against entire villages and nations to kill, plunder, and take as many captives as possible. "It is the design of the Iroquois," wrote one Jesuit missionary living amid the Huron, "to capture all the Hurons, if it is possible; to put the chiefs and great part of the nation to death, and with the rest to form one nation and one country." While competition over access to the fur trade might have reawakened traditional rivalries, epidemic diseases brought a new vehemence to the conflicts.[19]

Between 1648 and 1650, the Five Nations of the Iroquois League united their efforts and turned their focus toward the densely settled Huron villages in southern Ontario. In one attack in March 1649, over a thousand Iroquois warriors burned two villages, killing as many as three hundred, including several French missionaries who had established bases among the Huron. By early summer, most of the surviving Huron—already divided between Christians and traditionalists and decimated by a new round of epidemics—decided enough was enough. Many burned their own villages and stores to prevent them from falling into Iroquois hands and took refuge with other nations, including the Anishinaabeg to their north. Some fled eastward and formed settlements closer to Quebec. By the end of 1649, most Huron towns and villages were deserted, and the survivors scattered. The Iroquois then turned on other nations, including the French.[20]

•

Shocked by these developments, the French along the St. Lawrence believed they had lost most of their former allies. Few traders or explorers dared venture up to the *pays d'en haut*, and the only reports they received were from missionaries who had survived the attacks and who now followed small groups of shattered—and mostly Huron— groups as they traveled across the Lakes seeking refuge. The Jesuits were bewildered by what they encountered. Desperate to get some purchase on an alien world, these missionaries glimpsed what they thought was a world fragmented by persistent and horrific Iroquois attacks. Early French visitors to the *pays d'en haut* believed this world was in chaos. They could find no densely settled villages or towns like the ones they had seen in Huronia, or even Iroquoia. Unable to comprehend what they encountered, they heard what they could. Most of their informants were Huron, who only added to the horrific tales of

Iroquois persecution. The French concluded that all of the peoples of the *pays d'en haut* were only the remnants of—or refugees from—much larger groups of Indians similarly hammered by the Iroquois. The French thought that they were on their own.[21]

They were also soon fighting for their lives. Immediately after the fall of Huronia, they suffered more directly from Iroquois attacks. In 1652, for example, the governor of the fort at Trois-Rivières and twenty-one settlers were killed in a single attack. The post had been established in 1634 at Champlain's urging. Like other new settlements along the St. Lawrence, the town consisted of a simple log fort with barracks, a magazine, a storehouse, and a few houses for the French inhabitants. Over time, the Jesuits also built a mission and chapel and fur traders built a few cabins outside the fort. But while Trois-Rivières became one of the biggest and most important French settlements along the St. Lawrence, it still struggled to survive. It had been built to help protect the growing trade at the important nexus of waterways, but the Iroquois made a mockery of French plans. Only ten of the first forty settlers lived through Iroquois attacks in 1652. The following year, six hundred Iroquois laid siege to the post. Inhabitants feared more attacks. Many prepared to evacuate the town. Those who stayed lived in fear. There was no safe haven. Fearful of venturing out to tend their fields, inhabitants of the newly founded Montreal also starved, and by 1651, the Iroquois had reduced the population to less than fifty. Those who survived contemplated abandoning the settlement. As one Iroquois headman later boasted, "We plyed the French home in the warr with them, that they were not able to goe over a door to pisse."[22]

Under pressure of these attacks, the entire colony struggled to endure. Though many French had moved back and forth across the Atlantic since Champlain arrived in 1608, few had stayed, or survived. By 1625–1626, the population had climbed to a mere 43 souls. There were still in all of New France only 356 almost a generation later in 1640. Through natural increase supplemented by a trickle of new migrants, the population reached about three thousand in 1663, a thousand of whom were children. With Iroquois raiding parties ever vigilant to French vulnerabilities, most of these inhabitants clustered for safety in and around the relative stronghold of Quebec, where the population had grown to just under two thousand. Even many of these contemplated leaving rather than risking their lives further. In Quebec in 1660, the Ursuline nun Marie de L'Incarnation wrote that if something was not done, the Iroquois would "destroy the country and drive us all away by their warlike and carnivorous nature." She believed the Iroquois would have already exterminated them had not God intervened and blinded their enemies to French weaknesses. French alliances with the Huron and Algonquians had cost them dearly.[23]

In desperation, the colonists turned to France for help. When a new governor of New France took up post in Quebec in 1661, he immediately appealed for military aid from the French crown and sent an emissary to Versailles to explain the precarious situation of New France. Fortunately for the colonists, the new French king, Louis XIV, had only just taken the reins of power and saw an opportunity to tighten his grip. Since Champlain had founded Quebec, the colony had effectively been run by a group of shareholders, the Company of One Hundred Associates. But in 1663, the French crown used the Iroquois war as an excuse to revoke the charter of the company and assume direct control over the colony. The king entrusted Jean-Baptiste Colbert, the new and powerful finance minister, with its reorganization. In effect, the machinations of the Huron and Algonquian-speaking nations helped to reshape French colonial policy. Indian warfare not only brought down the company, it also helped make France a truly imperial nation. Not for the last time, events in the *pays d'en haut* reverberated across the Atlantic and helped alter world history.[24]

One of the first things Colbert did was to assert control over the defense of France's New World claims. He appointed a supreme commander over all French forces in the Americas on land and sea, and then he sent twelve hundred men in the Carignan-Salières Regiment to Canada to help the besieged colonists. They were the first French troops sent to North America. French officials told the soldiers they were there to put an end to the conflict with the Iroquois once and for all. The French crown issued orders "totally to exterminate" the Iroquois, who should be considered "perpetual and irreconcilable enemies of the Colony." Marie de L'Incarnation reported the "soldiers are being made to understand that this is a holy war." From the perspective of French *habitants* along the St. Lawrence, the arrival of the

troops seemed nothing short of a miracle. The harassed inhabitants
of the St. Lawrence believed that all their Indian allies were lost, or on
the run. Now the very existence of the colony was at stake. At the
edge of their known world, the French felt they were the protagonists
in an epic war that would decide the fate of North America.[25]

•

If God had been the only ally of the French, few vestiges of the colony
would remain today. The world of the *pays d'en haut* may have been
in flux in the middle of the seventeenth century, but it was not—as
the French feared—in a state of collapse. Even as the troops of the
Carignan-Salières Regiment landed at Trois-Rivières in 1665, they
were greeted by more than four hundred Anishinaabe warriors from
the Lakes. And if the nervous young soldiers of the regiment felt a
great weight at the task they had been given, their counterparts among
the arriving Anishinaabeg may have provided some reassurance.

If the Natives could or did communicate with the French soldiers,
they would have certainly put the Iroquois-French conflict into a
broader context. While the French may have suffered heavily from the
Iroquois attacks, they were only at the edges of this conflict. Indeed,
from the perspective of the Anishinaabeg, the French were merely
minor players in an Indian conflict that stretched over generations. The
Iroquois may have won some important battles in the first half of the
seventeenth century, especially over the Huron, but by 1665 the Anishinaabeg and their Algonquian allies had set them back on their
heels. The Huron were only one of many powerful nations that inhabited the *pays d'en haut*. The Huron may have been shattered and
dispersed by the Iroquois, but not all nations suffered equally.[26]

The Anishinaabeg were still a force to be reckoned with, and they
were soon again on the offensive against their ancient rivals the Iroquois. To be sure, many Anishinaabeg were alarmed at the destruction
of the thickly settled Huronia. At least some of their own kin—
primarily the Kiskakon Odawa who had lived with and near the Huron at the south end of Georgian Bay, off Lake Huron—had suffered
along with them. Shortly after the Iroquois forced the Huron to flee
their villages, the Kiskakon also fled northward together with the Tionnontaté and Huron. They joined their Anishinaabe kin on Manitou-

lin Island and beyond. With local resources under pressure by an influx of almost two thousand new people, the Kiskakon, Huron, and Tionnontaté subsequently migrated westward, probably first to Rock Island at Green Bay in 1651. Two years later, some moved farther northwest, to Chequamegon Bay on the southern shore of far distant Lake Superior. Some of the French Jesuit missionaries followed and wrote of a community of refugees. But they were likely there to share resources with their kin, the Anishinaabe Ojibwe of western Lake Superior.[27]

Moreover, if war with the Iroquois forced some Anishinaabeg such as the Kiskakon to relocate among kin living elsewhere around the Lakes, the movement was merely temporary. The Anishinaabeg as a whole never lost their grasp on the northern and central stretches of the *pays d'en haut*. Even as the Iroquois extended their raids, many Anishinaabeg managed to maintain their hold on important places such as Michilimackinac and Manitoulin Island—both relatively protected strongholds. From these secure bases and with their numbers swollen with kin and displaced allies from the south, the Anishinaabeg held off the Iroquois. In 1654, for example, a large Iroquois force penetrated far into Anishinaabe country near Michilimackinac. A combined force of Sinago Odawa and Bawating Ojibwe attacked and defeated the Iroquois as they tried to cross the straits. Anishinaabe canoeing abilities no doubt helped keep the Iroquois at bay. A later report noted that the Iroquois "dare not venture with their sorry Canows to cross the Streight." Four years later, the Iroquois again invaded the Michigan peninsula with a force of sixteen hundred warriors. They sought revenge for the death of thirty Iroquois at the hands of the Algonquians the year before. They were once more turned back.[28]

Under pressure of these attacks, the Anishinaabeg made the most of the kinship ties that bound them together. Indeed, Anishinaabe women who had married out and made important connections with different communities were crucial in defending Anishinaabewaki. They provided vital links between Anishinaabe and other Algonquian villages in the region. Those uprooted by the conflict could find shelter and hospitality with their kin in more distant places. But just as important, Anishinaabe ogimaag and warriors could request help from their relations right across the Lakes when forming war parties against the Iroquois.[29]

The Anishinaabeg drew on these extended networks to put together coalitions of their Algonquian-speaking neighbors and the numerous Hurons who had sought refuge with them. By 1652–1653, Anishinaabeg at Michilimackinac were preparing a counterattack, plotting a joint attack with a two-thousand-strong force of Huron, Nipissing, Petun, Ojibwe, and even Susquehannock warriors. The turning point came in 1660, when western Anishinaabeg managed to secure a temporary peace with the Dakota and northern lowland Cree, presumably to buy some time for the Anishinaabeg to focus on the Iroquois. Less than two years later, a combined Anishinaabe force wiped out an invading force at Iroquois Point in northern Michigan. Thereafter, Anishinaabe-led war parties consisting of hundreds if not thousands of warriors launched punitive counterattacks deep into Iroquois territory. At the time, the French were only dimly aware of the battles being fought outside their view. But it is clear in hindsight that the Iroquois could not press home their advantage against the French because they had their hands full against the Anishinaabeg and their allies.[30]

•

Trading voyages to the St. Lawrence were a measure of the confidence of the Anishinaabeg. Though devastating Iroquois raids on the *habitants* of the French colony continued through the 1650s and early 1660s and often prevented them from farming, the Anishinaabeg found time amid the conflict to hunt for furs and bring them down to the St. Lawrence. This was no easy journey. From Michilimackinac, it could take up to twelve weeks to reach Montreal by canoe. The main route took the Anishinaabeg across Lake Huron, up the French River, and finally down the turbulent Ottawa River, requiring some thirty or more portages. But as skilled canoeists, the Anishinaabeg were unafraid of the waters they traveled and unperturbed by the hardships of the portages and long spells of paddling. The first reported fur convoy from the *pays d'en haut* arrived in Montreal in 1654, shortly after the Huron dispersal. As the Anishinaabeg had reportedly told the French in 1652, they were eager to continue trading with the French "in order to render themselves more formidable to the enemy." But while the destruction of Huronia alarmed the Anishinaabeg, it also created new opportunities. They suddenly found themselves in a good position to fill

p. 6.

Sauuage de La f. 10. Nation

outaouaks.

Pipe

Iae apectun

Indian warrior of the Ottawa Nation, c. 1675. This sketch by Father Louis Nicolas depicts a heavily tattooed warrior with a pipe and tobacco pouch. (*Les Raretés des Indes, Codex canadiensis*. Reproduced by permission of the Gilcrease Museum, Tulsa, Oklahoma) the void left by the loss of Huron-French trade. They no longer needed to use the Huron as intermediaries between themselves and the French.[31]

At the same time, the Odawa in particular asserted their leadership over both war parties and trading convoys, strengthening their position across the Lakes. From Chequamegon Bay, one early French trader-explorer in the region, Nicholas Perrot, reported that the "Outaoüas went away to the north and sought to carry on trade" with other nations. The Odawa were savvy traders. They extorted beaver pelts in exchange for "old knives, blunted awls, wretched nets, and kettles used until they were past service." "For these," Perrot noted with some irony, "they were most humbly thanked." Moreover, the Odawa gained a great deal of influence over their neighbors. Perrot observed, "Those people declared that they were under great obligations to the Outaoüas for having compassion upon them and having shared with them the merchandise which they had obtained from the French." In exchange, the northern nations were generous. They gave the Odawa "many packages of peltries, hoping that their visitors would not fail to come to them every year, and to bring them the like aid in trade-goods." Both the French and western nations were dependent on the canoe skills of the Anishinaabeg to facilitate trade. As one official noted, the western and northern nations were "not expert at managing canoes," so they could not come and trade directly.[32]

Nor would the Odawa let them. Even while in supposed exile at Green Bay and later Chequamegon, some of the Anishinaabeg there told the French that the Ottawa River belonged to them, and "no nation can navigate it without their consent." The French complained that the Anishinaabeg acted "as peddlars, between these nations and us, making us pay for a round-trip of three or four hundred leagues." A group of mainly non-Anishinaabe Indians from Green Bay later told officials at Quebec that the Odawa "gave them to understand that the French would burn them alive if they came down here." Since the French received them peacefully, the visitors believed the Odawa "kept them in that fear so they could have their pelts for nothing and come to trade themselves."[33]

The role the Odawa played across the Lakes may also explain their movement farther west between 1650 and about 1670. As other land-based nations withdrew farther into the interior, some of the Odawa may have taken advantage of kinship relations in the west to bring the marketplace to those in exile. Chequamegon Bay, for example, was reportedly the rendezvous point for "twelve or fifteen distinct nations" who came from the north, south, and west to fish, but also "to transact their petty trading with one another, when they meet." These included the Sauk and Fox from the Green Bay–Fox River region as well as the upper reaches of the Mississippi, Cree from the northwestern shores of Lake Superior, and even small parties of Dakota from the far southeastern end of Lake Superior. In one trip alone, almost two hundred canoes made the journey. The Illinois, too, made the long trek from the Illinois River region in the south "in great numbers, as merchants, to carry away hatchets and kettles, guns, and other articles which they need." In return, they traded not just furs but "a great many slaves." The slaves were Indian war captives that were used as barter among many Algonquian communities at the time. In facilitating this trade, the Anishinaabe Odawa made themselves key players in the world of the *pays d'en haut* even in the midst of the war with the Iroquois—and probably because of it.[34]

Though it would not be clear to the French for some time, the trade convoys and military victories presided over by the Anishinaabeg meant that by 1665, the Iroquois were already on the defensive. While French histories celebrate the arrival of the Carignan-Salières Regiment as a turning point in the colony's history, the Anishinaabeg should get the credit. By the time the French troops arrived, most of the Iroquois were ready for peace. Algonquian attacks from the north had taken their toll. Anishinaabe warriors had even begun to make incursions into traditional Iroquois hunting territory in the Richelieu River valley. Moreover, the Seneca, Cayuga, Onondaga, and Oneida of the Iroquois League now had their hands full with a conflict with the Susquehannock to their south, who had forged important ties with Dutch traders in the Delaware Valley. When New Netherland fell to the English in 1664, the Iroquois grew increasingly uneasy about their own multifronted wars. Entangled in destructive conflicts, most of the Iroquois were in no mood for further conflict. In December 1665, with nary a French shot fired, Seneca, Cayuga, Onondaga, and Oneida leaders came to Quebec and agreed to a comprehensive treaty with the French. The following year, after two largely unsuccessful French expeditions, even the more belligerent Mohawk Iroquois recognized the need for peace. The French colony would survive. The Anishinaa-beg had helped ensure it.[35]

•

As the Iroquois threat waned, many Anishinaabeg regathered around Michilimackinac. Even those who had sought temporary refuge with their kin farther west seemed intent to return as quickly as possible to the region. Prior to 1670, there were already reports of Odawa along with others on the islands of Lake Huron, and especially Manitoulin Island. Others had continued to winter over in the area. In 1669, one Jesuit noted that in early November they had come across two French men with several natives at present-day St. Ignace, on the north shore of the straits. More arrived with each passing year. By the late 1660s, most of the rest of the Anishinaabe Odawa and Ojibwe who had moved to Chequamegon Bay moved eastward, together with the remnant groups of Huron and Tionnontaté who had sought refuge with them. Some moved first to the Sault, others moved back to Manitoulin Island, while a few lived a short while with kin at Green Bay. But over the next ten years many traveled back to Michilimackinac. By 1679, there were concrete reports that as many as eighteen hundred Huron and Anishinaabeg—primarily Odawa and Ojibwe—lived at the straits. There were probably more. The Anishinaabeg were coming home.[36]

Anishinaabe movements would again have far-reaching effects on European affairs. As they returned to the straits, the Odawa espe-cially showed an inclination to trade where they were rather than bring pelts east. While large fortified trading convoys down to the St. Lawrence made sense during the conflict with the Iroquois, after 1665 there was far less need for them. More and more young French traders were happy to accompany the Odawa back to Michilimacki-nac, and the Odawa were pleased to avoid the long journey to the St. Lawrence. Convoys were difficult to organize, and they took the better part of the short growing season to complete. They were also risky. Not only did the flotillas chance Iroquois attack as they approached the St. Lawrence, but perhaps more important, they left vulnerable fam-ilies behind to grow corn and maintain villages.[37]

Concern over leaving their settlements unprotected grew markedly in the early 1670s when hostilities with the Dakota began anew. Western Anishinaabeg—mostly Ojibwe—had long been at war with the Dakota on their western flank. While a temporary peace in 1660 had helped the Anishinaabeg to unite against the Iroquois, renewed hostilities against the Dakota may have helped convince many to move back to Michilimackinac in the first place. Then, in the summer of 1672, after supplying themselves at Montreal with arms and ammunition, the Sinago Odawa led a disastrous campaign against the Dakota in the upper Mississippi Valley. The loss put the Anishinaabeg at Michilimackinac on the defensive again. Though the French seemed largely unaware of the turmoil to the west, the renewal of war with the Dakota made summer-long large convoys to the St. Lawrence almost impossible. Indian conflict—even far beyond the ken of most Europeans—could have a powerful effect on European empire. Almost immediately, Odawa at the straits pushed for more French traders to come out to them. They also agitated for the establishment of an official French post.[38]

•

Odawa demands would severely disrupt French plans for a stable and productive colony on the banks of the St. Lawrence. Anishinaabe success against the Iroquois had bought the French some valuable time to put the colony on a much firmer footing. As part of his plans for the royal takeover of New France in 1663, the French minister of finance, Jean-Baptist Colbert, wanted to make the colony self-sufficient—both militarily and economically. To aid in this, he persuaded the crown to invest more than 200,000 livres per year in the colony (in today's currency, this was roughly equivalent to about $4,500 for each of the five hundred or so families in the colony). He encouraged immigration, settlement, agriculture, and even the development of industry—in shipbuilding, brewing, and fishing.[39]

Colbert had plans for the long-term defense of the colony as well as its growth; indeed, the two in his mind went hand in hand. Though the officers of the Carignan-Salières Regiment were told that they could expect to be back in France within eighteen months, Colbert hoped to entice many soldiers to stay. The king told the *intendant* (a newly created senior administrative officer in the colony who reported directly to the king), Jean Talon, Comte d'Orsainville, to offer the soldiers a small "gratuity" in the king's name to give them the means to stay. The king was also eager to grant them land. In New France itself, Intendant Talon was delighted, and he hoped the soldiers could farm the land and help defend it. Talon wanted to people the neighborhood of Quebec as thickly as possible, "mingling," he said, "soldiers and farmers, so that they may mutually instruct one another in the cultivation of the soil and be aiding to each other when necessary." At the heart of the metropolitan vision of empire was a colony of farming families along the St. Lawrence River.[40]

Plans to populate the colony worked: 30 officers, 12 noncommissioned officers, and 404 enlisted men out of the original twelve to thirteen hundred, or some 40 percent, are known to have stayed along the St. Lawrence. In addition to the settlement of soldiers, Colbert planned to send as many as 500 more men and 150 women a year to the colony, using royal subsidies. Though these efforts were not always successful, the population nevertheless grew quite dramatically. Indeed, the arrival of the Carignan-Salières Regiment coincided with and helped fuel a wave of immigration to the colony that started in 1665 and continued until the end of the decade. As many as twenty-five hundred new migrants to the colony arrived by 1671. It had taken about fifty-five years for the population to reach approximately three thousand; the spurt of immigration from 1665 doubled that number within a few years. And the colony continued to grow through natural increase—to nearly ten thousand by 1683, fifteen thousand by 1700.[41]

But if Colbert's plans for the demographic growth of the St. Lawrence Valley worked, his economic plans were largely undermined. Many of the new soldiers struggled to turn swords into plowshares. Some found themselves on poor lands with little to provide for large and growing families. The dense woods, short growing season, and mediocre soils along the St. Lawrence meant even seasoned farmers often struggled. Many went into debt to merchants at Quebec or Montreal. Some eventually abandoned their seigneuries to their creditors.[42]

Against these discouraging prospects lay the lure of the fur trade. While struggling along the St. Lawrence, *habitants* watched each year as hundreds of canoes laden with rich, thick pelts landed at popular trading sites. Moreover, by 1665, the Anishinaabeg had initiated a practice of inviting a handful of traders to accompany them back to the *pays d'en haut*. When one of the first convoys arrived in Trois-Rivières in 1654, for example, the Anishinaabeg asked for some French traders to return with them. They took back two Frenchmen including Médard des Groseilliers, a famous French explorer and fur trader, whom they may have known since he worked for some years with the Jesuits among the Huron. Groseilliers and his companion returned in 1656 with their Indian escorts along with hundreds of pounds of furs in their canoes worth a small fortune. The Anishinaabeg were happy to have them along: the French traders bolstered their status among their kin and other nations of the *pays d'en haut*. On their return, two ogimaag went directly to the governor and asked that he send more Frenchmen back with them.[43]

The Anishinaabeg continued to invite French traders to accompany them on subsequent trips. There were plenty of volunteers. The sudden influx of migrants, military and civilian, gave a new impetus to the fur trade as footloose newcomers sought quick riches rather than cold winters. Newly arrived soldiers especially eyed the fur trade as their farms failed. Many of the soldiers who stayed—and their sons and grandsons—got involved in some way with the fur trade.[44]

At first, the French colonial governor granted trade licenses to the lucky few whom the Anishinaabeg invited to accompany them. But as more and more traders spent time with their Anishinaabeg hosts, some of them began venturing out on their own. The decreased chances of Iroquois attack made this possible after 1665, but they were also aided by the return of the Anishinaabeg to Michilimackinac. With the Odawa back at the straits, French traders could safely access the trade of the *pays d'en haut* with a fully provisioned canoe. More important, traders could rely on their Indian counterparts to meet them at Michilimackinac to exchange winter pelts for French goods. That meant the French could make a round-trip journey in a single season. The Odawa, in turn, began welcoming western Indian nations to come and trade with them at the straits. They still maintained control over the trade, but they no longer had to spend as much time bringing furs down to the St. Lawrence and French merchandise out to the western edges of the *pays d'en haut*. The Odawa also invited some of the traders to winter over with them, so they could be well supplied during their winter hunts. French traders were happy to comply, as it gave them access to a more secure supply of pelts. It usually meant they were relatively safe, too. Isolated traders with no connections in the *pays d'en haut* were vulnerable.

Indeed, though European histories have often glorified the exploits of trader-explorers such as Groseilliers and his later companion, Pierre-Esprit Radisson, we should make no mistake about how they were able to move in the interior: they were invariably there on the invitation of native peoples, and usually dependent on them. Radisson and Groseilliers later boasted that they were conquering "Caesars" on their trips through the *pays d'en haut* in the late 1650s and early 1660s. But the "poore miserable" Indians they encountered and described would have reminded them that they survived only with their help. One Anishinaabe account notes that after the two adventurers had become separated from their escorts, some young Ojibwe eventually found them on the verge of starvation. They brought them to their village, "where, being nourished with great kindness, their lives were preserved." Others were not so lucky, especially if they were less welcome. When the Jesuit missionary Father René Ménard tried to reach a group of Huron in the spring of 1662, his Indian hosts abandoned him. Ménard perished when he got lost looking for supplies. Because much of the early trade in the *pays d'en haut* was concealed, we have little idea how many other Frenchmen died without the protection of Indian hosts.[45]

As the number of men who slipped away to the Lakes rose, French officials along the St. Lawrence and at Versailles grew alarmed. Many, like Colbert, were desperate to create a stable colony, and they saw containment of it in the St. Lawrence Valley as key. Colbert allowed voyages of exploration westward after 1666, but mainly to continue looking for a western route to a southern sea and to forestall other European nations that might make claims on the fur trade. And while he was eager to see the expansion of the fur trade, he wanted it confined to the existing French settlements. Native Americans, he believed, should come to them. The flood of individual traders westward not only might play havoc with their delicate relations with the Indian nations upon whom they relied, he thought, but also might weaken the main colony, as fewer men would be available to cultivate farms.[46]

French officials, desperate to keep their young men—and any fur trade profits—within the colony, outlawed unlicensed trade in the interior. But they could not enforce the ban. With the Anishinaabeg providing refuge when they arrived in the *pays d'en haut*, prospective traders had only to make it out of the St. Lawrence. As one official complained, "the country is so open, and the difficulty so great to ascertain precisely when they depart or when they return." The French simply did not have the resources to police all the pathways to the *pays d'en haut*. Nor was there much will to do so among local colonial officials. Almost everyone stood to profit from the illegal trade—the *habitants*, the principal merchants, and many of the colony's most "considerable families" were implicated, right up to the governor. In 1680, the intendant complained that "there is not a family of any condition and quality whatsoever that has not children, brothers, uncles, and nephews" among the illegal *coureurs de bois*.[47]

Within a few years of the peace settlement with the Iroquois, Intendant Talon estimated that there were some three or four hundred *coureurs de bois*—literally, runners of the woods, referring to illegal fur-traders—active in the west, mostly on private fur-trading missions. By 1680, his successor guessed there might be as many as eight hundred. Though they were no doubt exaggerating, subsequent officials echoed Colbert's complaints and despaired of the colony's future as the number of illegal traders increased. One wrote that many farms in the St. Lawrence Valley lay uncultivated "from the scarcity of people." The governor complained to the king in 1685 that the illegal traders had let their farms "lie fallow" and that married men had deserted their wives and children or gone into debt to the merchants. Those who had left had also taken with them most of the serviceable arms available for self-defense. At the very least, a substantial proportion of the able-bodied young men of the colony were spending much of their time away from it. The governor worried for the future of New France. The fur trade endangered empire. Their trade with the Anishinaabeg was leading them down the path of "complete ruin."[48]

•

Unconcerned about the disruption caused along the St. Lawrence and the complaints emanating from Versailles, the Odawa at Michilimackinac welcomed traders to the straits. While war with the Dakota threatened their western flank, the presence of the traders made good sense on a number of fronts. *Coureurs de bois* ensured a steady supply of provisions and arms that could be used in any conflict. Their presence at the straits, too, meant the Anishinaabeg did not have to leave their families and settlements unprotected to make the journey to Montreal. But the traders also effectively created an alliance between the Anishinaabeg and the French against the Dakota. Even if the French were not yet ready to join them in war, the Dakota would have interpreted their trade with their enemies as a hostile act. At the very least, if the Dakota killed French traders while attacking the Anishinaabeg, they risked the wrath of officials along the St. Lawrence.[49]

But hosting independent French traders in Anishinaabewaki was attractive for another, equally important reason. While welcoming the respite, the official French peace treaty with the Iroquois rang alarm bells for many Anishinaabeg. While our Eurocentric accounts make much of the negotiations for peace between Europeans and Indians, the prospect of peace between the Iroquois and the French was not so universally welcomed throughout Indian country. As far as the Anishinaabeg were concerned, peace between the French and Iroquois endangered the balance of power between themselves and the Iroquois. If the French began trading with the Iroquois, they would become more powerful enemies. And given how weak the French had been in the face of Iroquois attacks before 1665, there was every reason to believe they might prefer an alliance over further war. Under normal circumstances this would have been alarming enough. But renewed hostilities with the Dakota to the west put the Anishinaabeg in a precarious situation between two powerful rivals.

Such concerns were magnified when it became clear that under cover of the peace of 1665, the Iroquois established several villages along the north shore of Lake Ontario—Anishinaabe-claimed territory. Instead of blocking this expansion, the French seemed to welcome it. Machinations among colonial officials led to the establishment of Fort Frontenac on Lake Ontario in 1673. The newly appointed governor of New France, the Comte de Frontenac, Louis de Buade, was eager to engross the trade of the *pays d'en haut* under the pretense of erecting a bulwark against the expansion of English trade from the southeast. Yet Anishinaabeg at Michilimackinac were alarmed at the erection of an official French post so close to the heart of Iroquoia, and to the new villages in southern Ontario, as it seemed to give a formal stamp of approval to the expansion of Iroquoia.[50]

In this potentially dangerous context, having independent French traders at Michilimackinac facilitated a key Anishinaabe strategy. Supplies from illegal traders rendered them independent of French policies and officials along the St. Lawrence. This left the Anishinaabeg free to counter French moves to cozy up to their rivals. They did so by flirting with the Iroquois themselves. They even threatened an alliance with the Iroquois and their new English allies. As early as 1670, for example, the Odawa entertained some visiting Iroquois and wintered over with them, "to confirm their union, as they said." During the visit, the Anishinaabeg learned of the prices for furs offered by the English and in front of accompanying French traders vowed to open a trade with them via the Iroquois. A small party even traveled to Iroquoia to trade in the spring of 1671.[51]

As concerned as the Anishinaabeg were about the idea of a French-Iroquois alliance, the French themselves were terrified of the prospect of an Iroquois-Anishinaabeg alliance. It would be the end of the colony. One report in 1671 noted that were the old adversaries to join together, the French would face a "war more sanguinary than heretofore." The report directed all officials, including Jesuit missionaries, to sow the seeds of discord between the two nations. Though the French reassured themselves that they had succeeded in driving a wedge between the two on this particular occasion, the Anishinaabeg continued to dally with the Iroquois, keeping the French in a constant state of anxiety. In 1672, Governor Frontenac complained that the Iroquois were fetching furs from the Odawa to bring to the English. The following year, the governor traveled to Lake Ontario specifically to try to prevent the Odawa and Iroquois from concluding a separate treaty. But reports of Iroquois visits to Michilimackinac continued to come in over subsequent years.[52]

The Anishinaabe resettlement of Bkejwanong (near present-day Detroit) only inflamed French worries. Shortly after they moved back to Michilimackinac, at least some Odawa pushed south to challenge Iroquois claims to the region north of Lakes Erie and Ontario. Just as the Kiskakon Odawa moved to Michilimackinac, the Kamiga Odawa announced their intention of reestablishing a village at Bkejwanong. A spiritually important site, Bkejwanong also once formed a strategic part of the Odawa's western gateways. Though the region had been abandoned during the long conflict with the Iroquois, the Kamiga were eager to reestablish a presence there as hostilities subsided. Some of the refugee Tionnontaté accompanied them. They planted several villages there in the early 1670s. The settlements at Bkejwanong helped bolster Anishinaabe claims to the southern Lakes vis-à-vis the Iroquois, but they worried the French because it brought the two rivals closer. Nor did it escape French attention that the new villages helped secure Anishinaabe control over French trade to nations farther west. Between Bkejwanong and Michilimackinac, the Anishinaabe Odawa controlled all east-west movement across the Lakes. If the French wanted to trade across the lower Lakes, they would have to come through Anishinaabewaki.[53]

•

French dependency on the Anishinaabeg paid dividends for the latter when the Iroquois renewed their hostilities with the western nations starting in the late 1670s. The Iroquois were again growing confident of their strength because they had secured their southern and eastern flanks. In part because of the violence of the conflicts known as King Philip's War in New England and Bacon's Rebellion in Virginia, New York authorities approached the Iroquois to broker a series of historic treaties with the English and several longtime foes, including the Delaware and Susquehannock. This "Covenant Chain" between the English and the Iroquois and other nations brought diplomatic and economic benefits and ushered in a sustained period of peace. With fewer enemies to worry about and even the prospect of English allies joining them, the Iroquois grew bolder. Along with the planting of new villages on the north shore of Lake Ontario, they launched attacks against the Illinois at the southern end of Lake Michigan. Professing continued peace with the French, a large Iroquois force then invaded the Illinois country in 1680. They kept striking, reaching as far west as the Mississippi and as far north as Green Bay. As the Iroquois went on the warpath, Anishinaabeg at Michilimackinac and Bkejwanong grew concerned. Even French officials believed that it was only a matter of time before the Iroquois would turn north and attack the Anishinaabeg at Michilimackinac.[54]

Still, the French were terrified of the prospect of renewed war with the Iroquois and hesitated to act. Some even contemplated siding with the Iroquois. The Anishinaabeg were alarmed and annoyed that the French would stand by and allow these Iroquois attacks to continue, even arming them through further trade. They took matters into their own hands. When a visiting Illinois warrior "accidentally" killed a visiting Iroquois elder in an Anishinaabe village at Michilimackinac in 1681, a real opportunity arose. The elder had been killed in front of a party of Frenchmen, and he had been killed with a French knife. Whether the killing was accidental or not, the Anishinaabeg made good use of the incident. The following spring, a large delegation of Odawa traveled to Montreal to tell the governor this incident would mean war. They noted that the Iroquois were on the move against the Miami and Illinois nations and they would almost certainly attack Michilimackinac at the same time. An alarmed Frontenac insisted that the Odawa immediately make amends with the Iroquois and cover the dead. But the visiting delegation refused. Instead, they insisted they would defend themselves if attacked and pushed Frontenac to renew hostilities with the Iroquois. Though the governor stopped short of ordering an offensive against the Iroquois, he did promise the delegation that he would immediately issue orders to the French in their country to unite with them and repel any attack if it came. That was enough. The Anishinaabeg knew that if traders fought against the Iroquois, the French would be embroiled in the conflict. The Iroquois would not distinguish between the actions of illegal French traders and colonial policy. They would renew their war against the French settlements. The Anishinaabe strategy of hosting French traders had worked. The delegation departed, Frontenac reported, "better satisfied than they had appeared to be in the voyages of former years."[55]

The next year, in 1683, the French moved further to appease their allies and hold on to the fur trade. Amid more rumors of planned Iroquois attacks on Michilimackinac, the new French governor, Joseph-Antoine de La Barre, issued orders to establish a fortified post on the north side of the straits (present-day St. Ignace). He immediately dispatched six canoes with thirty men and a great deal of powder and lead from Montreal under Olivier Morel de la Durantaye, a French officer. They were to rendezvous with fifteen canoes full of trade goods and provisions under Daniel Greysolon Dulhut and other traders and fortify the post. By all accounts, they hastily threw up a few small wooden cabins, and they counted on protection from the Huron and Odawa at the straits should they need it, despite the fact that they had orders to ready themselves for a "determined defence."[56]

The French had no choice but to side with the Anishinaabeg over the Iroquois and establish an official post at Michilimackinac. Despite their desire to maintain good relations with the Iroquois, the French realized they were dependent on the Anishinaabeg. By 1681, the intendant had admitted that the Odawa were the most useful nation to the French since they were so critical to the fur trade. It was they who used their canoe skills to negotiate and trade with the more distant Indian nations in the Lakes. There were no other nations who could supply the French as the Odawa could. Nor would the Odawa allow it. The intendant claimed the Odawa continued to "intimidate" the other nations, "in order to be the carriers of their Merchandise and to profit thereby." While controlling the trade to rival nations, the Odawa not only strengthened their position at the straits but also became indispensable to the French.[57]

Anishinaabe strategy also played into the hands of expansionist-minded Frenchmen. Though Finance Minister Colbert and the crown wanted to limit French expansion and keep existing settlements secure, others used Odawa threats to argue for new interior posts to protect French interests. Eager to control the trade that flowed through illegal routes, some French believed a post at Michilimackinac could channel all of the far western trade at this strategic location. And with the Jesuits now at Michilimackinac, support for their endeavors also played into these arguments. Men such as Frontenac asserted that they needed such bases to keep the Anishinaabeg from trading with the Iroquois, who in turn would trade with the English. When news came that the Odawa themselves had been in touch with the new English governor Edmund Andros of New York, all agreed the threat was real. Though some among the French realized that Odawa were deliberately applying pressure to establish a post at the straits, there was little they could do but comply. The Odawa thus compelled the French to change official policy restricting trade to the St. Lawrence Valley and establish a post at Michilimackinac. They had forced the French to expand their empire in order to secure their own.[58]

•

With the Anishinaabeg back at Michilimackinac and a French post at the straits, it quickly became a point of preeminent importance to both the Indians and French. Between about 1670 and 1700, Michilimackinac flourished and became one of the central sites of the fur trade. Soon, French visitors reported vast summer markets taking place along the shorelines each year. Both natives and newcomers flocked to take advantage. Hundreds of Native Americans from around Lakes Michigan and Superior would make the voyage to the straits to meet French traders coming up from the St. Lawrence. In the words of a later French traveler, Michilimackinac became "the landing-place and refuge of all the savages who trade their peltries." Consequently, Michilimackinac rapidly became the "general meeting-place for all the French who go to trade with stranger tribes."[59]

At Michilimackinac each summer, thick furs and deer hides from as far west as Lake Nipigon were traded for French goods. The post quickly became a major node in an expanding trade network that stretched from Europe through to the upper reaches of the Mississippi. The French were delighted. By 1688, one visitor thought Michilimackinac was of "great importance to our Commerce." A little later, one of the first post commanders at the straits, Antoine de La Mothe, Sieur de Cadillac, boasted that it was no longer an outpost, but a "centre, as it were, for all the rest of the colony, whence everything is distributed . . . and is in the midst of all the nations having relations with us." By 1695, Cadillac claimed the village at Michilimackinac was "one of the largest in all Canada."[60]

Michilimackinac did become central to the French empire. But if the post at the straits seemed a symbol of growing French imperial power, Michilimackinac was still very much Indian country. On the surface, the straits in the 1680s seemed a good example of a "middle ground" between Natives and newcomers, where neither side could dominate. But numbers alone should make us pause to consider the balance of power at the straits. The French population at the straits in the 1680s consisted of a couple of Jesuit missionaries, a few resident traders, and at most a dozen or two French soldiers. These latter were housed in some roughly constructed houses along the shoreline of Moran Bay. The French would not complete a fort, Fort de Buade, until 1690. A few hundred legal and illegal traders who came and went with the trading season supplemented the European population, but they rarely stayed for long. The tiny number of more or less permanent French numbers at the straits lived alongside two large and fortified Huron/Tionnontaté and Odawa villages, with thirty-foot-high palisades. More Odawa villages could be found a few miles away at Gros Cap. In all, as Cadillac noted, some six or seven thousand Anishinaabeg along with hundreds of Huron refugees lived within an hour or two canoe's journey to the straits. They encircled the tiny French post in dozens of villages. Cadillac exaggerated the number of French troops and residents at the post, but his claim about the size and importance of the community holds true when Anishinaabe numbers are counted. This reality belied French claim of possession. The French were there because the Anishinaabeg wanted them there.[61]

The Odawa also dictated the terms upon which the French could remain at Michilimackinac. Upon his arrival in 1683, Durantaye was compelled to distribute trade goods, provisions, and equipment to the Indians of the region, initiating a tradition, and creating an expectation, that would last for more than a century and cost the French dearly. By 1702, the Jesuit Étienne de Carheil complained that the giving of presents had created a shrewd and savvy diplomatic practice. The Indians at Michilimackinac, he noted, were "exacting in requiring that they be solicited; to make it necessary that all their actions and all their emotions be purchased by dint of presents; and, finally, that they do nothing that they should do voluntarily, except in return for something which is given them and which they exact." Carheil was right: for the Odawa and many other nations, presents were "evidence of their leaders' ability to extract tribute from imperial governments." Across eastern North America, many Native Americans traded in multiple markets and deployed their military strength in ways that kept rival empires guessing at their intentions in order to maintain a "diplomatic system that featured substantial annual transfers of arms, cloth, and tools."[62]

Nor did the Odawa give much ground to the French Jesuit missionaries who hoped to proselytize at Michilimackinac. The French were quick to trumpet the need for new interior posts to help missionaries in their labor for Indian souls. The Jesuits had made some progress among the Huron earlier in the century, but there is little evidence that the Jesuits gained many converts at Michilimackinac. Before 1660, the Jesuits' main contacts among the Anishinaabeg were the Kiskakon Odawa who lived near the Huron in southern Georgian Bay. When the Kiskakon and Huron fled to Lake Superior during the Iroquois wars, the Jesuits followed. Though claiming some success with the Kiskakon Odawa, Father Jacques Marquette reported that the Sinago were "very far removed from the Kingdom of God," while another Odawa doodem simply said they were not interested. Moreover, and more generally, he complained, the Odawa were "superstitious to an extraordinary degree" and "seem to harden themselves to the teachings that are given them" even while they were "very glad to have their children baptized." Only the Kiskakon, he claimed, were ready to call themselves Christians.[63]

When the Kiskakon moved back to rejoin kin at Michilimackinac in 1671, Marquette accompanied them, founding the first Jesuit mission at St. Ignace. The missionaries looked forward to the move because they knew how important the region was in the Anishinaabe world. They would have easy access not only to so many who lived in the area, but also to the numerous nations who passed through the straits. But the Jesuits would be disappointed. They continued to struggle. In 1688, one French official heaped scorn on the Jesuit efforts at Michilimackinac among the Odawa and Huron after visiting the post and mission. He thought the Indians desired baptism only when they were dying, or for "inconsequential people." Even as late as 1698, a visiting Jesuit noted that the priests at Michilimackinac admitted they had made "very little progress, even though they have worked for a long time, with so much zeal, for the conversion of the Huron and Ottawa natives, who are here in great numbers." The Jesuits loom large in our historical literature and consciousness, of course, but they do so only because they left the most, and the richest, records. But they could describe a world at Michilimackinac to which they had only limited access. In reality, they made only tentative inroads among the Anishinaabeg in and around the straits. In the end, the Jesuits were allowed a foothold at Michilimackinac, but it was more an enclave than an invasion.[64]

•

Instead, Michilimackinac continued to be an Indian world, one in which the Anishinaabeg played a central role. The French were dependent on their hosts from the start. That dependency grew as the Odawa took advantage of the growing numbers of French and Indians alike who came yearly to the straits to establish a flourishing provisioning trade. The Odawa were perfectly positioned. A canoe leaving Montreal early in the spring could reach the straits by early summer and be back down the St. Lawrence just in time to see their cargo off with the last ships leaving for Europe. Moreover, the capacity of the canoes that were used by French and Indians alike limited the distance paddlers could travel with adequate provisions. The seven hundred miles or so from Montreal to Michilimackinac along the Ottawa River was about the maximum span for journeys before travelers had to reprovision. If traders wanted to move any farther into the interior, they had to restock and often replace their canoes at Michilimackinac. This was particularly important because if traveling any farther west or north of Michilimackinac, traders would inevitably have to winter over in the *pays d'en haut*. For that, they had to be prepared.[65]

Michilimackinac was thus a critical stopping point for any fur trade voyage undertaken by natives or newcomers alike. The Odawa took full advantage. They sold fish to visiting nations, surplus corn to the French. They also sold beans and squash and meat to the soldiers of the French garrison. When they chose to work, as one French chronicler noted, they made and sold canoes to desperate travelers. Their technical skills were renowned. They also provided timber for houses and sold strawberries and other fruits to pay for their vermilion and glass and porcelain beads. There was no question who were the beneficiaries of such exchanges. "They make a profit on everything," complained the French. The Odawa compensated for any excessive prices for French goods by setting exorbitant charges for their own commodities, especially fish and corn. The French, though frustrated— like other Indian nations—could do little. They were dependent on Indian corn for their subsistence. As one group of traders protested, even in the first year of the post, they had to buy provisions from the Odawa at a "very high price, without which they would all be dead of starvation."[66]

The Odawa at Michilimackinac did well enough from the provisioning trade to meet most of their needs. This made them immune to any official French pressure to change their practices. When some officials in Quebec suggested they ought to conduct trade along the St. Lawrence instead of at Michilimackinac, for example, officials at the straits scoffed at the suggestion. They said the Odawa would not bother to go to Montreal in search of French goods when they could get what they needed at home: "Interest alone governs them; their sole desire is to live comfortably and to be clothed." Even as they depleted large game and beaver stocks nearer the straits, the local inhabitants did not worry. One French observer concluded those "who dwell there do not need to go hunting in order to obtain all the comforts of life." The provisioning trade alone gave them what they needed. Moreover, with a temperate growing season, the Huron and Odawa of Michilimackinac grew plenty of corn, peas, beans, pumpkins, and watermelons and lived well off the "great abundance" of fish. The French who visited thought there was not a family that could not catch enough fish for the entire year.[67]

The Odawa used their advantageous location and their relations with the French to establish economic security. They trapped some beaver themselves. When local stocks were scarce, they used their canoe skills to range widely in search of furs. One Nipissing ogimaa accused the Odawa of destroying the beaver stocks in his country. But they mainly took advantage of the thousands of western and northern nations who came yearly to Michilimackinac to trade. These nations complained that the Odawa often plundered them before they arrived. Others complained that once there, the Odawa forced them to trade their furs for poor prices. They would then sell them to the French for a profit.[68]

•

Finally, the growing importance of the straits and the trade conducted there also meant the Odawa consolidated an important political role in the region. The more prominent Odawa doodemag at the straits, including the Sable, Sinago, Kiskakon, and at some point, the Nassauakueton, or Nation de la Fourche, reaped the economic and political benefits of their location at Michilimackinac. They took particular advantage of the large numbers of Huron who lived with them as refugees. They had come to the straits along with the Kiskakon Odawa, with whom they had close relations at Nottawasaga Bay. While relations between the Huron and Odawa were sometimes strained, their presence reinforced the diplomatic importance of the straits. In addition to the Huron, other Anishinaabe doodemag lived near Michilimackinac. An important community of Ojibwe, for example, lived a short canoe trip up the St. Mary's River at Sault Ste. Marie. There were smaller settlements of Ojibwe closer to the straits. Because of kinship politics, most of these communities were mixed—that is, Ojibwe could be found in primarily Odawa villages and vice versa. They were also connected by kinship relations to other Anishinaabe and Algonquian villages across the Lakes. These connections, along with the economic and strategic advantages of the straits, made Michilimackinac one of the most important Indian centers in the *pays d'en haut*. As Cadillac noted in 1695, Michilimackinac was "the rendezvous of the chiefs of all the nations in the surrounding country."[69]

In the midst of this Anishinaabe-dominated world, the Odawa in particular had a powerful voice at the straits. For one thing, because they had such a widespread network of relations among Indian peoples in the region, they were seen as important mediators. Not only could they intervene in disputes between the French and visiting nations, but they also conciliated inter-Indian conflicts. Something of this role can be glimpsed in the episode that led to Daniel Greysolon Dulhut's negotiations with the Odawa at Michilimackinac over the winter of 1683–1684. Left in charge of the hastily erected post, Dulhut learned that a mixed group of Menominee (allied-Algonquian speakers, but not Anishinaabeg) and Ojibwe warriors had killed two French traders near Sault Ste. Marie. Dulhut knew he had to tread carefully. He noted that the Menominee warrior had gone to Sault Ste. Marie only "on account of the number of allies and relatives whom he had there." Another of the accused had a brother, sister, and uncle in the village of the Kiskakon Odawa. Before he could do anything to bring the killers to justice, then, Dulhut was compelled to consult with all the chiefs of the Odawa Sable, Sinago, and Kiskakon doodemag, together with ogimaag from the Ojibwe of Sault Ste. Marie and the Huron.[70]

Though risky, Dulhut hoped the Anishinaabeg would treat the murders as they did internal disputes, as opposed to disputes between themselves and the Iroquois—they would kill the murderers themselves, man for man, in order to prevent a war. Once the accused had been identified as Menominee and Ojibwe, the Odawa stepped in to mediate—to avoid an outright war with the French. Eventually Dulhut agreed to execute only two of the murderers. Two days after the executions, the Kiskakon, Sable, and Sinago Odawa gave six belts of valuable wampum to the French to cover their dead. Yet they also gave belts to the father of the executed Ojibwe and the relatives of the Menominee who were present. Odawa authority in the region, together with kinship ties to these two groups, was enough to prevent a new war between the Algonquians and the French.[71]

Though the French have often been represented as the "mediators" between Algonquians in the *pays d'en haut*, it was in fact the Michilimackinac Odawa who played that role. Any nation on the move across the Lakes had to come through the straits. Indians came to trade, but they also used the same route to make war on each other. So it was natural and "easy" for the Odawa "to stay their axes and become the mediators in all their quarrels, as they have been in the past." Andrew Blackbird recalled that the Odawa were "always considered" the "most expert on the warpath and wise councilors." Every nation of Indians from "far and near" deposited a peace pipe at Michilimackinac and pledged to let the Odawa settle disputes between them. One French post commander later noted it was useless to try to intervene in any regional disputes unless specifically asked to do so by the Indians themselves. Any agreement the French could negotiate was liable to be broken, and when the Algonquians "wish to end a war among themselves, they know better than we do the means for ending it." The Odawa, then, mediated between their kin and the French, and between their kin and others. They made themselves indispensable to all.[72]

Thus the Odawa at Michilimackinac took full advantage of the new opportunities they helped engineer. They carved out an important diplomatic, political, and economic place for themselves, acted in their collective self-interest, and played native and European empires against each other. They secured a steady supply of presents from the French and forced French traders to come to Michilimackinac, undermining the aims of French colonial and imperial officials. They procured what they needed and lived comfortably enough to protect themselves from the worst effects of periodic epidemics. The Odawa were not a "shattered" people living as "refugees." Despite the wars with the Iroquois and the effects of introduced European diseases, the Odawa were thriving.[73]

2

DEFENDING
ANISHINAABEWAKI

On one of their earlier trading voyages to the St. Lawrence, the French governor at Quebec asked visiting Anishinaabeg from the *pays d'en haut* to take a Jesuit priest back with them. Though the Anishinaabeg had invited some traders to return with them, they were not so sure about the missionary. After some discussion, they reluctantly agreed to take Father Claude Allouez. Soon after they were out of sight of the French settlement, though, one of their "chief men" told Allouez "in arrogant and menacing terms" of his and his people's intention to "abandon me on some desert Island if I ventured to follow them farther." When the French canoe broke upriver, the Indian party made good on that promise. They took the traders into their own canoes but abandoned Allouez. The determined Jesuit tried to follow, and after a series of mishaps and further rejections, Allouez finally managed to persuade one Indian to take him on board. Even then, he was treated with contempt, laughed at, and mocked. The Odawa stole most of his goods.[1]

Allouez's treatment should have been a warning to the French as they established a post at Michilimackinac in 1683. While some French traders no doubt profited from their toehold at the straits, French imperial interests were less well served. Officials thought that a settled trade was the best route to a military alliance with the nations of the *pays d'en haut*. As one observer put it, trade was essential to alliance with the Algonquians, for during times of war, "they always take the part of those with whom they trade." Subsequent historians have followed suit in asserting that trade relations underpinned the French-Algonquian alliance for much of the colonial period. Yet there is much evidence to suggest that trade was no guarantee of a formal alliance. At best, the Anishinaabeg formed relationships with particular traders. But they were loath to unthinkingly extend that alliance more generally to representative officials of the French colonial enterprise. In the same way they had encouraged illegal fur traders to come to Michilimackinac in the 1670s, the Odawa could undermine imperial interests when they did not serve their own ends. Subsequently, even as trade flourished at the straits, formal ties between the French and their Algonquian allies deteriorated rapidly. One seasoned observer called it a "great revolution" in French-Indian relations.[2]

•

While French officials hoped the establishment of the post at Michilimackinac in 1683 would assuage Anishinaabe concerns about a possible French-Iroquois rapprochement, they quickly learned that their Indian hosts expected much more. A thriving trade with French *coureurs de bois* and then an official French presence at Michilimackinac emboldened the Odawa themselves to push again for war against the Iroquois. Having consolidated their hold on the upper Great Lakes through the 1660s and 1670s, the Odawa grew alarmed at continued Iroquois aggression and advances to the south. But with the French now at Michilimackinac, Odawa there could strike back. They used French fears of an Iroquois-English alliance to push for greater military support. While the French dreamed of a peaceful and expansive western trading empire in the 1680s, the Odawa instead drew them into another round of destructive wars with the Iroquois.[3]

Even as Olivier La Durantaye arrived to set up the post in 1683, the stage was set for renewed hostilities. In the face of renewed Iroquois provocations, western Anishinaabeg had negotiated another temporary peace with the Dakota by joining with them to raid a common enemy, the Mesquakie, or Fox, in 1681. The way was clear for the Odawa at Michilimackinac to strike back at the Iroquois. Moreover, the Odawa insisted the French pay a price for the new French post beyond the gifts and presents Durantaye offered. They expected the French to aid them in their conflicts with their enemies. In Odawa eyes, the arrival of the French at Michilimackinac signified a renewal of war against the Iroquois. The Iroquois certainly interpreted it as such as well. Almost immediately, a party of French traders who had come up with La Durantaye was pillaged by a force of two hundred Iroquois on the Kankakee River south of Lake Michigan. The Odawa expected and pushed the French to take revenge.[4]

When news came in that hundreds more Iroquois had laid siege to the French post at St. Louis on the Illinois River, the French knew they were in a precarious position. The Jesuit missionary Father Jean Enjalran, who had recently arrived at Michilimackinac, told Governor La Barre in no uncertain terms that they either had to stand up to the Iroquois or would face attack and the loss of trade from "the nations of these quarters, who will become insolent to the last degree if you do not render to them the necessary protection." "We are obliged to listen to all those with whom we are allied," the Jesuit noted with concern, "until we are assured of a peaceful commerce, and that you protect it as much as they will want." The new French intendant, Jacques de Meulles, was convinced. He told the governor that war with the Iroquois was now essential. Otherwise, the Odawa and other allies would lose all respect for the French and ally instead with their enemies.[5]

Father Enjalran also suggested that internal politics among the Anishinaabeg increased the pressure exerted on the French. The decision to allow the French to establish a post at Michilimackinac in 1683 had not been a unanimous one. There were some among the families at Michilimackinac who had disagreed with the need for a French presence at the straits. But pro-French doodemag were able to persuade enough of their kinsmen to support the move. This did not stop critics from agitating against the French. As Father Enjalran noted a year after the French arrived, their opponents only waited for an opportunity to make an argument against the French presence—"which some bad-intentioned individuals have already supported, being pained to see Frenchmen here." Any perceived weakness on the part of the French toward Odawa enemies would give these factions succor and could easily result in a "mutiny." Another official at the post pointed out that the French should not make the mistake of thinking that the

establishment of the post meant sovereignty over the Indians. The nations there, he warned, were not in a "spirit of submission."[6]

The French had to act. They began planning an attack against the
Iroquois. Governor La Barre and Commandant Durantaye worked
desperately to mobilize their allies at Michilimackinac, as they were
hardly in a position to act on their own. But only the Huron taking
refuge with the Anishinaabeg initially accepted the hatchet offered by
the French. Most of the Odawa were content to let the French show
their mettle. They wanted proof that the French were serious about
attacking the Iroquois. Eventually, after many talks and a great deal of
gift giving, Durantaye managed to persuade some 400 Anishinaabeg
and perhaps another 150 Huron to accompany his smaller French
force of 150 troops and traders on an expedition. They were to head
southward and rendezvous with a larger French force under Governor
La Barre at Fort Frontenac. But the Anishinaabeg did not trust the
French; they worried the latter were still contemplating an Iroquois-
French alliance. They stalled, they threatened to turn back, and
when French pinnaces failed to show up at the Niagara River with
promised provisions and guns, they feared the French were leading
them into a trap. Eventually, a ship came up Lake Ontario from Fort
Frontenac, but instead of bringing supplies and reinforcements, it
brought only news that Governor La Barre had run short of supplies
and lost many of his troops to a bout of Spanish influenza. The Iroquois
forced him to sign a humiliating peace agreement that allowed them
to continue raiding Algonquian communities in the Illinois region.[7]

•

Imperial weakness gave anti-French factions among the Anishinaabeg
some influence. They exploited an astute understanding of the nature
of European rivalries to push their case. The year after the French
signed the peace treaty with the Iroquois, a party of Anishinaabeg
met with some Iroquois on the Ottawa River and told them they would
welcome English traders at Michilimackinac. Several months later,
eleven English canoes arrived at the straits and did a brisk trade with
the Odawa, who allegedly received them "cordially." The Odawa promised they would come to Albany to trade the following year if the
Seneca would lead them there. The English convoy caused a panic

among French officials. They believed they could lose the trade of the entire *pays d'en haut* to an Anishinaabe-Iroquois-English alliance. Another group of English traders came the following year, and two more tried to reach Michilimackinac in 1687. The Odawa welcomed the English in full view of the French garrison. Officials could do little but watch and report.[8]

Such pressure worked, especially in tandem with the turbulent world of court politics in France. For his failings against the Iroquois, the French king had replaced La Barre with a new governor, Jacques-René de Brisay de Denonville, the Marquis de Denonville. He arrived in the colony with a new mandate to act against the Iroquois, but he soon learned that the French had to move quickly or they would lose their valuable Anishinaabe allies. If that happened, the French would either lose the fur trade or their lives if the Iroquois renewed the war. Already, he lamented, "our reputation" is "absolutely lost both with our friends and our enemies." In desperation, Denonville in 1687 launched a hastily improvised campaign into Seneca country (on the western edge of the Finger Lakes region of what is now upstate New York), accompanied by a party of Odawa and Huron from Michilimackinac. Again, however, the French lost their nerve at the last minute. Denonville sued for peace prematurely, in part because war had broken out in Europe. The governor complained that he could do nothing more without considerable reinforcements from France.[9]

The Odawa and their allies, some of whom were still suffering attacks by the Iroquois, were furious. Kondiaronk (Sastaretsi, or "Le Rat" to the French), a Tionnontaté ogimaa at Michilimackinac, immediately undermined the French-Iroquois peace by manipulating the French at the post into killing an Iroquois captive. In response, while a huge Algonquian trade convoy was in Montreal in September 1689, an estimated fifteen hundred Iroquois warriors swept down on the village of Lachine, ten miles upstream from Montreal. They killed at least two dozen French and took as many as ninety more captive before burning more than two-thirds of the homes. The colony reeled from the attack. Yet Anishinaabeg in Montreal who witnessed firsthand the panic of the French had little sympathy. They were disgusted by French weakness.[10]

In a piece of diplomatic theater that would have rivaled any contemporary European court intrigues, the Odawa at Michilimackinac immediately called a council and unanimously resolved to open negotiations for peace with the Iroquois. At the very moment that peace between the French and Iroquois became impossible, the Odawa turned the tables. In an unusual move, they invited French observers at Michilimackinac to the council. They then showed great hospitality to several Iroquois prisoners, sending them off with the "famous calumet dance, which is a public Token of alliance." The calumet was a long pipe made from polished red stone that was often decorated with paint and feathers. Algonquian peoples used it in dances and ceremonies that ranged in purpose. As one Jesuit priest put it, they used the calumet "to put an end to Their disputes, to strengthen Their alliances, and to speak to Strangers." Yet given that the calumet and calumet dance had multiple uses, the French struggled to understand its meaning at any given time.[11]

On this occasion at least, Jesuit Father Étienne de Carheil thought the Odawa had another reason to perform the calumet dance: to impress on the French who were present at the ceremony "the contempt they felt for our alliance and for your [the governor's] protection." The Odawa had previously believed the "French man was warlike through numbers, through courage, and through the number and diversity of the implements of war which he could make." Now it was clear that they could expect nothing from the French. The French were "useless to them through his [the governor's] powerlessness." Moreover, their relationship with the French was becoming burdensome. It took away "the trade of the English, which was incomparably more advantageous to them." And the French gave little in return—from the start of the new war with the Iroquois, the French had done "nothing on his side against the enemy" and expected the Odawa to do "everything." Finally, in "seeking to save himself," the French governor had put the Odawa in danger of Iroquois vengeance.[12]

By the end of the open council, the French commandant and the Jesuits at Michilimackinac thought the post was in danger and that all the French in the *pays d'en haut* were about to be killed or thrown out of the Lakes in favor of an Odawa-Iroquois alliance. La Durantaye even believed the Odawa were about to attack the French fort at the straits. Carheil thought that the almost sure peace between the Iroquois and

Odawa would "take away our greatest strength from us, to give it to the enemy" and feared the imminent loss of the *pays d'en haut*. Carheil concluded, with some insight, "From this it will be seen that our savages are much more enlightened than one thinks; and that it is difficult to conceal from their penetration anything in the course of affairs that may injure or serve their interests."[13]

•

It is unlikely that the Odawa were serious about seeking peace with the Iroquois. This was high theater, designed to compel the French to act decisively against the Iroquois once and for all. The Odawa could afford to be pushy. They had benefited immensely from ongoing trade with the French at Michilimackinac. This had allowed them to push back against the Iroquois themselves, without French help. Once again, though French expeditions against the Iroquois had been inconclusive, the tribal histories of the Algonquian nations suggest that the Anishinaabeg and others launched numerous war parties against the Iroquois during this period but did so outside the purview of the French. These attacks were so successful that the Iroquois were in full retreat by the end of the 1680s. Though poorly documented because few French scribes were present, the histories of the attacking nations note the defeat of the Seneca in a canoe battle on Lake Erie, intertribal mobilization near Lake St. Clair, and a successful campaign across southern Ontario. A dramatic series of Algonquian victories over the Iroquois took place along the canoe routes through the old Huron settlements at the south end of Georgian Bay off Lake Huron and the chain of lakes and rivers along the Trent-Severn Waterway. A division of this joint campaign veered southward at Lake Simcoe toward present-day Toronto, aiming attacks at the western end of Lake Ontario.[14]

Raids led by Anishinaabe doodemag that included Odawa and Ojibwe warriors, their Huron allies, and many of their southeastern Anishinaabe kin, the Mississauga, forced the Iroquois away from their new settlements along the north shore of Lake Ontario. By 1687, the Iroquois had abandoned them and returned to New York. Then, in the final decade of the wars, the Mississauga Anishinaabeg and their allies defeated the Iroquois in several battles near the abandoned villages of old Huronia where so much fighting had taken place in 1649.

The wars had come full circle. Thereafter, the Mississauga occupied the northern lakeshore villages, and the Potawatomi gradually returned to more traditional locations along the south and eastern shores of Lake Michigan. No wonder, then, that at least some French felt the weight of the contempt in which they were held by their supposed allies. Around this time, the fur trader Nicolas Perrot noted that western nations like the Odawa held the "arrogant notion that the French cannot get along without them and that we could not maintain ourselves in the colony without the assistance that they give us."[15]

•

The French were only dimly aware of these inter-Indian battles, but they sensed that their fate once again lay in the hands of their native allies. Throughout the 1690s, letter after letter between Quebec and Versailles argued that the number of French troops in the colony would not be enough to defend it in case of a joint Iroquois-English attack. Nor were the French strong enough to eliminate the Iroquois themselves. For this, officials estimated they would need at least an additional four thousand troops. It would be easier, some suggested, to attack the English settlements instead. Given their vulnerability, the French believed that since they could not defeat the Iroquois without assistance, their alliances with the Algonquians were essential. As one chronicler of early French enterprises put it, "ultimately, as soon as these nations [of the Great Lakes] cease to defend our interests, it will be a catastrophe for Canada. They are our support and shield; it is they who curb the Iroquois in all the hunting parties they are obliged to make outside their territory for subsistence. Indeed, they go further, bringing fire and sword into the centre of [Iroquois] territory."[16]

The Anishinaabeg did just that. While the French claimed that their own important victories over the Iroquois finally brought them to the negotiating table, in fact they had their Indian allies to thank. In 1691, even while the Odawa and Huron again told the French they would pursue peace with the Iroquois, they went on the warpath. The French heard various reports that perhaps as many as eight hundred Indians from the upper Lakes were out on war parties against the Iroquois. They could only infer their success by the "marked inactivity" of the Iroquois and the abandonment of a Seneca village. When the French appeared to treat for peace again with the Iroquois in 1694, the Anishinaabeg entertained the Iroquois separately and warned the French they were on the verge of peace. They then renewed their efforts to wage war. The commandant of Michilimackinac at the time, Cadillac, estimated that as many as nine hundred warriors had gone out on war parties from the straits in the summer of 1695.[17]

Yet most of the Anishinaabeg and other Algonquians refused to join in the final French campaign against the Onondaga and Oneida Iroquois in 1696. In French lore, Governor Frontenac led a famous expedition against the Iroquois that year. It resulted in one Iroquois death. That same year, in separate expeditions, Odawa and Potawatomi warriors killed fifty, and perhaps as many as seventy, Iroquois and took captive another thirty. The Anishinaabeg continued their own punishing raids in league with others from the *pays d'en haut*, attacking in 1697, 1698, 1699, and 1700. One Iroquois chief pleaded to the French governor in 1699 in Montreal, "I beseech you, my father, make your allies stop coming into our territory every day and breaking our heads." The Iroquois were forced to seek peace. When trouble began again with the Dakota on their western flank, the Anishinaabeg themselves finally seemed ready to stop the conflict with the Iroquois. They made peace with them in 1700. In turn, this paved the way for a general peace treaty in 1701 between the French, the Iroquois, and the Anishinaabeg and other Algonquians of the *pays d'en haut*. Once again, the French colony on the banks of the St. Lawrence owed its misfortune—and ultimate survival—to its native neighbors.[18]

•

The Great Peace of Montreal of 1701 has long been seen as a turning point in French-Indian relations in North America. With more than thirteen hundred Native Americans in attendance from as far away as the Mississippi Valley in the west and Acadia in the east—representing at least forty different nations—it was certainly an unprecedented gathering. The French saw the outcome of the conference as an unmitigated success. They established a peace between themselves and the Iroquois, gained a promise of Iroquois neutrality in the case of war between England and France, and seemingly brokered a peace between all the nations of the *pays d'en haut* and the Iroquois. The French

positioned themselves as official mediators in any further disputes between the Algonquians and the Iroquois. Anyone attacked by another
was told to come to the French before taking revenge. The French
governor would seek satisfaction from the offending party or use the
force of the alliance to compel them to do so. Having asserted their
authority over the peoples of the *pays d'en haut*, the French thought
they could look forward to a long era of peace and trade with their old
and new Native allies.[19]

Yet within a few years, the Anishinaabeg of Michilimackinac once
again made a mockery of French officials' dreams. While the treaty did
initiate a long period of peace between the French and the Iroquois, it
only papered over the underlying tension between the Iroquois and
the Anishinaabeg. The latter were still wary of the intentions of their
ancient rivals. Moreover, the peace brought to the fore divisions between
some of the Algonquian nations of the *pays d'en haut*. It was not long
before the region was in turmoil again—only this time the protagonists
were primarily the Algonquian-speaking nations whom the French
hoped to retain as allies. In spending years trying to unite the western
nations to work with them against the Iroquois, the French misunderstood the nature of the long-standing rivalries that divided Native
Americans in the Lakes. Formal peace with the Iroquois gave some
of these nations more freedom to pursue their own interests. French
plans for a far-flung, peaceful, trade-based empire quickly gave way to
a new reality in Indian politics. Within a few years of the Great Peace,
the French were again embroiled in a world of Indian warfare.

The French inadvertently ignited this new fuse. First, they announced in 1696 that they were closing their western posts and with-
drawing their traders from the *pays d'en haut*. Citing a glut in the
market for beaver furs, and continued frustration with their inability
to regulate the movements and trade of the *coureurs de bois*, the crown
decided to restrict all trade to the St. Lawrence Valley. The king also
noted his anger at the wartime machinations of their supposed Indian
allies and the resulting cost of the protracted war. An expansive empire
would only lead to further costly wars. He wanted the colony to focus
more on farming on the St. Lawrence and less on hunting and trade with
the western nations. The post at Michilimackinac would be closed.[20]

Simultaneously, wrangling among colonial officials in New France led to the creation of a new French post at *le détroit*, or Detroit, in 1701—an initiative almost single-handedly spearheaded by the grasping and ambitious Cadillac, who had glimpsed the riches possible with a monopoly over the western trade during his short tenure at Michilimackinac. But Cadillac well knew who controlled the trade at the straits. The Odawa there were the ones who had encouraged the illegal traders who eventually flooded European markets. The Odawa also carefully regulated which Native nations could trade, and only those allied to the Anishinaabeg were allowed to bring their furs to the straits. Cadillac knew he needed an alternative to Michilimackinac. He wanted to circumvent the Odawa. While hoping to engross a larger portion of the trade for himself by excluding illegal traders, Cadillac convinced others of the value of his scheme by citing the danger of English trade advances. In the absence of other trading posts in the *pays d'en haut*, Cadillac argued that a strong French presence at Detroit would serve as a barrier against further trade and alliance initiatives between the northern Indians and the Iroquois and English—an especially worrisome prospect since peace had now been restored, but doubly so because the French had stopped trading at Michilimackinac. It was not that much harder to travel to Albany via Iroquoia than Montreal.[21]

Cadillac's scheming found a ready audience, because of course French officials had long fretted about the possibility of increased contact between the northern and western nations and the Iroquois and the English. After some Anishinaabeg made their way to the Detroit region in the 1680s, for example, Governor Denonville had ordered a post built at Detroit, specifically noting, "We know perfectly well of what importance it is to hold all of the passages which link the Ottawas to the English." Though this early order came to naught, Cadillac exploited these same fears to push through his project in 1701—at the very moment the French abandoned all other posts.[22]

A post at Detroit, though, also served other imperial purposes. With it, the French could bypass Michilimackinac and use Detroit to concentrate trade with the nations farther to the west. The French had long coveted trading relations with the nations and peoples west of the Great Lakes whom they had glimpsed on exploratory missions over the course of the seventeenth century. They also knew that the

Odawa at Michilimackinac had often blocked their attempts to trade directly with them. Most French officials were eager to establish good relations with as many fur-trading nations as possible in order to keep their European rivals from trading and allying with them. In pursuing this goal, however, they often curried new alliances with long-standing rivals of the Anishinaabeg. As early as 1679, for example, a group of French and Fox smoked the calumet together in an attempt to initiate a long, peaceful, and profitable relationship. In 1695, separate delegations from both the Fox and the Dakota Sioux visited Montreal.[23]

War with the Iroquois had, at least in part, kept the French from pursuing these links. Some French—like Cadillac—saw the Great Peace and the post at Detroit as an opportunity to expand and monopolize more profits from the fur trade. Officials in Versailles gave grudging assent because they were desperate to secure and expand their alliances with western nations to exclude the English. Though some warned that this would only lead to conflict among the western nations, Cadillac's silver tongue and a general desire to cultivate new allies and trading partners farther westward helped arrest opposition.[24]

The French put this thinking into practice starting in 1701. For example, the governor invited the Fox to the Great Peace conference as full partners rather than enemies of the French-Algonquian alliance. Then, when Cadillac established the post at Detroit, he signaled French intentions to make welcome all the western nations. He also claimed they would help mediate peace between nations in conflict, usurping the Anishinaabe role at Michilimackinac. Colonial officials dreamed of an extensive and more peaceful western alliance that would bankroll and secure their foothold in North America. Cadillac dreamed of the personal riches that would accrue to him by making Detroit the preeminent post for a vastly extended trading network. Yet few French officials understood the true nature of the politics of the *pays d'en haut* and the central position of the Odawa of Michilimackinac. They would pay dearly for their ignorance.[25]

•

French moves alarmed many Anishinaabeg. Most Odawa at Michilimackinac saw the end of the war with the Iroquois in a significantly different light than did the French. As the war in the east wound down, many thought it high time to put their western affairs in order. While the French looked forward to expanded trade relations with the far western nations, the Anishinaabeg looked back to settle some old scores. They were champing at the bit. Throughout the 1670s, 1680s, and 1690s, the Anishinaabeg had joined with Illinois and Huron war parties to raid the Fox in particular. The source of the conflict between the Anishinaabeg and the Fox was unclear, but it may have had something to do with the eastward movement of the Fox from the upper reaches of the Mississippi to the Fox-Wisconsin River region. There, they may have competed and come into conflict with mixed groups of Anishinaabeg and the nations of the Illinois region farther to the south. Kinship ties and wartime obligations would have drawn the Anishinaabeg of Michilimackinac into the conflict. There was also an increase in skirmishes with their long-standing western rivals the Lakota Sioux. The Nassauakueton Odawa, for example, launched an unsuccessful expedition against a group of Siouan speakers. Then, in 1695, possibly in response to this attack, word came from western Lake Michigan that the Mascouten and Fox were forming an alliance with the Sioux, and possibly with the Five Nations.[26]

The Anishinaabeg repeatedly sent delegations to Montreal demanding that the French help fight against the Sioux and avenge the death of the chief of the Nassauakueton. The French insisted they would not do so while still at war with the Iroquois, but they made promises that as soon as that conflict ended, they would help with the western war. After the Peace of Montreal, then, the Anishinaabeg expected military support, not French mediation. Indeed, the renewed war in the west may have been one of the few reasons the Anishinaabeg accepted peace with the Iroquois. By 1703, they pressed the French to make good on their promises to war with the Sioux. By this point, they were further angered that French traders with permits had crossed their lands and villages on their way to trade with the Sioux, who were in turn using their newly acquired French arms against the Anishinaabeg. After one skirmish, the Anishinaabeg found the bodies of two French men who had died fighting alongside the Sioux.[27]

Under the circumstances, then, the Anishinaabeg were infuriated with the stoppage of French trade at Michilimackinac at the very moment when they needed it most—as they pursued a multifronted war in the east and west. The withdrawal of the French could only be seen as a hostile act—particularly in light of French diplomatic outreach among the Fox and Sioux. The Anishinaabeg were having none of it. As Onanguissé, a chief visiting Montreal, threatened in 1697, if the French quit the *pays d'en haut*, "you shall never see us again." They would never return to Montreal. French officials attending the council were shocked by his vehemence. The following year, the Sable and Kiskakon Odawa told the French of their intention to leave Michilimackinac and set up shop closer to English trade.[28]

•

Threats such as these initially helped bolster Cadillac's argument for a new post at Detroit. But when it became clearer to the Anishinaabeg that the French intended to reestablish a post at Detroit and would welcome all nations to trade with them there, the relationship grew poisonous. Cadillac had failed to appreciate, or at least publicly acknowledge, the enmity between some of those nations and the Anishinaabeg. The Anishinaabeg feared that rivals such as the Fox and Sioux would use the Detroit post to arm themselves. It might even become an axis along which the Iroquois, Miami, and Fox could unite. When the Fox boldly attacked Ojibwe near the southeastern corner of Lake Superior in 1703—shortly after they began trading with the French at Detroit— Anishinaabe fears were realized.[29]

Cadillac's post at Detroit also represented a direct threat to Anishinaabe security on their southeastern flank. As the Sable and Kiskakon Odawa threats made clear, the Anishinaabeg had designs of their own on the Detroit area, and successes against the Iroquois in the previous decades had motivated at least some from Michilimackinac to migrate there already. They had long claimed Detroit as their own. Now, with the Iroquois set back once again, the fertile lands and long growing season of the southern Bkejwanong region—as the Anishinaabeg called it—were even more attractive. Moreover, the Anishinaabeg had long coveted Bkejwanong to reinforce the boundaries of their southern flank, preventing any encirclement by either their western enemies or the Iroquois. Not coincidentally, of course, a presence at Bkejwanong would also help the Anishinaabeg keep a door open to the English.[30]

But the Peace of Montreal in 1701 and the French move to Detroit gave many Anishinaabeg pause. While still at war with the Iroquois, some had actually lobbied for a French post there to help protect their interests in the region. They had, however, expected the French to pursue the war with the Iroquois with greater vigor. Both Governor Denonville in 1687 and Cadillac as recently as 1695 had promised to prosecute the war with the Iroquois until they had achieved the "entire destruction of the common enemy." Yet in 1701, the French abruptly changed tack and seemed keen on "sparing and Preserving" the enemies of the Anishinaabeg. Whereas prior to 1701, the Anishinaabeg believed they could "peaceably enjoy" the lands around Detroit once the Iroquois were eliminated, after the Great Peace was signed, many Anishinaabeg had "completely Changed their minds, and no longer look upon Detroit in any other light than That of an Enemy's country, where they can have no Wish to dwell, and where there can be no security for them." The closure of the French post at Michilimackinac, combined with the opening of Detroit, seemed to signal a change in French policy that could only favor their old enemies.[31]

That feeling grew as so many rival nations—and potential allies of the Iroquois—moved to Anishinaabe-claimed land around Detroit. For amid the tense situation, Cadillac made the further error of not just welcoming trade but also of inviting all the western nations to come and live at the new post. The Huron who had taken refuge among the Anishinaabeg at Michilimackinac immediately took advantage of the offer and moved to Detroit. Crucially, many of those who moved resented their forced stay with the Anishinaabeg and/or were Iroquois sympathizers. Though Iroquois speaking, the Huron had a long history of enmity with the Iroquois. But their enforced period of refuge among the Anishinaabeg had created tensions between the former trading partners. A later French report noted that the Huron were held in a "sort of slavery" while living alongside the Odawa at Michilimackinac, a situation that grew worse once the French abandoned the post.[32]

Some Huron were also eager to open up trade links with the English. Some planned to move closer to Albany; others were plotting with the Miami and thinking about moving even farther southward. A few saw the move to Detroit as an opportunity to renew relations with the

Iroquois. One group traveled to Albany in 1702 and told the English and the Iroquois "not to trust the [Ottawas] for they are a brutish People." Evidence also suggests that an increase in intermarriages between the Huron and Iroquois began almost immediately after the Great Peace of 1701. By 1704, some Iroquois families had even moved in to the new Huron village at Detroit. In Anishinaabe eyes, the Huron who had moved to Detroit appeared to be actively seeking new alliances with the Anishinaabeg's rivals to bolster their own power in the region.[33]

In light of perceived Huron machinations, Anishinaabeg at both Michilimackinac and those who had already made the move to Detroit were alarmed further when more groups of rival Algonquian nations began arriving at the new post. Groups of Miami, Mascouten, Kickapoo, and Sauk came to live at Detroit. They likely came from the Fox-Wisconsin River region and may have moved under pressure from the eastward-drifting Fox. Though Algonquian speaking, the Anishinaabeg apparently had few ties to these different nations and could therefore command no allegiances. Without the glue of kinship, these nations were rivals and could be wooed away by the Anishinaabeg's enemies. The Anishinaabeg were horrified. They were now in danger of being surrounded—and overwhelmed—by foreign nations. As more peoples arrived in Detroit, delegation after delegation of Anishinaabeg traveled to Montreal to warn French officials of the grave consequences that would follow if the resettlements were not stopped. And still they came.[34]

These developments would have been alarming enough to most Anishinaabeg in the region. But the Odawa at Michilimackinac in particular were in jeopardy of losing their carefully constructed position within the politics of the *pays d'en haut*. The closure of the Michilimackinac trading post was a significant blow to their economic security. For some time now, the Anishinaabeg around Michilimackinac had relied less on trapping and trading furs themselves and more on supplying the valuable provisioning trade that flourished at the straits. With Indians now expected to bring their furs to Detroit or Montreal, the Anishinaabeg would lose their place as crucial intermediaries in the trade. Not only would they have to resume trapping for their needs, they would also have to travel afar to trade those furs.

At places like Montreal and Detroit, they would be one group among many competing for European goods in return for their furs. They would be at the mercy of French merchants while leaving their families vulnerable to western enemies.

While Odawa fortunes declined, the Huron's grew. Experienced horticulturalists, they quickly stepped in to become the primary provisioners at Detroit. They seemed eager to reestablish the prominence in the fur trade they enjoyed up until the middle of the seventeenth century, when the Iroquois had shattered Huronia. The Huron resented the fact that the Anishinaabeg had not only suffered much less than they had from these attacks but even seemed to benefit from them in the long run, by usurping their position in the burgeoning fur trade. Envious of the Odawa, at least some Huron had long wanted to make peace with the Iroquois and English in order to counter Odawa power. Even as early as 1687, then-governor Denonville had noted that the Huron hoped to become "master of the entire trade of the other Far Nations."[35]

The new French post at Detroit also threatened Odawa political and military security because it split the community at the straits. Facing the loss of the lucrative provisioning trade and their preeminent position among the thousands of French and Indians alike who gathered yearly at Michilimackinac, the Odawa were torn over how to respond. Some left to go to Detroit to salvage what they could from the situation there. Yet many others, despite making early promises to move, refused to go. Over time, without the provisioning trade to anchor them at the straits, many Anishinaabeg did migrate, but to greener pastures farther afield. Some went to their wintering grounds at Grand River, along the eastern shore of Lake Michigan; others went to Saginaw, on the western shore of Lake Huron; and some went to Manitoulin Island, northeast of Michilimackinac. Still others who went to Detroit either drifted back to Michilimackinac or followed kin elsewhere. It seemed to some at least that Anishinaabe dominance at Michilimackinac was over.[36]

Certainly, without the provisioning trade, the Odawa who remained could no longer command the respect and authority over the other nations in the region. Their vaunted role as peacemakers was lost. Their central position in the French empire was in jeopardy. But the Odawa also faced the disintegration of the very settlements that had put them in such an advantageous position. As Koutaouiliboe—an ogimaa at Michilimackinac—complained in 1712, before the establishment of Detroit, "All the tribes respected us because they were obliged to come here for what they had need of," but that was no longer the case. The Odawa used to be, he lamented, "people of importance."[37]

•

The division of the Odawa could not have happened at a worse time. With war in the west against the Dakota again a possibility, the French enjoying a cozy relationship with the Iroquois, the Huron growing in strength and stature, and more of their rivals moving into Detroit every day, the Odawa felt isolated and vulnerable, and they quickly grew hostile. It was only a matter of time before the once simmering trouble boiled over.

The Odawa of Michilimackinac struck first. Less than three years after the French celebrated the Great Peace of Montreal in 1701, a party of Odawa attacked an Iroquois village located adjacent to the French Fort Frontenac (near present-day Kingston, Ontario). They did so while on an ostensibly peaceful mission accompanied by a group of Huron and Miami. But their purpose was clear. They planted a distinctive Huron club on a dead Iroquois warrior to try to drive a wedge between those two nations. Then, to demonstrate to the French what they thought about the Great Peace and the rapprochement between the French and the Iroquois, the party deliberately canoed past the French fort at Detroit, parading thirty captive Iroquois. The Odawa wanted to provoke another war between the French and the Iroquois and thus wreck their plans for Detroit. They later told the Iroquois the French had instigated the attack. Governor Philippe de Rigaud, the Marquis de Vaudreuil, who had been appointed in 1703, believed the Odawa struck because they wanted their kin at Detroit to return to Michilimackinac. Their plan almost worked. Pro-English Iroquois agitated among their kin to attack the Odawa. The French had to engage in frantic negotiations with the Iroquois to prevent a revenge attack that would have turned Detroit inside out. As it was, the attack succeeded only in further souring Odawa-French relations. The French even contemplated war against the Odawa. If a conflict between the

Iroquois and Anishinaabeg arose, Governor Vaudreuil concluded, it would be necessary "to take the side of the Iroquois."[38]

Amid the tense stand-off, further trouble at Detroit seemed inevitable. Relations between the Huron and the Anishinaabeg worsened as the former strengthened their relations with both the Miami and Iroquois through trade and intermarriage. As early as 1702, one Jesuit missionary predicted that resentments between the Odawa and the Huron would "explode one day" soon. The Odawa later claimed the Miami and Huron taunted them about the loss of the French post at Michilimackinac. The Huron had said the Odawa no longer had a father, as he had abandoned them—the proof was that they had no more gunpowder. Le Pesant, a Sable Odawa chief living at Detroit who was unhappy with what the French had done there, claimed the Miami had actually attacked them twice. In turn, the Huron conspired further with the Miami and Iroquois. Years of resentments built up while living as refugees among the Anishinaabeg encouraged Huron enmity. Because of the "just causes" for Huron retaliation against the Anishinaabeg, Governor Vaudreuil told the king's ministers at Versailles, "we know they are only waiting for an opportunity to fly at each other's throats."[39]

That opportunity came when Anishinaabe warriors left to attack the Sioux in June 1706. A Potawatomi warned them that in their absence, the Huron and the Miami would attack the Odawa village at Detroit and kill those who remained. The war party turned back and instead, joined by warriors from Michilimackinac, launched a preemptive attack on a group of Miami chiefs, killing five and driving the rest back to the French fort. During the ensuing melee, the French fired on the attacking Anishinaabeg and killed a young warrior. In retaliation, angry Anishinaabeg killed a French Recollect priest outside the fort and a soldier who tried to rescue him. A fierce and deadly fight followed. Before anyone could blink, as many as three Frenchmen, thirty Odawa, fifty Miamis, and an unknown number of Hurons were killed.[40]

The Odawa involved in the fighting fled to Michilimackinac, and for almost a year after, the French and Odawa stood poised on the brink of war with each other. The Jesuit missionary Father Joseph-Jacques Marest, who had stayed behind at the straits, told the governor that he was worried about the safety of their countrymen, both at

Detroit and at the straits. Though they were horrified at the flagrant killing of the priest and soldier, French officials were even more worried about the prospect of a major war with one of their most powerful allies. They well knew that should they go to war with the Odawa, they would have to contend with at least eight or ten allied Algonquian nations. From the other side, the Huron and Miami pressed the French to avenge the deaths of their warriors. If the French did not appease the Huron, they might find themselves at war with a Huron-Miami-Iroquois alliance. French officials engaged in frantic negotiations, but throughout, Governor Vaudreuil noted that the Odawa neither desired peace nor feared war.[41]

The French were forced to back down. Though Vaudreuil had earlier contemplated allying with the Iroquois against the Odawa at Michilimackinac, events at Detroit ruled it out. The now real prospect of an Iroquois-Huron-Miami alliance against the Odawa was unthinkable. The French had to take the side of the Odawa. They did so because they feared the Iroquois and were dependent on the Odawa as a counterweight to them—to prevent the Iroquois from becoming too powerful again. Vaudreuil explained to the king that if the Huron, Miami, and Iroquois united, they would drive the Odawa from Detroit and Michilimackinac, and if the Odawa at Michilimackinac were pushed out, the Iroquois would be free to "wage a bloodier war than ever against us," because they would have "nothing more to oppose him above." Moreover, the French would lose a "considerable trade" and create another powerful enemy. If the Odawa were driven out of Michilimackinac, the governor concluded, they would simply "take refuge in Lake Superior," trade with the English at Hudson's Bay, and "continue the war as long as the memory of what they will have suffered dwells among them."[42]

Kinship politics shaped the denouement. From his post at Detroit, Cadillac declared the Sable Odawa ogimaa Le Pesant responsible for the French deaths and demanded retribution. But the seventy-year-old chief had already fled north to Michilimackinac. In council after council with Cadillac and the governor, the other Odawa ogimaag insisted that they could not turn him over. Vaudreuil thought it was a matter of authority: "The savages have no sufficient authority over each other to be able to hand anyone over." But the question of authority was intimately tied to doodemag politics. The Odawa insisted that the aged and well-connected Pesant was too influential and had too many allies around the Lakes simply to turn him over. Whoever did so would be responsible for his fate and would have to answer to all his kin. When Cadillac issued an ultimatum, the Odawa gathered at Michilimackinac and found waiting not only Anishinaabe kin from Sault Ste. Marie, Detroit, and St. Joseph's, but also Menominee representatives and even some Sauk, Winnebago, and Fox from the Green Bay region. All of them were keenly interested in the fate of Le Pesant, because "he is allied to almost all of them." Though the French were not privy to these inter-Indian discussions, the Odawa must have brokered a deal. Just after the visiting nations left, a group of Odawa ogimaag brought Le Pesant down to Detroit. Conveniently, though, the overweight septuagenarian somehow escaped over a palisade wall soon after he was handed over to the French. Still, the Odawa were absolved of any further responsibility even while the king continued to insist on punishing someone. The Miami and Huron were also furious that Le Pesant had escaped, and attacked the French. They threatened to raise war parties with the Iroquois against the French and Odawa. But French colonial officials stood their ground. They brought no Odawa to justice for the killings.[43]

•

Still, the theatrics did nothing for French-Anishinaabe relations. For their part, the Odawa were still angry with the French for maintaining the post at Detroit and abandoning Michilimackinac. Those at the straits were annoyed further by Cadillac's insistent demands that they only trade at Detroit or, if they wanted to bring furs to the St. Lawrence Valley, that they do so by traveling via Detroit. The Odawa had long favored the route to Montreal across Lake Huron and via the French and Ottawa Rivers. The journey down to Detroit and then across Lakes Erie and Ontario was not only longer, but brought them closer to their enemies, including the Iroquois. On top of this, Cadillac kept insisting that the remaining Odawa at Michilimackinac come to Detroit to live. The Odawa at the straits were having none of it. Surely, they told Vaudreuil, Cadillac should be "content with having divided our village." Though there was some talk of the Anishinaabeg abandoning

Detroit altogether, many decided to remain. Most were irritated that the French allowed the Huron and Miami to stay at the post, but they could not afford to abandon the site to their rivals. "Those of our people who are with him," Odawa from Michilimackinac noted about Cadillac and his post, "were settled with him before." "We do not regret that," they concluded.[44]

But relations with the French remained troubled. The Anishinaabeg used all the muscle they could muster short of outright war, including threats to defect to the English. And given the circumstances, these were potent warnings. The War of the Spanish Succession (1701–1714) had spilled over into North America, where it was known as Queen Anne's War. The French and some of their eastern native allies had taken the opportunity to harass settlements in New England, culminating in a famous raid on Deerfield, Massachusetts, in 1704 in which more than a hundred captives were taken and brought back to Indian settlements near Montreal. In retaliation, New England colonists made plans to take Port Royal, Montreal, and even Quebec. Given that the English tried to persuade the Iroquois to join them, the Anishinaabeg were likely aware of the threats to invade New France. The French were petrified at any rumors that the Anishinaabeg might join the English, however unlikely. As the Jesuit priest and colonial historian Pierre Charlevoix put it, "If these people ever joined the English and the Iroquois, one solitary campaign would suffice to oblige all of the French to leave Canada."[45]

The situation was serious enough for the French crown to intervene directly. The bloodshed at Detroit, the threats against the French, and the Anishinaabeg's own complaints to the governor of New France pushed the minister of marine to act. In 1708 he sent an emissary, François Clairambault D'Aigremont, a forty-eight-year-old naval commissary who had the ear of the intendant in New France and the crown at Versailles, to the Great Lakes to assess the volatile situation. The minister asked Clairambault to inspect the trading posts and report on any illicit trading by post commanders. Rumors flew across the Atlantic that not only was Cadillac mismanaging Indian affairs, but he was also involved in trading with the English himself. Clairambault was to inspect the old and new trading posts and determine the "usefulness or otherwise of each post" so that the king might maintain the important ones and abandon the others.[46]

Clairambault spent a considerable amount of time at Detroit, and the bulk of his report was a damning indictment of Cadillac's governance and the decision to establish a post there. His main concern was that the post had, as the Odawa complained, brought many Indians and illegal French traders into closer contact with the Iroquois and English. The French lost a substantial amount of valuable furs this way, Clairambault concluded. He believed that even with all the Indians settled peacefully at Detroit, they would not get one-tenth of the pelts they would get from Michilimackinac because of its proximity to the Iroquois. The furs would be diverted through Iroquoia to the English. The Huron helped make these vital connections, and many Indians "have gone that way." But there would never be peace at Detroit in any case, Clairambault noted, so the trade would never be settled. The Huron, Miami, Wea, and Kickapoo were conspiring to form closer relations with the Iroquois. The Anishinaabeg would never allow it. He wrote a long report of the 1706 affair, effectively exonerating the Anishinaabe Odawa from any wrongdoing.[47]

In contrast, Clairambault took a highly favorable view of Michilimackinac. He concluded it was "the most advantageous post in Canada." The straits were vital, he said, because they were the conduit for all the superior, thicker pelts that were funneled through there from colder northern climes. The beaver furs brought to Detroit were of a poorer quality and less thick, as were many other kinds of pelts brought there. The only quality items traded at Detroit were deer hides that were used by French habitants along the St. Lawrence. The northern furs brought through Michilimackinac, he claimed, were worth perhaps twice as much as the southern furs. But without a post at the straits, the French were cut off from the supply. Moreover, traders were unable to reprovision there, so some were taking their furs to Hudson Bay instead. Nor would the Odawa bother to come down to Montreal with the furs they accumulated. They usually sold their furs to other Indians on the way, who in turn took them to Albany.[48]

While stressing the importance of Michilimackinac to the French fur trade enterprise, Clairambault also emphasized the part played by the Odawa and the terms on which they expected the trading post's reestablishment. He noted that the Odawa wanted the return of an official French post with a garrison of thirty men. They even asked for a specific commander they knew. A garrison was essential if the French were not to "lose the natives in the Upper Country who are allied to us," Governor Vandreuil would later write. Sending only a post commander, he warned, "instead of inspiring respect in the natives, it will only serve to make them despise us." But Clairambault also thought the Odawa wanted the soldiers as a market for their provisioning trade. He said the soldiers must grow no crops of their own, for that would "cause disputes to arise between the soldiers of that garrison and the natives." They also wanted to sell to visiting Native Americans. The Odawa sold corn to Indians from upcountry, often in exchange for their furs. This supplemented their own hunts and gave the Odawa a reliable supply of tradeable pelts of all types. They grew enough, despite the poor soils at the straits, to sell to both visiting natives and the French.[49]

The Anishinaabeg convinced Clairambault of the strategic importance of the site as well. They reminded him it was the point of "resort of all the tribes" that came down from Lake Superior, Green Bay, and St. Joseph's River. That meant the Odawa were central to all the exchanges that took place at the post. The French did much of their trading with the Odawa, who in turn traded with the visiting Indians. But it also meant the Odawa wielded great influence over these nations. Anyone on their way to the lower settlements, the Iroquois, or the St. Lawrence would have to come through the straits. Michilimackinac also was a formidable stronghold. It was difficult to approach it from any direction without being discovered, and was "inaccessible to the most powerful of their enemies," Clairambault wrote. Neither the Miami nor the Fox "were people of the canoe."[50]

French officials, desperate to keep the Anishinaabeg as allies, relented. Alarmed by the bloodshed among their valued allies, concerned about the future of the fur trade, they agreed with almost all of Clairambault's recommendations. At Versailles, the minister of the marine endorsed his report and, in June 1709, ordered the reestablishment of the post at Michilimackinac. Clairambault thought the post so important to maintain, and the Odawa so central to the smooth running of the fur trade, that it was worth enforcing an artificially high price for beaver pelts to stop them from trading with the English. Without this added incentive, they could not keep them from doing so except by force. And that would be a disaster, since the Anishinaabeg would simply join with the Iroquois in making war on the French, "which would be extremely unfortunate for this Colony."[51]

Governor Vaudreuil agreed. In his report on the colony in 1708, he told the crown they were doing all they could to retain cordial alliances with the Indians, as "only this alliance can secure the happiness and safety of this Colony." They had to maintain a steady stream of costly presents to keep pace with the English, "who practice every art to attract them." They were also unable to effectively punish the Anishinaabeg responsible for the killings in 1706 because that, too, would mean war. They had to do everything in their power to prevent further conflict, either between themselves and the Anishinaabeg or the Anishinaabeg and other Native nations. That meant appeasing the Odawa at Michilimackinac. By 1710 most French officials were in agreement that they had to reestablish the post.[52]

•

But it was too late. Even as French imperial strategists in Quebec and Versailles finally came around to the idea, local officials at Detroit made a deadly mistake. In the wake of Clairambault's damning report, Cadillac had been punished in the time-honored manner—with a promotion to the governorship of Louisiana. This left the post at Detroit in the hands of the relatively inexperienced Jacques-Charles Renaud Dubuisson, a military officer who had spent most of his time at Quebec. Dubuisson invited a new group of nations—including the Fox—to come and live at Detroit. The French were still interested in mediating peace between the Fox and their enemies. They thought they could realize their expansive vision of a western trade alliance only if the Fox were at peace. As the English pressed their advantage in Queen Anne's War and the Iroquois again threatened to join the fray, the French believed it was now essential that they ensure Fox loyalty. But they seemed oblivious to the enmity between the Fox and other nations at Detroit, most especially the Anishinaabeg. When a thousand Fox, Kickapoo, and Mascouten arrived at Detroit in 1710–1711, the area was primed for further conflict.[53]

The arrival of the newcomers gave the Anishinaabeg the excuse they needed to right the wrongs of the past decade. Most had grown frustrated with unfulfilled French promises. Since Clairambault's visit, the French had promised to reestablish a post at Michilimackinac but had not yet delivered. The Anishinaabeg, already angry that they had lost so much ground to so many of their rivals, were aghast at the invitation extended to the Fox. Now, "the most savage and unreasonable of the nations," they protested, could trade and live at Detroit "in as great numbers as they wish" and "buy their powder and trouble their allies."[54]

The Anishinaabeg and their allies moved to end once and for all French dreams of an expansive western trade and alliance system. As the Fox and Mascouten began to hunt in territories north of Detroit that the Anishinaabeg had long claimed for their own wintering grounds, violence erupted. Once again, a war ogimaa from Michilimackinac, Sakima, began the conflict. Amid rumors of Fox overtures to the Iroquois and the British, a series of raids and counterraids culminated in a massive attack on a group of Mascouten in the winter of 1711–1712. In the spring, the Mascouten poured into Detroit seeking mediation from the French and protection from the Fox. A mixed group of largely Odawa and Potawatomi then surrounded the Fox village and threatened to kill all those inside unless they released their prisoners and returned to their own lands west of Green Bay.[55]

As they massed against the Fox and Mascouten, the Anishinaabeg made amends with the Huron in the face of a common threat. They also conspired to convince the French that the Fox and Mascouten had been in the midst of launching an attack on the French themselves. The Anishinaabeg claimed they had thwarted them. When the Fox appealed to the French to make good on their promises to mediate, the naive post commander Dubuisson instead joined the attack. By the time the slaughter ended, nearly a thousand Fox and Mascouten were dead or captured, and French hopes for peace were shattered. As Kinongé, a Sable Odawa ogimaa at Detroit, put it to Vaudreuil in 1713, "this war that we have with the Outagamis [Fox] is your war just as it is our war, because you were killed by them just as they killed us." But the French were more deeply implicated in this new conflict than that. In the aftermath of the battle, the victors enslaved many Fox women and children and then sold them to the French. Much against French wishes, the Anishinaabeg had ensnared them in a near-genocidal conflict with the Fox that would last a generation.[56]

Indeed, this was only the beginning of an increasingly destructive, decades-long wasting war with the Fox initiated and encouraged by the Anishinaabeg and their allies. Significantly, as the historian Brett Rushforth has shown, their most successful strategy was to continue to raid Fox villages for captives, then sell or give these to the French, driving a deep wedge between the French and their potential allies, the Fox. Even while officially pushing for peace, French colonists' unwillingness to give up their slaves helped ensure that the Fox would rebuff any official overtures for peace. Though the French knew the Anishinaabeg and others were actively wrecking any chance for reconciliation with the Fox, they could do nothing about it.[57]

•

In the short run, the Anishinaabeg at Michilimackinac got what they wanted. While this first phase of the war with the Fox destabilized the region once again, the outcome was very different from the peace of 1701. For one thing, the war made the French realize that an immediate return to Michilimackinac was imperative. Governor Vaudreuil wrote to Versailles that this was precisely what he feared when he warned the previous year that a full-scale war between Algonquian nations was imminent. He reiterated his belief that only the reestablishment of the post at Michilimackinac could put an end to it. The French promptly started reissuing trade *congés*, or licenses, and reoccupied posts at Michilimackinac, Green Bay, Ouiatenon, Chequamegon, and St. Joseph's and in the Illinois region. In 1715–1716, they undertook the construction of a new fort on the south side of the straits at Michilimackinac, near one of the main Odawa villages. By 1717, one report noted that there were six hundred Frenchmen back in Michilimackinac for the trading season.[58]

French traders were greeted by a newly reunified Odawa community. As early as the summer of 1712, reports noted that conflict with the Fox had "brought the greater part of them together again at Michilimakinac [sic]." Those who had moved to Grand River and Saginaw, and even some from Detroit, had already returned. Others who had moved to Manitoulin Island were expected to come back soon. Only the arrival of a group of French reinforcements at Detroit had stopped all of the Odawa from returning to the straits. With both the numbers of traders and Anishinaabeg increasing at Michilimackinac, at least some of the Odawa there even began to wonder whether they needed an official French post any longer. Father Marest noted they scoffed at continued French promises to return, saying they had been assured of this for so long they did not believe it now, nor did they any longer rely on it.[59]

A permanent post commander, Louis de La Porte de Louvigny, also arrived at Michilimackinac in 1716. He had commanded the post between 1689 and 1694, in the heyday of the fur trade at the straits. A contingent of Odawa had specifically asked for his return. Louvigny then did precisely what the Odawa there were eager for the French to do: he immediately organized a joint expedition against the Fox from Detroit and Michilimackinac. This time, there was less uncertainty among the French and Anishinaabeg about their respective roles. Indeed, even while they were jockeying over the precise shape of the conflict, the war inevitably gave the French and Anishinaabeg a common purpose. It also helped knit together again divided communities among the French and Anishinaabeg. Not only did many *coureurs de bois* and renegade fur traders join Louvigny's punitive expedition, but so too did both Michilimackinac and Detroit Indians. In the end, four hundred Canadians joined four hundred Anishinaabeg to lay siege to one of the primary Fox villages at the southern end of Green Bay, which surrendered soon after.[60]

In the long run, the Anishinaabeg used the conflict to clear their flanks of a serious rival that had threatened an alliance with their enemies for years. The Anishinaabeg in the upper Lakes did not let the matter rest. The next ten years were punctuated by periodic raids, threats, and rumors of new anti-Anishinaabe alliances. The Odawa at Michilimackinac were particularly irritated by continued Fox raids on allies such as the Menominee in Green Bay and kin among the Ojibwe on the south shores of Lake Superior. When the Fox again threatened an alliance with the Sioux in 1727, the Odawa secured French help and raised a large joint force of Anishinaabe Odawa, Ojibwe, and Potawatomi warriors to march into Fox country with Canadian and French soldiers. After this expedition failed to find the Fox, the Anishinaabeg again pressed the French to pursue the war. They were particularly eager to take advantage of a growing rift between the Fox and the Fox's erstwhile allies the Sioux, Mascouten, and Kickapoo. The French, for their part, believed they had to act to "animate" the Anishinaabeg and "Prevent them from having the contempt for the French."[61]

Emboldened by Fox squabbles with potentially dangerous allies, and urged on by the Winnebago, who had also fallen out with the Fox, the Odawa and Ojibwe did not wait for the French to "animate" them; they struck an outlying Fox village in the autumn of 1729, killing thirty men and almost seventy women and children. Encouraged by their success, more warriors from the same villages joined the group and surprised a large party of Fox villagers who were returning from a buffalo hunt in Iowa. More than two hundred warriors pressed the Fox, inflicting heavy casualties and taking many captives. They claimed to have killed seventy-seven warriors and three hundred women and children. Employing the same strategies they had before, the Anishinaabeg made sure to distribute Fox captives as slaves both to allied Indians and incoming Frenchmen, including new post commanders.[62]

Soon after these new attacks, the Fox realized they were completely isolated and decided to take flight. In June 1730, three hundred warriors and six hundred women and children quietly slipped out of the Fox-Wisconsin waterway, down to the Illinois River, just downstream from its junction with the Fox River. They had some notion of joining the Iroquois, but instead they ran into trouble with the nations of the Illinois Confederacy, notably the Cahokia. While they were on the run, it became clearer that the Fox had become pariahs in the *pays d'en haut*. Kinship relations among the Illinois and Algonquians meant the Cahokia were soon joined by Potawatomi and even Kickapoo and Mascouten warriors. By September, two hundred more Huron, Potawatomi, and Miami joined the siege from Fort Miami. Egged on by their Algonquian and Illinois allies, the French were willing to take no quarter. The result was another massacre. Only three hundred Fox warriors faced up to twelve hundred attackers. The allied forces killed perhaps as many as two hundred warriors and three hundred women and children. The French seemed almost surprised by the extent of the devastation. By the end of 1730, the new governor of the colony, Charles de la Boische, the Marquis de Beauharnois, estimated there might have been only about 450 Fox still alive anywhere, and the majority of those were captives in the hands of French-allied Indians. The French had come a long way in a short time. At the Great Peace of 1701, they had invited the Fox to Montreal as allies. In 1710, they invited them to come live with them at Detroit as friends. Yet by 1730, the French boasted of the "almost total destruction" of the Fox.[63]

If the French harbored any doubts about who was pulling the strings in this conflict with the Fox, the end of the wars would help lay those doubts to rest. In 1736, a delegation of Odawa and Ojibwe arrived in Montreal and told colonial officials they were finally putting an end to the Fox Wars and that the French must do so as well. French officials puzzled over the turnaround in Anishinaabe sentiments toward the Fox. The governor thought they were concerned about French power. Beauharnois told officials in Paris, "You may imagine . . . that the Savages have a policy as we have Ours, and that they are not greatly pleased at seeing a nation destroyed, for Fear their turn may come."[64]

Yet had Beauharnois listened carefully, he might have understood there was a little more to it than that. In fleeing from Anishinaabe and French attacks, many Fox had taken refuge among the Sauk living at Green Bay. But few nations of the pays d'en haut had a quarrel with the Sauk. Some were intermarried with them. The Sauk had particularly close relations with and kin among the St. Joseph's River Potawatomi community, on the eastern shore of Lake Michigan (near present-day Niles, Michigan, almost directly opposite Chicago). In turn, the St. Joseph's Potawatomi community had close relations and kinship ties with the Odawa at Michilimackinac and the Ojibwe at Sault Ste. Marie. They were all Anishinaabemowin speakers and were intermarried with one another.[65]

Under the circumstances, the Odawa and Ojibwe had to tread carefully. They first tried to get the Sauk to give up the Fox among them. But as it became clear that the French wanted to punish the Sauk for harboring the Fox, the Anishinaabeg balked. As the Odawa had explained to a French officer at Michilimackinac, they did not want to make war on the Sauk, "whom they looked upon as brothers." The following year, a group of Sauk took refuge with their kin by moving in with the Potawatomi at St. Joseph's River. The Odawa could not and would not tolerate a French war with the Potawatomi, with whom they were intermarried. Kinship shaped Odawa policy. They led two delegations down to Montreal, one in 1736 and another in 1737. They wanted the French to call off an expedition against the Sauk and end the war with the Fox. "All the Evil Hearts Had been destroyed," they claimed.[66]

The French, faced with the loss of their crucial allies, could do little else but abandon their plans for another genocidal campaign against the Sauk and Fox. In fact, this intervention signaled the end of the Fox Wars. The Odawa, who had helped initiate the conflict in 1712, also brought it to a close in 1737.

•

From French imperial officials' perspective, the Fox Wars were a disaster. The conflict drained the royal coffers for war provisions and supplies, men, and presents to keep their allies happy. The conflict with the Fox also "claimed thousands of lives and destabilized the Upper Country . . . for the better part of thirty years." The war certainly frustrated French efforts to expand their trade westward to the Mississippi. In 1730, they could only cling to the hope they had finally gained the hold on the *pays d'en haut* they had thought they secured almost thirty years ago. Beauharnois boasted that "peace and tranquillity . . . now reign in the upper Countries." But it was a very different kind of peace and tranquillity from that envisioned by French officials in 1701, or 1712, or even as late as 1726. The Anishinaabeg had made certain of that.[67]

In contrast, from the perspective of the Odawa, the Fox Wars were a success. The origin of the conflict was of course largely a product of Anishinaabe anger over the French decision to abandon Michilimackinac and welcome rivals to a new base at Detroit. In starting a war with the Fox, the Odawa wrecked that plan. By 1730, the French post at Detroit was a shambles. From about 1712, French colonial officials effectively ignored Detroit for a generation or more, and Michilimackinac reemerged as the most important trade hub in the *pays d'en haut*. The Odawa were thus able to resume their role as the main suppliers of canoes, equipment, and provisions for the network of commerce that extended throughout the upper Lakes basin, as well as the entire upper Mississippi area. In defending this position, the Odawa also made certain that trade at the straits would be conducted on their terms. The western trade of the French empire was still highly contingent on very uneasy relations with the Anishinaabeg.[68]

3

EXPANSION

As the denouement of the Fox Wars showed, in the turbulent world of the *pays d'en haut*, whom you knew was just as important as who you were. And the glue that held most people together was kinship. The end of the Fox Wars demonstrated that the Odawa had developed kinship connections that extended deep into Sauk country on the western side of Lake Michigan. While we have long focused on European expansion across the continent during this era, the relations that defined Anishinaabewaki also increased rapidly in the first half of the eighteenth century. Europeans may have infiltrated the continental interior in the late seventeenth and early eighteenth centuries, but most of the time the French could only follow, not lead. French imperialism took place against a backdrop of continued Anishinaabe growth across the central Lakes. The movement and expansion of the Odawa, Ojibwe, and Potawatomi Anishinaabeg was predicated on the incorporation of new peoples through the extension of doodemag or kinship relations. When we begin to understand the nature and implications of these kinship alliances, it is just as easy to say that by the 1730s, an expanding Anishinaabewaki stretched from the Mississippi deep into the St. Lawrence Valley. The Odawa at Michilimackinac were comfortably at the heart of this sprawling Anishinaabe domain.

•

The Anishinaabeg of the *pays d'en haut* have long been a people on the move. Considering their relationship with the waters of North America, this should perhaps not be surprising. Oral histories, archaeological evidence, and linguistic markers all point to a history of movement and expansion westward via the major waterways from points of origin in the east. As the Anishinaabeg moved, they inevitably came into contact and conflict with other nations. Their journeying up the Ottawa River may have been a result of conflict with the Iroquois that predated the arrival of Europeans. Ojibwe Anishinaabeg who traveled across Lake Superior ran headlong into Dakota territory, initiating a long war on their western flank. The Odawa Anishinaabeg warred with the Winnebago for control over the central Lakes. Oral stories also talk of a violent conflict with a group called the Muscodesh— most likely the Mascouten—near the straits of Michilimackinac. While we think of genocide as a practice introduced by Europeans, the Odawa tell of a near-genocidal war with former allies. Indeed, the violence may have resulted from a contempt born of familiarity. The Mascouten had lived in peace with the Odawa for many years. An insult to a famous Odawa war leader—"Saw-ge-maw"—who had already suffered defeat triggered a war of conquest that gave the Odawa control over the straits, which continued after the arrival of the French.[1]

Yet as the longer-term relationship with the Mascouten suggests, not all expansion was accompanied or facilitated by conflict. The long history of the Anishinaabeg provides much evidence of the peaceful incorporation and absorption of new peoples, too. The relations between many of the Algonquians east of Michilimackinac who call themselves Anishinaabeg—including the Algonquin, Nipissing, and Mississauga—is evidence of that incorporation. The relationship between the Ojibwe, Odawa, and Potawatomi is also testimony to long periods of peaceful relations during which diverse communities evolved and changed and yet maintained crucial kinship ties with one another. But the Anishinaabeg also created "confederations" with other, more culturally distinct nations. The special relationship between the Anishinaabemowin-speaking Kiskakon Odawa and the Iroquois-speaking Tionnontaté at the southern end of Georgian Bay off Lake Huron was one example of such cultural connections. The nineteenth-century Odawa writer Andrew Blackbird later also spoke of a relationship between the Siouian-speaking Osage and the Ojibwe. The historian Michael Witgen has more recently shown that even the lines between the Anishinaabeg and the Lakota Sioux may have been considerably more blurred than we are accustomed to thinking.[2]

Conflict and cooperation in Anishinaabe expansion was dictated by social organization. As Witgen has noted, "In the world of the Anishinaabeg there were two categories of people—inawemaagen (relative) and meyaagizid (foreigner)." Relations with meyaagizid were almost invariably conflict-ridden, since there were few rules dictating or circumscribing conduct and the terms of relationships with outsiders. There were no guidelines about reciprocal rights and responsibilities and access to resources and land. There were no agreed-upon ways in which wrongs could be righted. Without some kind of kinship relation, meyaagizid could end up as perpetual enemies. For the most part, the Iroquois and Fox remained foreigners for much of their early history with the Anishinaabeg.[3]

To create new relations, or end a conflict, it was imperative that the Anishinaabeg transform enemies, or foreigners, into relatives. One important way they did this was through the Feast of the Dead, a ceremony possibly borrowed from kin among the Huron. Usually held in the early spring, as the Anishinaabeg began returning from their winter hunts, the Feast of the Dead brought inawemaagen and specially invited meyaagizid together. Over the course of two weeks, the Anishinaabeg engaged newcomers in dance, games, gift exchanges, and especially ritual adoption and arranged marriages. The hosts capped the ceremony with a feast in which the living ate alongside their dead relatives and then gave all their goods to their guests as gifts. With their relatives buried together and new relations secured, former enemies were now joined together as family: "Enemies literally and ritually had been transformed into allies by being made into kin. They were now inawemaagen, relatives."[4]

The key to turning foreigners into relations, then, was through kinship building. Apparently this could be done—at least in part—by creating fictive relations with other individuals or groups. We see this at work in the label that Algonquian nations gave to the French governor: they called him Onontio—"Father." This was likely a deliberate ploy. In the patriarchal world of the French, all authority stemmed from the father—from God the Father, to the king, to the father at the head of the household. When a father commanded, his children obeyed. But the Odawa and other Anishinaabeg understood this relationship differently. In the Algonquian world, a father was generous, kind, and protective. Though his children might owe him respect, a father could not compel obedience. This creative misunderstanding, as the historian Richard White has characterized it, served to build an initial bridge between the Anishinaabe and French officials. But it was clearly a fictive kinship relation. As such it was frail. If Onontio failed to provide for the needs of his children—whether it be through generous gift giving or a strong and effective military alliance—there was little to hold the relationship together. The turbulent relationship between French officials and the Anishinaabeg over the Iroquois war and the settlement of Detroit reflected the limits of that fictive kinship relation.[5]

Instead, marriages were the real glue of kinship relations. As we have seen in the introduction, most Algonquian nations practiced some form of exogamy, and among the Anishinaabeg, daughters and sisters created crucial new links by marrying outside their doodem. They knitted together their old doodem with their new one. While a new wife kept and represented her father's doodem, her children would take her husband's. Women thus played an enormously important part in creating bridges between lineages and clans, and even between villages and nations. New bonds of kinship compelled extended families to cooperate because of the mutual rights and obligations. This cooperation could extend to trade, warfare, and subsistence.[6]

Something of this can be glimpsed in a French report of a war party against the Dakota as early as 1670–1671. A Sinago Odawa ogimaa called upon warriors from his own doodem at Michilimackinac. Yet he also called upon relatives among the Kiskakon Odawa and in turn the Tionnontaté, who were living at the straits at the time. As the party traveled west across Lake Michigan, they were reinforced at Green Bay because the Sinago Odawa ogimaa had a brother-in-law who was a chief among the Sauk living there. His brother-in-law could in turn call on relatives among the Potawatomi. By the time the war party reached Dakota country, they had collected a thousand warriors. When necessary, hundreds if not thousands of Algonquians from all across the *pays d'en haut* could be mobilized to meet a common threat—such as the Iroquois or the Fox. In the absence of formal alliances, such relationships were crucial for maintaining and expanding commercial and military ties.[7]

There were of course limits to these expanding relations. Evidence suggests that the Huron and Anishinaabeg did not intermarry in numbers, despite their close proximity for many years. But their relationship was complicated by the limited intermarriage that did take place between the Kiskakon Odawa and the Tionnontaté. The two groups had intermarried and lived near each other in the early part of the seventeenth century at the southern end of Georgian Bay. But while the Kiskakon Odawa did not generally intermarry with the nearby Huron, the Tionnontaté did. The relationships between the Kiskakon, the Tionnontaté, and the Huron were likely the reason why many of the latter found themselves living among the Anishinaabeg after 1649–1650, when the Iroquois forced the Huron into exile. These connections may also have prevented a full-blown war between the Huron and Odawa when tensions between them threatened to boil over. Yet when the Huron moved to Detroit starting in 1700, there was a marked increase in marriages between them and the Iroquois, while Anishinaabe-Iroquois marriages remained rare. The increase of Huron-Iroquois marriages at Detroit only added to the complaints of the Anishinaabeg— forever wary of a Huron-Iroquois alliance. In turn, the lack of marriages between the Iroquois and Anishinaabeg, and between the Fox and Anishinaabeg, seems to have accounted for the fury of the conflicts between them. Once there was an accumulated weight of grievances between two warring groups, it was difficult to reconcile in the absence of extensive kinship connections.[8]

•

If kinship relations often dictated peace or conflict with other Native groups, kinship patterns also helped ameliorate conflict within Anishinaabe communities. This role was particularly crucial given the system of governance within Anishinaabe societies. In the absence of coercive powers or a culture of obedience, leaders had to earn respect. "Each person is free to do as he pleases," one French report noted: the chiefs "can have influence, but they do not have authority." In turn, this influence derived from a leader's ability to mobilize resources on behalf of his extended family. Heredity may have contributed to attaining chiefly status among the Anishinaabeg, but an ogimaa could hold his position only if he could prove that he could guide his community through any crisis, whether it be famine, disease, or foreign invasion. As one French observer later put it in more crude terms, the influence of a village or war chief over his warriors and kin depended on his "attention to keeping their kettles full, so to say."[9]

The power to live, to grow crops, to heal the sick, and to defeat enemies was usually seen to derive from *manidoog*, or spiritual forces. *Manidoo* represented the "ability to make things work in the world in a way that an ordinary human being was not capable of doing on his or her own." People could possess manidoo in the sense that they could control access to a source of extraordinary power. Trade goods, the production of surplus crops or other goods, and success in war could all be sources of power and influence. Thus kinship alliances could bring badly needed economic, material, and spiritual resources to an ogimaa and his people. An extensive network of kinship relations enhanced an ogimaa's chance of success in keeping kettles full and enemies at bay. In short, more relatives gave an ogimaa more influence.[10]

In turn, kinship alliances enhanced an ogimaa's political ties both with neighboring nations and with other Odawa doodemag as well. But the power derived from these kinship alliances was highly decentralized. Ogimaag could represent only their extended family when in council with other Odawa, or with other nations such as the French. Though they often tried to single out particular leaders, the French were constantly compelled to deal with many different ogimaag, even from the same village or town. Yet even these ogimaag had relatively little coercive power over their extended family let alone the rest of the community. They could only try to persuade, and their ability to do so was contingent on how much influence they could command at any given moment.[11]

The decentralized nature of authority and decision making played havoc with French efforts to get the Anishinaabeg to act in concert. In 1696, for example, the Odawa were split about whether to continue war with the Iroquois. Some wanted to make peace with the Iroquois so they could focus on avenging the death of one of their ogimaag at the hands of a western nation. Others were wary of rumors of a separate French peace with the Iroquois and wanted to preempt it. When confronted with evidence of new peace overtures to the Iroquois, Cadillac called a general council. Pro-war Odawa spoke up, but made clear the limits of their authority. One Odawa ogimaa from Michilimackinac, Onaské, for example, declared himself in favor of carrying on the war with the Iroquois and said he had "some young warriors" who would not abandon him. But he also announced, "I urge no one to follow me; let every one act as he will think fit, and let me do as I like." Eventually a small coalition made their way down to Detroit to act against the Iroquois, but it was a close-run thing. The governor reported that Onaské persisted "despite the belts presented to him by people belonging to his own Nation, and the considerable presents they offered him." "Faction ran so high," French officials reported, "that his canoes were cut in the night" before the party was to leave.[12]

This so-called factionalism did lead to a fair amount of fluidity in Anishinaabe communities. Amid the troubles of the 1690s and early 1700s, some doodemag clearly took advantage and jostled for prominence at Michilimackinac by exploiting obvious divisions among the French, making promises to both Cadillac on one side and the Jesuits on the other. Still others used the crisis to flirt with the English and other rivals. Such strategies could have threatened to tear communities apart. Yet the decentralized decision making of the Anishinaabeg also meant that when factions did develop, there was always an out. Families could and did leave villages to join different communities, or to establish new ones—in a process that we might call fissioning. In this way, they could avoid outright conflict with one another. But they invariably moved along existing kinship lines, often leaving tendrils of relations behind in the villages they left. So even if families left because of sharp disagreements across communities, there were established rules of behavior among kin that promoted cooperation rather than competition between them. While particular doodemag and ogimaag jostled for place and prominence within a region or across a set of villages, marriages and doodemag still knit them together. In this way, even amid conflict, an expanding Anishinaabewaki could be created and secured across the region.[13]

·

The rise of the Nassauakueton Odawa at Michilimackinac helps illuminate doodemag politics among the Anishinaabeg at the straits. While many other doodemag took their names from various animals, Nassauakueton meant "the people of the fork." While likely referring to a topographical feature such as a fork in a river, historians are unsure of the precise etymology or significance of the name. The French often called them the Nation de la Fourche, and in the late seventeenth century, they listed their ogimaa as either La Fourche or Nissowaquet (sometimes written Nansouakouet). The name Nissowaquet was handed down to successive ogimaag as they took on the leadership of the Nassauakueton. Like their name, their origins are also murky. The available evidence suggests the Nassauakueton may originally have risen to prominence in the Green Bay region and had ties to the Potawatomi living there in the mid-seventeenth century. But by the time French officials arrived and stayed at Michilimackinac in the 1680s and 1690s, they were most commonly listed as one of the four main Odawa doodemag at Michilimackinac along with the Kiskakon, Sable, and Sinago. A Nassauakueton delegation from Michilimackinac attended the Great Peace of Montreal in 1701, where the first recorded Nassauakueton pictograph appeared in the formal record.[14]

Subsequently, during the crises that rocked the *pays d'en haut* after 1701, the Nassauakueton took on an increasingly prominent role in negotiations and diplomacy at Michilimackinac. They appeared to do so by exploiting their kinship ties with the Potawatomi, and pushing for greater cooperation with the French. In 1687, for example, when the Anishinaabeg at Michilimackinac were divided over whether to help the French attack the Iroquois, "Chief Nansouakoüet alone took sides with the French," one report noted. He made the decision to aid the French upon the arrival of a group of Potawatomi warriors at the straits who had already declared they would go on the warpath against the French. Amid the turmoil of the late 1680s and early 1690s, some French observers believed that Nissowaquet was "the only friend of the French" among the "Outaouaks." He had been an opponent of the English "in spite of his tribe." Over time, Nissowaquet helped build a coalition of pro-French Odawa ogimaag at the straits. In the early 1690s, for example, he was chosen by his warriors to avenge the death of another pro-French Anishianaabe ogimaa who had died during a

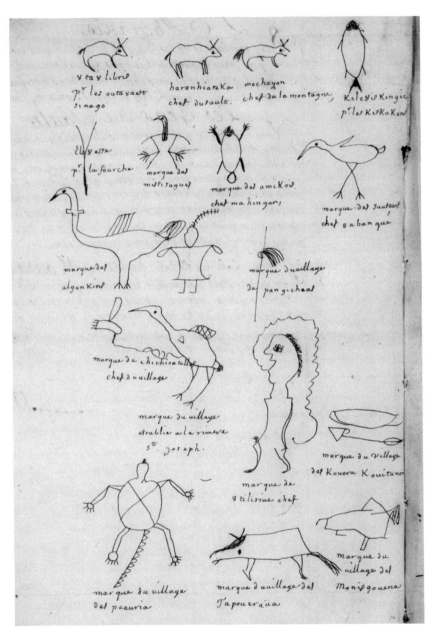

Pictographs from the Great Peace of 1701. Elaouasse signed the treaty on behalf of the Nassauakueton, or the Odawa of "La Fourche" (the Fork), with a Y-shaped drawing that probably depicted a fork in a river. ("Ratification de la paix . . . ," Aug.–Sept. 1701, MG 1, Série C11A, vol. 19, fol. 41–44v, Library and Archives Canada, e000790882. Courtesy of the Archives *nationales d'outre-mer* [ANOM, France])

campaign against Indian nations in the west. French reports later noted that Nissowaquet's brother-in-law was also a pro-French ogimaa at Michilimackinac and that his nephew had died fighting the Iroquois alongside the French.[15]

The Nassauakueton created a place for themselves at Michilimackinac by courting the French and exploiting this influence among their kin. But they also drew on their kin relations to create some powerful alliances with other Indian nations. When Nissowaquet died during the revenge mission against the western nations, for example, it was Onanguissé, a renowned ogimaa of the Potawatomi at Green Bay, who demanded that the French help avenge the death of "this great chief." The Potawatomi at Green Bay in turn had kin living among the Sauk, and probably among the Illinois farther south. Onanguissé himself was likely of Sauk origin, and the Potawatomi at Green Bay lived in mixed villages, which brought a number of other nations into their orbit and under their influence. At the Great Peace of Montreal in 1701, Onanguissé spoke on behalf of the Sauk, Illinois, and Potawatomi, and on some key issues seemed to speak on behalf of most of the nations of the Great Lakes. Nissowaquet and his doodemag clearly had some powerful allies around the Lakes.[16]

The kinship connections beween the Nassauakueton and the Potawatomi benefited the other Odawa doodemag living at Michilimackinac. Immediately after they signed the peace treaty of 1701, Onanguissé and many of the Potawatomi from Green Bay moved to St. Joseph's River in the southeast corner of Lake Michigan. Other Potawatomi moved to Detroit. Because of the close relations between the Nassauakueton and the Potawatomi, the Odawa from the straits secured crucial wintering grounds south of Michilimackinac in the Grand River region, near St. Joseph's. But perhaps even more important, both the Potawatomi at St. Joseph's and those at Detroit also aided and supported the Odawa from Michilimackinac during the conflicts that engulfed Detroit after 1701. They were invaluable allies who helped protect Anishinaabe interests in the face of the new threats they faced in the region.[17]

More generally, these kinship ties gave the Nassauakueton and their Odawa kin an extended circle of relations that reached down to Detroit, across to Wisconsin, and even into the Illinois country.

While other Odawa doodemag at Michilimackinac maintained close relationships with Anishinaabe Ojibwe to the north and west and Mississauga and Nipissing to the south and east, the Nassauakueton helped maintain relationships—and secure Anishinaabe interests—to the south and west. So these kinship alliances and the political power they represented also helped firmly ensconce the Nassauakueton within the sociopolitical landscape of the *pays d'en haut*. But the establishment and maintenance of these kinship alliances also created an expansive, ever-thickening, and important buffer against rivals across a wide arc of territory. They made Michilimackinac, and indeed the central Lakes, an even more secure Anishinaabe stronghold.

•

The Nassauakueton also illuminate the creative and adaptive responses that many Native Americans made to changes in their circumstances over time. For in the midst of the troubles that started with the withdrawal of the French, the Nassauakueton, like others in the region, pursued a novel strategy. They strengthened the fictive kinship ties between themselves and the French governor by forming real kinship relations via marriages between Anishinaabe women and French men.

During the years of the great Michilimackinac trade fairs in the latter half of the seventeenth century, there was no real need for Anishinaabeg to marry French traders. Trade was certainly important to the Odawa at Michilimackinac. But as French officials at the time, and historians since, have noted, most Indians looked only to supply their needs—or *besoins*. For the Anishinaabeg at the straits, there was generally enough of the new material goods on offer from the visiting French to make themselves comfortable without transforming their lives. The French traded or gave away stockings, shirts, beads, thread, mirrors, kettles, iron axes and knives, hoes, blankets, tobacco, alcohol, guns, gunpowder, and lead shot. These items made for an agreeable addition to a dwelling, but more important, they helped the Odawa maintain themselves against rivals. In turn, guns and gunpowder directly contributed to the ability of the Odawa to defend themselves, but these and other trade goods could also be redistributed by ogimaag across their family lines in order to enhance their prestige and influence. They were a way of demonstrating the strength of the doodem and the ogimaa. Anishinaabeg at Michilimackinac could obtain plenty of these goods by direct trade for beaver and other fur pelts, or via the provisioning trade at the straits, in which Odawa families could sell corn, fish, meat, sugar, canoes, and other necessities to itinerant traders, visiting Indians, and hungry soldiers at the post. Odawa ogimaag also extracted a healthy and continuing supply of presents at least twice yearly from French post commanders. By these means, the Odawa did quite well for themselves.[18]

The withdrawal of the French from Michilimackinac and the creation of a new post at Detroit threatened this prosperity and stability. Not only did doodemag heads lose the valuable supply of presents that post commanders were obligated to provide each year, but Anishinaabeg at the straits also lost the valuable provisioning trade with visiting Indians and the garrison at the post. Though some individual traders still ventured to Michilimackinac, an increasing number of legal traders followed the Indian trade and headed for Detroit, drawn by the protection offered by the French post there. Without traders, fewer other Indians visited Michilimackinac. Those left at the straits were faced with a dwindling supply of goods and diminished political power.[19]

As we have seen, many remaining Odawa reacted violently to these changes. Yet some also sought more peaceful means to secure access to French trade goods. In 1702, Étienne de Carheil, the Jesuit priest who stayed behind at Michilimackinac, noticed the rise of a new practice. Indian families had begun welcoming French traders into their villages and encouraging them to marry Odawa women. Carheil noted that while the French had a post at the straits, it was a rare occasion when traders would visit Indian villages at all, let alone consort with Indian women. If any trader was obliged to live in the Odawa villages, it was only out of "extraordinary necessity." And to do so, a trader had to notify the commandant and missionary, "so that he might be assigned to a Cabin about which there was no suspicion, that he might lodge there without scandal." But since the post commander had left, the Anishinaabeg had allowed French men to seek out women in their villages and even "to go to live with the women in their Cabins." Carheil spoke of "husbands," implying that some of these relationships had been formalized, at least in his eyes.[20]

From the perspective of the Anishinaabeg, more intimate relations with French traders was a desirable development because it gave Odawa families privileged access to trade goods. Marriage meant that on their return from the St. Lawrence Valley, French traders would guarantee their new kin a fresh supply of commodities, and better prices for them. In turn, kinship gave particular families a monopoly over the now scarce trade goods coming into Michilimackinac. Any surplus that French men could bring upcountry might then be exchanged along kinship networks. Such exclusive access to trade goods only enhanced doodem leaders' prestige both within the family and without, strengthening kinship bonds and trading partnerships throughout the *pays d'en haut* via mobile French traders who effectively acted on behalf of their Indian families.

If there was any doubt about how these relationships facilitated the fur trade in favor of the Anishinaabeg, it was dispelled in Carheil's description of the role women played in the seasonal activities of traders. The Jesuit noted that Odawa women helped feed French traders while at Michilimackinac and kept them stocked with wood and clean clothes. They repaired and made "savage shoes, Garters, and pouches, according to their fashion, and other similar articles." But they also accompanied them on their journeys both to and from the St. Lawrence and across the *pays d'en haut*. Odawa women inserted themselves directly in the business of the fur trade. Thus they could oversee not only the supply side of the trade at Montreal or Trois-Rivières but also the distribution of goods among their kin.[21]

Indeed, Anishinaabe women were not mere pawns of French or Odawa men. Scholars have shown that among the Anishinaabeg, trade was a family affair. Given the importance of trade, it should be no surprise that women and children participated in almost all stages of the fur exchanges that took place at Michilimackinac. Even though French records rarely mention women, they played a vital part in the trade. French traders and post commanders brought a wide variety of goods that were clearly aimed at women and children, such as kettles, combs, mirrors, hoes, and fabrics, and in return they needed much more than Anishinaabe men alone could provide. For example, growing crops was largely the work of women, and so they supplied the corn and maple sugar necessary for the sustenance of a trader. Because they stocked their canoes mostly with trade goods, and not provisions, most traders were literally dependent on Odawa women for their daily bread by the time they got to Michilimackinac. Women also processed furs and aided in the making and maintenance of canoes. Indian men may have been more involved in ceremonial and ritualized trading, gift giving, and credit trading, but given their role in trading a wide variety of food and supplies, there is suggestive evidence that women were more often involved in direct trade than men.[22]

Under the circumstances, native women usually benefited from marriages with French men. They did not so much marry out, but rather "incorporated their French husbands into a society structured by native custom and tradition." The living arrangements of mixed couples corresponded closely to traditional marriage practices among the Anishinaabeg, wherein new couples would spend time living among the wife's kin before they moved to live with the husband's doodem. Though the precise nature of Anishinaabe understandings of French kinship relations is unclear, the fact that recently married French traders soon established a village apart from both the French and Indian communities is suggestive. In effect, they seem to have set up their own doodem, or family line, and like other Anishinaabe doodem, they marked it with a settlement apart from the others. In addition, Native women continued to enjoy close relations with the doodem from which they had come. A fur trader's presence enhanced the kinship network he joined, as well as his wife's "authority and prestige among her people."[23]

The rise in Anishinaabe-French marriages also coincided with new trade practices that more firmly embedded French traders into Odawa society. Before French officials withdrew from Michilimackinac and other posts, every spring and autumn the Odawa would call on the post commander to give and receive ceremonial presents. The Odawa would often give food and provisions, and in return post commanders would give out cloth, utensils, powder, and alcohol that would be useful for the winter hunt. Post commanders would simply label these items as "gifts" and claim them as expenses from the king. When French officials formally abandoned the posts, traders had to fill this void and still balance the books. Usually upon their arrival in the autumn, traders would exchange gifts of alcohol for food and provisions. Then they would distribute clothing, utensils, and powder for the winter hunt, but they would do so on credit. They would collect on this credit when families returned from the winter hunt laden with new furs.[24]

With a post at the straits, traders could and often did wait out the winter with the French garrison. But after the French withdrew the post, vulnerable French traders started wintering over with Anishinaabe families. Not only did this ensure they could collect on the furs for which they had given credit, but it also meant they had more secure access to food and shelter during the harsh winter months than if they stayed at the post or wintered on their own. Traders would normally have to pay for those provisions and reduce their profit margin, but marriages meant they would be well looked after over the winter. In return, the Odawa had year-round immediate access to French trade goods at a reduced price that could make the difference between life and death. The new system worked. Even after the French reestablished a post at the straits, the practice of wintering over continued. In 1720, the post commander at Michilimackinac complained about the French who "run after their debts" by spending the winter "in the woods." These traders weakened the strength of the post and ranged widely with their Indian families. The post commander noted that the Anishinaabeg were only too happy to facilitate this practice, since they were able to keep the French "in order" rather than the other way around.[25]

Why did French traders agree to marry into Anishinaabe families and risk restricting the market for their goods? Because they had no other choice. In the absence of the French post, not only were they more dependent on Indian women to feed and clothe them, but they needed the protection that Anishinaabe women could provide. As relations between the French and the western nations soured through the 1690s, the *coureurs de bois* found themselves on their own, and vulnerable. Despised by Jesuits and colonial officials as lawless and uncontrollable, they were increasingly at the mercy of those on whom they were most dependent—the Indians. Without a French post at the straits, traders scrambled to find families who would help provision them and protect them. They were vulnerable enough even when there was a French post at the straits. Without it, most traders knew that they could be plundered and pillaged at any time.

Such risks grew as ties between the French and Anishinaabeg became strained to the point of breaking in the early years of the new century. In June and July 1706, just after the French and Odawa fought at Detroit, traders who had stayed at Michilimackinac found themselves living "as if the tomahawk were suspended over their heads." Two "principal women" in the village, who had always been friendly to the French until then, "went weeping from hut to hut, demanding the death of the French who had killed their brother." The French traders at the post doled out generous presents to the Anishinaabeg, and some of the ogimaag tried to reassure them that they would be safe. Still, the traders began fortifying a post. Father Marest, the Jesuit priest who also stayed at the straits, believed that "no one can depend upon the word of the natives, since the chiefs, however good their intentions, are not masters." Indeed, one Odawa ogimaa later told the governor that at a council, the Anishinaabe chiefs decided to bring the French into their own homes before leaving for Montreal because they worried what their "young men" might do, "who were sorrowing for the loss they had sustained."[26]

In such dangerous circumstances, savvy traders had to innovate. The most successful were those who adapted best to Indian ways: the "Competent" young men, "who know the places, the customs, and the language of the savages; who are Acquainted with the persons; who have the most experience, skill, and strength in Managing Canoes." With their knowledge of Indian customs, those traders also knew that taking an Indian wife was likely the best chance they had of surviving the turbulent politics of the *pays d'en haut*. They might just have understood, too, that marriage into an Indian family would knit them into an extended kinship network across the region, allowing them both to travel freely and conduct trade with an expansive number of natives who could provide the vital protection that the metropole could not. Yet if French traders saw advantages to more intimate relationships with native women—and flattered themselves that Indian women liked "the French better than their own Countrymen"—they could profit from them only because their Anishinaabe trading partners sought new opportunities. Isolated traders were hardly in a position to coerce native support.[27]

·

The Nassauakueton were one of the doodemag that adopted the new strategy of marrying out to French traders in the early eighteenth century. Relatively recent arrivals at the straits, the Nassauakueton seemed uninterested in following the French to Detroit in 1701. Instead, they remained at Michilimackinac, helping to agitate for the return of an official French post and working to smooth over the troubled waters between the Odawa and the French more generally. The Nassauakueton continued a policy of negotiating a pro-French position even while they demonstrated their worth to other Anishinaabeg at the straits. But as trade goods at Michilimackinac began to dry up, the valuable access to French goods that enabled Nassauakueton influence in Anishinaabe councils also wavered. So, too, did their influence in the region via kinship alliances. The Nassauakueton ogimaag struggled to provide for their families. They needed a new source of power and influence.

They initially found it in the union of Domitilde and Daniel Joseph Amiot Villeneuve. Daniel Villeneuve was born in Quebec in 1665. Though not much is known of his early life, he probably grew up along the banks of the St. Lawrence. There, he would have witnessed the convoys of fur traders and Native Americans who regularly plied those waters, and heard boastful tales of the riches of the west. If Villeneuve dreamed of trading himself, he was fortunate enough to have the connections to facilitate such ambitions. His uncle was Charles Amiot, a Quebec fur trader and merchant who was the son of one of the earliest migrants to New France. Amiot in turn had traveled extensively in the hinterlands of Quebec with Father Henri Nouvel. Nouvel would later become chief missionary at St. Ignace at Michilimackinac (from 1672 to 1681, and again from 1688 to 1695) and would continue to proselytize in the *pays d'en haut* until his death in 1701 or 1702, at Green Bay.[28]

Villeneuve probably called on those connections when he secured a contract to travel with François de la Forest's trading venture to Fort St. Louis on the Illinois River in 1690 (about ninety miles southwest of present-day Chicago). But the twenty-five-year-old Villeneuve had already spent some time in the Illinois country. On this trip, during which he helped fortify the French post, the commander noted that Villeneuve already had "half his back tattooed in the same manner" as the local Illinois Indians, who were inked from shoulder to heels.

Villeneuve had become one of those "competents" noted by Father Carheil. In the early 1700s, he found himself in Michilimackinac. Then, in the midst of renewed troubles in the *pays d'en haut*—as the French and Odawa stood poised for war with each other—he took refuge with Marie Kapiouapnokoue, an Odawa woman who hailed from the straits.[29]

Little is known of their relationship, only that the two traveled together and married in Montreal in September 1709. Soon after, they had a child, possibly in Quebec, whom they named Marie. But by 1712, the elder Marie was dead. Villeneuve had firsthand knowledge of how crucial a local marriage was to his future in the Great Lakes, and after the death of Marie, he quickly remarried. By the end of 1712 he had had a child with Domitilde. Domitilde was a Nassauakueton and the sister of a young boy who would become his doodem's primary ogimaag, Nissowaquet, or La Fourche. Marie and Domitilde may have been from the same family; it was not unusual in Algonquian societies for the families of deceased wives to find new partners for their widowed in-laws.[30]

Viewed from a native perspective, the marriages of Daniel Villeneuve were a clear sign of the Nassauakueton effort to expand their kinship network eastward into French ranks. With his connections in the St. Lawrence, Villeneuve could guarantee an annual supply of trade goods for Domitilde and her extended family. Yet Villeneuve—who had extensive experience in the *pays d'en haut* and who had spent some time among the Illinois—was also a valuable asset to a doodem looking to consolidate its hold at Michilimackinac and influence among Anishinaabe allies like the Illinois who lived to the west and south. Villeneuve could help strengthen the hand of the pro-French Odawa at Michilimackinac, in particular the emerging new alliance between the French and the Nassauakueton. The efforts of the Nassauakueton paid off when Villeneuve was hired as an interpreter by the first French officer sent to the straits in 1712. The position of interpreter at these isolated posts was a crucial one, given how few Europeans were conversant in Native languages. The Nassauakueton now had unmediated access to French councils and all discussions between the Anishinaabeg and French. They could have a direct say in affairs at the post, and also a privileged place in the conversation. The importance of this kind of influence cannot be overestimated.[31]

Domiltilde also helped negotiate a relationship with the French at the post. The Jesuits still struggled among the Odawa at Michilimackinac: even as late as 1735, one missionary claimed his colleagues labored among the Odawa "with little success." But another observed that on occasion, there were a very "few souls who, from time to time, give themselves truly to God, and console the Missionary for all his labors." Domitilde seems to have been one of those few. Though it is unclear whether she converted to Catholicism before or after she married Villeneuve, the Jesuits at Michilimackinac spoke highly of her. In one letter to the governor, Father Marest noted that Villeneuve continued to behave well, as did his wife. A year later, Marest claimed that Domitilde set a good example not just for the Indians, but also for the few French women at the post. He also noted that with her help, his colleague Father Chardon was planning to learn the Odawa language in the coming winter.[32]

Domitilde was not alone, of course. She was one of a very small but influential group of women who married French traders at the straits around the same time. The growing number of these relationships is testimony to their mutually beneficial nature. Indeed, historians have noted a rise in the number of intercultural marriages beginning in the 1690s throughout the *pays d'en haut* but particularly at Michilimackinac. By the time the French reestablished an official presence at the straits, these relationships had flourished. When a French officer arrived at the former French post in 1712, he found the log and bark cabins of the *coureurs de bois* and their new families. The exact population of this early mixed settlement is unknown, but there were perhaps some forty *coureurs de bois*, many, if not most, living with Indian women.[33]

•

Over the next few decades, Domitilde helped the Nassauakueton and the Odawa navigate a prosperous future in the uncertain world of the *pays d'en haut*. In addition to providing the Nassauakueton with immediate access to French trade, Jesuit council, and the ear of the post commander, the Domitilde/Villeneuve family began creating a new set of important relations through their children. They baptized their first son, Daniel, at Michilimackinac on September 27, 1712. Domitilde and her husband then had another seven children between 1712 and 1725 (five girls and two boys), all but one of whom made it to adulthood. The Odawa saw these children as valuable assets, particularly in strengthening the doodem. As Cadillac had noted, Odawa children, once grown, "support the hut, that is, the house, either by their deeds as warriors or by hunting or else by the alliances they make, by taking wives of their own." These children were also important in elevating the status of Domitilde in both French and Odawa eyes. In Anishinaabe communities, widowed women with children generally found it easier to remarry, because the new husband became "the father and chief of the whole family, and is therefore a person of more importance." Rather than a burden, the children were seen by prospective husbands as important additions to their kinship network. Thus when Daniel Villeneuve died sometime around 1724, he left his widow, and her extended relations, a rich legacy.[34]

Domitilde did not wait long to take advantage. Indeed, if there was any doubt that her first union with a French trader was a strategic choice, her remarriage to another up-and-coming French trader in the 1720s put this notion to rest. Domitilde married Augustin Mouet de Moras sometime after 1724. Augustin was the grandson of Pierre Mouet, who had arrived as an ensign with the Régiment Carignan-Salières in 1665 and was one of the soldiers who stayed in the colony. Pierre Mouet had died in 1693, dividing the island he had been given as a land grant between his eldest son, also Pierre Mouet, and his youngest daughter, Thérèse. The younger Pierre Mouet, known as Sieur de Moras, used his small inheritance to secure a marriage with Élisabeth Jutras, a well-known granddaughter of the trader-explorer Pierre-Esprit Radisson. They quickly had seven children of their own.[35]

With only a small island to divide between them, Pierre and Élisabeth's sons looked elsewhere for their fortunes. One joined the military but died young. The two others, Didace and Augustin, also joined the troupes de la marine, but they, like so many others from Trois-Rivières, had an eye on the fur trade. There were plenty of stories and examples to inspire them. Trois-Rivières had long been a customary trading place for visiting Algonquian traders, particularly the Anishinaabeg. Their great-grandfather Pierre-Esprit Radisson had made his early home in Trois-Rivières. Of course, their own grandfather Pierre Mouet may also have passed along stories of the fur convoys of the 1660s and 1670s. One of their uncles, too, was already trading in the west, having served as an engagé, or voyageur, in 1702.

Initially, both Didace and Augustin may have traveled west with the *troupes de la marine*. Some records suggest they traded in the region from as early as 1716, when the Michilimackinac post was re-established. But the first official record we have of either traveling westward is in 1726. At this point, twenty-two-year-old Augustin, who took the last name Langlade, contracted with Louise Dubuisson to lead a canoe of five men out to the western posts. Dubuisson was the wife of Jacques-Charles Renaud Dubuisson, who had been the post commander at Detroit in 1712 but who in 1726 was commanding a post among the Miami. By 1729, he was appointed post commander at Michilimackinac.[36]

If Didace and Augustin dreamed of making it as independent fur traders in the turbulent world of the *pays d'en haut*, they had enough experience to know they would need help to do so. They were prospecting in the region in the middle of the conflict with the Fox. Family lore has it that Augustin Langlade—along with many other *coureurs de bois*—participated in the 1728 attack on the Fox at Green Bay. In the tense situation, Didace and Augustin, like Villeneuve before them, were desperate to make connections and secure protection in the *pays d'en haut*. They, too, turned to marriage. Didace married Louis de la Porte de Louvigny's daughter in 1727. Louvigny was well respected among the Odawa at Michilimackinac, and it was he who officially reopened the French post in 1716. At around the same time, Augustin married the recently widowed Domitilde. [37]

With seven children, three of whom were approaching adolescence, Domitilde would have been an even more attractive choice for a young Frenchman looking to make his way in the uncertain world of the *pays d'en haut* than she was when Villeneuve married her. Her children could not only support the household, they also represented an increasing number of kinship ties in the future. The example of Villeneuve and others over the previous generation had also made it clear that alliances by intermarriage were crucial to the success of any endeavors in the Great Lakes. Augustin would have been eager to establish a trade network. But if Domitilde was an attractive option for Augustin, he in turn offered his new wife and her kin a suitably well-connected replacement for Villeneuve. Integrated with the French military and trading communities, Augustin came with connections both commercial and strategic.

•

Domitilde and Augustin wasted little time in creating a family of their own. Their son, Charles-Michel Mouet de Langlade, was baptized at Michilimackinac in May 1729. Even at the moment of his birth, Charles Langlade inherited a complex and extensive kinship network in the region that would serve him well in future years. Domitilde still lived either with or close to members of her own doodem, and in the midst of several large Anishinaabe villages in and around Michilimackinac. In part because of Domitilde's marriages to French traders, her doodem, the Nassauakueton, had already risen to prominence in the village at the straits. In turn, Domitilde's brother, Nissowaquet, had already or would soon rise to power as an important leader (possibly, of course, because of Domitilde's French connections; we cannot be sure). With Domitilde's marriages, Nissowaquet's kin relations now stretched from Trois-Rivières to the east to Green Bay in the west, and possibly farther. Langlade, by virtue of his mother and uncle, could immediately count on Algonquian allies and support across a vast region.[38]

But if Domitilde secured for her son an important place among the Nassauakueton, she was also able to ensure that he was enmeshed within an extended métis family. Today, the Métis Nation is a legally recognized aboriginal group in Canada with homelands scattered across the country and into parts of the northern United States. Historians use the term for the eighteenth century to denote people of mixed Indian and European descent even though it is not always clear how they labeled themselves, if at all. Most immediately, Charles Langlade inherited up to three stepbrothers and four stepsisters, ranging in ages from five to seventeen, all of whom were métis. As they grew older, most of these children married into prominent trading families in the region and became close military or trading associates of Charles Langlade. Domitilde also played a crucial part in ensuring that the extended family was well integrated with one another by serving as godmother to her grandchildren and as a witness to their marriages.[39]

As these roles suggest, Domitilde also wove other kinds of associations that were something less—but at times no less important—than blood relations. Historians call them fictive relations. These were connections among and between the small but steadily growing multiethnic Catholic community at Michilimackinac. Domitilde had impressed the Jesuits at the straits when she was a younger woman. They would have been equally pleased that Domitilde was quick to baptize the children she had with both Daniel Villeneuve and Augustin Langlade. As she grew older, she was also careful to help prepare others in her family for baptism. In September 1752, for example, she became godmother to a fifteen-year-old woman who took the name Marie and took her first communion immediately after. The young woman, according to Father Pierre du Jaunay, a Jesuit priest living near Waganawkezee, had "been instructed for a long time" and greatly desired baptism. She was also Domitilde's slave. Likely a war captive from an earlier conflict, Marie was just one of a number of Indian slaves held by the Langlades. The historian Brett Rushforth has found that these slaves were held for much of their lives in Algonquian societies and lived increasingly precarious and marginal lives on the edges of Native communities over the course of the eighteenth century. Yet Domitilde saw fit at least to bring them within the Catholic orbit at Michilimackinac.[40]

Domitilde continued to play an important role in the slowly expanding Catholic community, agreeing to become godmother to at least dozens of French, métis, and Anishinaabe children and adults. She was one of the most active women in the small Catholic community at Michilimackinac. It is impossible to tell just what Domitilde and others who participated in these Catholic ceremonies made of church doctrine and theology, and how they may have adapted them to suit their own needs. But it is clear that in taking on this function, she helped knit together a wide and diverse network of prominent trading families, military officers, and Anishinaabeg.

These relationships mattered. In September 1744, for example, Domitilde agreed to serve as godmother to a young girl who was enslaved to a trader named Boiguilbert. Her act may have secured good husbands for two of her daughters. The following year, her eldest daughter, Anne Villeneuve, married the godfather in the ceremony. Then, Agathe, her youngest daughter with her first husband, Daniel, married the slaveholder Boiguilbert himself. Domitilde's role as a godparent in the small Catholic community brought her and her family to the attention of French traders and officers. The fictive relations she created often translated into real relationships and expanded kin lines.[41]

Domitilde and her family's position within the Catholic community of the *pays d'en haut* secured important alliances for Charles Langlade and the Nassauakueton among not just the French Catholic trading and military community at Michilimackinac but also among the few Catholic-leaning Anishinaabeg in and around the post. On February 1, 1747, for example, Domitilde served as godmother for a twenty-year-old Ojibwe woman who took the name Marie Athanasie. Two years later, Domitilde became godmother to Rose, a thirty-five-year-old Ojibwe woman of La Pointe who came in to be baptized along with her son Alexis. As the historian Susan Sleeper-Smith has shown, the kinds of fictive and familial relationships that women like Domitilde could weave under the umbrella of Catholicism strengthened and expanded an already complex indigenous kinship system. They also enhanced the importance of women such as Domitilde.[42]

The ubiquitous presence of the Langlades in the baptismal and marriage records of Michilimackinac give us only a glimpse of the connections that knit these communities together. Yet given the numbers of French traders in the region, they also speak volumes about the prominence of the Langlades among the wider community at the straits, especially those involved in trade. While the French population in more fertile areas of the southern *pays d'en haut* grew considerably toward the middle of the eighteenth century, it remained small at Michilimackinac. The Langlades were thus at the nucleus of a relatively small number of either French or mixed families living north of Detroit. As late as 1749, a French report on Michilimackinac noted there were only ten French families living at the fort. Three of these were mixed families. One of them was that of Augustin and Domitilde.[43]

•

Certainly, this prominence within complex and dense kinship relations of the French and Indian communities around Michilimackinac helps account for the Langlades' success in extending their trade relations. Starting with a relatively secure trade connection via his Odawa wife's family at Michilimackinac, Augustin quickly expanded his operations. Traveling back and forth between Trois-Rivières along the

St. Lawrence River and the *pays d'en haut* for several years during his young son's early life, Augustin managed to cobble together enough capital by the summer of 1731 to buy into a joint venture that would become known as the Second Sioux Company. The company was set up by a group of prominent merchants and traders in Trois-Rivières who wanted to expand trading relations deep into the Mississippi. Because of the expense and risks involved, it was left to private groups of traders to pool their resources and share the profits. The company might have admitted Augustin into their ranks because of his marriage to Domitilde and his links with the Anishinaabeg. His connections could secure a smoother passage across the *pays d'en haut*.[44]

As it turned out, the Second Sioux Company failed because of renewed hostilities between the Sioux and the Anishinaabeg. The French traders found themselves in the middle of the conflict and lost much of their goods. Yet Augustin could still fall back on the relatively safer trading networks his family had already secured within the Anishinaabe-defined triangle of Michilimackinac, Grand River, and Green Bay. By the time Augustin started trading, the Grand River region was a popular wintering quarters for the Michilimackinac Anishinaabe Odawa, while trade at Green Bay was facilitated by the good relations the Odawa increasingly enjoyed with the Menominee and Anishinaabe kin who lived there. Though Augustin moved back to Michilimackinac around 1737, he secured a license to trade at Green Bay in 1746. His son Charles would continue to trade at Grand River and eventually secured a monopoly on trade in the region in 1755.[45]

Successful trading relations were but one measure of the importance of the Langlades at Michilimackinac. They also enjoyed a growing influence with colonial French officials at the straits. Their close relationships with the Anishinaabeg in the region, particularly the Odawa community at Michilimackinac, gave them access to several important ogimaag and their extended families at the straits and beyond. This kind of access was invaluable to incoming French commanders who had little knowledge of the politics of the *pays d'en haut*. Officers at the post had to rely on go-betweens like the Langlades to communicate with the Anishinaabeg and smooth relations between them. Post commanders would often ask the Langlades to use their trade goods to cover the dead and provision their Indian kin during wartime, for example. But Augustin and later his son's kin connections and trading experience also meant that they could serve as intermediaries between the French and other Indians in the region.[46]

Yet the French were not the only ones eager to capitalize on the union of Domitilde and Augustin. Indeed, neither trade nor the creation of a wide fictive Catholic kinship network was sufficient to explain the Langlades' role in Odawa affairs. But Domitilde's family ties were. In the patrilineal world of Anishinaabe doodemag, uncles were especially important in the lives of their sisters' children. Charles Langlade's uncle was no less than Domitilde's powerful brother, Nissowaquet. He seemed to take a special interest in the son of Domitilde and Augustin. Charles Langlade later told a story that Nissowaquet brought him along on a successful war party against the Chickasaw when he was but a child. After this, Nissowaquet brought the young Langlade on many more war parties. While the details of these stories may have been romanticized by Langlade or his descendants, they speak of an important and early relationship between Charles Langlade and his Nassauakueton uncle. Subsequent events would show it was a lasting one.[47]

Many questions still remain open about the Langlades' activities in the region. For example, Augustin submitted receipts for presents and provisions he gave out to the Odawa. However, it is unclear whether he acted independently, under the authority of the post commander, or at the direction of his Odawa kin. Regardless, in distributing these goods he acted much like an Anishinaabe ogimaag. But we do not know how his Odawa family viewed him in kinship terms. Though normally Domitilde would have been expected to join her husband's doodem, there was no clearly established procedure for the incorporation of those—such as the French—who in Indian eyes lacked a doodem. They may have been adopted into an existing doodem. There were certainly accounts of French traders simply taking up with Indian families and villages. Or they may have been seen to have their own doodem. Certainly, both Augustin and his son Charles seemed to hover between the two worlds. They were trusted by both the French and the Odawa to help maintain good relations between the two groups.[48]

Indeed, that trust helped the Langlades' Odawa kin, including Nissowaquet, to become firmly knitted into the French and métis communities at the straits. While their doodem, the Nassauakueton, had maintained good relations with the French from a very early stage, the partnership of Augustin and Domitilde helped strengthen the tie. Nissowaquet continued to be an important advocate for the French in Anishinaabe councils. With an expanded kin network that reached deep into the heart of the French colony, he could now claim even greater influence over his own family and the village at Michilimackinac. But because of the Nassauakueton's extensive ties with Anishinaabe and Algonquian families to the south and west of Michilimackinac, he also became a powerful advocate for the French across the region.[49]

•

Marriages such as the one between Domitilde and Augustin were particularly important because the number of such unions was relatively small. Though the French reported hundreds of illegal traders in the region in the 1670s, 1680s, and 1690s—the height of the great trade fairs at Michilimackinac—the number of French traders dropped precipitously once the post had been abandoned. Without the protection of the post, anyone who wanted to stay and trade had to ingratiate himself into the world of the Anishinaabeg. This was no easy venture, and it took a willingness on the part of Anishinaabe families as well as some good fortune. Even then, few French or even mixed families were able to establish more permanent roots at the straits—perhaps less than a dozen. While the families of Domitilde, Daniel Villeneuve, and Augustin Langlade were prominent in French eyes, the number of identifiable, intermarried, and permanently settled trading families remained small for most of the colonial period.[50]

We also need to keep such marriages, and the métis offspring they produced, in broader perspective. Marriages between French traders and Odawa women were only a part of a more expansive growth in Anishinaabe power and influence across the Lakes. While we have no access to records that would give us the same kind of picture for inter-Indian marriages as the French records do for European-Indian relations, the language of kinship and the actions of different communities throughout the Lakes suggest a remarkably wide arc of networks. Those alliances extended north and northwest from Michilimackinac through the Ojibwe to the shores of Lake Superior and north into Cree and Assiniboine country, and southwestward to the Mississippi basin. They connected peoples all around Lakes Michigan and Huron and their riverine systems (extending to the Mississippi, the Illinois country, and down to Detroit), and eastward across to the Ottawa River, the mixed nations of Catholic Indians near Montreal, and now, with the marriage of French traders, even into the heart of European settlements along the St. Lawrence.

The Odawa at Michilimackinac enjoyed a privileged and secure position in the center of this expansive Anishinaabewaki. By the 1730s, they had eliminated any potential direct threats to the straits and created useful buffer zones of kin on all sides. To their east lay the Nipissing, Algonquin, and Algonquian kin who had intermarried with the Huron and other Algonquians settled along the St. Lawrence. Between them and the Iroquois sat the Mississauga in southern Ontario to their south. Though their relationship with the Huron at Detroit and the potential for harmful alliances with the Iroquois and other rivals to the south remained high, they could still count on a thick weave of Anishinaabe relations at Detroit and St. Joseph's to counterbalance that threat and protect their interests. To their north, kin among the Ojibwe across the northern Lakes provided a measure of security against any direct threats from the Sioux. Finally, war with the Fox and intermarriage with many Menominee, Sauk, and even Winnebago in the Green Bay region helped the Anishinaabeg create a protective layer of allies on their western flank (see map on pages 120–21). Though slow to take shape and often difficult to discern clearly, in the midst of so-called French imperial expansion, the Anishinaabeg had stamped their presence firmly across the *pays d'en haut.*[51]

•

So, while the Nassauakueton at Michilimackinac enjoyed the fruits of Anishinaabe expansion in the form of extended kinship alliances throughout the region, they and their French kin were only a small, if still influential, part of a much larger whole. Moreover, even though Domitilde and her indigenous kin were able to expand their network of informal relations deep into the heart of New France, this still did not ensure a smooth *formal* relationship with colonial French officials. While Nissowaquet may have cultivated good relations with the French, he was only one among many ogimaag at Michilimackinac. He could make arguments in favor of the French in councils, but he could not force others to agree. Nor could he even guarantee that his own network would follow him. While his relationship with the French and his privileged access to trade goods may have helped increase his influence over his village, they still did not give him the authority to force compliance with his wishes. In addition, the limited influence he might wield lasted only as long as the resources he could command. If French supply lines were to dry up, the Nassauakueton voice in council would diminish rapidly.

The particular loyalties of French and métis traders also worked against smooth imperial governance. We have often assumed that French and even métis traders among the Indians acted as official and unofficial agents of empire. We have done this despite the fact that French officials themselves constantly complained about the lawlessness of the *coureurs de bois*. Those complaints were often accompanied by assertions that the traders were acting against the interests of both French officials and the Indians with whom they traded. But colonial officials usually had a vested interest in the trade themselves, and they were frustrated by those who had better access to their trading partners. The inroads French traders made in Anishinaabewaki often frustrated the best-laid imperial plans for trade and empire building. They evaded licensing requirements, they lived where and with whom they wanted, and they often traded with whoever gave them the best deal, which sometimes meant the English. When discussing the reestablishment of the French post at Michilimackinac in 1713, the intendant thought a garrison would be necessary—not to protect against the Indians but to overcome the forty or so *coureurs de bois* who "remain[ed] masters" there. They were seen as a necessary evil by some in the absence of the post in order to prevent the Indians from going to the English. But once the post was reestablished, most officials wanted to get rid of them altogether.[52]

While French officials believed they were independent renegades, it is more likely traders who stayed upcountry were working on behalf

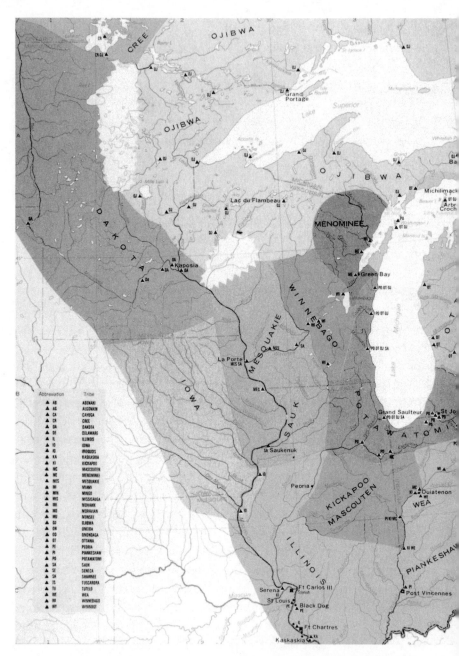

Indian Villages and Tribal Distribution, c. 1768. Though from a slightly later date, and showing only the major Indian towns and villages of the *pays d'en haut*, this map shows the impact of Anishinaabe expansion across the Lakes by the middle decades of the eighteenth century. Note also the Odawa at Michilimackinac

Indian Villages and Tribal Distribution c. 1768

were surrounded by a ring of Anishinaabemowin-speaking nations, including the
Ojibwe, Potawatomi, and Mississauga. (*Atlas of Great Lakes Indian History*, edited by Helen
Hornbeck Tanner. Copyright © 1987. University of Oklahoma Press. Reproduced with permission. All
rights reserved)

of their Indian kin. The new trade practices that compelled traders to winter over with Indian families and extend credit meant a much closer relationship was imperative. The racist complaints of officials implied as much. Governor Vaudreuil told the king in 1709 that they should forbid mixed marriages because "bad should never be mixed with good." The Frenchmen who married Indian women had become, he complained, "licentious, lazy and intolerably independent; and their children have been characterized by as great slothfulness as the savages themselves." "It seems that all children born of them," he concluded, "try to create as many difficulties as possible for the French." Vaudreuil knew, too, that traders married into Indian families had not only illegally brought furs down to the new colony on the lower Mississippi, but some had also accompanied Anishinaabe canoes traveling to Albany to trade with the English. In other words, French and métis traders facilitated illegal Indian trade. Later, in 1737, relations between the *coureurs de bois* and French officials came to a head once again in Michilimackinac. The post commandant wrote the governor that, in June, nearly thirty of them demanded passage through the straits, contrary to French prohibitions against independent traders. They were "armed with Swords, guns, and Pistols wherewith to fight those who might oppose their passage." Significantly he added, "Those people had many Savages on their side," and thus he was "not strong enough to stop them." Whether they had married into Indian families or were simply dependent on them, French traders had to adapt to survive, and that usually meant working on behalf of the Odawa—not of the French empire.[53]

•

Still, kinship alliances such as those created by the Nassauakueton may just have been significant enough to help sustain a French-Anishinaabe alliance for as long as it did work. Through these networks of kin, the Odawa especially managed to maintain a privileged position within the French empire even while they maintained an independence that was often at odds with imperial interests. French imperial officials had long struggled to establish a harmonious alliance with the Anishinaabeg. The Odawa and others sometimes paid lip service to the fictitious kinship relationship the French wanted to cultivate by calling the governor Onontio, or Father. But history had shown time and again that this diplomatic gesture would never translate into a formal and reliable alliance. As the English began to make inroads into Indian country starting in the 1740s, there was even less evidence that the Odawa and other Indians of the *pays d'en haut* would maintain any formal loyalty to to the French empire. In that evolving context, the connections forged by the Nassauakueton and other families in the first quarter of the eighteenth century would become crucial in nurturing a relationship with the French through some trying times. While their numbers were small, their connections were vital. Indeed, it might be no exaggeration to say that without the intimate kinship ties that created real bonds between the Anishinaabeg and the French, the latter would have lost their empire in the *pays d'en haut* long before they did.

4

THE BALANCE
OF POWER

When the Anishinaabe Odawa at Michilimackinac signaled their
intention to move from the straits in the late 1730s, alarm bells rang
at Versailles. Imperial strategists in the metropole saw the intended
move as a major blow to France's territorial ambitions. Paranoid about
the growing threat of English trade and influence among the nations
of the Lakes, the French believed the Odawa move was a grave sign of
their waning power in the region. They could not afford to lose such a
valuable ally. No less than the governor of New France, the Marquis
de Beauharnois, pored over maps of the region, made suggestions for
new locations closer to the straits, and ordered the post commandant to
winter over with the Odawa for two successive years. Beauharnois also
sent report after report back to France about the progress of negotiations
over the new village. In their obsessive interest in the move of the Odawa,
it would seem as if the entire French North American imperial edifice
rested on the outcome.

Of course, most French officials could not help assuming the
move was all about them and the English. Increasing trade between
the English and the nations of the Great Lakes certainly did affect
both Indian politics and their relationship with the French. The Anishinaabeg had long maintained some connections with English traders at Albany, but in the 1720s they took increasing advantage of the
opening of a new English trading post at Oswego, established in 1722

on the southeastern shore of Lake Ontario. Some eighty Indians and their families from Michilimackinac and Detroit made the journey in the spring of 1723 alone. In 1725, the French governor reported that the Odawa had told the Iroquois that all the Lakes were theirs, and they had the right to trade with whomever they wanted, and wherever they liked. The Anishinaabeg and other Indians of the *pays d'en haut* were happy to have an alternate source of trade as it gave them some leverage over the French. Desperate to keep the beaver pelts flowing to Montreal rather than Albany, the French countered these moves in the 1720s with increased subsidies and concessions to the nations of the Lakes. The Anishinaabeg could only benefit from the competition between the French and the English.[1]

French fears about the influence of the English were exacerbated when their struggle to maintain influence in the *pays d'en haut* culminated in an abortive French-Indian war in 1747, followed by a series of significant Indian defections and movements into the Ohio Valley. Because their imperial claims in the region were so heavily dependent on the Native peoples who lived there, the French thought they were on the verge of losing their empire. French officials despaired over the state of their relations with their erstwhile allies. Having long recognized the "spirit of independence" that prevailed among most of the western nations, some French officials began to openly admit the vaunted Algonquian alliance system was a fiction. In 1736, Governor Beauharnois reported that "the natives have their policy just as we have ours . . . All that they outwardly express toward the French is never sincere."[2]

But Indian politics through the 1730s and 1740s, at least at Michilimackinac, were more complicated than these accounts suggested. They were also more consistent with earlier Anishinaabe concerns about the balance of power than they first appeared. It is unlikely that the Odawa at the straits were overly concerned about the growing power of either the French or English. Unlike other more eastern nations, there weren't growing numbers of settlers on their frontiers. And neither the French nor the still geographically distant English seriously threatened to disrupt the comfortable position they had forged at Michilimackinac. But wary Indians at the straits did have to keep an eye on the balance of power both between the French and English and among their Indian neighbors. Though the Anishinaabeg had brought an end to the Fox Wars in 1736, a new round of conflict with the Sioux threatened their western flank (and likely helped hasten the push for peace with the Fox). To their south, renewed Huron outreach to the Iroquois and other traditional rivals of the Anishinaabeg threatened to bring further conflict to the region. Increased Indian trade overtures to the English exacerbated Anishinaabe worries about the balance of power to their south. As their rivals seemed to gain power all around them through increased trade with the English, there was a growing worry among the Anishinaabeg that they had tied their fortunes to the wrong horse.

The Anishinaabeg response to these developments was, as in the past, complicated by kinship. Some ogimaag and their doodemag wanted to throw their support behind the French, others the English, and still others preferred to adopt a wait-and-see attitude. But as more and more of their own kin, both at the straits and at Detroit, began to flirt with the English and English-allied Indians, Odawa at Michilimackinac began to realize that further entanglement with Europeans might lead to civil war. They had to tread carefully. Torn between maintaining good relations with the French and being left out of a pro-English Indian alliance, the Odawa at the straits tacked between reaffirming a military alliance with the French and outright war against them. At the same time, some agitated for a pan-Indian alliance to protect against further European-inspired conflict between them. Ultimately, only the intimate connections the Odawa had fostered with the French community at Michilimackinac and other Indians across the region would help turn sentiments in dramatic fashion at a critical moment—and trigger a world war.

•

In 1736, the same year that the Anishinaabeg called a halt to the Fox Wars, they suddenly found themselves facing the threat of another major conflict. Skirmishing between the western Anishinaabe Ojibwe and the Dakota Sioux endangered a decades-old détente between the two. Why the forty-year uneasy peace ended is still unclear, but by 1736 a renewal of a major conflict between the Anishinaabeg and Sioux seemed inevitable. Communities throughout the *pays d'en haut* prepared for war. Kinship obligations would invariably draw eastern Anishinaabeg into the conflict. Sure enough, by the summer of 1737, the Sioux had struck the Anishinaaabe Ojibwe at Chequamegon Bay at the far western end of Lake Superior. The Ojibwe in turn began calling on their kin and allies to the east for help. Within a few years, war parties of the Anishinaabeg and their allies, some from as far away as Lake Ontario, had mobilized to aid the Ojibwe, even as the French tried in vain to stop them.[3]

The Anishinaabeg also faced another potential conflict on their southern flank. Trouble once again stemmed from the uneasy relations between the Anishinaabeg and Huron at Detroit. While the Fox Wars had temporarily unified the two groups, a new round of trouble began when some Huron at the post initiated a peace with ancient rivals the Catawba and some of their southern allies sometime in the 1720s. The Siouan-speaking Catawba, who lived far to the southeast in the Carolina Piedmont area, had been a longtime target of northern war parties from all over the Lakes, both Algonquian and Iroquoian. But as English-armed Catawba began to drift northward into the Ohio Valley, at least some Iroquois and Huron saw the newcomers as potential allies, to the detriment of former alliances. Early councils between the Huron and Catawba soon caused all the other nations around Detroit to turn on the Huron, and there were even reports that Potawatomi and Odawa at Detroit were raiding the Huron village there in the early 1730s.[4]

The situation was only complicated by the further occupation of the upper reaches of the Ohio River and its tributaries. Under pressure from English encroachments on their land and conflicts with other Indians, diverse groups of Indians began moving to formerly unoccupied regions of the Ohio Valley beginning in the mid-1720s and intensifying through the 1740s. Among these were mixed groups of Iroquois, Shawnee, and Delaware Indians. The occupation of this region alarmed many of the northern Algonquians. The Ohio Valley had long served as a natural buffer—a neutral zone—between the nations of the upper Lakes and their main rivals to the south and east. Iroquois claims over the area in particular helped keep the region free from any major settlement, and kept the numerous and powerful nations of the south—including the Catawba—at arm's length. But as newcomers arrived, including some Iroquois-allied (and dependent) communities, northern Anishinaabeg worried about confronting a new Iroquois-led alliance—supplied by the English and now on their very doorstep. Rumors were also rife of a peace treaty between the Iroquois and the Catawba that might even involve the Cherokee. The Iroquoian-speaking Cherokee were a powerful Native group who lived along the western edges of Georgia and the Carolinas and who were allied with the British. While the Anishinaabeg had occasionally sparred with them, the expanse of the Ohio Valley and the distance between them had prevented a major conflict.[5]

Amid this increasingly uncertain situation, in the spring of 1738, the Huron at Detroit announced they had made a formal peace with the Catawba. They invited the Anishinaabeg to do the same, but the Odawa at Detroit in particular were furious and refused to do so. The Odawa, along with the Ojibwe and Potawatomi, immediately formed a war party to move against the Catawba to show their contempt for the Huron-initiated peace. But shortly after they got under way, they were ambushed. The Odawa claimed the Huron had warned the Catawba and may even have participated in the attack. When word of the ambush spread, the Anishinaabeg were furious, calling the Huron "dogs" who were capable of killing their brothers and fathers. The Huron, in fear of retaliation, withdrew into their village at Detroit, fortified it with palisades, and asked the French and their kin in the mission villages of Quebec to intervene.[6]

There was much at stake in this confrontation. With the Huron and Anishinaabeg at each other's throats, the entire region teetered on the threshold of an inter-Indian war. Even the French realized the danger. The Iroquoian-speaking Huron now had deep connections with the Iroquois themselves, and the Algonquian-speaking Odawa would draw all the other nations of the Lakes into the conflict. The French commandant at Detroit warned that the ambush of the Anishinaabe war party could be the start of a major conflict: "the bloodshed it has caused makes me fear lest all the savages should take sides in it; for these two tongues affect all the tribes of this country." To try to stave off an escalation of the conflict, the Odawa sent runners with belts to the Iroquois, asking them not to take sides. The French immediately prohibited sales of arms to either side for fear of dragging the French into the conflict by looking as if they were taking sides. The Huron did not trust the French to protect them and believed the Anishinaabeg were in the midst of organizing a coalition to exterminate them. Eventually, several groups of Huron made a permanent move to new villages around Sandusky Bay, in the southwest corner of Lake Erie, halfway between present-day Toledo and Cleveland and about a hundred miles south of Detroit. Out from under the watchful eye of the French at Detroit, they immediately made contact with British traders and made peace with some of the English-supported southern Indians.[7]

•

New conflicts with the Sioux and Huron were one significant factor forcing the Anishinaabeg to rethink their relations with the French. With war threatening on their western flank, their rivals to the south were growing in power, apparently with the aid of English trade goods and arms. The Huron alliance with the Catawba was proof of the potential of a dangerous axis that could stretch from Albany across Iroquoia into the Ohio Valley and up into Anishinaabewaki via Sandusky and Detroit. As they contemplated these dangerous combinations, many Odawa at Michilimackinac looked for reasons to maintain good relations with the French instead of allying with the English themselves. But if pro-French advocates among the Odawa hoped for a sign of strength to counter those favoring accommodation with their enemies and the English, they would be sorely disappointed. For at the same moment, the French got embroiled in a divisive and ultimately disastrous conflict with the Chickasaw, far to the south along the Mississippi watershed.

The French had established a new North American beachhead at the Gulf of the Misssissippi in the late seventeenth century, which was quickly followed by the founding of New Orleans in 1718. French planters, eyeing the fertile lands of the Mississippi watershed, began moving upcountry, which led to a series of vicious wars with the local Natchez Indians. When some of the Natchez took refuge with the Chickasaw in 1730, the stage was set for a complex and protracted war. The Chickasaw, who were then living along the Mississippi in what is now Tennessee, had long been a thorn in the side of the Louisiana colony because of their trade links with the English. Now they were a powerful enemy. In retaliation for French and allied-Indian attacks, the Chickasaw raided far and wide, hitting both the French and allied nations north of the Ohio and along the Wabash and other vital routes into Illinois country. They also preyed on French shipping on the Mississippi, and they began to entice the Choctaw over to their side with the promise of British trade. The Choctaw were another powerful confederacy of native peoples in the Gulf Coast region with whom the French had so far been able to maintain friendly relations. The governor of Louisiana began to despair. In 1733 he complained that only the "entire destruction" of the Chickasaw would secure the safety of the French settlement at Louisiana.[8]

Yet it was not until 1736—the same year the Anishinaabeg had put an end to the Fox Wars—that the French felt secure enough to strike en masse. In that year, the veteran Louisiana governor Jean-Baptiste Le Moyne, Sieur de Bienville, collected an army of six hundred, which included newly settled French planters and their African slaves, at Mobile. But they were routed when they prematurely attacked the well-fortified Chickasaw town of Chocolissa. They were cut to pieces by defensive fire, then encircled and trapped by warriors from another town. Many of the prisoners, including one of their officers, were burned alive by the Chickasaw. After a second deadly loss, the Chickasaw forced the French into a demeaning withdrawal. To add insult to injury, that summer a group of four hundred Chickasaw, Natchez, and Cherokee, newly equipped with vast amounts of plundered French ammunition, stores, arms, and clothing, came north to settle on the Ohio River two hundred miles above its mouth, bringing several English traders with them. Bienville thought they were there to sway more Ohio nations to their side. Almost immediately, they attacked a canoe with six voyageurs on their way to the Illinois, killing four.[9]

There was more at stake in this humiliating sequence of events than the direct threat posed by the southern nations. Governor Bienville and other French officials knew that all of the western nations were watching. The fragile balance of power all along the Mississippi watershed depended on Indian ideas of the relative power of the French and English. Most of them were only too happy to play off the French against the English to pursue their own interests. The Choctaw, for example, would help the French only if they could bring to the field their northern Indian allies. But the northern Algonquians were reluctant to commit themselves to a losing cause. Though the Odawa and Huron at Detroit swore revenge for the killings on the Ohio, little came of their initial efforts. The situation was critical. Almost immediately after the defeat in 1736, Bienville asserted that the king would have to undertake a second campaign "without which the reputation of our arms would be destroyed among the Indian nations from which we should not obtain the same assistance after too long a delay . . . all the Indian nations are waiting to see the method that we shall adopt." Though it had already spent 120,000 livres (or close to $1,000,000 in today's money) on the disastrous campaign of 1736, the Ministry agreed and promised more money and regular troops to restore the "honor of France."[10]

The Chickasaw War thus became a test of French power. Yet they continued to falter. Poor planning, diseases, and the weather conspired against French plans to attack the Chickasaw again until 1739. A new plan called for help from the Odawa at Michilimackinac as well as many other northern Indian groups. The governor of Louisiana thought that without their help, "it would not be possible to undertake anything against the Chickasaws." The French also hoped that mobilizing the northern nations would intimidate the Choctaw into a more secure alliance. By 1739, though, most of the Anishinaabe Odawa were reluctant to get involved. Only pro-French doodemag such as the Nassauakueton agreed to send warriors. The rest held back. The expedition suffered lengthy delays and supply problems. Eventually, the warriors from the north grew impatient and abandoned the war party. Without his Indian allies, the governor admitted he could do little against the Chickasaw, and he negotiated a peace. Though he would try to put a good spin on it, the peace achieved little. The Chickasaw signatories demanded that the French prevent further Indian war parties from raiding their villages. Bienville agreed because he could do little else under the circumstances, but he hardly had the power to enforce such a provision.[11]

The French failure did little for their deteriorating relations with the nations of the *pays d'en haut*. One officer complained just after the 1739 expedition turned back that their Indian allies would now "treat us as women, and in a way they will be right." He predicted that they would "offer us all sorts of insults" and demand extraordinary presents. They did more than that. The nations who had joined the French expressed their disdain for the negotiated peace by attacking isolated Chickasaw hunting parties. Despite pleas by Governor Bienville to stop the raids, they continued through 1742, extending also to the Cherokee. In 1741, several hundred warriors from Detroit, St. Joseph's, and Michilimackinac sent out war parties against the Chickasaw and Cherokee. They seemed happy to embroil the French in further conflict while settling old scores. The Chickasaw Wars only increased the contempt many felt for the French.[12]

•

It was in this troublesome context that the Odawa at Michilimackinac announced they were moving their village. They said they wanted to move far to the south, nearer the Potawatomi at St. Joseph's River on the eastern shore of Lake Michigan. The Odawa claimed that the soil was growing weak around the straits, exhausted by years of intensive agriculture. There was likely a great deal of truth to this claim, but the French worried that their main aim was to move away from them and closer to the English. The French were desperate not to lose their valuable suppliers, and allies, from Michilimackinac. The governor of New France immediately invited the Odawa to Montreal for talks and suggested three sites for resettlement that were much closer to Michilimackinac. Though he claimed his suggested locations were still too far off, he tried to remind the Anishinaabeg what they might give up: "Think of the pleasure you will experience in being near the French, who purchase your canoes, your guns, your corn, your fat, and every thing that industry causes you to produce, whereby you are furnished with the means of living more comfortably with your families, which you would not find farther off." But both Beauharnois and the Odawa knew there were advantages to a move farther away. The governor took note of their previous visits to the English. Under the circumstances, he could not be critical. Instead he had to promise he would provide for all their needs.[13]

The Odawa were only too happy to play on French fears. They told the French they were considering sites all along the eastern shore of

Lake Michigan, as far south as the Muskegon and Grand Rivers on lands that many Odawa had used as wintering grounds. The Odawa were not ready to abandon the French altogether. But keeping the French at arm's length was beneficial on a number of fronts. Maintaining contact with the English and other Indian nations who traded with them was important in keeping an eye on developments farther to the south. As their rivals moved into the Ohio Valley and renewed the threat of an Iroquois-inspired alliance against them, the Odawa needed to keep their options open. Being able to host visitors and conduct councils free of a French presence allowed them to do just that. Many also wanted to continue to use the English as alternate suppliers when French goods were scarce or prices too high. But given the central role the Odawa played in the Michilimackinac provisioning trade, most agreed that the possibility of an alternate trade was more important than the reality. It gave them leverage over the French.

The pressure worked. Eventually, the Odawa settled on Waganawkezee, or Crooked Tree—about twenty miles southwest of the straits on the eastern shore of Lake Michigan. It was named after an old and bent pine tree that leaned out over the lake from a ridge above. It served as a visible waymarker for canoes on their way to the new settlement. The Odawa made the move in 1742. Though they had initially told the French governor that they wanted to move farther away, it was likely they had Waganawkezee in mind all along. Odawa oral stories suggest a long familiarity with the site, which provided excellent land for growing corn in a warm microclimate between the Lake and coastal bluffs. Odawa from Saginaw Bay had almost moved to the site in 1739. For the Odawa from Michilimackinac, it was perfect. It was far enough away from the French to maintain their independence, yet close enough that they could keep their hold on the strategic straits—and thus to continue the valuable trade upon which the French post depended (see second map at front of book).[14]

The Odawa also knew the French would be compelled to reward them for their apparent loyalty in choosing a site closer to the French garrison. They were right. In addition to the presents the French plied them with throughout the decision-making process, the French promised they would even send troops out to help the Odawa clear the land to sow in the spring. The Odawa also got the governor to agree to send a French blacksmith to maintain and repair their arms and other iron goods. Beauharnois told the French minister at Versailles that he had conceded so much to the Odawa because French trade in the region was dependent on them. If they moved any farther from the straits, it would have been "very prejudicial to the Commerce of the Upper Country." But he knew there was more to it than that: "the stratagems resorted to by the English to attract our Savages, compel me to use great Circumspection toward Them, and to Content them as much as I can."[15]

•

For the French, the consuming negotiations over the resettlement of the Odawa at Waganawkezee were only a prelude of worse to come. The Detroit Odawa, for example, continued to trade more or less openly with the English. But the governor also suspected the Michilimackinac and Saginaw Odawa of forging relations with the English. He worried the Odawa would seize the "first pretext to break the word they have given me were I to fail to keep mine." Yet his word was about to get much harder to keep. Just after the Odawa finalized the details of their move and left Montreal in the summer of 1742, the French Ministry announced a new trade policy that restricted the number of trade licenses and established monopolies at the smaller French posts. The crown wanted to make more money from the fur trade by selling the licenses and monopolies directly and cracking down on clandestine dealings. But the new regulations would invariably slow down the flow of trade to the *pays d'en haut* and drive up prices for French goods—encouraging the Indians to trade with the English. Restricting the number of licenses issued for trade at places such as Detroit and Michilimackinac also hurt particular families with established connections and contributed to growing anti-French sentiment in the region.[16]

On top of these changes, the outbreak of a new French war with the English in 1744 quickly brought things to a head. King George's War (1744–1748) was the North American branch of the European War of the Austrian Succession. Nominally caused by a struggle over the Austrian throne, the conflict provided a pretext for the French and British to fight again over their increasingly valuable imperial holdings in the Caribbean and North America. Though the war was largely confined to skirmishing along the eastern seaboard—in northern Massachusetts and New York, and around the maritime colonies of Nova Scotia and Acadia—it had an adverse effect on trade in the interior. Very early in the war, Governor Beauharnois reported a dramatic decrease in trade goods taken up to the *pays d'en haut*. The increasing prices of trade goods, combined with lower prices offered for beaver pelts during the war, discouraged potential traders. The fall of the commanding and impressive French fortress of Louisbourg, at the eastern end of Île Royale, or Cape Breton Island, jutting out into the Atlantic Ocean, in June 1745 then drove up prices further: the French lost control of the Gulf of St. Lawrence to the British Royal Navy, and virtually no supply ships made it to Quebec until the end of the war in 1748. Beauharnois noted he had to sell licenses to trade at the posts for practically nothing, especially to Detroit. The governor warned the Ministry that the growing scarcity of goods would cause problems for their alliance with the Indians, and "may produce among them great change towards us."[17]

By 1747, the situation was dire. The French crown blamed Governor Beauharnois for the loss of Fortress Louisbourg, and he was replaced with the relatively inexperienced and uninterested naval commander Roland-Michel Barrin de la Galissonière. New France thus lost a governor who had gained valuable experience dealing with Native Americans over his twenty-year administration. The new governor struggled to maintain the western trade. He reported that they now had to pay voyageurs to take the king's provisions up to the posts rather than sell the licenses. Even then, only nine canoes left for Detroit and ten for Michilimackinac. They were running desperately short of the fabric that the Indians coveted, too. Without these, the new governor reported, "The Trade of the Upper Countries And the Beaver trade in particular cannot be kept up." But as inexperienced as Galissonière was, he seemed to understand the consequences. The shortages, combined with English machinations, would have disastrous results.[18]

Even during peacetime, post commanders struggled to keep up with the constant demand for provisions and presents that Indians demanded in return for French posts in their territories. During wartime, and particularly when asking for help from Indian war parties, dwindling supplies meant that post commanders could not act as important war chiefs ought to act. They could offer little to those contemplating warfare. In turn, this inability to act as generous war chiefs was taken as a signal of French weakness in general. Coming on the heels of the humiliation of the Chickasaw War, this was not a good look. For those already wary of the French, inadequate supplies made good arguments for forging better relations with the English.

Moreover, the English promised much. As early as the summer of 1745, Huron, returning to Detroit from a visit to the English post at Oswego, boasted that an officer there had assembled all the nations and made a present of a large cask of brandy for each village. He told them they must look to the English from now on, as they had great fleets coming across the seas to take Canada. The French would no longer be able to supply them. The post commander at Detroit said reports of this conference spread quickly and had "so great an Effect in the Village of this post, that they are leaving continually without saying a word."[19]

The French clung to any signs that they still had supporters among the nations of the *pays d'en haut*. In 1744, for example, they celebrated the fact that Kinousaki, an Odawa ogimaa at Detroit, was able to raise thirty-five warriors to scare off a British patrol in the Ohio Valley. But even when apparently acting as allies of the French, most warriors pursued their own interests. In 1745, sixty Odawa and Ojibwe warriors from Michilimackinac, including Nissowaquet, promised to head for Montreal, and several parties of Detroit Indians had set out to attack toward the Carolinas. The French governor celebrated the fact that so many warriors had traveled so far to participate in raids against the Anglo-American colonists and allied Indians. But English-allied Indians observing preparations of the Anishinaabeg in Montreal reported a misunderstanding over their war aims. The French, hoping to strengthen their alliance with the Anishinaabeg against their own foes brought out a calumet and danced "after the Method of the Indians with the Heads of Beasts in their Hands, saying, thus will we carry the Heads of the English." Yet the Indians "in their turns danced, but said, thus will we carry the Heads of the Fflattheads [Catawbas]." The war dance, the spies concluded, made the French "look very down."[20]

•

The deep ambivalence in Indian country about the French and their strength as allies helps explain the confused events of 1747. While historians often make much of "Pontiac's War" in 1763, a similar pan-Indian war almost broke out sixteen years prior—only that time it was against the French. The year began promisingly enough for the French. Reports from Michilimackinac indicated that many there looked forward to traveling to Montreal to help the French in the spring. By early July, 192 Indians from Michilimackinac, St. Joseph's, and Green Bay arrived, though unusually, 80 of these were women and children. The French should have taken note of the uncommon composition of the group. Indeed, hot on the heels of their arrival came news from Detroit that the disaffected Huron at Sandusky had killed five Frenchmen. Soon reports flew that "all the Indians of the neighborhood, except the Illinois, had formed the design to destroy all the French of Detroit on one of the holidays of Pentecost, and afterwards to go to the fort and subject all to fire and sword." Native Americans presumably hoped to take advantage of French inattention on the Catholic holiday. The premature attack at Sandusky, along with a warning by a Huron woman, were all that prevented a full attack on Detroit from going ahead, according to later reports.[21]

Even after the attack on Detroit was preempted, anti-French factions among the nations of the *pays d'en haut* took advantage. Most pro-French warriors and chiefs were down in Montreal. Given the presence of women and children with them, they may have gone to Montreal deliberately, to steer clear of the attacks and await the outcome. On August 13, the governor received news from Michilimackinac of "the confusion that prevails among all the Nations of that post and neighborhood." The Saginaw Odawa had killed three Frenchmen who were going from Detroit to Michilimackinac, while some Ojibwe from La Cloche (an island north of Manitoulin) had attacked two French canoes. Nearer Detroit, Ojibwe on Grosse Isle stabbed another Frenchman. Yet even those at Michilimackinac threatened. On July 3, the French called a council at the fort after they heard a report of the conspiracy at Detroit. But the council ended abruptly when a crowd of young warriors forced their way in and insulted the

French. Subsequently, the commander barred the Indians from the fort, but they continued to offer "divers insults and threats at the fort, and in the vicinity." They killed all the horses and cattle they could not take with them, and the officers believed they were planning a siege of the fort itself.[22]

According to French reports from Michilimackinac, the Mississauga and Ojibwe had been won over by the anti-French factions, and the Odawa of Michilimackinac would have taken part against them "had it not been for the portion of the village which is in Montreal." The post commander at Detroit, Paul-Joseph Le Moyne de Longueuil, also heard that the Ojibwe and Odawa of the Lakes were on the verge of attacking his fort. The situation was deadly serious. A later report noted that "no respect was paid to the commandant" at Michilimackinac and that voyageurs were robbed and maltreated at Sault Ste. Marie and across Lake Superior. "In fine, there appeared to be no security anywhere." Longueuil wrote from Detroit that the Odawa ogimaa Kinousaki was the only one that remained friendly to the French at that post. Mikinac, another Odawa ogimaa, was allegedly only waiting for reinforcements from the Odawa and Ojibwe of Michilimackinac to declare against the French. Letters from officers at Forts Frontenac, Niagara, and Chartres and among the Iroquois all confirmed that anti-French sentiment had spread throughout the entire *pays d'en haut* and down into Illinois country. The extent of the conspiracy and how close it came to being far worse for the French can be glimpsed in none other than Pontiac's speech sixteen years later. The reputed leader of one of the most famous pan-Indian wars against the English claimed in 1763 that it was he who had defended the French when "the Chippewas and Ottawas of Michilimackinac, and all the northern nations, came with the Sauk and Foxes to destroy you."[23]

A decade later, Nissowaquet and his Odawa warriors also claimed they had intervened in the attacks and even warned Longueuil of the plot in advance. Yet at the time, at least, pro-French Anishinaabeg and others who had joined the French campaign in 1747 protested their surprise at events in the *pays d'en haut*. We will probably never know whether that surprise was genuine or whether they had left the region on purpose so as to avoid any conflict at all. But as it became clear the attacks had been preempted, they moved to restore order. On

August 28, the Potawatomi at Montreal, hearing the same news as the French, demanded leave to return home to clear their name. They claimed to regard the attacks of their fellow Anishinaabe Odawa and Ojibwe as made against them. A few days later, ten other Odawa along with one Ojibwe from Michilimackinac arrived in Montreal to see the governor. But they also wanted to return home immediately and said they were surprised by the reports of the attacks there. Both groups promised to take revenge on those living on Bois Blanc Island (adjacent to Mackinac Island), who they claimed were responsible for the attacks.[24]

The return of the pro-French Anishinaabeg to Michilimackinac seemed to bring an end to the crisis. On the way back from Montreal, they did what they could to prevent a further escalation of hostilities. Captain Jean-Baptiste Jarrett de Verchères, the post commander at Michilimackinac, had captured an Odawa warrior with property belonging to one of the dead Frenchmen in his sack, along with a scalp. Two Odawa canoes just returning from Montreal then claimed the prisoner, assuring Verchères that "he belonged to the family of Koquois, a chief who is attached to the French and known to Mr. De Verchères." They then reneged on their promises to burn the village of the disaffected on Bois Blanc Island, knowing that would only inflame the situation. Instead, they quickly and quietly got the rest of their kin to disperse for their winter hunts. Lieutenant St. Pierre, who commanded a convoy up to Michilimackinac in October, said he arrived there without incident—all the nations there had gone to their winter quarters. But he also noted they had done so "without giving any token of repentence for the outrage they had perpetrated."[25]

Pro-French Anishinaabeg believed they had to tread carefully to rebuild a fragile peace. The French would demand justice for the attacks. Indeed, the new governor, Galissonière, detained all the voyageurs and their goods the following spring, and told the Indians that he would not send any traders into their country until they delivered the murderers of the Frenchmen and restored the plundered goods. But pro-French factions knew they were in no position to deliver what the French wanted, and if the traders were stopped, it would anger their kin further. In Detroit, Longueuil reported that a few Odawa and Potawatomi came to the post to renew their alliance with the

French, and that the ogimaa Mikinac brought some thirty families down from Saginaw to make peace. But they refused to bring in any of the perpetrators of the attack. The only compensation they offered was a slave who they said was anti-French. Though this was likely all they could offer under the circumstances, Longueuil worried they were only trying to procure supplies before they "discover a favourable opportunity to betray us irrevocably."[26]

At Michilimackinac and Saginaw, pro-French Odawa managed to convince some of their kin to turn themselves in, but only on the understanding that the French would pardon them. They each sent a prisoner down to Montreal accompanied by some of the most pro-French ogimaag in their midst. They expected this gesture would be enough to repair relations; the French could then release the prisoners. But the inexperienced new governor did not abide by Indian rules. Galissonière detained the prisoners despite repeated requests to liberate them. The Anishinaabeg were horrified and feared the consequences of returning to the *pays d'en haut* without them. In desperation, they went on the warpath against the English to show their fidelity, and they renewed their requests for the prisoners on their return. The governor grew so concerned about their increasingly insistent demands that he sent the prisoners up to Quebec. On the way, they somehow managed to escape, killing eight escorts in the process. An embarrassed Galissonière first blamed the escape on the negligence of the guards, but he later admitted that the captives were probably helped by some of the Odawa who were in Montreal. The newly freed prisoners joined the Michilimackinac and Saginaw Odawa returning home. The governor could do nothing to stop them.[27]

Pro-French Anishinaabeg also pursued another strategy to deflect further French-Indian conflict. They tried to channel the blame for the uprising toward the Huron at Sandusky. Still uneasy about the prospect of a Huron-Iroquois-English alliance, the Anishinaabeg tried to use the conflict to force the French to act against the Huron. Even in the midst of the attacks, one pro-French Odawa named Nequiouamin came to the fort at Michilimackinac and told the post commander and missionary that the Iroquois, Huron, and Catawba "had come to an understanding with the English to destroy the French and drive them to the other side of the sea." After the uprising failed,

Mikinac and a Potawatomi chief at Detroit promised they would help punish the rebellious Huron. They told Longueuil that if the French sent a force of a hundred Indians and French to Detroit in the winter, and another hundred in the spring, they would take revenge on the Huron.[28]

In the end, Galissonière believed that it was only the arrival at Detroit of a convoy of merchants and traders, accompanied by about 150 French troops, that saved the post in September and forced the nations there to back down. The arrival of the troops was likely enough to allow pro-French factions in the region to reassert themselves. Yet the governor and other French officers only dimly glimpsed these internal political divisions. They were convinced there was a general conspiracy against them, which included plans by some of the Odawa and Ojibwe along with the Catholic Huron to destroy Detroit. Of Michilimackinac, Galissonière thought that, though farther from the English, "their invitations and intrigues had been, in some degree, the cause of more disorder there; scarcely any of the Nations had been exempt from the general seduction." But Galissonière also admitted that their friends among the same nations might well have saved the French.[29]

For at least some French officials, the pan-Indian assault was more than just a result of English intrigues. Rather, it was a sorry indictment on the French inability to assert their authority over their own empire or even insinuate themselves among their so-called allies and friends. In the aftermath of the 1747 uprising, the aging governor of Montreal, Josué Dubois Berthelot de Beaucours, drew on a lifetime of experience with Indian diplomacy but could only conclude the Anishinaabeg and others were little interested in the French per se. Even in Montreal, and almost 150 years after the French planted a colony, Beaucours sensed he still lived very much in Indian country. He felt surrounded by Native Americans: they were vulnerable and exposed whenever they traveled. Perhaps more significant, he noted that some time ago "the Red skins made a treaty . . . not to kill one another, and to let the whites act against each other." Beaucours might have had in mind Odawa diplomatic efforts to keep the Iroquois neutral in their conflict with the Huron at Detroit in 1738. French fears of an Iroquois-Anishinaabe alliance against them still haunted many colonists who could recall the precarious position the French had found themselves in at the end of the seventeenth century. Indeed, Beaucours thought he detected a sinister new plot: their so-called allies had since stood aside while their enemies attacked the French. Now they were ready to strike themselves. The French could never be safe, he concluded, "not knowing the secrets of their hearts."[30]

In this bleak context, the few remaining friends of the French were about to become even more crucial. Promises to reform the licensing system, as well as an infusion of much-needed supplies at Quebec in the spring of 1748 as King George's War wound down, helped woo back some of those who had joined the conspiracy. But resentments continued to simmer in the *pays d'en haut*. The governor remained wary of Indian intentions, and after the massacre of the escort of the Indian prisoners, renewed his determination to punish the perpetrators. He only succeeded in alienating more potential allies. Concerned about retaliation, some of the Odawa and Ojibwe who had been involved or implicated in the murders fled Michilimackinac and sought refuge with their more rebellious kin at Saginaw, out of the immediate reach of the French. Farther south, French determination to punish the killers resulted in further defections of some of the already wavering nations, especially those near Detroit who had a longer history of trade with the English.[31]

But the biggest threat to French claims over the *pays d'en haut* emerged when a coalition of disaffected Miami Indian families moved to a new settlement on the banks of the Great Miami River in the Ohio Valley. The village was called Pinkwi Mihtohseeniaki (the village of the "people of the Ashes" in the Miami language). The English called it Pickawillany (see first map at front of book). From this new settlement, a global war and then a revolution would come.[32]

•

The unlikely leader of the breakaway group at Pickawillany was Memeskia, known also as "La Demoiselle" by the French and "Old Briton" by the English. Memeskia was, like so many other Algonquians of the Lakes, of mixed parentage. He had a Piankashaw father and a Miami mother (the two groups were closely related). Living amid the Miami, Memeskia was originally only a minor figure in the village of

Kekionga (or Kiskakon), one of two main Miami villages on the upper reaches of the Maumee River. The French considered Le Pied Froid the head chief of the Miami and regarded Memeskia as only one war chief among many in Le Porc Épic's clan. Both Piedfroid and Le Porc Épic were staunch advocates for a French alliance, the latter tied by marriage to the French.[33]

On the surface, at least, Memeskia's rise to power, like that of the Nassauakueton earlier in the century, revealed the fluidity of Algonquian kinship politics in action. Through connections on his father's side, an awareness of the opportunities provided by the British trade offensive, and some daring, he began jockeying for power during the events of 1747. At the time, he led a party of warriors to sack the French post at the Miami village when he was not even a band or clan leader. The attack gained him notoriety among the French and adherents among their enemies. Though the main group of disaffected Miami from Memeskia's village rejoined the French after the revolt, the Shawnee Indians of the Ohio Valley—keen to gain allies in their claim to the contested lands of the upper Ohio—persuaded Memeskia and his followers to establish a new town at Pickawillany.[34]

Once at Pickawillany, Memeskia was quick to create new alliances with Pennsylvania traders who were surging into the region. The Pennsylvanians had made inroads among the new communities of Shawnee, Delaware, and Mingo who had moved to the Allegheny and upper Ohio by the early 1740s. When French trade to the Ohio Valley virtually collapsed during King George's War, English colonial traders moved in quickly to fill the vaccum. Not only did they trade with the new communities filling the Ohio Valley, but they also reached out to older communities of ostensibly French-allied Indians farther west and north. There were reports that some had even ventured within sight of the French fort at Detroit to trade with Indians there. By 1748, there were more than twenty colonial traders from Pennsylvania in Logstown alone, and a similar number at Pickawillany. Memeskia also persuaded the English to formalize their relationship, traveling almost five hundred miles eastward to Lancaster, deep into the English colonies, to sign a treaty of friendship and alliance with commissioners from Pennsylvania on July 23, 1748. To the English, Memeskia claimed to be at the forefront of a new wave of defections from the French. He said he spoke on behalf of twelve villages lying west of Pickawillany who were ready to repudiate the French and join with the British. He also boasted that there were twenty villages on his river and a thousand warriors, and they blocked French access to their posts on the lower Mississippi. The commissioners from Pennsylvania were impressed. They pledged free trade with the English and "assistance on all occasions."[35]

Better trading relations was certainly a key goal of Memeskia and others who joined him. Like many other Algonquians in the Lakes, Memeskia and the Miami had suffered from poor supplies and high prices at the hands of the French. The increasing availability of cheaper English goods combined with French shortages over the past decade convinced many that the future lay with the English. The reforms promised by the French after 1747 came too late to make a difference to those farther to the south. In places like Michilimackinac, the French had a more effective and well-established supply network that could rectify problems quickly. There was also a market not only for beaver and other furs but also for venison, canoes, fish, corn, and bear oil. Thus, price concessions in furs, and price reductions for supplies to the Algonquians of Detroit and Michilimackinac helped win back many after 1747. But in the south, the French struggled to get supplies out to all the trading posts, and French merchants were still hesitant about accepting the many deerskins that remained at the heart of the trade on the Ohio. The British were more than happy to take them.[36]

More troubling for the French was the fact that Memeskia was not alone. Though the French singled him out, he was one of a new group of rebels who wanted to revive an English-Iroquois trade and alliance axis for their own political gain. Orontony—one of the Hurons behind the move to Sandusky in 1736 from Detroit—had long been in regular contact with British traders from towns on the headwaters of the Scioto River. Yet the Huron had also continued to make overtures to British-supported southern Indians. When the 1747 uprising failed, Orontony and other Hurons moved from Sandusky in 1748 and eventually established a town called Conchake on the Muskigum River across from modern Coshocton. From here, like Memeskia, they continued to make overtures to the British and the Iroquois. By welcoming British traders into their towns, these new villages put French claims over the entire Ohio Valley in jeopardy. But given the recent trouble in the Lakes, they also worried that they would lose the entire *pays d'en haut.* French officials were desperate to stop the defections.[37]

The new villages of Pickawillany, Conchake, Sonnontio, and Logstown did not just represent a threat to French trade and claims. They also engendered a new political alignment that threatened the stability of inter-Indian relations across the *pays d'en haut.* Indeed, the breakaway groups along the Ohio and its tributaries also constituted a critical movement away from the dominance of other—and often pro-French—nations around Detroit and the central Lakes. In particular, most of the rebels, like Memeskia, came from nations who were less thickly woven into the larger Anishinaabe alliance around the *pays d'en haut.* The Miami, of course, had a long history of conflict with the Anishinaabeg, particularly in the Detroit region. Other breakaway groups, such as the Huron under Orontony, also simmered with long-standing resentments against their Algonquian neighbors. Instead, both the Miami and Huron had historic and social—if sometimes uneasy— relations with the Iroquois.[38]

In these circumstances, Memeskia signaled his intentions by reaching out to other nations beside the English. Alienated from pro-French Algonquians around the Lakes (including those in his own former village), Memeskia first sought out the Iroquois and other southern nations. Indeed, the treaty at Lancaster in 1748 was as much a pact between the Miami and the Delaware, Shawnee, and Iroquois as it was between the Miami and the English. According to Pennsylvanian officials, the breakaway Miami, Huron, Piankashaw, and other nations pressed the Iroquois to accept them into the Covenant Chain (the historic set of alliances and treaties initiated in the 1670s primarily between the Iroquois and the English). The French believed that Memeskia was the "concocter" of a league against the French that stretched from Iroquoia in the east through the Ohio and as far west as the Illinois region.[39]

Knowing what was at stake, Memeskia moved carefully and also worked to turn kinship politics to his advantage. Memeskia knew that formal alliances with the English and Iroquois were unlikely to ensure his survival, so he pursued a more important strategy. He quickly began building a fictive kinship network that emanated from his village into the heart of the *pays d'en haut*. He did this by welcoming in strangers and capitalizing on their connections. Like other rebel towns on the Ohio and its tributaries, Pickawillany rapidly became a gathering place for many disaffected groups. One French report in 1749 noted that the new town of Scioto had attracted Indians of all nations. Though it was mostly inhabited by Iroquois and Shawnee, there were Indians from the Catholic villages near Montreal as well as Miami, Delaware, and "some from nearly all the tribes of the Upper Country, all entirely devoted to the English." Near Pickawillany, there were another six cabins of Miami at the White River. They had Seneca with them. The French believed this was a deliberate "policy of these tribes" to "always have some of the latter with them who are shields for them."[40]

It worked. The French were unable to penetrate the webs of kinship that emanated out from the peoples whom Memeskia had welcomed at Pickawillany. An initial French military campaign against him in 1749 failed disastrously when expected Indian reinforcements from Detroit never materialized. The Detroit Indians worried they might end up fighting against their own kin. After boasting they would "whip home some of our children," the French lost even more face among the nations of the *pays d'en haut*. Indeed, the failed expedition spurred further defections and emboldened Memeskia. For example, he sent delegates into all the winter quarters of the Miami bands of Le Pied Froid. He also contacted other mixed-Miami villages of closely related Wea and Piankashaw living at the French Fort Ouiatenon on the Wabash River (near present-day West Lafayette, Indiana). He capitalized, too, on the presence of Miami among the Potawatomi as far north as St. Joseph's. Here, a small group of previously pro-French Miami living among and intermarried with the Potawatomi began to act as agents for Memeskia.[41]

Again, his strategy worked. By early 1750, the commandant at Fort Miami reported that all these communities promised to take their furs to Pickawillany in the spring, and the Wea at Fort Ouiatenon (on the Wabash River, about sixty-five miles northwest of present-day Indianapolis) made plans to settle there. Le Pied Froid also feared the rest of his warriors would leave, despite his protestations; none of those who went to Pickawillany the previous autumn had yet returned. In the summer of 1749, there were only forty or fifty warriors at Pickawillany. Over a year later, there were as many as four hundred families, including whole clans and minor chiefs of the Wea and Piankashaw.[42]

Memeskia's successful defiance also encouraged other disaffected groups to flirt with the English. In 1749 and 1750, large numbers of Odawa, Ojibwe, and Huron from Lakes Superior and Huron carried furs to the English post at Oswego. The commandant of Michilimackinac at the time, François Lefebvre Duplessis-Faber, told the governor in Quebec that "the greater portion" of the nations in his region had gone to the English via Sault Ste. Marie (i.e., simply avoided the Michilimackinac stop-off), and had taken more than three hundred packages of furs. Chiefs and would-be chiefs quickly realized there was political capital to be gained by opening relations with the English and Iroquois. Many warriors, for example, pledged to follow Noukouata, a Michilimackinac Odawa, if he accepted the position of a British chief offered him by the English. The French believed the English were sending messages via the Iroquois to lure the visiting nations away from the French. Odawa and Ojibwe even carried British brandy to Green Bay, arousing French fears of British influence there, too. For French officials, worse was to come. In the spring of 1750, the disaffected Odawa and Ojibwe still living in exile at Saginaw after the 1747 uprising promised to join Memeskia the following year.[43]

The French were desperate to stop Memeskia. His defiance and open relations with the English effectively threatened all French claims over the Ohio Valley. If Memeskia continued, it was only a matter of time before the French would be completely locked out and the English instead could make good their claims over the same region. But Memeskia's defiance also threatened another round of conflict with those whom the French hoped to keep as allies against the English. In a state of siege, the French had to repair their relations with as many Indians as possible, no matter what their recent transgressions. So, early in 1750, the French declared a general amnesty for those who had attacked them in 1747. The new governor who had taken over from the short-tenured Galissonière, Jacques-Pierre de Taffanel de la Jonquière, then held councils in Montreal to give out presents and medals. He met with some success, drawing off a few rebel Huron who deserted their leader Orontony, and Jonquière eventually won back over the Sinago Odawa in exile at Saginaw, who promised to return to Michilimackinac. But the French could do little right at this stage. The pardons granted to the rebels of 1747 only angered other allied nations. Wea living at Ouiatenon along the Wabash River, for example, concluded that "it costs no more with the French to be a scoundrel than to be honest men." By mid-May 1750, those at Ouiatenon had committed to Memeskia, assuring the English and Memeskia that before the summer was over they would strike the French themselves.[44]

Despite their promises to help, even the majority of pro-French Indians refused to budge. It was too dangerous. In desperation, the French tried to organize another campaign against Memeskia in 1751. At Detroit, the different nations there deliberated for twenty days before finally concluding that while they were happy to move against the British, a full attack on Memeskia and the rebel town of Pickawillany was another matter. It would ignite a civil war. English reports noted that the Odawa and Ojibwe at Detroit told the French any attack on Pickawillany would be an attack on their "brothers" and they would be compelled to strike the French in retaliation. "The Twightwees [disaffected Miami] were married and intermarried among them," an Odawa ogimaa explained, and if any other Indians dared attack them "he would have their scalps, or else they his." Without Indian support, the French backed down and canceled the expedition. The commander thought if he left Detroit to attack Pickawillany, the Indians would destroy the post in his absence.[45]

In the face of French weakness, many rebels seized the moment and struck first. By the end of 1751, the Piankashaw on the Vermilion River declared war on the French and killed five traders. Others plotted. Rumors flew that the Piankashaw planned to meet up with the Illinois and Osage to coordinate a general attack on the French. Another report noted the Illinois, Wea, Piankashaw, Miami, Delaware, Shawnee, and Iroquois planned to meet at Pickawillany—to discuss an alliance that would extend from the Hudson to the Mississippi River. Many nations secretly promised to remain neutral. A Potawatomi chief at St. Joseph's reportedly told a Piankashaw chief they would never raise the hatchet against the Miami. Even the Michilimackinac Anishinaabeg, despite promises to aid the French, refused to budge.[46]

Memeskia's key strategy seemed to work. He had quickly built a formidable network that extended throughout the *pays d'en haut*. It served as a shield for his town. In April 1752, the acting governor, Charles Le Moyne de Longueuil (who had temporarily taken over when Jonquière died in office), told the French minister that every party of Indians who went to the Miami village had left people there "to increase the rebel forces." With each new occupant at the village, dozens more around the *pays d'en haut* became reluctant to attack, even if they were pro-French allies. The commandant at St. Joseph's, for example, said he could not control the nations there because the rebellious Miami were near relatives. There was even one report that Memeskia's son was married to an Odawa woman.[47]

Longueuil despaired. After surveying the sentiments of many of the nations of the *pays d'en haut*, he concluded that very few would act against Memeskia, and even those that "promised wonders" were only deceiving the French, for "at heart, they preserve the same feelings of attachment for those rebels to whom they are connected by blood." Longueuil told the French Ministry at Versailles that all the post commandants had said the same. They were facing a "general conspiracy" and could do little to stop it without substantial reinforcements from the metropole. Colonial officials in New France prepared to face their enemies alone. While it looked as if they would lose the Ohio Valley, they also thought they were on the verge of losing the entire *pays d'en haut*.[48]

•

Fortunately for the fate of the French empire in North America, there was more at stake in Memeskia's defiance than European rivalries. By welcoming disaffected groups and individuals who had their own kinship connections across the Lakes, Memeskia thought few would dare oppose him. But in creating this fictive kinship alliance, Memeskia had also provoked the ire of pro-French doodemag among the nations of the *pays d'en haut* whose own grip on their towns and villages was slipping. But even those uncertain about their relationship with the French could fear the possibility of an English-backed southern confederacy composed of many of their ancient rivals. Not only did this prospect threaten a developing aim to maintain as far as possible the balance of power between the English and the French, but it also jeopardized the uneasy détente between the Anishinaabeg and their allies and the Iroquois and theirs. At worst, Memeskia's machinations threatened to ignite a war among the Indian nations at a moment when many were more actively pursuing a policy of limiting bloodshed between them.

Heated councils took place across the *pays d'en haut* as towns and villages deliberated and considered the new reality. Among the Odawa at their new settlement at Waganawkezee, younger warriors and disaffected chiefs made the case against the French. Their supplies and provisions had been inconsistent over the past couple of decades; prices had been high. English traders at Oswego and elsewhere were willing to give much more for the furs and skins brought down from the *pays d'en haut*. This could only be a result of French haughtiness. The new forts they built, the new colony they planted in Louisiana, gave the French a confidence they did not deserve. Their war of extermination against the Natchez revealed another side to the French. So, too, did the causes of that war show that some French planters coveted Indian lands as much as the English. Yet against real adversaries, the French were weak. The Chickasaw humiliated them. The Huron taunted them. Now Memeskia and others openly defied them, killing their soldiers and traders. Morever, the recent succession of French governors and post commanders seemed to indicate the French were divided among themselves. They were too weak to move against even one village. It was foolish to make an alliance with a nation that possessed so little power and influence. With the Dakota a threat to their west and a pro-English alliance to their south, Odawa at Michilimackinac would be isolated and vulnerable. As the nations to the south benefited from English trade and began forming alliances against them, many Odawa argued that they, too, should join this alliance and rid themselves of the French. And they should do so now while they had a chance. Some could have pointed to the fact they had kin among the rebel villages who could facilitate it.

Against this arsenal of arguments, cooler heads advocated for patience. The French had for decades provided for their *besoins*, or needs. Well-worn trade networks and kinship alliances meant they wanted for nothing. Yes, the English were selling cheaper goods and giving away much more liquor, but the Odawa had to travel far and often into Iroquois territory for it. They could not become dependent on their former enemies. Besides, the French showered them with presents and in return asked little. As their history with the French had shown, the forts the French built throughout the *pays d'en haut* were little more than trading posts and provided some safety from attack. The English, on the other hand, wanted their land. It was now clear that settlers almost always seemed to follow behind the English forts and trading posts and quickly swallow up Indian lands. The long and bloody history of English-Indian relations and conflicts over land since they arrived in North America was apparent to everyone. The Odawa should do what they had always done: simply use the leverage they had by playing off the European nations against each other. With both sides keen to woo them, the Odawa could always count on help when they needed it, wherever and whenever a threat arose. This need was more pressing in the current circumstances, when the drift of more rivals into the Ohio Valley threatened to upset the balance of power between themselves and their potential enemies. Many worried that now was not the time to repudiate the French. It would only be a matter of time before their old rivals—strengthened with English arms and new alliances—turned on them.[49]

The Odawa moved cautiously. First, they sent a delegation to Pickawillany to see if they could resolve the crisis peacefully. In early 1751, four Odawa ogimaag traveled down to meet Memeskia. They brought a French flag and gifts of tobacco and brandy. They told Memeskia that the French would forgive him if he stopped trading with the English and returned to the Maumee River. In the midst of courting the Wea and Piankashaw, and with English traders in his midst, Memeskia took the opportunity to score some points with his would-be allies. He heard the delegation out, and then insulted them. Memeskia taunted the ogimaag about their own loyalty to the French. He also reminded them of his new connections. Boasting that he had been "taken by the hand" by the English, the Iroquois, Shawnee, Delaware, and Huron, Memeskia openly dared the Odawa and their French friends to attack him. He was ready for them. In his defiance, Memeskia confirmed the worst fears of those concerned about the alliances he was constructing. His insults demonstrated the place

Memeskia envisioned for the Anishinaabeg in this new configuration. The Odawa began preparing for war.[50]

Before they could strike, though, they still needed some kind of guarantee that conflict with Memeskia would not embroil them in a wider war with the English or the Iroquois. Thus, a few months later, in June 1751, fourteen canoes of Anishinaabeg from Michilimackinac arrived at Oswego to warn the English that there was likely to be a war between the Odawa and the disaffected at Pickawillany. But at the same time, the delegation reassured the English they had no quarrel with anyone else. The Odawa then moved down the St. Lawrence to attend a council between the French and Onondaga Iroquois in July. Though we have no records of any private discussions or separate councils between the Odawa and Iroquois, they did speak to each other at least once in the presence of the French. It was a rancorous meeting, but ultimately reassuring for the Odawa. The Onondaga re-stated their claims to the lands of the Ohio River Valley and made it clear they were not happy about recent settlements. They asserted that they had told the English to leave as well as the other Indian na-tions, including the Odawa. The Onondaga accused the Detroit and Michilimackinac Odawa of trading with the English themselves and going to live among the rebels. They demanded that the Odawa ogi-maag warn off their young warriors from the area. And while they did not denounce Memeskia and the other rebels, the Onondaga at the council did not affirm a commitment to defend them either. Instead, they claimed they would "not permit any Nation to establish posts there; the Master of Life has placed us on that territory, and we alone ought to enjoy it, without anybody having the power to trouble us there." Though they would not enforce their own edicts to clear the Valley of non-Iroquois settlements, they did open the door to others doing so.[51]

•

Even with a green light from the Iroquois, the Anishinaabeg struggled to put together a coalition of the willing. Who would risk such an attack? The kinship alliances of Memeskia's followers looked too strong to penetrate without risk of a massive war in which the Anishinaabeg faced a multination alliance. At this critical juncture, though, kinship politics once again played a vital role. Memeskia managed to attract converts to Pickawillany and cobble together a diverse kinship network that helped protect his village. But another young upstart would prove his match. At Michilimackinac, one of a vital few men who were products of the intimate alliances made in the uncertain first half of the century was about to come of age. Enmeshed from birth in a world of densely woven Indian and French relations that continued to thicken through his young life, Charles-Michel Mouet de Langlade would put a decisive end to Memeskia's dreams of an expansive southern anti-French alliance.

Langlade, at the age of about twenty-three in 1752, was already firmly embedded in both the Nassauakueton and French worlds by virtue of his mother and father. His mother, Domitilde, had rooted him in a French-Anishinaabe Catholic community. By 1750, his father also secured him a cadetship in the French troops. In turn, Charles drew on these connections and also married an Odawa woman, while enjoying extensive trade relations with the Odawa both at Waganawkezee and their wintering grounds at Grand River. He was in a perfect position to help push a pro-French agenda among his Indian kin. Langlade's trade interests also depended on keeping the English at bay. Finally, Langlade's real and fictive kin network was dense and influential enough that with his Nassauakueton kin, he could put together a coalition of warriors willing to strike out against Memeskia. Thus, he could not only claim to carry out French orders but also further the interests of his extended Indian family.

Langlade and his kin recruited warriors over the winter of 1751–1752. Langlade likely spent most of his time in the Grand River region wintering with the Waganawkezee Odawa. There, they would have also made contact with Potawatomi from St. Joseph's. As the ice broke up around the Lakes, Langlade returned with his Indian kin to Michilimackinac and continued recruiting among the Ojibwe who stopped at the post. By early June, they were ready. Approximately 270 warriors from among the Odawa, Ojibwe, and Potawatomi left the straits on June 3. Stopping at Detroit, about 30 of the group left the expedition when they heard the Miami had been hit by smallpox. Langlade continued with some 240 Indians and one other unidentified Frenchman. They moved quickly, arriving at Memeskia's village less than three weeks after leaving Michilimackinac. By the morning of June 21, they stood watching from the edge of the Miami clearings for the right moment to strike.[52]

At about nine in the morning, Langlade and the Anishinaabe warriors charged the stockade, catching women in the cornfields and forcing defenders back to the safety of a hastily constructed fort. The attackers may have killed as many as thirteen Miami in this initial skirmish and captured four women and several children. Three English traders sought shelter in some of the houses outside the stockade, but they quickly surrendered. These captives, fearing for their lives, told Langlade's force there were only twenty defenders in the stockade and that they had little water. They also told them how many English were still in the fort. Langlade's force kept up a heavy fire on the stockade well into the afternoon. Then, under a flag of truce, Langlade told the rebels they only wanted submission, not war. If they promised to return to their former homes, they could go peacefully. They also said they only wanted the English traders. Langlade offered up the captured Miami women and children in return for the traders, whom they promised not to harm.[53]

Those in the stockade, facing so many attackers, appeared to comply. They thought it better to deliver up the English and their supplies of beaver and other goods than to risk annihilation. But both sides failed to honor the agreement. The defenders sent out only three of the five Englishmen they were holding. One of them was a blacksmith who had been wounded in the fighting. Langlade's forces immediately set on him, stabbed him to death, scalped him, and ripped his heart out. They ate it in front of the defenders. They also somehow managed to seize Memeskia and drag him out of the stockade. Ordering the rest of the defenders to stand along the wall and watch, Langlade and his allies then killed, boiled, and ate Memeskia in front of his family and kinsmen. While reports of ritual cannibalism are rare in this era, the Anishinaabeg were one of the few Indian peoples who did practice it. As one captive later suggested, they turned to cannibalism not "for want of food, but as a religious ceremony, or rather, from a superstitious idea that it makes them prosperous in war." The attackers literally reabsorbed the rebellious chief and his powers—or manidoog—into their own alliance. After the feast, they released the women they had taken and headed for Detroit with four captured traders and £3,000 worth of goods (or well over $300,000 in today's money). The number of casualties varies—newspaper accounts put the figure at thirty dead, yet English reports list only seven dead: Memeskia, the blacksmith, one Mingo, one Shawnee, and three Miami.[54]

Reports of the terrifying attack at Pickawillany circulated widely, no doubt as Langlade and his Anishinaabe allies intended. But it was a masterful piece of theater. The limited casualties at Pickawillany—given the unequal odds—point to a carefully orchestrated attack. Though the surviving Miami later stressed the surprise nature of the attack in order to save face, many at the town had been warned. While moving through Detroit, the attacking force made it known they were going to persuade the Miami to come back to the French or "else cut them off." At least one visiting Mingo heard the news and hurried off to the Ohio. Then, ten days before the attack, an advance party of Indians arrived at Pickawillany. The Miami later told Virginia governor Dinwiddie they had been given "Wampum, & a fine French Coat, in token of Peace & good-will," which made them believe it was safe to go out hunting. But what the desperate Miami did not tell the governor was as many as twenty-five Piankashaw and Miami families took the opportunity to leave Pickawillany to go back to their French-allied villages. The warnings and the advance visit had an effect. By the time of the attack, only a few intransigent rebels were left in the village. The Miami claimed there were a mere eleven men of able-bodied age at the town when the attack came, plus nine English traders. Memeskia could barely muster his own family in his defense. He paid the price.[55]

The attacking Anishinaabeg were also careful to return Miami women and children in exchange for the English traders. Only Memeskia and the wounded blacksmith were purposefully executed. In a world of extended and complicated kinship alliances, the Anishinaabeg knew what was at stake if they killed indiscriminately. It was too risky. Not only was there a danger of reprisals from those who had kin elsewhere, but there was also a concern that an indiscriminate attack against pro-English rebels would reignite a general Indian war. Langlade and the Anishinaabeg thus alerted most of the village and limited the casualties. Their main target was Memeskia, who had more fictive than real kin. The attack was effectively a political assassination.[56]

The Anishinaabeg also gambled that in limiting casualties, the rebellious Miami would be isolated. With few casualties outside Memeskia's own kinship circle, the surviving Miami would be unable to call on allies to avenge the attack. They would also be blamed for it. In the midst of the battle, the Anishinaabeg taunted Memeskia and his kin. Once Memeskia surrendered the blacksmith, they said they need not kill all the Miami because the British and Iroquois would hold them responsible for the deaths and captives. Sure enough, the English refused to help the rebels. The surviving Miami first turned to the governor of Virginia for help, requesting at least arms and ammunition so they could defend themselves. They stressed how sorry they were that the English had been killed and captured. They also tried to incite the English against the French. Though they acknowledged only two Frenchmen had participated in the raid, thereby counting Langlade as French, not Indian, they improbably asserted that there were as many as thirty more in the woods nearby. The Miami knew they were in a precarious situation. In desperation, they also wrote to the governor of Pennsylvania, declaring that they now "look upon ourselves as lost People, fearing that our Brothers will leave us."[57]

They did. English traders fled the region in droves. The ferocity of the attack struck fear into vulnerable British traders isolated along the Ohio River. Far in advance of any formal military protection, the attack at Pickawillany showed that the rebels who wooed English traders could not protect them. So, too, did Memeskia's erstwhile allies abandon the village. In the face of the attack and with English traders on the retreat, most of the rebels returned to their hometowns and to the French fold. Some early reports suggested several families from Pickawillany even left with the attackers. Others fled in the days following the raid—many back to their former Miami, Anishinaabe, and Huron villages. By early autumn, the Wea and Piankashaw returned home to the Wabash River professing fidelity to French, and the Miami as a group refused further trade with the British. A very small band that included Memeskia's wife and child sought refuge with nearby Shawnee. They were all that remained of Memeskia's seemingly formidable alliance.[58]

The French, of course, were quick to claim the attack as a great success that demonstrated the strength of their alliances with the

Indians in the face of English attempts to woo them over. But there was more to the victory than met the eye. Most of those involved in the battle took great pains to stress that it was primarily aimed at Memeskia. If it benefited French officials, that was only coincidental. Even some of the Anishinaabeg played down their relationship with French officials, at least in front of other Native Americans. Later accounts noted that after the initial attack, a mortally wounded Iroquois (probably the Mingo) demanded a talk with the Anishinaabeg. At that point, a Miami with a flag in his hand came up to them and reproached the Anishinaabeg as "they had become the slaves and dogs of the French, who forced them to fight and destroy each other." The Anishinaabe warrior replied it was the last time they would listen to the French. The attacking party then reportedly sent belts to the southern nations to "confer and to agree no longer to take arms against each other, which would imply a sort of league against the French." For months after the attack, the *pays d'en haut* was alight with rumors not of revenge attacks on the Anishinaabeg, but of pan-Indian councils to smooth over relations and blame either the French or the English for the attack instead.[59]

Certainly, the Anishinaabeg from the *pays d'en haut* were cheered and relieved by the Iroquois response to the attack. Though there were reports of planned retaliatory raids, Anishinaabe diplomacy ahead of the battle won the day. The Iroquois did not strike back. Despite Memeskia's boasts of belonging to an Iroquois-English alliance, his demise was simply not worth the risk of an inter-Indian war, especially when the Iroquois themselves were coming to question the worth of their relations with the English. There were many rumors that relations between the English and the Iroquois were strained. Anishinaabeg in the *pays d'en haut* along with Shawnee and Delaware Indians in the Ohio Valley then learned that in June 1753, the Mohawk—among the staunchest allies of the English—repudiated their close relationship with the New York authorities.[60]

•

The Anishinaabeg and other Indian nations across the *pays d'en haut*, then, could draw two important lessons from the turbulent events of the middle decades of the eighteenth century. The first was that it was more important than ever to play off the English and French against each other in order to limit their power. As Europeans grew in numbers along the St. Lawrence and eastern seaboard of America, Native Americans immediately west of them had experienced the destructive effects of their increased presence. New diseases, the encroachment of settlers on Native lands, a lack of control over a now global trade network, and several devastating European wars against Indian nations such as the Natchez all pointed to the need to watch both Britain and France very carefully and not allow either side to gain the ascendency. In that respect, both the uprising against the French in 1747 and the attack at Pickawillany in 1752 can be seen as efforts to check the power of Europeans. As Governor Galissonière noted at the end of 1752, echoing his predecessor Beauharnois, the so-called Algonquian allies of the French "love us hitherto a little, and fear us a great deal, more than they do the English." But there was a clear logic in the policy of nations such as the Odawa. Many of them knew it was in their best interests to play off the French and English, he thought, "so that through the jealously of these two nations those tribes may live independent of, and draw presents from, both."[61]

Simultaneously, though, by 1752 there was a growing awareness among Native nations of the *pays d'en haut* that the best way to restrain European power was by keeping the peace among themselves. In the seventeenth century, Native Americans such as the Anishinaabeg could generally mobilize the English or French to aid them in their wars and advance their own interests. As European numbers and power on the continent grew, however, Indians in the eighteenth century found themselves being drawn into largely European conflicts and divided among themselves over whom to support. This meant they were increasingly in danger of facing off against one another as Europeans pushed them to choose sides.

The second lesson of Pickawillany, then, was that traditional rival powers in the *pays d'en haut* should and could put aside their differences in the face of the growing European presence and influence in the region. While pro-French and pro-English factions among them might still edge each nation to closer relations with one European power or another, fewer Indians north of the Ohio River seemed prepared to go to war with each other over those relationships. As we have seen, the governor of Montreal, Berthelot de Beaucours, suspected that the Indians of the *pays d'en haut* had around 1737 made a peace treaty among themselves. This came hot on the heels of the Fox Wars, and in the midst of the trouble between the Huron and the Odawa over the alliance with the Catawba. While we may never know for certain whether there was such a treaty, or its details, conflict between the nations of the *pays d'en haut* did susbside considerably after 1737 or so. When Memeskia threatened to blow apart that peace, he was taken out. The attack on his village combined with the lack of repercussions in Indian country in its aftermath was a good sign that the growing pan-Indian movement for peace among the northern nations could hold under duress. These lessons came at a particularly opportune moment. For while the attack on Memeskia did not trigger an inter-Indian conflict, it did have a massive effect on European politics. At Pickawillany, Charles Langlade and his Anishinaabe kin helped seal a peace between Indian nations. But they also provoked a war between Europeans.

5

THE FIRST
ANGLO-INDIAN WAR

The attack on Pickawillany in June 1752 proved a critical turning point in the history of the modern world. A conflict in Indian country ignited one of the world's first truly global wars. From European perspectives, it helped initiate a series of events that would explode into what we now know as the Seven Years' War. Had the French been unable to dislodge Memeskia from Pickawillany, they might not have risked further conflict in the region. Instead, the successful attack explicitly raised questions—and the stakes—over imperial boundaries and thus provoked an increasingly heated exchange between England and France about their claims to the Ohio Valley. From this squabbling, France and England quickly locked themselves into an almost decade-long war that spanned three continents and eventually drew in more than a dozen European nations together with countless colonial communities around the world. The war would reshape the modern geopolitical landscape and forever change the course of North American history.[1]

If Native Americans helped trigger this war, we have often misinterpreted their subsequent role in it. Historians have traditionally seen the attack at Pickawillany as an important victory for the French. The blow supposedly secured the "allegiances" of most of the rest of the western nations of the *pays d'en haut* for the duration of the new war. The ferocity of the attack seemed to demonstrate French power at a vital moment. So closely did the attack allegedly knit together European and Native American interests that the ensuing war has long been mistakenly called "the French and Indian War." In this historical framework, Native Americans are driven by European concerns, mere auxiliaries of the French or (very rarely) the British. Few historians have tried to explain the presence and motives of the Anishinaabeg and other Indians at important battles throughout the war. They have seen them as mere pawns in a European chess game. The main contest was between Britain and France, and the prize in North America was control over the Ohio Valley. In this story, from June 1752 onward, Native Americans could act as allies to only one or the other of the central players. In that respect, historians have at least recognized that Native alliances were crucial to the balance of power during the war, and especially critical to the French. Yet in assuming that the European story was the only one to explore, we have lost sight of the fact that Native nations around the *pays d'en haut* had their own agenda during the ensuing conflict. We have lost sight of how much Native Americans drove the story of the Seven Years' War.[2]

Viewed from Indian country, the Seven Years' War began as a pan-Indian effort to roll back recent English advances and restore an older equilibrium. From an Anishinaabe perspective especially, the conflict could equally be labeled the first Anglo-Indian War, for the successful attack on Pickawillany signaled the possibility of inter-Indian cooperation among the nations of the *pays d'en haut*. The unanswered blow to the English and the lack of Indian reprisals—combined with unusual French vigor in pushing the war effort—gave Native Americans an unprecedented opportunity to rebalance the politics of the *pays d'en haut* after years of French weakness and English advances. Pro-French feeling among the northern nations melded into anti-English resentment farther to the south. Moreover, Pickawillany had shown that the Iroquois would likely remain neutral. For the nations of the Ohio Valley and *pays d'en haut*, never before had such an opportunity presented itself—to roll back not just English trade but especially settler advances over the past decade or two. Once that goal had been achieved, only ardent pro-French factions continued to support the French war effort.

But it would not be enough to save the French empire. Early Indian successes in the war raised the stakes for British colonial and metropolitan empire builders. Just as most Native Americans ended their war, the British stepped up their efforts against the French in North America. If Indian support had often propped up French imperial endeavors over the past century or so, the withdrawal of that aid in the middle of the Seven Years' War would unknowingly help spell the end of the French empire in North America.

•

Buoyed by the attack on Pickawillany, French officials along the St. Lawrence and at Versailles initiated plans to back up their claims to the Ohio Valley. Whereas just prior to 1752 they had virtually given up on reclaiming the Valley because of Indian hostility in the region, in 1753 they sent a large expeditionary force out from Quebec to mark their territory once and for all. They built a fort at Presqu'île on the eastern shore of Lake Erie (near present-day Erie, Pennsylvania) and built a road south, to the headwaters of LeBoeuf Creek (present-day Waterford, Pennsylvania). Along the way, the French took captive any English traders they found in the area and brushed aside remaining Indian complaints about their presence. The French were confident that, given the lack of reprisals for the attack on Pickawillany, they would not face much opposition from either the Iroquois or other Indians in the region. After their efforts in 1753, French forces followed the rivers south to the Allegheny in early 1754, then to the confluence of the Allegheny and Monongahela Rivers (present-day Pittsburgh, Pennsylvania), where they started building Fort Duquesne. The new fort gave them command of the entire upper Ohio Valley.[3]

English colonial officials and land speculators in both Virginia and Pennsylvania were alarmed by the formal French move into the upper Ohio Valley. Investors in the Ohio Company, which had bought up vast tracts of land in the region, stood to lose thousands of pounds if the French upheld their claim. Investors included no less a personage than the governor of Virginia, Robert Dinwiddie. In October 1753, Governor Dinwiddie sent the Virginia Regiment to warn the French to leave the region. A twenty-one-year-old major named George Washington led the force. His brother was also an investor in the Ohio Company. Washington met with the French at Fort LeBoeuf; they politely told him that they had no intention of leaving, and gave him a history lesson detailing why the French claim to the area was stronger than that of the English. Washington returned to Williamsburg in early 1754 with the news that the French had arrived in the upper Ohio Valley in force and were not going to leave.[4]

Across Indian country, the attack on Pickawillany also set in motion events that would lead to war. Most important, the successsful attack strengthened pro-French sentiments. The audacity of the attack and the lack of repercussions were a sure sign of great manidoog—it enhanced the standing of pro-French families at the straits, and also the influence of the Michilimackinac Anishinaabeg throughout the region. Pro-French Anishinaabeg were now able to argue convincingly for an all-out offensive against the English. While the French had showed only signs of weakness over the past decade or two, the English had made considerable inroads into Indian country to the south. As the flagrant defiance of Memeskia had shown, the possibility of a strengthened pro-English alliance across the southern frontiers of the *pays d'en haut* could threaten the stability of greater inter-Indian relations. In the aftermath of Pickawillany, too, there were likely more disgruntled groups who would join in attacks on the English than groups who would oppose them. Even some of the pro-British villages in the Ohio Valley were disgusted that the English had done nothing to avenge the attack on Pickawillany. It showed the British wanted land, but would offer no protection for their Indian allies. Many communities to the south were also angered by long-standing grievances against the English or unfulfilled promises. Some of the Shawnee and Delaware, for example, were reportedly enraged at the English for putting some of their chiefs to death. They sent out wampum belts to many other nations, too, inviting them to come and avenge the insults. These belts, made of precious white and purple shell beads, were used by many nations across the eastern seaboard and *pays d'en haut*. Designs carefully stitched into the belts could convey important political messages between Indian nations. They were not to be taken lightly.[5]

The fact that the Iroquois did nothing to avenge the death of Memeskia also signaled a significant shift in their attitude toward both the English and the Algonquian nations to their north. Not only did it demonstrate a rapprochement of sorts between the Iroquois and the Anishinaabeg, but it also showed a frustration with the English in their midst. As English settlers poured over the Appalachian Mountains in the footsteps of traders, Indian country was alight with renewed concern over the greed of the newcomers. In secret councils with delegates from the Tuscarora, Oneida, and Cayuga Iroquois in October 1754, for example, their Iroquois kin living among the mixed Catholic villages near Montreal noted it was time to distinguish between the English and the French. The lands around French forts were still good hunting grounds, since the French "fixed [themselves] in those places we frequent only to supply our wants." The English, however, "no sooner get possession of a country than the game is forced to leave it; the trees fall down before them, the earth becomes bare, and we find among them hardly wherewithal to shelter us when the night falls." Even if there were some who still harbored resentments against the French, most were convinced this was a good opportunity to strike the English.[6]

Thus even before the French and English formally began to trade blows in the Ohio, Native Americans went on the offensive. Indian raids began in 1753, triggered by Shawnee outrage that some South Carolina militia had taken captive a war party who were on their way to attack the Catawba. They soon received reports that the governor of the colony was holding their warriors hostage and that one of their leaders had died in prison. The Shawnee took to the warpath against the English. Anishinaabeg from Michilimackinac may have joined in the attacks. Certainly, rumors of their involvement caused much anxiety on the English frontier. The ferocity of the attack at Pickawillany had been widely reported in British colonial newspapers. Now, new reports of Odawa and Ojibwe war parties on the colonial frontiers struck terror into the hearts of colonists. When George Washington met with the French in late 1753, his scouts warned him that the Odawa, Ojibwe, and most other Algonquians had taken up the hatchet against the English. When the party came across seven scalped settlers at the head of the Kanawha River, Indians with him claimed that it was the work of the Odawa.[7]

Fears of further Indian attacks weighed heavily on Washington's mind when he returned to the Ohio Valley the following year. As soon as Governor Dinwiddie had learned of French activities in the region in early 1754, he sent Washington back to help build a fort at the forks of the Ohio. As he approached the area in May 1754, an anxious Washington found out the French had already arrived in numbers at the forks and begun erecting a fort of their own. Yet he was most worried about the possibility of ambush from reinforcements. He heard new rumors that in addition to two groups of French on the move, there were six hundred Ojibwe and Odawa coming down the Scioto River to join them. So, when Washington stumbled upon a detachment of Canadian militia escorting the French emissary Ensign Joseph Coulon de Villiers de Jumonville, he panicked. Jumonville had been sent to find the Virginians and to urge them to leave the region peacefully. Though not yet officially at war with the French, Washington's party killed Jumonville and twelve of his men in an ambush. Enraged, Jumonville's older brother diverted seven hundred Canadians and Indians on their way from the St. Lawrence to reinforce Fort Duquesne to avenge his brother's death. The Virginia Regiment, who took refuge in the hastily erected and aptly named Fort Necessity, had no chance. Washington surrendered to avoid a massacre. But the damage was done. Washington's "assassination" of Jumonville caused a diplomatic uproar in Europe. Most historians consider the one-sided Battle of Jumonville Glen as the informal start of the Seven Years' War in America.[8]

•

If the Battle of Jumonville Glen signaled the opening of the European war in America, the official start of the Anglo-Indian war was arguably initiated at Michilimackinac. In July and August 1754, the Odawa brought together some twelve hundred delegates from at least sixteen different nations from across the *pays d'en haut*. They included many of the Anishinaabeg of the immediate region and their kin among the Algonquin and Mississauga, but also the Huron, Menominee, and Winnebago. Yet another measure of the enhanced standing of the Michilimackinac Anishinaabeg was the presence of older rivals and more distant nations too. These included representatives from the Fox, Miami, Mascouten, Kickapoo, Wea, Sioux, Pawnee, and Assiniboine. They gathered not only to talk among themselves about the impending conflict, but also to hold formal talks with the French. A detachment of the French force sent to build Forts Presqu'île and LeBoeuf had headed north to Michilimackinac to drum up support. The French sent as many as two hundred regulars and as many more militia to the straits to quell any remaining doubts about their strength and demonstrate how serious they were about fighting the English. As a sign of respect to the Odawa and Ojibwe at the straits, the French headed straight for Michilimackinac to hold their talks.[9]

Over twelve days, the Odawa hosted three different councils. The first council was held outside the walls of the fort. The French commander of the expedition, Captain Michel-Jean-Hugues Péan, spoke first and claimed he represented the governor of New France. Well aware of the debate that had raged within most Indian communities over the past few years, the officer alluded to rumors that some of them had thought about turning their arms against the French and in support of the English. Indeed, the French were still very unsure of the loyalties of those they came to impress. One French soldier, Charles Bonin, later said they purposely held their first council under the guns of the fort and kept their arms close, and loaded. With such a large gathering of delegates with unclear intentions, the French were "forced to take precautions against a surprise attack." They were very much concerned "in case of any evil intentions on their [the Indians'] part." Even after initial Indian assurances of support, the French remained under arms.[10]

But the French need not have worried. The Odawa had already smoothed the way. The successful attack at Pickawillany carried great weight among their allies and erstwhile rivals. It quieted anti-French talk. Instead, pro-French ogimaag were able to convince any remaining doubters that the way was clear for a pan-Indian assault on the English. By the time the French arrived, there was little disagreement. After Captain Péan spoke, each chief stood up and spoke and in turn affirmed his intention to war against the English, backing this up with carefully made strings of wampum that sealed their words. They had obviously prepared their speeches before the French arrived. They said they would "levy all their young men to go to war against the English, who had already deceived them, and to whom they would listen no more." According to Bonin, who wrote his account many years after the visit, the visiting delegations then affirmed their resolution with several war rituals. The delegation first formed a circle and all together gave a war cry. Then they sat down and began to paint themselves red and black, the colors of war. They also smoked the calumet. But to signal their intention to go to war together, they smoked through a hollowed-out tomahawk instead. It was a sign of cowardice to refuse to smoke it when offered. After this, the Indian representatives danced the rest of the day and into the night. Though the French and Indian delegates met in council twice more over the following week, it was a mere formality. The Anishinaabeg and their allies across the Lakes were going to war.[11]

•

The formal Indian declaration of war at Michilimackinac in turn led to the formal start of hostilities between the English and the French. Upon hearing news of Washington's foray to the Forks of Ohio, the English sent an expeditionary force from Europe to dislodge the French from Fort Duquesne. The French upped the ante and made plans to send a much larger force to North America. But before these troops could be deployed, Native Americans started the war on July 9, 1755, with a famous victory over three thousand British regulars—once again in Indian country.

In the battle we now remember as "Braddock's Defeat," a British expeditionary force under Major General Edward Braddock set out to take Fort Duquesne. But they ran headlong into a trap. More than six hundred Native Americans lay in wait for them, along with just over two hundred French *troupes de la marine* and Canadian militia. The Indians spread themselves along the line of the British column and on a signal began firing into the flanks of the advance guard. When the redcoats tried to retreat, they ran pell-mell into a group of reinforcements moving forward. In the confusion, Indian marksmen made their shots count. Fifteen of eighteen officers in the advance guard were killed or wounded within the first ten minutes of battle. A long and fierce fight ensued during which most of the disciplined regulars could hardly see their enemies. Eventually the besieged and terrified British began to give way, encouraged by "a whoop of the Indians, which echoed through the forest, [and] struck terror into the hearts of the entire enemy." Thousands of troops fled the area, and the French thought a thousand British were left dead or wounded on the field of battle, including most of their officers. Despite the fierce fighting, the Native Americans and the French lost only twenty-two men, and sixteen wounded.[12]

Ironically, Charles Langlade is perhaps now best remembered for his role in this decisive and opening battle of the Seven Years' War. A well-known painting hanging in the Wisconsin Historical Society depicts Langlade as one of the leaders, if not the commander, of all the French and allied forces. Distinguished from his kin in the 1903 image by his European clothing and his pistol, Langlade appears to be directing the movements of Native Americans during the battle. He is depicted not as a warrior himself but as a go-between, a métis officer among the French forces leading Indian warriors. Yet while Langlade was promoted to ensign on March 15, 1755, there is no contemporary evidence of his presence at the battle. All extant evidence comes from English sources, written after the Seven Years' War. No French sources at the time list or note Langlade's involvement. It is highly unlikely he was there.[13]

Edwin Willard Deming, *Braddock's Defeat*, c. 1903. Charles Langlade, on the left, is depicted directing an Indian attack on General Edward Braddock's troops in 1755. (Image number: Whi-1900, Wisconsin Historical Society)

Significantly, though, Langlade's Anishinaabe kin *were* at the battle. French accounts specifically mention the participation of at least 637 Indians, including many Odawa and Ojibwe from Michilimackinac, and Potawatomi and Huron from Detroit. Though often listed—and remembered—as "French Indians," or auxiliaries, they were there as independent allies. And the French were fortunate they were. One of the earliest accounts of the event notes that the commandant of Fort Duquesne learned of the approach of the three thousand British troops only on July 7, when they were only twenty miles from the fort. Though he had not anticipated this, the large number of Native Americans at the fort allowed him to act immediately even though his own forces were so few. When the British killed a French officer early in the skirmishing, the regulars and militia were thrown into further confusion. But the Anishinaabeg and Huron placed themselves along the flanks of the British column. The result was a rout. Though many French officials claimed credit for the victory, the Anishinaabe and Huron warriors won the day.[14]

While Britain and France would not formally declare hostilities against each other until the spring of 1756, Native Americans made it inevitable. And as diplomats in Europe engaged in a preliminary war of words, Indian warriors continued to attack British colonial settlements. Within a few weeks of Braddock's defeat, for example, thirty-five Virginian settlers were reported dead. Hundreds streamed back over the mountains. By the autumn, more than a hundred Virginians had been killed or taken captive and the roads east were choked with "Crowds of People who were flying, as if every moment was death."[15]

The early string of Indian successes that stretched from Pickawillany to Fort Duquesne in turn helped win more converts to what would amount to a pan-Indian assault on English holdings. By 1756, most of the Shawnee, Delaware, and Mingo in the Ohio Valley had begun preparations for war. The new French governor, Pierre de Rigaud de Vaudreuil de Cavagnial, also boasted that the Odawa, Menominee, Sauk, and Fox had told him how pleased they were to see him in power and had claimed that they could bring to the warpath the more remote Indians of the *pays d'en haut*. News also soon reached Montreal from Detroit that all the Indians of that quarter were inclined to attack the English, including the Miami and Potawatomi at St. Joseph's. The latter reportedly sent out a steady stream of war parties, killing or capturing 120 English. The war plunder, scalps, captives, and ransom money brought back from these raids and Braddock's defeat helped spur the confidence of the western nations and whet their appetite for further attacks. In addition, evidence of Iroquois neutrality and signs of British weakness gave the green light to many nations in the *pays d'en haut* and the Ohio Valley to pursue old grievances and settle scores. Apart from a few Mohawk, the English were completely bereft of Indian allies by the start of 1756.[16]

With the way across and up the Ohio Valley clear of any English-allied Indians, attacks on western settlements increased, with devastating effect. By March 1756, some seven hundred people had been killed or taken prisoner in raids by Indians. In April alone there had been at least twenty expeditions of Delaware and Shawnee, who were reportedly joined by warriors from more than sixty-five nations. In June, the newly arrived French general Louis-Joseph Montcalm gleefully reported that the Indians from the *pays d'en haut* "carry off entire families," which kept the English busy constructing rude forts. They attacked despite "the presents and solicitations of the English."[17]

Among those harassing the English were the Anishinaabeg of Michilimackinac, accompanied by Charles Langlade, who had spent the winter at Grand River recruiting warriors from the families from Waganawkezee. As they traveled down to the Ohio, they joined hundreds of other warriors of mixed nations. The French commandant at Fort Duquesne believed that in his region alone there were as many as 3,250 French and Indian troops, including as many as 700 from Michilimackinac. Only rumors of smallpox at Niagara prevented even more from joining them, as some Indians were unwilling to risk getting infected. Many of those who went on the warpath took advantage of generous French supplies and encouragement, and continued to attack deep into the autumn. By the end of the year, the commandant at Fort Duquesne said he counted five hundred scalps and had two hundred prisoners with him. The attacks effectively rolled back the Pennsylvania frontier to Carlisle, about a hundred miles from Philadelphia. Governor Vaudreuil was elated; he thought the Indians alone could force an end to the war. He told the ministers at Versailles that he would continue to encourage war parties to move against the

English colonies, because "Nothing is more calculated to disgust the people of those Colonies and to make them desire the return of peace."[18]

•

As Vaudreuil's comments hint, these initial attacks were crucial to the survival of the French colony. By 1755, the population of the English colonies in North America was upward of ten times the number of French habitants along the St. Lawrence and its hinterland. As the French began the war, they knew the cards were stacked against them. Fortunately, the new French governor knew full well the key to their survival. Vaudreuil, son of a former governor of the colony, was a long-standing officer in the *troupes de la marine* and had already served as the governor of Louisiana. He was familiar with the *pays d'en haut*; as a young man, he had even joined an aborted expedition on the Fox in 1727. Most important, the governor had seen firsthand the value of securing Indian allies. Not long after he took over, he complained to the Ministry that the upper country had been "greatly neglected in every respect." He believed they should spare no effort or expense in trying to repair their relations with the nations of the *pays d'en haut*. The fate of the colony, he believed, had always rested in the strength of their alliances with the nations of the west. They were doubly important now.[19]

If Vaudreuil understood the value of his Indian allies, he also had some insight into how best to nurture those relations. Though instructed by the crown to keep Indian expenses to a minimum, Vaudreuil thought they had to spend a great deal to counter English presents and trade. He also knew the importance of men like Charles Langlade. As part of his plan, Vaudreuil sent colonial officers throughout the *pays d'en haut* to establish new posts among the Indians—against the inclinations of the crown. In late 1755, for example, it was he who had sent Langlade to the Grand River region to establish a new and official post to ensure those wintering over there were well supplied and in constant communication with the French. The governor also knew he had to treat his would-be allies as sovereign, and equal, nations. In early 1756, for example, he revived an old tradition and made plans to welcome the chiefs of all the nations to Montreal to talk about their plans for war. He hoped by this to render their attachment to the French "inviolable."[20]

Yet much like alliances between European nations at the time, good relations between the French and their many would-be allies was predicated on a convergence of interests. French colonial officials were reminded of this when they tried to woo the Carolina-based Catawba away from their alliance with the English. It quickly became clear the only way to do this was establish a peace between the Catawba and the nations of the *pays d'en haut*. But the upper nations were having none of it. When they stopped at Fort Duquesne in the summer of 1756, the commandant tried to broach the subject of a peace with the Catawba. Turning the tables and echoing the words of many a French governor at council fires in Quebec, the natives of the *pays d'en haut* told the commandant there in no uncertain terms that "having left their village with my axe, every other matter must surcease; and that they could only think of making war on the English." The nations of the *pays d'en haut* fought as independent allies, not as French auxiliaries.[21]

This independence was also evident in their refusal to help the French take Fort Oswego. Despite their enthusiasm to roll back the English frontier settlements, few Native nations were interested in supporting the governor's plans to strike the English on Lake Ontario. In French eyes, Fort Oswego had long been a source of irritation. Vaudreuil knew many English traders used it as a base for illicit trade, and that because of its convenient location, Indians of all nations used it as an alternate place of exchange and meetings with the English and Iroquois. In short, Vaudreuil believed it to be "the direct cause of all the troubles that have overtaken the Colony, and of the vast expense they have occasioned the King." But for the same reasons, he knew most of his allies would be uninterested in taking it down. While some cited rumors of smallpox for their reluctance, and others were engaged elsewhere during the campaign, many warriors had for several decades at least maintained more or less good relations with English traders at Oswego and used it as a meeting place with the Iroquois. Indeed, in the spring of 1756, no one could yet be sure they would not face Iroquois warriors across the ramparts. The post was in Iroquois territory. It was unclear how the Iroquois would respond to this French incursion on their lands.[22]

As it turned out, the Iroquois stood down, and the French took the post in August 1756 with only a handful of Indian allies accompanying them. It was a vitally important victory for the French. It helped blunt a renewed British offensive and bought the French some crucial breathing space. A week after the surrender, British troops under Major General Daniel Webb on their way to reinforce Oswego heard the news and beat a hasty retreat all the way back to German Flats, about seventy miles west of Albany. At the end of 1756, this was Britain's westernmost post in New York. Perhaps more important, though, and as Vaudreuil initially hoped, the victory appeared to cement the alliances of an unprecedented number of native groups from far and wide. Vaudreuil knew that as far as his native allies were concerned, talk was cheap. European diplomacy was no different. The French needed the victory at Oswego to show they were worthy allies. Pierre Pouchot, commandant at Fort Niagara, believed the fall of Oswego "produced the greatest effect upon all the Indian tribes . . . We may say, that since this event, they have redoubled their attachment and friendship for the French." As early as October 1756, the commander at Presqu'île also wrote that "news of the taking of Oswego created a sensation in the western country, that a great number of Indians appeared full of ardor to come next season and hit the English."[23]

Some historians attribute this renewed enthusiasm to the tales of plunder at Oswego that spurred on others to share in it. But if the spoils of war helped kindle enthusiasm for the French alliance among native communities, few contemporaries suggested it as a root cause. Indeed, more astute commentators on the ground suggested Vaudreuil had been right to strike Oswego for political and symbolic reasons. While William Johnson, the British superintendent of Indian affairs, and the English had held many secret councils with western Indians to persuade them away from the French alliance, Vaudreuil had acted with determination, and successfully. Pouchot at Niagara noted the decisive action was key: "the English had affected a decided superiority over us, and by their braggadocio on their power and their courage sought to make the Indians believe that we should not be able to resist them. The latter saw with what ease we took a post which had as many defenders as assailants." For Native nations who had watched the French suffer humiliation after humiliation in the 1730s and 1740s at the hands of both other Indians and the English, the victory was indeed impressive. Pouchot believed that though the French might attribute the renewal of their alliance to some inherent preference for the French, "on account of their easy habits of life and their gayety," the Indians' renewed interest in the alliance resulted from a more stark realpolitik: "the principal motive of their conduct came from this, that they knew very well the advantage of being on the strongest side, for, although some of them may have been very affectionate, they still loved Europeans according to their interest." For the few still undecided natives of the *pays d'en haut*, the successful siege of Oswego was a sign they ought to tip their hands.[24]

Of course, inter-Indian politics also played a part in the enthusiasm generated by the fall of Oswego. Many of the nations of the *pays d'en haut* were at least equally cheered by the fact that the Iroquois neither resisted the French at Oswego nor retaliated. It was as much a sign of their neutrality as it was of French military superiority. That view was confirmed when Vaudreuil made it clear he was eager to press home the French advantage and launch a campaign down the Champlain Valley into the heart of the English colonies. The governor wanted to prevent a counterattack, but his plans meant an expedition through Iroquois territory. The Anishinaabeg and other Algonquians immediately pushed Vaudreuil into calling a council in Montreal in December. Vaudreuil thought he could capitalize on their enthusiasm to finally bring the Iroquois to act against the English. Even the French general Montcalm thought it was one of the biggest and most important conferences in New France for some time.[25]

At the council, the native participants acknowledged the changed relations between them. An Onondaga Iroquois delegate spoke first, noting that not only had they been at peace for many years, but even new kinship ties had grown between them more recently. He reminded the western nations they were no longer just friends, but also brethren, "by the marriage of several women, Outaouacs, Pouteoutamis, etc." They repeated this message, "in order that we might all work anew at good business." While Vaudreuil kept trying to use his native allies as a stick to beat the Iroquois into neutrality at the very least, his allies were more circumspect. The governor had threatened to use his native allies to launch a "never ending war against them" if they attacked the

French. But at the conference, the Algonquians, including representatives from the Odawa at Waganawkezee, kept insisting this was a quarrel between the English and French. The last thing they wanted at this stage was a renewal of intertribal conflict. Native communities should take advantage of the opportunity. As one Nipissing ogimaa put it, "I hate the Englishman. I thirst for his blood. I am going to bathe in it." To reinforce the message, an Odawa ogimaa sang a war song calling to the others, "Father, we are famished; give us fresh meat; we wish to eat the English." The Iroquois reaffirmed their neutrality. Some even hinted they would join them.[26]

•

The ensuing campaign of 1757 simultaneously represented the fulfilment of French dreams of a vast Indian alliance and revealed its limits. Indeed, while French and Indian successes during the expedition up the Champlain Valley that year have been interpreted as epitomizing the special relationship that existed between the two, the details and realities of the campaign display the tensions that continued to exist between the French and a very diverse group of autonomous nations. While France's native allies were no doubt responsible for the success of the campaign, the French could not dictate the terms. Once more the fate of New France lay in Indian hands, and the French could do little about it.

With Iroquois neutrality secured and as returning warriors reported on the successes of 1756, Indian country was alive with the possibility of driving back the British even farther. Governor Vaudreuil made it clear that in 1757 he wanted to launch a major campaign against the English colonies via the Lake Champlain–Hudson River corridor that connected Montreal with New York via Albany. In anticipation, many Indian warriors took the unprecedented step of wintering over at Montreal and farther south at Fort Carillon (later Fort Ticonderoga). Among these were Langlade and many of his Odawa kin. While waiting for both French and Indian reinforcements, they went on the offensive in early 1757. They faced off against the British who had ensconced themselves at the head of Lake George (Lac Saint Sacrement to the French) at Fort William Henry. The Odawa played a vital role in curbing English scouting. In late January, for example, they ambushed a party of Robert Rogers's rangers. A few weeks later, they joined a joint French and Canadian attack on an English construction depot outside Fort William Henry. The raiders harassed the post for four full days, burning all of the fort's outbuildings, which included a palisaded barracks, several storehouses, a sawmill, and a hospital. But more damaging was the destruction of a sloop that was half built, and more than three hundred bateaux. Soon, Langlade and Odawa, Ojibwe, and Potawatomi warriors pushed their advantage and claimed the land between Fort Carillon and Fort William Henry as their own. Significantly, they also cut off communications between Fort William Henry and Fort Edward, the next nearest English post at the falls of the Hudson River—which in turn was less than fifty miles from Albany.[27]

As summer approached, reinforcements of warriors from the *pays d'en haut* grew dramatically. Doodemag relations and obligations contributed in bringing warriors to the field. An astute young Louis Antoine de Bougainville, the future French admiral and Pacific explorer, served on the campaign in the Lake Champlain–Hudson River corridor as aide-de-camp to General Montcalm. He took note of the doodemag of different groups of Odawa as they joined the French, along with their war ogimaag. At one point, he noted thirteen different Odawa ogimaag participating in a single skirmish. After questioning some of his new allies, he observed how they came from all over the *pays d'en haut*, including Detroit, Green Bay, and Michilimackinac. He thought the Odawa alone could furnish one thousand to twelve hundred warriors. But he also glimpsed the nature of the entwined relations between what the French believed to be different nations. He noted that the Potawatomi were sending several of their warriors with the Odawa "solely to fulfil their obligations to the other nations."[28]

Kinship alliances and obligations helped multiply the number of warriors heading to the low country. Post commandants reported great gatherings of Indians at Detroit and Niagara. Pouchot, at Niagara, noted that even some Fox who had had nothing to do with the French since their wars with them had come to the post. They had been living with the Delaware and Seneca. Then, on July 1, at a council at Niagara, an Iroquois delegation told an assembled group of Huron, Wea, Miami, and Odawa they had taken up the hatchet for the French and would not put it down again. The number of Indians continued to swell. Bougainville, in Montreal, confirmed that "canoe loads of Indians arrive every day. The number come from the Far West now passes a thousand. Some are come from a nation so far away that no Canadian interpreter understands their language." Among the new arrivals were almost three hundred Odawa warriors from Michilimackinac, including Langlade's uncle, Nissowaquet. They were quick to demand an audience with the highest French officials. They also wanted to meet with Montcalm, acknowledging his power in taking Oswego: "We wished to see . . . this famous man who, on putting his foot on the ground, has destroyed the English ramparts."[29]

But if the Odawa and others were happy to pay their respects to the chiefs of their alliance partners, they were also keen to act. French officials had failed to lay in sufficient provisions for such a large contingent of arriving allies. Nor were the Nations of the *pays d'en haut* particularly interested in prolonging the campaign by observing European war tactics. They pressed the French to take action, even against what many thought was the numerical superiority of the British forces that were massing at the other end of Lake George. Despite the odds, one observer noted "on account of the state of feeling among the Savage Tribes, the greatest success was expected."[30]

Governor Vaudreuil shaped French strategy to suit his Indian allies. Provisions were running low along the St. Lawrence, as a bad harvest did nothing to relieve French supply lines already suffering from English naval superiority. As the number of western Indians who passed through Montreal reached a thousand, the governor gave orders to Montcalm to take nine thousand troops to capture Forts Edward and William Henry. He wanted to keep the Indians on the offensive. He also knew the spoils of war resulting from a campaign would make up for some of the lost harvests of that year. That meant his Indian allies fought with few provisions. The governor also told Montcalm that after taking the forts, he should disband the Indians and form them into detachments for the purpose of laying waste the nearby settlements of Orange and Corlac. Montcalm—the professional soldier—was loath to make the campaign so dependent on native allies, but he had to admit their importance. He was "obliged" to gratify the Indian nations to the point of participating in ceremonies he considered tiresome. Early

in July, he held a war council with the upper Indians and joined in
their war dances and feasts. Montcalm did so because he, too, was
convinced that the Indians held the balance of power in their hands:
"Our Indians are equally capable of determining in a quarter of an hour
the gain or loss of an affair." As even veteran French regular officers
were forced to admit, their Indian allies were "a necessary evil."[31]

Montcalm's words were prophetic. The official campaign against
the English opened with a brisk sweep of the territory between Forts
Carillon and William Henry. A combined Indian-colonial force, including Anishinaabe warriors, pushed to the outskirts of the English
fort and took thirty-three scalps. Then the Odawa put their canoe
skills to good use. They suggested a project that would ultimately seal
the fate of the fort and its defenders. Their target was a flotilla of
twenty-two whaleboats or barges led by Colonel John Parker, who
had brought five companies of New Jersey and New York militia down
the Lake to destroy a sawmill and take prisoners. Langlade and the
Odawa cut off his retreat. It was an upper country affair, made possible
by the canoe skills of the participants. The Odawa, Ojibwe, Potawatomi, and Menominee totaled some five hundred warriors alongside
about fifty Canadians. Lying in wait to launch an amphibious ambush, they took the first six boats in silence, without a shot fired. The
Indians who were on the shore then fired on the following barges.
Those in canoes pursued the remnants of the group, sinking or capturing all but two boats that escaped. Fewer than a hundred of Parker's
350-strong expedition made it back to Fort William Henry. A hundred
men were shot, drowned, or hunted down in the forests when they
fled, and the Anishinaabeg took another 150 prisoners. Only one warrior was slightly wounded. Though Montcalm praised his own officers
in official reports, he also claimed "the whoops of our Indians impressed them with such terror that they made a feeble resistance."[32]

Montcalm, who had only just arrived at Fort Carillon, was eager to
take the credit for the decisive and demoralizing expedition. But it
was Langlade and his Anishinaabe kin who paved the way for the success of the French campaign in 1757. Previous scouting and skirmishing by Indian patrols had kept the English in the dark about French
plans and strength. The destruction of Parker's force, along with so
many English barges, was the final nail in the coffin for the forces at

Fort William Henry. The French were now free to bring up their heavy siege artillery by water. Lord Loudoun, on board HMS *Winchelsea* off Halifax, told the secretary of state after hearing of the fate of Parker's expedition, "from their having permitted the Enemy to get the Superiority of the Lake . . . I look upon that Place and Garrison, as lost, with the whole Troops there."[33]

If the French and English realized the value of the Indians as allies, they also got a taste of what such an alliance meant. Bougainville was horrified by what happened after the ambush of the barges. The Odawa, he said, boiled and ate three prisoners—perhaps more—in front of their terrified companions and French officers who were powerless to stop them. Bougainville thought only the Odawa practiced this ritual, which was reminiscent of the scenes at Pickawillany. Not understanding the cultural origins of the practice, Bougainville first blamed the alcohol captured in the attack. He thought it caused the Anishinaabeg to "commit great cruelties." But a Jesuit priest reported the Odawa recommenced the feast in the cold light of the next morning. Then, a few days later an English corpse came floating down the lake. The Anishinaabeg "crowded around it with loud cries, drank its blood, and put its pieces in the kettle." French officers were horrified.[34]

There were other signs of the independence of France's native allies. Many who took part in the battle on Lake George wished to go home. They considered the war party a success, and to continue on would only tempt fate. The Anishinaabeg also wanted to take their prisoners to Montreal to reap a promised ransom. Montcalm, desperate to take further advantage of their presence, quickly drew up an order of march on Fort William Henry. He then convened a general council on July 26–27 with all of his Indian allies. At the council, Bougainville tried to get the diverse nations to act in unison. He presented a massive belt of six thousand beads in the king's name "to bind all those different tribes to each other and to him, so that they may act together and not separate from each other, nor quit him before the close of the expedition." Immediately objections arose from the Odawa who had participated in the battle on Lake George. They claimed "it was tempting the Master of Life to continue to expose themselves to the dangers of war, after such a beautiful affair as they had just accomplished." After protracted negotiations, they agreed to stay and send their prisoners back to Montreal with only a small escort. Soon after, however, perhaps as many as two hundred Odawa and Mississauga left anyway, just on the eve of the siege of Fort William Henry.[35]

French officers grew increasingly frustrated with their native allies, but they could do little in response. When Montcalm called a council to complain about their insubordination, he was rebuked. The gathered Indians were angry and instead complained about Montcalm. They said that they had been left in the dark about French plans and that their advice had not been followed. They wanted an equal say in war councils. Instead, they lamented, they were treated as "though they were slaves." They forced Montcalm to apologize and promise more war councils. At times it seemed the French were working for the Indians. Bougainville wrote that Montcalm had to submit plans each day to all the Nations. They requested detailed and daily information about the march of the army, the route to be followed in the woods, the day of departure, and many other arrangements. Though Montcalm continued to chafe at this interference, Bougainville admitted these deliberations were essential. "For these independent people whose assistance is purely voluntary, require to be consulted; everything must be communicated to them, and their opinions and caprices are oftentimes a law for us." French dependence on their native allies continued to frustrate military leaders and colonial officials. In that respect, little had changed since the middle of the seventeenth century. Native Americans still shaped the law, and the historical landscape, of early America.[36]

•

In the end, almost eighteen hundred Indians took part in the siege of Fort William Henry. They fought alongside six thousand French regular troops, colonial troops, and Canadian militia. The gathering of Indian nations was unprecedented. It was perhaps the largest pan-Indian force ever assembled. In official French accounts, almost twenty different nations were represented, and as many more groups from within the different nations. One Jesuit accompanying the expedition reckoned there were thirty-six nations present in total. The French assigned an officer to provide liaison with different groups of Indians. These officers were mostly veteran soldiers and warriors such as Langlade with long experience in the ways of Indian warfare. The French also made sure there was an interpreter for each group and missionaries for the "domesticated" Indians. Altogether, there were perhaps about 820 Indians from the mission villages around the St. Lawrence, and about 1,000 from the *pays d'en haut*.[37] The latter included some 337 Odawa drawn from at least seven separate doodemag, including that of Langlade's uncle, the ogimaa Nissowaquet.[38]

The superior numbers of French and Indians and the scouting undertaken by the Anishinaabeg and others meant the actual siege of Fort William Henry was a relatively short affair. On August 3, Canadians and Indians slipped around the fort, cut off the route to Fort Edward, and commenced sniping at the palisade walls. Montcalm began entrenching and steadily moved his cannon closer to the walls of the fort. On August 7, Montcalm showed the English commander, Lieutenant Colonel George Monro, an intercepted letter from General Webb, at Fort Edward. He would send no reinforcements. Under steady fire, his own batteries reduced by half from overuse, and almost out of ammunition, Monro asked for terms of surrender. Two days later, Montcalm offered a capitulation that paid homage to the defense undertaken by the commander. The entire garrison would be granted parole and escorted to Fort Edward. In return, they had to promise they would not rejoin the conflict before eighteen months had elapsed. The defenders were also allowed to retain their personal effects, small arms, unit colors, and a symbolic brass fieldpiece—in short, all the traditional spoils of war.[39]

Though these terms were not unusual by European standards of the time, they were guaranteed to anger France's native allies. And despite his consultations during the siege, Montcalm called a council of the war chiefs only after the Articles of Capitulation had been agreed (just before they were signed). The Indians, after several months of service without pay, were expected to let the British walk away. They would get nothing for their efforts. Some had spent all winter in the east and missed out on winter trapping. They were often poorly provisioned. Now they were supposed to return home with no war trophies, scalps, or captives to ransom or replace their own dead. They would lose face among their compatriots, and the ogimaag in their ranks would lose influence. Though the surprised war chiefs allegedly "agreed to everything and promised to restrain their young men," they likely knew they could do no such thing under the circumstances.[40]

French officers, including Montcalm, also knew this. Despite the presence of intermediaries, the independence of the Indian nations made French control over them difficult from the start to the end of the siege. And Montcalm was aware that his allies fought for different stakes: they told him so. Before leaving Montreal, a council of Indians from the *pays d'en haut* warned him not to expect them to give quarter to the English. They explained they had with them "young men who have never yet drunk of this broth. Fresh meat has brought them here from the ends of the earth. It is most necessary that they learn to wield the knife and to plunge it into an English heart." Montcalm had listened. Early in the siege he warned the British commander of the fort that once the fighting had started, "perhaps there would not be time, nor would it be in our power to restrain the cruelties of a mob of Indians of so many different nations."[41]

Even as the English evacuated the main fort, Bougainville reported they felt it "necessary" to let the Indians and Canadians in to pillage all the remaining effects, while the French tried to save the provisions and munitions. Some of the Indians also scalped and killed wounded soldiers within the fort. In this race for some kind of reward for their efforts, it is not surprising the aggrieved Indians then turned their attentions to the entrenched camp across from the fort, where they searched for provisions and equipment. French officers, including Montcalm, claimed they did all they could to stop them. But Bougainville blamed some of the French and Canadians who were attached to them for encouraging and participating in the plundering. "We will be most fortunate if we can avoid a massacre," Bougainville concluded before he left the fort to bring word of the victory to Montreal. By nine in the evening, order seemed to reign in the camp, and Montcalm was able to arrange that in addition to some of the French troops, two ogimaag of each nation would escort the English troops as far as Fort Edward, to try to keep an eye on their own warriors.[42]

But alarms continued through the night, as the guards struggled to "prevent disorder." At one point the French decided that the paroled prisoners should march out after dark, "because it was known that the Indians almost never acted during the night." Then they held back because they were warned that six hundred Indians lay in ambush. At daybreak on August 10, the English, "who were inconceivably frightened by the sight of the Indians," pushed to leave before the French could organize a proper escort. They abandoned their trunks and other heavy baggage and started to march. Confusion grew when some of the English allegedly gave the Indians rum to drink in an effort to placate them.[43]

The Indians, faced with the imminent loss of their quarry, grew desperate. Some took more scalps from the sick and wounded who lay in the tents that served as a hospital. Others plotted an attack on the retreating columns. Bougainville, who was on his way to Montreal and thus heard reports of what happened only secondhand, wrote that some Abnaki of Maine started the attack. They claimed they had "recently suffered from some bad behavior on the part of the English." According to Bougainville's report, the Abnaki "shouted the death cry and hurled themselves on the tail of the column which started to march out." The English, "instead of showing resolution, were seized with fear and fled in confusion, throwing away their arms, baggage, and even their coats." Their fear supposedly "emboldened the Indians of all the nations," who started pillaging, killing soldiers, and taking captives. French officers, they later claimed, were powerless to stop the infamous "massacre" of Fort William Henry.[44]

Reports of the attack—many of which were carried on the tongues of terrified English soldiers fleeing the Indians—unsurprisingly amplified the numbers killed, and ran them into the hundreds. Yet Bougainville claimed only that "some dozen soldiers" were killed in the attack. A Jesuit reported "hardly more than forty or fifty" killed. Most Native Americans were after captives, not scalps. Prisoners were more desirable because they could be ransomed back to the French or English. Some nations may have wanted to adopt them into village communities to replace dead warriors lost on the campaign. It was only when French officers tried to intervene and take back prisoners that more were killed. In lieu of a captive, warriors would invariably take a scalp. Later estimates of the total number killed after the surrender range anywhere from 70 to 185 soldiers and camp followers (including the wounded killed the first day). The Indians took far more captive— somewhere between three hundred and five hundred prisoners.

Montcalm claimed to have taken back or ransomed as many as four hundred more captives on the spot. With tensions between Montcalm and his erstwhile allies at a peak, all but a handful of mission Indians disappeared with their captives and war booty that same day.[45]

A few days later, many of the Indians arrived in Montreal with their prisoners—perhaps as many as two hundred. They clearly believed they had done little wrong. As in the past, they expected ransom money for their prisoners, and rewards for their efforts. Instead, Vaudreuil "scolded" them for having violated the capitulation and told them they must give up the prisoners. The following day, to mock Vaudreuil's demands, they killed one of the prisoners "in the presence of the entire town," boiled him in a kettle, and "forced his unfortunate compatriots to eat him." Bougainville, disgusted, thought the French Canadian officers had spurred them on.[46]

Indeed, Langlade himself may have been involved in the proceedings. Bougainville wondered aloud whether those in Europe could believe that the Indians alone were responsible for the alleged atrocities. While Bougainville was one of the more astute observers of Indian cultures, he found it hard to understand some of their practices and instead blamed them on European greed. He seemed to take particular umbrage at the plunder of African slaves from the English. Slaves could of course be found throughout colonial America at the time, and there were certainly a number of them among the surrendered garrison of Fort William Henry. They were most likely owned by officers, or had been hired out to the army to help bolster the defenses of the fort. Bougainville, probably not familiar with the practice of Indian slavery either along the St. Lawrence or in the *pays d'en haut*, wondered whether the "desire for the Negroes and other spoils of the English has not caused the people [the interpreters and Canadian leaders of the Indians] who are at the head of these nations to loosen the curb, perhaps to go even farther?" Bougainville did not doubt it. That day, he noted he saw "one of these leaders, unworthy of the name of officer and Frenchman, leading in his train a Negro kidnapped from the English commander under the pretext of appeasing the shades of a dead Indian, giving his family flesh for flesh." Yet the officer was most likely trying to help. Knowing that his Indian kin would be satisfied with the replacement of their dead family member by a captured slave (whether Indian or black), the officer was probably trying to exchange a British soldier for the slave, in compliance with Vaudreuil's request. Whatever part Langlade may have played in the "massacre" and its aftermath, it ultimately met with the approval of Vaudreuil. On his return through Montreal with his Anishinaabe allies, Langlade was promoted to second-in-command at Michilimackinac, under Captain Louis Liénard de Beaujeu.[47]

Ultimately, Governor Vaudreuil knew he had to back down from his demand that the Indians simply hand over their captives. Native Americans forced French officials to pay an average of 130 livres (which was about equivalent to the annual pay for French soldiers at the time), along with thirty bottles of brandy, for each captive. Then they demanded a series of councils, or "farewell audiences." Vaudreuil had to lay on ample gifts and provisions for the Indians returning home. Each received a set of new clothes, "Varying according to the rank which each holds in his village," and what Bougainville called "village presents" consisting of tobacco, vermilion, lace, and brandy. Despite his initial reaction, Vaudreuil knew it was the price the French had to pay for the defense of New France. In official letters, the governor defended the actions of the Indians and blamed the English who surrendered for giving the Indians rum. In his report of events to the Ministry, Vaudreuil betrayed little remorse about the incident. Given the initial Abnaki complaint and the expense of the ransoms paid, he believed that the English should instead be grateful for French efforts to return the English captives.[48]

Indeed, in the short run, despite the historic legacy of outrage that the "massacre" engendered, most French officers, including Montcalm, were not overly concerned. Montcalm initially wrote that the terms of capitulation "suffered some infraction on the part of the Indians." But what would be an infraction in Europe, he claimed, "cannot be so regarded in America." He repeated his arguments to Webb and Loudoun to ensure they had no pretext to break the terms of the surrender. It was only afterward, when the outrage of the British grew and French defenses began to weaken, that Montcalm tried to distance himself from what had happened. As late as September 18, he continued to boast of his influence among the Indians and Canadians—even as they left him in droves.[49]

The events of 1757 will forever be shrouded by accusations of blame. Only one thing is clear: we have no Indian voice to explain what happened and why. Still, the evidence we do have suggests that Native Americans had good reasons for their actions at Fort William Henry. They were not paid, of course, and many had wintered over in the Champlain Valley instead of hunting and trapping. Even provisions and presents received at the posts through which they passed to get to Carillon were running low by the summer of 1757. In this light, whatever warriors could take from the campaign itself was vital. Nor were Indian allies properly consulted about the terms of capitulation. They were thus shocked to find that the English were allowed to leave with all their possessions. After pursuing the English for months, many Indians were appalled that the enemy they had been chasing for so long was simply walking away, free to fight another day.

For most Native Americans, there was much more at stake in this conflict than French honor. At the very least, after several years of skirmishing, and a long campaign throughout 1757, many Indians had some old scores to settle with the English. Some desperately wanted captives to replace the dead they had lost in recent campaigns and the siege itself, or wanted ransom money to make up for a lost summer harvest. Others—particularly many of the Ohio Indians—had long suffered at the hands of the English. For some Indians at the siege, these same soldiers threatened their land and livelihoods. The conflict had become, in effect, a war of extermination. Moreover, openly declaring in favor of the French left many exposed to English retaliation should the opportunity present itself. Now, Native Americans would have to face these same warriors again. If the French, as they promised, would not push the campaign to its full conclusion, their Indian allies would. There were, in the end, many different reasons why Native Americans at Fort William Henry acted as they did. With close to forty different nations present at the siege, it would be a mistake to think any one motive was preeminent.[50]

•

From the perspective of Indian country, the campaign of 1757 was noteworthy for a number of different reasons. Not only did it again expose the limits of the so-called French-Indian alliance, but it also marked a significant turning point in the history of Indian-English relations. While "Pontiac's War" of 1763 garners much attention in the literature on pan-Indian unity and resistance to European imperialism, many Native American communities had declared war on the English six years or more before Pontiac and achieved considerable success. But because we have tended to see this as a "European" war, where Indians served only the interests of the French, we have failed to appreciate just how significant the early conflict was.

We have also failed to acknowledge how successful this first pan-Indian coalition was. The coincidence of Native interests and degree of cooperation among such diverse nations was truly remarkable, and unprecedented. It also reinforced ideas that a pan-Indian alliance was possible. Never before had Iroquois, Anishinaabe, Abnaki, and Fox warriors fought alongside each other. And they did so in a campaign that capped a series of stunning victories over the far more numerous English. Despite the tensions between French officials and Indian warriors during and after the 1757 campaign, Native Americans returning from the Champlain Valley could be well pleased with the results of the last few years of the war. Indian attacks on English settlements virtually emptied the region west of the Appalachians of Europeans. Indian raids on the frontiers of British colonial settlements between 1753 and the end of 1756 were so successful that in early 1758, Vaudreuil reported "nothing very important" had happened in the Fort Duquesne region throughout most of 1757. It was not for want of trying. Rather, "all our parties have carried terror among our enemies to a point that the settlements of the English in Pinsilvanie, Mariland, and Virginia are abandoned. All the settlers have retreated to the city or into the forest." On top of this success, Native Americans from across the Great Lakes country had taken the battle further and had brought down a major army closer to the heart of the English colonies. They had rolled back the English almost to Albany. For many Indians of the *pays d'en haut*, their objectives had been achieved. Growing English power had been curbed. The balance of power between the English and French had been restored. And they had achieved this while maintaining intertribal unity between most of the major players.[51]

•

Yet if there was any remaining doubt about whose interests most Native Americans served during the Seven Years' War, events the following year—in 1758—dispelled them. As warriors returned to their winter camps at the end of 1757, many paused to take stock. As the Odawa had pointed out to Montcalm after their success on Lake George, it would be tempting fate to continue the war. But the outbreak of a smallpox epidemic across the Lakes forced a more serious reconsideration. Reports of the often deadly disease had circulated in New France at least since the beginning of the conflict. Almost all Native Americans would have heard about the pain and devastation smallpox could bring to both individuals and whole villages. Some would have had firsthand experience. It had been a scourge in Indian country since first contact with Europeans. While the disease had become endemic among European populations, Native Americans who had no prior exposure to the disease were still susceptible to epidemics such as the one that had devastated Huronia in the seventeenth century. While the evidence suggests the Anishinaabeg avoided the worst effects of these epidemics, they were often quick to take action to avoid contact with it. As we have seen, some Anishinaabe warriors held back from joining the 1756 campaign because they heard there was smallpox at Fort Niagara. But as the war progressed and new troops arrived from Europe, it was more and more difficult to avoid.[52]

In the midst of the campaign of 1757, officials reported the disease amid the English at both Forts William Henry and George, as well as at Albany. By the autumn of 1757, smallpox was among the French and Indians, and as winter approached, reports reached Montreal that the disease had spread to the *pays d'en haut*. French officials speculated that returning warriors from the 1757 campaign either picked it up from the English they killed and captured, or from the French on their way through Montreal and the other posts. Some reportedly died on their way home from the campaign. Others lived long enough to bring it back to their villages. Detroit, St. Joseph's, Michilimackinac, and Green Bay were hit hard. Pouchot thought that the Potawatomi suffered most and "almost entirely perished of this epidemic." A later report from Michilimackinac noted "a great many Indians" died at that post, too. Later Odawa accounts noted that "lodge after lodge was totally vacated—nothing but dead bodies lying here and there in their lodges—entire families being swept off . . . the whole coast of Arbor Croche [Waganawkezee] . . . entirely depopulated and laid waste."[53]

French officials knew this was a disaster in the making. Native Americans would invariably want to hold someone or something accountable for the deaths. The French did their best to spread the rumor that the English were to blame. At least some Indians did blame them. Initial French reports from Michilimackinac at the end of October 1757 declared that the Odawa there "seem to be satisfied with the campaign and with us." Odawa oral tradition told of returning warriors who brought back a tin box they had bought from the British. The British had told them to open it only when they got back to Waganawkezee. Shortly after they opened the box, smallpox laid waste the village. The Odawa initially blamed the British, who they said had disguised the disease in the tin box. As late as April 1758, Montcalm announced that fortunately for the French, the ogimaag "have always declared, in the different Councils held at Michillimakina, Detroit &c., that the English had thrown *that Medicine* on the Indians."[54]

Yet as the death toll mounted, French hopes that their Indian allies would cover the dead by avenging themselves on the British in the new year faded. With so many killed, they could not afford to send more warriors out. Instead, they expected compensation from the French. As Bougainville noted, "Their custom in such a case is to say that the nation which called upon them has given them bad medicine. The commanders of the posts must dry their tears and cover the dead." As Montcalm came to realize this, he remarked, "This is a real loss to us, and will cost the King considerable in consequence of the expenses it will occasion at the posts to treat them, cover the dead and console the widows."[55]

The French could ill afford the expense. They were under siege and struggling to feed themselves. New France, having suffered two of its worst harvests in 1756 and 1757, barely managed to survive on supplies brought by ships arriving from France. But as the British brought their superior naval forces to bear on the conflict in America, the shortages of food would get much worse. They focused on blockading the St. Lawrence corridor, so that the French could not even count on imported supplies. Prices everywhere were on the rise. The shortages were felt in the *pays d'en haut*. Post commanders reported they could no longer give out presents to the Indians. Bougainville fretted that "their ignorance of Indian customs" meant the post commanders did not properly cover the dead of their allies. Already angry about the scarcity of provisions laid in for them during the campaign against Fort William Henry, many Indians expected more, not fewer, presents to persuade them to join again with the French in 1758.[56]

Debate raged once again around council fires about what to do. Most native groups did what they could to shift for themselves. At Michilimackinac, Langlade tried to rustle up support for the French, but the Odawa were going nowhere. They conserved what they could. The Odawa also drove a hard bargain with the traders and garrison who were dependent on their corn, forcing them to give "as much as seven fist-fulls of powder, three hundred balls and [one line here illegible] per sack." Nor did the situation look as if it would get better. "This is a year of crisis and desolation for us Michilimackians," one observer lamented.[57]

In the difficult circumstances, communities were torn. Former allies began turning on the French, whom they now blamed for the deaths in their midst. The Menominee, some of whom had served at Fort William Henry, actually invested the fort at Green Bay and killed twenty-two Frenchmen. Eventually, pro-French Menominee managed to send seven of the attackers down to Montreal for punishment. But when Vaudreuil had three of them shot in the town square instead of pardoning them as usual, he only succeeded in undermining his remaining allies in the Menominee camp. By May, Bougainville said the situation was getting worse: "Great unrest among the Indians of the Far West." The Iroquois stopped traveling to Niagara to trade with the French, and there was "fermentation and discontent . . . among the Indians of St. Joseph, the Miamis, and Outias [Wea]." Disaffection spread quickest where smallpox hit hardest. Bougainville noted the Potawatomi "seem indisposed." Even the Odawa, he claimed, "have evil designs." As the English prepared to throw everything at the French, Bougainville concluded ruefully, "Finally [the relations of] all these nations [with us] are on the decline."[58]

•

French officials were correct in their assessments, but the decline was not attributable just to smallpox. Most Native nations had come to similar conclusions about the war at about the same time. Those who failed to convince their kin that peace was necessary over the winter of 1757–1758 had only to point to the toll smallpox took and juxtapose that with the massive reinforcements from Britain to push their point as a new campaign began. The British also sent out emissaries seeking peace. Recognition of Native American success in the war was then capped in part with the Treaty of Easton, signed in October 1758. In front of more than five hundred Indians from across the Ohio Valley and the Lakes, chiefs representing at least thirteen nations negotiated an agreement that promised to end English colonial settlement west of the Appalachians. The government of Pennsylvania even agreed to give back lands the Iroquois had ceded several years before. In the eyes of many Indians, this was a formal acknowledgment of the success of their campaign in the first years of the conflict. It signaled the end of their conflict with the British. The first Anglo-Indian War was over.[59]

The treaty was signed just as British general John Forbes advanced on Fort Duquesne at the Forks of the Ohio in late October into early November. The successful negotiations induced many formerly French-allied Indians to desert the post. The Delaware under Kuskuski kicked around the French commandant's proffered war belt and told his emissary he had "boasted much of his fighting; now let us see his fighting. We have ventured our lives for him; and had hardly a loaf of bread [in return]; now he thinks we should jump to serve him." A few days after receiving this news, the French commandant abandoned the undermanned post to the advancing British. In turn, the fall of Fort Duquesne in November caused more defections. It was the British who now benefited from the good news of victories. General Forbes gleefully reported that having stayed neutral during the siege, the Ohio Indians now seem "all willing and ready to Embrace His Majesty's Most gracious Protection." Two months later, they were still coming "in Shoals every Day . . . pretending the utmost Freindship."[60]

As more and more warriors laid aside their weapons, Native nations across the region attended numerous councils to persuade others to do the same, especially those farther west. After the successes of the past years, few wanted to risk a rupture among themselves over the continuing conflict between the English and French. Both French and English officials heard similar messages. Something of these talks can be glimpsed in the secret embassy of mission Indians from near Montreal to the Iroquois a year later. Iroquois reports of this meeting note they carried a message from twenty or more western nations— including the Odawa at Michilimackinac—who wished to keep an open and clear path between themselves and the Iroquois, which they said the war between the British and the French had blocked. But there was a greater good at stake than an alliance with either European power. "Tho' the English and French are at frequent Variances," the delegates concluded, "let us abide by Our Old Engagement of Friendship, and not meddle with their Quarrel otherwise We shall be ruined, to Join One or the Other, while both bear hard upon Us, who are the Native Owners of the Land they fight about." The statement was another sign that many Native Americans made a distinction between their own conflict with the English and the one in which the French were still engaged. It was also a plea to maintain the unity they had enjoyed to great effect earlier in their war with the English. They had to be equally vigilant against all European powers.[61]

•

The politics of the *pays d'en haut*—which, of course, should have come as no surprise to eighteenth-century European diplomats—had a dramatic impact on the Seven Years' War that by 1758 had become global. Naval skirmishing in the Mediterranean and a new British alliance with Prussia meant that the conflict had begun in earnest in Europe in 1756. But because both England and France had many overseas colonies, the war quickly spread to India, coastal Africa, the Caribbean islands, and even the Philippines. Given the increasing importance of the colonies to the European powers, it was perhaps inevitable that British failures early in the war led to the downfall of one ministry and the rise to power of William Pitt, who saw victory in North America as the key to the global conflict. Starting in late 1757, Pitt poured thousands of British regulars into the continent, and he promised incentives for colonies that could raise more men and provisions for the campaign. In the campaign of 1758, a force of perhaps as many as thirty-eight thousand, consisting of British regulars, colonial militia, and a small contingent of Native Americans, confronted as few as eight thousand French troops at Louisbourg, Fort Carillon, and Fort Duquesne.[62]

In these critical battles of 1758, few Native Americans joined the French. Montcalm boasted as late as February of that year of his influence over his former allies, but as he and Vaudreuil made desperate efforts to reinforce Fort Carillon in the face of a massive British expedition back down the Champlain Valley, few Native Americans answered the call. Of the two thousand or more warriors who aided Montcalm in 1757, only sixteen were with him when he pulled off an improbable defense of the fort on July 8, 1758.[63]

Though the British offensive stumbled at Fort Carillon, it continued apace in other quarters. By the end of July, Fortress Louisbourg was in British hands, rendering Quebec vulnerable and the resupply of the suffering colony precarious. By the end of August, Fort Frontenac was also theirs, giving them a stranglehold on the St. Lawrence Valley. The combined loss of goods and vessels at Fort Frontenac crippled the trade and supply route between Montreal and the *pays d'en haut*, further alienating Native communities there, who were still waiting for compensation for their losses. Knowing the rest of the French posts south and west could not be defended, some British officers tried to persuade their superiors to follow up the victory with an expedition into the heart of the Lakes. But there was no need. As Indian defections continued, the French posts in the interior were already withering on the vine.[64]

The withdrawal of Indian support had other significant consequences. The independence of their native allies contributed to a deepening and debilitating rift between French metropolitan and colonial officials at this crucial moment. With the French panicking over poor supplies and the loss of their Indian allies, Vaudreuil argued that French strategy had to take into account Indian diplomacy. But it was not just a matter of keeping them on their side. The governor believed the Indians were crucial for the survival of New France. If the British were to get ahold of the Champlain Valley and the lower reaches of the St. Lawrence, most Native Americans would not only abandon their alliance with the French but also join the English. "Indubitably," Vaudreuil concluded, "the Indian Nations, believing our defeat inevitable, would pounce from all points on the heart of the Colony and total ruin would be the result in a short time."[65]

By the end of 1758, however, French metropolitan officials had had enough. They were in part swayed by the arguments of officers such as Montcalm who chafed at the cost and utility of their Indian alliances. Montcalm grumbled that the claims for Indian expenses from Michilimackinac alone totaled 1.1 million livres, while those at Green Bay amounted to another 600,000 livres. Yet French officials at Versailles needed little persuading. The minister had already complained to Governor Vaudreuil about the "excessive expenditure" in the colony that year, which was estimated to be some 20 million livres (or about 10 percent of France's total projected military and naval spending across the globe for the following year), along with another million livres to cover the expenses of the Indians who had died of smallpox.[66]

In February 1759, the king told Montcalm that he would send no reinforcements that year for fear of losing them. The French were unwilling to throw any more money at a losing cause. They cited the expense of keeping their Indian allies on side, their seeming unpredictability, and the lack of a tangible return on such a massive colonial investment. While there had always been a faction who argued the colony was not worth keeping, the campaign of 1758 helped sway the rest. The massive commitment of British forces and resources to North America was certainly a major factor in the declining fortunes of the French in 1758. Yet the loss of their native allies at such a critical moment was at least as heavy a blow. Their absence contributed substantially to the inability of the French to defend themselves at this crucial turning point. But for some key decision makers, the cost of simply keeping Indians as allies called the whole colonial project into question.[67]

•

From the perspective of Versailles, then, the campaign of 1759 was over before it began. The same feeling was also prevalent among many Native nations of the *pays d'en haut*. If there was any remaining support for the French in the last years of the war, it was in no small part due to men such as Langlade and his pro-French kin. With the very existence of the colony at stake, colonial officers and intermediaries like Langlade pressed the French case with the nations of the *pays d'en haut* throughout the colder months of 1758–1759. Perhaps fittingly since they had helped precipitate the global war in 1752 and more formally in 1755, Langlade and his Anishinaabe kin played a part in the last act of the drama in North America. Though reports of Indian participation in the final English campaign along the St. Lawrence in 1759 are surprisingly sketchy, there was a sizable contingent from Michilimackinac who came down with Langlade. They probably understood the consequences of losing the French altogether.[68]

As the British closed in on Quebec, Langlade and his Anishinaabe kin skirmished several times with British troops near the falls of Montmorency. The Odawa were also involved in a skirmish on August 11, when a detachment of some seven hundred Canadians and Indians attacked a British work party. The raid was successful, with over one hundred English reportedly killed or wounded while the French suffered only seven injured. Yet it was on the Plains of Abraham that Langlade and the Odawa may have taken on their most significant role. As French and British regular troops faced off outside the walls of the citadel of Quebec, some eight hundred Indian warriors, Canadian militia, and colonial regulars slipped into the woods on the left flank of British general James Wolfe's troops. For several hours before the main battle, they poured a deadly fire into the ranks of the British, forcing Wolfe to detach four of his eleven battalions to protect his exposed side. Had Montcalm held steady, this skirmishing would have pinned the British down long enough for French reinforcements to arrive and deploy artillery. But Montcalm ordered a premature charge that ended in disaster and retreat. The militia and Indian warriors could only help cover their hasty withdrawal. They may also have killed General Wolfe. In death, Wolfe secured a famous victory. A subsequent series of errors, including an unnecessary withdrawal from the heavily fortified city, sealed the fall of Quebec, and the fate of New France.[69]

The following year, a contingent of Anishinaabe Odawa again traveled down the Ottawa River. Langlade and other pro-French ogimaag persuaded some warriors to make one last foray to help keep the French alive along the St. Lawrence. They arrived in Montreal in April and joined the Chevalier de Lévis, François de Gaston, Montcalm's second-in-command, who had mounted an expedition to try to retake Quebec City. But the siege was foiled by the arrival of a British convoy of ships. Langlade and his kin then traveled briefly to Trois-Rivières on August 17—the place where he and many of his kin could trace their roots and recall stories of early encounters. From there, they retreated to Montreal in the face of British advances. Then, on September 3, Governor Vaudreuil ordered Langlade to leave Montreal and escort his Indian kin back to Michilimackinac. Five days after leaving Montreal, Vaudreuil sent a courier to tell Langlade that Montreal—indeed, all of New France—had fallen to the English. When the group brought this news back to Michilimackinac, the post commander, Captain Beaujeu, decided to move the garrison to Louisiana to avoid surrendering to the British. In his absence, Langlade—who stayed to take his chances with his kin—took charge of the post. Thus when the British finally did make it to Michilimackinac, it was the last post surrendered by the French, and Charles Langlade one of the last serving French officers in New France.[70]

That Langlade was also an Anishinaabe Odawa warrior when he surrendered the post has largely been overlooked. It is symbolic of the elision of Native Americans from one of the most important global wars in modern history, a conflagration that may have cost the lives of upward of one million or more people worldwide. It also changed the face of the British Empire, as Britain gained Spanish Florida, several lucrative Caribbean islands, Senegal in West Africa, and a more secure foothold on the Indian subcontinent. Yet some of the most important changes took place in North America, where Britain secured the bulk of New France, inheriting a French settler population along the St. Lawrence and claims to a vast region to the north and west. This result, of course, would eventually give rise to and shape the new nations of Canada and the United States. But few now remember that the war that transformed global imperial politics began and ended in Indian country; that there was an Anglo-Indian War within the global conflict we call the Seven Years' War. In pursuing their own goals, the indigenous peoples of the *pays d'en haut* played a remarkable part in changing the course of world history.

Yet ominously for the British, Langlade's role in the closing days of the French empire in North America was also symbolic in another sense. His command and last instructions revealed the lack of real control the French ever had over the *pays d'en haut*. Vaudreuil told Langlade to look after the French inhabitants at the post of Michilimackinac. He still hoped the colony would be returned to the French at the peace table. But the astute governor also appealed to Langlade, the Anishinaabe ogimaa. Though Article 40 of the capitulation terms stipulated the Indians would "be maintained in the lands they inhabit, if they choose to remain there," Vaudreuil worried this would not be sufficient to appease them, since the French had effectively sold them out in the peace negotiations. He thus put Langlade in charge of all the Indians of the *pays d'en haut* and asked him to watch them carefully, to ensure they did not turn too quickly on the French in the region in retaliation for the loss and peace terms. He pleaded with Langlade to "encourage them always in their attachment to the French nation." To the end, French imperial officials were never able to rest easy about their relationship with the nations of the *pays d'en haut*, despite their reliance on men such as Langlade. The British, in inheriting French claims over the region, would also inherit their uncertain relations with the indigenous owners of the land.[71]

6

THE SECOND
ANGLO-INDIAN WAR

In the autumn of 1761, on the sandy shores that narrow at the straits of Michilimackinac, several groups of Anishinaabe Odawa and Ojibwe Indians prepared to receive new visitors. They had gotten word that a flotilla of canoes bearing a detachment of British troops and an emissary from the English king was on its way. Many had anticipated this moment for more than a year. Some of the Anishinaabeg had participated in the pivotal battle of the Plains of Abraham between the British under Wolfe and the French under Montcalm and had witnessed the surrender of Quebec in 1759. The following year, one of their kin, Charles Langlade, had brought news that the French had officially surrendered their colony—stretching from the St. Lawrence to the Mississippi—to the British. The Anishinaabeg expected that if the newcomers wanted to make good on this claim, they would have to make the journey up the lakes and rivers from Montreal to Michilimackinac. The strategic straits served as a door to the rest of the continent. And the Anishinaabeg knew that they, as always, held the key. The British, like the French before them, would have to pay their respects to the Anishinaabeg on the banks of these vital waters.

From the perspective of most Anishinaabeg and other Native nations around the Lakes, the British might have defeated the French, but they had not conquered the Indians. Even after Quebec fell, the

British Indian agent and trader George Croghan knew the English would have to tread carefully, because while "they may say we have beat the French . . . we have nothing to boast from the war with the Natives." Far from it. The Anishinaabeg at Michilimackinac especially had enjoyed some spectacular successes. Together with kin and allies from across the *pays d'en haut*, the Anishinaabeg had defeated the mighty General Braddock and his warriors. They had rolled back the English frontier. They had been central to one of the most successful campaigns of the conflict, in 1757. And though they had suffered much through epidemics, shortages, and famine, few had been bettered in direct conflict with British troops. Most had stayed at home in the disastrous year of 1758, when the French lost so much ground. Even those who had served in the campaigns of 1759 and 1760 acquitted themselves well. The British had marched only as far west as Niagara before the French surrendered. Most of the *pays d'en haut* was left untouched.[1]

In these circumstances, one thing was clear to the nations of the straits. If the British wished to occupy the French posts and establish a trade with the western nations, they would have to do so on Indian terms. Through constant negotiations and not a little violence, the Anishinaabeg had made themselves central to the French empire, and indispensable to the French in their midst. For more than a century, the French had viewed the Odawa at Michilimackinac in particular as one of their most important allies. Though the feeling was not always mutual, French dependence on the Anishinaabeg meant they worked hard to keep their Indian allies happy. The Odawa benefited from generous presents, good trade relations, and a privileged position in French councils. They also used the French to maintain an influential role in the inter-Indian politics of the region as well as a balance of power between themselves and their rivals.

The Odawa at Michilimackinac saw no reason for this privileged position to end with the coming of the British. At a minimum, the newcomers would have to follow long-established customs in return for their occupation of the posts and their trade with the Indians. As the British readied themselves to take over the western posts, the Anishinaabeg expected them to make peace by covering the dead of the many kin they had lost during the war. They also expected them to flood the region with badly needed supplies and provisions. Not only had British agents like Croghan promised this would happen, but also the gears of the Indian trade had to be properly oiled by these gifts and presents to work. It was a matter of respect. Anything less would be seen as an act of war.[2]

•

In the wake of the first Anglo-Indian War of 1752–1757, there was a great deal of uncertainty in Indian country about the intentions of the British. As early as 1759, for example, there were rumors afoot that the British, in revenge for their losses earlier in the conflict, "had a design to cut of [sic] all the Indian Nations." As the European war in the east wound down, there were reports the British would send an expedition to the *pays d'en haut*. Would they come to conquer, settle, or trade? Not since the seventeenth century had the Anishinaabeg been faced with such uncertainty about the intentions of Europeans.[3]

Even the capitulation of the French was accompanied by reports that they would soon be back. Vaudreuil told Langlade that he ex- pected the colony would be returned at the formal peace settlement. Rumors of a French return gave pro-French advocates a continuing say in inter- and intratribal relations. Their position was bolstered by the conflicting reports that swirled around the *pays d'en haut*. Though many pointed to an Iroquois-inspired conspiracy to rid the country of the French, then the English, some worried that without the French as a counterbalance, the Iroquois could just as easily turn on their old rivals. The Iroquois had, after all, suddenly switched sides and joined the British when they laid siege to Fort Niagara in 1759. The move wor- ried and angered many. Croghan reported in early 1760 that some Odawa, Ojibwe, and other Indian delegates called the Iroquois-speaking Huron to a "great Council" near Detroit to complain about Iroquois ac- tions at Niagara. The Iroquois allegedly killed and scalped several of their people and in particular two great ogimaag. They were willing to forgive these transgressions, but the Iroquois had not bothered to send anyone to cover their dead and repair relations. The Anishinaabeg suspected that the attack was evidence the Iroquois had designs against them and had allied with the English to accomplish their aims. Some even suspected that the British would cultivate an alliance with

the Huron at Detroit again. Under the circumstances, some Anishinaabeg argued that they should support a French return to the *pays
d'en haut.*[4]

Others used these events to argue precisely the opposite—that it
was time to throw in their lot with the British and see what they had
to offer. The French were no longer able to supply their needs. The
British had promised much in their councils with Indians through the
war. After they had taken Fort Duquesne, for example, and in an effort to woo the western nations to their side, the British pledged that
if they were successful against the French, "all the Rivers were to run
in Rum, that presents from the great King were to be unlimited, [and]
that all sorts of goods were to be in utmost plenty and so cheap as a
Blanket for two Beavers." If they did not cultivate good relations, pro-
British Anishinaabeg argued they would not have access to these promised goods. More worryingly, their rivals would. The growing number of
British traders in the Ohio Valley, combined with the new British stranglehold on the lower Lakes via Niagara, would invariably attract and
strengthen Indian communities on the southeastern flank of the Anishinaabe world. They might even bring back Iroquois towns to the
north shore of the Lakes. Anishinaabe influence over the British was
the only way to avoid being left out of these developments. Almost
certainly, welcoming the British was one of the few ways of stopping a
pan-Indian conspiracy against the Anishinaabeg. They needed to establish formal ties with the British, and to make Michilimackinac and its
peoples as important to them as it had been to the French.[5]

•

It was against the backdrop of these discussions that the British approached the *pays d'en haut* in the late fall of 1760. For the Odawa at
Michilimackinac, these early British efforts immediately raised alarm
bells. For one thing, the British made the mistake of heading for Detroit
first. There, George Croghan, on behalf of William Johnson, met with
the Odawa, Potawatomi, and Huron. At these councils, Croghan offered the covenant belt of alliance to "Renew and brighten the Ancient
Chain of Friendship" between the British, the Iroquois, and the "several Western Nations to the Sun setting." He also promised a reopening of trade. Croghan and Johnson were pleased with the outcome of

these initial negotiations and surprised by how little formal or overt resistance there was to the occupation of Detroit. They believed they had secured peace across the entire *pays d'en haut* with all the "western nations." They were so sure of themselves that they did not bother to press on to Michilimackinac that year.[6]

Johnson and other British officials could perhaps be forgiven for assuming that control over Detroit meant control over all the western nations. They were largely in the dark when it came to the politics of the *pays d'en haut*. The superintendent had long experience in native affairs, but Johnson had never ventured much farther west than Iroquoia. And few British officials fully understood the French-Indian relationship in the region, let alone the complex political and kinship network of the northern nations themselves. Their experience with most of the nations across the central region was limited to brief trading visits to Oswego by small groups of Anishinaabeg and their families. Most officials lumped the nations of the upper Lakes into one undifferentiated category. Johnson's lack of intelligence was revealed in a series of questions he asked of the interpreters and other "Intelligent Persons" at Detroit. He wanted to know some basic facts. How many Indians were at each post? And what were their names and residences, connections, dispositions, and current conflicts? How many posts did the French have, and how many troops at each? Did the Indians like the French, and how was trade between them conducted? What post was best for trade, and what did the French pay for furs? The level of ignorance betrayed by these questions would cost the British dearly in the years to come.[7]

In lieu of a sound understanding of native politics in the *pays d'en haut*, Johnson focused his efforts on Detroit because that is where his native informants led him. Johnson's knowledge of the nations of the upper Lakes was mostly limited to what he had learned from one of the Anishinaabeg's main rivals—the Iroquois. More recently, the superintendent had met with delegates from another group who had a vested interest in talking up the importance of Detroit—the Huron. Because of the increasing number of intermarriages between the Huron and Iroquois, and the disaffection of many Huron from the Anishinaabeg and French at Detroit, there was a growing number of Huron visitors to Iroquoia in the years leading up to 1763. Most of these visitors were eager to cultivate better relations with the English and Iroquois—some in defiance of their own pro-French kin. Whether accessing intelligence directly from these delegates from Detroit or from their kin among the Iroquois, Johnson not only came to believe that Detroit was one of the most important centers for Native Americans in the *pays d'en haut*, but also that the Huron were the main players in an Indian confederacy emanating from there—because that is what many of his native informants wanted him to believe. They had an interest in making such assertions—the British would take them more seriously if they thought they spoke on behalf of all the nations of the *pays d'en haut*. As the historian Andrew Sturtevant has shown recently, the Huron were eager to use the transition to the British regime as a way to leverage greater influence at Detroit.[8]

In believing Huron claims of influence in the region, Johnson also misunderstood the nature of kinship politics in the *pays d'en haut*. In his dealings with Indians along the Cuyahoga-Sandusky-Detroit axis at the southwest end of Lake Erie, Johnson met with many Odawa, Potawatomi, and Ojibwe warriors and chiefs who he presumed spoke for or represented each of their "nations." At times, this seemed to be what they told him. Representatives of the nations near Detroit, for example, told the arriving British in 1760 that "All the Indians in this Country are Allies to each other and as one People." But in an important sense, that assertion of a relationship was only about their connection to one another. While the nations of the Lakes *were* connected with one another in complicated ways—largely through generations of intermarriage and kinship networks—this guaranteed only that they were unlikely to fight each other. It said very little about their individual or collective relationship to the incoming British. Though the Michilimackinac and Detroit Anishinaabeg could still work together at times and entertained an idea of creating a larger pan-Indian confederacy, there was certainly no evidence that Detroit was central to these machinations. Nor did it mean, as Johnson thought, that the Odawa at Detroit were the same as those at Michilimackinac. Yet Johnson wanted to believe that the nations of the Great Lakes moved to the beat of the same drummer.[9]

It was perhaps inevitable, then, that Johnson would focus his efforts on Detroit, believing it to be the center of the "western confederacy."

But that focus would anger the Michilimackinac Anishinaabeg. Allowing the Huron to take the lead at Detroit was irritating enough, but Johnson's assumptions about the importance of Detroit in general were an insult to the influential role of the Anishinaabeg at Michilimackinac, and particularly the Odawa. In their eyes, early British efforts at forming new political and economic alliances lacked an appreciation of the long history of Indian-European relations in the region and the importance of the people at the straits in particular.

Perhaps more immediately, British strategy undermined the very people who might have eased their way. Advocates among the Anishinaabeg who believed British promises of a lucrative trade were at a loss to explain why they had failed to come immediately to Michilimackinac. Anti-British factions could argue that if the newcomers chose not to establish a base at Michilimackinac, the Odawa would lose the valuable provisioning trade that had proved so durable and reliable over the years, and their coveted political position as mediators, too. Finally, the new focus on Detroit allowed pro-French advocates to resurrect older fears that the British intended to create a southern axis of allied Indians that stretched across Iroquoia and into Detroit. Johnson's special treatment of the Huron confirmed this worry. The British seemed to be bent on exploiting divisions between Indians that many Native nations had worked hard to overcome in recent years. The northern Anishinaabeg could and would be isolated.[10]

•

While the initial British base at Detroit raised concerns among the Michilimackinac Anishinaabeg, early contact with them was not promising, either. Anxious to set out on their winter hunts and hopeful that the newly arrived British would end the wartime dearth of supplies and provisions they had suffered through for the past few years, Native Americans poured into Detroit with requests for provisions and ammunition. The new British commander there, Captain Donald Campbell, could barely keep up with the requests from neighboring nations. The British failure to reach Michilimackinac put the Indians there in a particularly precarious position. The French officer in charge of the post had taken most of the provisions when he departed. This left

Langlade, the interim commander, short of everything he needed to supply the Indians for their winter hunt. Under pressure from the Odawa, Langlade sent a delegation down to Detroit seeking provisions and especially ammunition. Campbell told his superiors that he "was obliged to give them what [he] could spare," but he admitted he could not keep up with their requests. He expected more Indians to come in from all quarters. He was at a loss as to what to do with them all.[11]

Over the winter, debate raged within Anishinaabe communities. The situation did not look promising for the British. Ogimaag at Waganawkezee apparently stopped a winter war party against the British at Detroit only after "much Trouble." Early in the spring of 1761, the Jesuit priest living near Waganawkezee, Father Pierre du Jaunay, warned the British that the Ojibwe in particular would oppose the arrival of any British forces at Michilimackinac. Though he said the Odawa had been "very tranquil" over the winter, the spring had brought fresh troubles. Several times, parties of warriors had threatened to attack the British at Detroit. Jaunay said the Jesuits, Langlade, and every Frenchman at the post were doing all they could to secure the peace. Though Jaunay thought the ogimaag of the Odawa returning from their winter hunts at Grand River had "peaceful intentions," he still feared some "unhappy occurrence" should the British march for Michilimackinac. Campbell stayed put. He would not spare any of his garrison for what looked like a dangerous trip up to the straits.[12] Yet the longer Campbell delayed sending a garrison up to Michilimackinac, the more discontented the Anishinaabeg of the straits grew. A year later, one report noted that the Michilimackinac Indians kept asking the British "what is ye Reason that we always was Calling them to Council During ye Warr & giving them presents & Now Take No Notice of them."[13]

Anti-English factions at Michilimackinac made the most of British neglect to further their own plans. In mid-June 1761, Campbell again reported alarms on account of the "discontent and bad designs" of the Indian nations. He thought they originated from two quarters—the Anishinaabeg around Michilimackinac, where the British had yet to secure a foothold, and the western parts of Iroquoia, especially Seneca country. One report noted that several Odawa brought belts as far east as the Abnaki at St. Francis, on the south shore of the St. Lawrence

River about seventy miles downstream from Montreal, near Trois-Rivières. Campbell thought the Seneca Iroquois had sent belts to all the Indians from Gaspé (at the far eastern tip of present-day Quebec, near the mouth of the St. Lawrence) to the Illinois region, inviting them to take up the hatchet against the English. Two Seneca deputies had even been so bold as to visit Detroit to propose the attack and invite the nations there to a grand council with the Delaware and Shawnee. Campbell believed the plans involved a pan-Indian conspiracy to act in concert to seize British traders and their goods at Sandusky and cut off all communications between Niagara, Fort Pitt, and Detroit. The attacks would start within two weeks.[14]

The British had to act. The commander in chief of the North American colonies, Major General Jeffery Amherst, wanted to prepare for war. He told Johnson he was willing to send as many as three hundred troops to help Campbell take the upper posts in order to keep "the Whole Country in a proper Subjection to the King." In the meantime, he wanted to end the provision of gunpowder to the nations of the Lakes. But Johnson knew it would take much more than force to bring the *pays d'en haut* into the English orbit. He was beginning to learn from post commanders like Campbell that the Indians expected presents and provisions before they would even contemplate a "due and proper attachment." Campbell told Johnson that the nations around Detroit had told him "the French have a different manner of treating them from us."[15]

Johnson decided to venture to Detroit himself. He planned to bring the council fire to the western nations. Along the way, he held talks with hundreds of Indians from Iroquoia through to Detroit. All professed peaceful intentions, but few hesitated to voice their complaints. When he arrived on September 9, he found already waiting for him ogimaag and principal men from the Shawnee, Delaware, Mohican, Huron, and Iroquois. They were soon joined by Detroit-based Huron, Odawa, Potawatomi, and Ojibwe, and more distant Saginaw Indians, Kickapoo, and Miami. At one point, Johnson boasted that there were more than five hundred Indians in attendance. Significantly, though, there was not one clear reference to the presence of Indians from Michilimackinac. There is no extant evidence that any Michilimackinac nations were even invited to the meeting.[16]

While at Detroit, Johnson made only empty promises to the gathered nations, and ignored many of their demands.[17] But if the superintendent failed to quell the concerns of the Detroit Indians about the supply of provisions and powder in the Lakes, he infuriated the Michilimackinac Anishinaabeg. Johnson effectively made the trip to the *pays d'en haut* to squash a rumored pan-Indian revolt and to secure Michilimackinac. He believed the nations of the straits were the source of many problems for the British. Yet he traveled only as far as Detroit. There he kindled a council fire that further alienated the northern nations. Johnson seemed to think that the presence of Odawa, Potawatomi, and Ojibwe from Detroit meant that the nations of the north were represented. The status he accorded the Huron at Detroit made the situation worse. He even singled out the Huron and declared "he looked upon them as the head of the Ottawa Confederacy." His handling of the situation alienated both the southern and northern Anishinaabeg.[18] Yet Johnson had no clue. He told Amherst shortly after returning he believed matters were "Settled on so stable a foundation there, that unless greatly Irritated thereto they will never break the Peace Established with them." Events would prove otherwise.[19]

•

British ignorance of Indian politics in the *pays d'en haut* almost led them into making a fatal error as early as 1761. Officials at Detroit felt reassured enough by Johnson's council to send a detachment of nearly two hundred soldiers under Captain Henry Balfour, a British officer, to secure the northern posts, including Michilimackinac. There is no evidence to suggest Balfour sent runners or belts ahead of this expedition. Nor did he bother to send one of his own Indian agents. He seems to have thought that a peaceful reception at Detroit meant that Michilimackinac was secure. Indeed, Balfour was under the impression that the Michilimackinac "Chiefs, or their Deputys" had assented to the renewal of the Covenant Chain at the recent meetings at Detroit and Niagara.[20]

Balfour's arrival at Michilimackinac almost started a war fifteen months before Pontiac struck at Detroit. By the time he reached the straits, the Anishinaabe Ojibwe and Odawa were already on the verge of plundering several English traders who had ventured up ahead of the military force. Balfour, who had very little diplomatic experience with Indians—let alone with the nations from the *pays d'en haut*—called a meeting with the Anishinaabeg who had remained at the post following their confrontation with the traders. His minutes reveal that he ignored all Indian diplomatic protocol and made a speech instead of holding a council. He first thanked the Indians present for assembling to meet him, oblivious to what had brought them to the post. He repeated many of the platitudes of Johnson, but like the superintendent he mixed empty promises with blunt threats. He offered wampum to console the Anishinaabeg for their losses in the war, but he also demanded a return of all British prisoners. Balfour offered an alliance, but he emphasized only the consequences of not acquiescing. Anything less than peaceful relations, he noted, will draw upon the Indians "inevitable ruin, on you, & your families" and oblige the British to treat them as "Brutes, and not as Men."[21]

Surprised by the tone and language of his speech, the assembled Anishinaabeg tried to test British intentions. Using the diplomatic language of poverty, they told Balfour they feared for the lives of their wives and children this coming winter as they had neither provisions nor ammunition. This was the British cue to distribute presents and provisions like a generous father, as had the French. It was customary. They were thus taken aback by Balfour's response. He accused them of trading all their furs away for rum at Niagara. Missing the point, he asked how they could expect the British—strangers—to pity their wives and children more than they themselves did. In the end, Balfour concluded, he could not consider them men, because they preferred rum to their elders and wives and children.[22]

The assembled Odawa and Ojibwe were less than impressed. Crucially, both groups avoided making any formal commitment to the British. They left the door open to war. The Odawa speaker, Quinonchaming, noted they were there only by "accident" and had no authority to speak for the rest of their people. He promised to bring Balfour's offerings to Waganawkezee, but he said he could not accept his belt of alliance. Instead, he told Balfour they would give it to the Ojibwe to hold until they could come back with an answer in the spring. For their part, the Ojibwe only claimed that all their great chiefs and fine speakers were dead. In their absence, they hoped the British would not hold them responsible if their foolish young men should strike the English. It was not just rhetoric. A later account noted that before the British troops arrived the Ojibwe had declared they had signed no treaty with the English and thus would "not suffer an Englishman to remain in their part of the country." One ogimaa had told an English trader that "although you have conquered the French, you have not yet conquered us. We are not your slaves." Despite the warnings, the British still didn't have a clue. When Amherst received the notes of the council at Michilimackinac, he told Johnson that it was clear that the Indians there, "to all appearance, seem pleased with the change of their neighbours."[23]

•

From this inauspicious start, relations between the British and the Anishinaabeg at Michilimackinac deteriorated rapidly. Indian suspicions about British plans only grew as it became clear they wanted to starve them of powder and lead in particular. Amherst was adamant that the British should not arm potential enemies. Communication between them broke down, too. Johnson's Indian Department was hopelessly understaffed and Johnson could not or would not send out officers with the new garrisons that set out from Detroit in September. That left Indian relations in the hands of young and inexperienced post commanders—Lieutenant William Leslye at Michilimackinac and Ensign James Gorrell at Green Bay. Leslye complained his orders contained "very little respecting Indians" and he had been given no wampum with which to renew peace.[24]

When Johnson did finally get around to sending an assistant, the gesture was feeble and came too late. A mere ensign, Thomas Hutchins of the 60th Regiment of Foot, traveled through the *pays d'en haut* in the early summer of 1762 and spoke with Indians at Michilimackinac, Green Bay, and St. Joseph's. He reported that all the Indians he met "behave very Sively," but they were clearly underwhelmed with his lowly rank and even less impressed with the meager presents he brought with him. Hutchins reported that the Odawa and Ojibwe of Michilimackinac professed peace with the English and claimed (probably ironically, given the circumstances) they were "much obliged to Sir William Johnson for taking so much Notice of us as to send you to visit our Country." But they still went away "much dissatisfyed." His interpreter told him they expected presents, though they said nothing to Hutchins about it.[25]

Summarizing his trip, Hutchins said in private conversations that the Indians all told him the French gave them presents three or four times a year and always allowed them sufficient ammunition at the posts. They now "think it very strange that this Custom should be so immediately broke off by the English." They had not even enough ammunition "to Kill game sufficient for the support of their families." Hutchins concluded that only with the "greatest difficulty" could the post commanders "keep them in a good Temper." Though the officers of the posts had given them some presents, they looked on them as "mere trifles, and are in great Expectation of having Presents sent them from Sir William Johnson." Finally, many of the Indians reminded Hutchins of British wartime promises of bountiful presents and a free-flowing trade. Even the French, the Indians noted, who were "butt a poor peple," "allways Cloathed any Indians that was poor or Naked when they Come to see them."[26]

On hearing Hutchins's initial reports, Johnson immediately wrote to the Lords of Trade demanding changes. Though he still did not quite understand the specific grievances of the Anishinaabeg at Michilimackinac, he began to grasp that the "too sudden change" of treatment from the French to the English was at the root of the trouble more generally. The Indians were "not only very uneasy, but jealous of our growing power." The French encouraged them to think that British power "would prove their destruction, as we should hem them in and in the end extirpate them." "A people Jealous of their libertys as the Indians" were sensitive to these changes. The Indians took note of new posts to the south, of restrictions on trade and powder, and saw this as proof of British designs. Johnson thought a small amount of presents would accomplish far more than war with the Indians. They had little choice but to emulate the French. A war would be expensive and bloody, and the Indians could easily lay siege to their posts and wreak havoc on the frontiers. So they had to win them over with friendship and esteem—and prove they planned to adhere to their promises.[27]

•

Yet even as Johnson penned his letter, many Native nations—including the Anishinaabeg at Michilimackinac—were preparing for war. In failing to act like the French, the British had managed to strengthen anti-English factions throughout the *pays d'en haut*. If unfulfilled promises and rumors of British intentions to war against the Indians were not enough, anti-English factions within Native communities even at Michilimackinac could point to what was happening in the Ohio Valley for evidence of what to expect from the British. The war parties sent out throughout the Seven Years' War served as intelligence-gathering operations. For the first time, thousands of warriors from the *pays d'en haut* traveled to far-flung places such as the Champlain Valley, the Shenandoah Valley, and the Appalachian Mountains. The evidence was clear. The English were numerous, and they were on the move. Few Native Americans of the *pays d'en haut* could be in doubt that British occupation would likely bring settlement. Despite repeated promises to the Ohio Indians that even the soldiers would not stay at Fort Pitt (formerly the French Fort Duquesne, at the Forks of the Ohio River), for example, the place had been quickly flooded with settlers. These settlements were all bigger and more intrusive than those built by the French, and it was clear that the English were there not just to trade, but to hunt and farm, which would put them in direct competition with the Indians. More ominously, they were now under the protection of larger, well-armed contingents of troops.[28]

However, it may have been British attitudes that most irritated Native nations. The British threatened more than they promised. They promised more than they gave. They gave only with an accompanying rebuke. Lurking behind these actions was an assumption that the nations of the *pays d'en haut* were now a conquered people, at the mercy of British power. Amherst gleefully passed on the news of James Grant's successful campaign against the Cherokee to Johnson while he was on his way to Detroit. In 1761, Grant had destroyed fifteen towns and driven five thousand men, women, and children into the woods and left them to starve. He told Johnson that he should not fail to "make use" of this intelligence in his upcoming meetings, as an example that the Indians may be convinced that we "have it in our power to Reduce them to Reason."[29]

Prudently, Johnson did not make use of the news in such a way, at least not in open council. Yet Amherst's contemptuous behavior was just the beginning. Major Henry Gladwin, who replaced Donald Campbell at Detroit, not only restricted presents even further but also allegedly called the Indians there "hags and otr. Names, telling them to get along & go about their business, & would not hear them." Daniel Claus, a German-born Pennsylvanian serving in the Indian department at Montreal under Johnson, was also frustrated by English attitudes. He overheard one British officer boasting to a delegation of Indians that the English could crush them "whenever they pleased." Claus complained, "we are so intoxicated with providential Success that we will presently stumple over the whole Universe, if no Block should happen to lay in our way."[30]

But the British were about to be blocked. Throughout 1762, many Indians around the Lakes started testing the waters by harassing the English. By July 1762, Campbell at Detroit predicted war in the upper country. He thought his neighbors "only want a good opportunity to fall upon us." Just over a month later, post commander Leslye at Michilimackinac mused that the Indians had come to the post "to do some mischief." But Leslye had been warned, and was on guard, so the Indians left him alone. Then, in mid-September, news came that there had been a "great Council" at the Odawa town above Detroit in the summer, attended by the chiefs and principal warriors of the Huron, Ojibwe, Odawa, Potawatomi, and "some other Tribes who live amongst those Indians on Lake Superior, above Mechelemackinac and Fort La Bay [Green Bay]." The council was kept "a great Secret from all Indians Except those of the greatest note amongst their Nations." As soon as the council broke up, deputies were sent out to the Miami, Ouiatenon, Kickapoo, Piankashaw, and other tribes settled on the Wabash, and from there to the Shawnee.[31]

By the winter of 1762–1763, it seemed no longer a question of whether there would be another Anglo-Indian war, but rather when, and where it would start. Few accommodationist chiefs could still garner any support. The final catalyst was news of the official Treaty of Paris, formally ending the Seven Years' War. The preliminary articles of peace were signed on November 3, 1762, and word reached the east coast of America by the end of January 1763. By the time the western nations began returning from their winter hunts, the country was alive with new reports of the complete cession of French-claimed lands east of the Mississippi. The Illinois country would be turned over to the English. Spain would take Louisiana (see map on page 214). Twenty British regiments were to remain in North America. The French were not coming back. Croghan reported from Fort Pitt that the Ohio Indians had been "very Jelous of our Growing power, Butt Sence I acquainted them of ye paice & Lett them know that all North America was Ceaded to Greatt Britian they Seem Much More So." By April, officers at the interior posts also reported similar sentiments. Croghan told Amherst that from the letters he received from Gladwin and Campbell, "I understand the Indians in them parts seem uneasy in their minds, since they have heard so much of North America is ceded to Great Britain." Nearer to Fort Pitt, the Indians were "Dissastisfied since they heard it, and says the French had no right to give away their country; as, they say, they were never conquered by any Nation." In light of these reports from the field, as it were, it is hard not to conclude the British had been warned. They should have been prepared.[32]

•

The first cut was not the deepest. An Anishinaabe Odawa ogimaa called Pontiac planned a surprise attack on the British fort at Detroit on May 7. But a Huron woman warned the commandant in advance. Though they failed to take the post, Pontiac's forces laid siege to it on May 9, killing or wounding twenty British soldiers and traders and taking fifteen more captive. A week later, they captured a convoy of supply boats approaching from Niagara, killing and capturing at least fifty more soldiers and bateaumen. A few days on, the besiegers took nineteen more prisoners when they intercepted another party on its way to the fort. With every success, Pontiac's forces grew. But the attack on Detroit was only the start. Word of the siege spread among Indian communities faster than the British could send warnings. As if they had been waiting for a signal, Native nations throughout the *pays d'en haut* struck. Just over a week after the siege of Detroit began, Huron warriors farther south surprised and seized Fort Sandusky near the west end of Lake Erie, fifty miles from Detroit. Nine days later, on May 25, a group of Potawatomi demanded a conference with Ensign

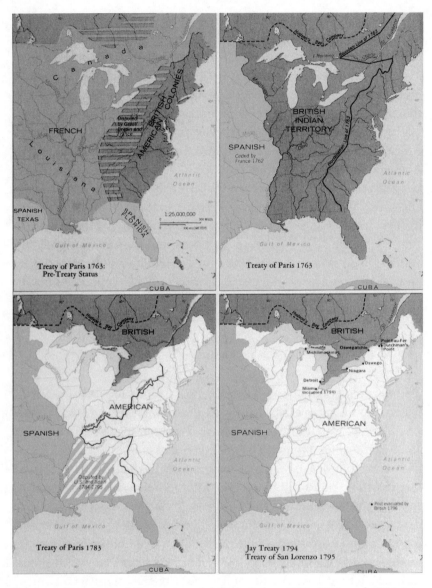

European Treaties and Claims over the Great Lakes, 1763, 1783, and 1794 (*Atlas of Great Lakes Indian History,* edited by Helen Hornbeck Tanner. Copyright © 1987. University of Oklahoma Press. Reproduced with permission. All rights reserved)

Francis Schlosser, the young post commander at St. Joseph's. They ended the meeting by killing nine of his fifteen-man garrison and taking Schlosser captive. Two days later, the Miami took the British post on the Maumee River, then persuaded Kickapoo, Mascouten, and Wea warriors to join them in a raid on Fort Ouiatenon on June 1.[33]

Indian attacks rolled across the *pays d'en haut* like shock waves pulsing outward from the epicenter at Detroit. At Michilimackinac, on June 2, Anishinaabe Ojibwe famously surprised the fort while pretending to play a game of lacrosse. They killed or captured the entire garrison within minutes. By June 21, a nervous James Gorrell abandoned his isolated post at Green Bay and barely managed to escape with his life. By that time, Delaware and Mingo warriors had shed the first blood in the upper Ohio country when they overran Colonel William Clapham's settlement twenty-five miles up the Monongahela River from Fort Pitt. Seneca war parties—sometimes accompanied by Odawa, Ojibwe, and Huron warriors—attacked English posts and settlements in the Ohio Valley in mid-June. All of the new forts leading from the south shore of Lake Erie to the Forks of the Ohio were next to go. Fort Venango fell on June 16, its garrison killed. Fort LeBoeuf was taken on the eighteenth, and Fort Presque'île on the twenty-first.[34]

Almost simultaneously, Delaware and Shawnee warriors cut off the newly named Fort Pitt from the east by destroying settlements along Forbes Road and attacking Forts Ligonier and Bedford in quick succession. By the end of June, Fort Pitt itself was under attack and every British post west of Detroit had fallen to the Indians. Both Detroit and Fort Pitt were still in British hands but were cut off from supply bases on the Great Lakes and in Canada. In addition, Delaware, Shawnee, and Mingo war parties began raiding Pennsylvania settlements again as far east as Carlisle and down to the Virginia backcountry as far south as North Carolina. Colonel Henry Bouquet, a British officer who had helped take Fort Duquesne in 1758, reported a "general Panick" among English settlers near Carlisle. Rumors swirled that Indian attacks were just the start of something larger. Slaveholders along the eastern seaboard heard that Indians attacking the frontiers were "saving and caressing all the Negroes they take" and feared this might "be productive of an insurrection." The Second Anglo-Indian War rocked the British Empire.[35]

•

Most historians see 1763 as the end of the Seven Years' War. Others see it as the start of events that would lead to the American Revolution. It was both, and they were connected by another event—a revolution in Indian country, a turning point in British imperial relations with indigenous peoples. Its effects would transform the world in which we live today. But what it was not was an Indian "rebellion," "uprising,'" or "conspiracy." Nor was it "Pontiac's War." It was a second Indian war against Britain. While the first was primarily an attempt to rebalance power between the English and the French, this second conflict aimed to rebalance power between Native Americans and the English. In effect, it was a war for Native autonomy against an imperial power bent on controlling and restricting their independence. Angry at British talk of conquest and new imperial policies, and anxious about white encroachments on their lands, many Indians throughout the *pays d'en haut* came to the same conclusion at the same time: the British had to be chastised and brought to heel. They had to be made to recognize native sovereignty just as the French had done. In that respect, the Second Anglo-Indian War might be seen as the first war for American independence in North America. And it was remarkably successful.

But like most revolutions, and like much of the politics of the *pays d'en haut*, the Second Anglo-Indian War was a complex event. Though historians have argued about its causes for many years, it has defied easy generalization. Invariably, local circumstances dictated communal responses. Inter- and intra-Indian politics were as important as Indian-British relations. So, too, were the relationships between Canadians, Métis, Indians, and French. Nowhere was this complexity more obvious than during the tense hours and days following the initial attacks. While most Native Americans could agree that it was time to chastise the haughty British, there was less consensus about exactly how that should be done. For the most part, the goal of the war was not to eliminate the British from the *pays d'en haut*, but to restore the status quo that existed prior to the Seven Years' War. Much like the conservative origins of the American Revolution (in which many colonists simply wanted to return to the status quo before the Stamp Act), many native peoples wanted a relationship with the English much like the one they had with the French, in which they maintained the upper hand.

Significantly, though Pontiac and the story of the attack at Detroit took center stage in the accounts of the British and subsequent historians, events at Michilimackinac complicate the traditional story of the war. There, as tensions between the British and the Anishinaabeg boiled over, differing and often conflicting interests came to the fore. At Detroit, the Odawa ogimaa Pontiac appeared to orchestrate events. Yet at Michilimackinac, Odawa ogimaag worked hard to "save" the British garrison from the hands of their Ojibwe kin. The Ojibwe and Odawa at Michilimackinac and Detroit shared many of the same grievances against the British, but they differed over how best to redress them. The Second Anglo-Indian War reveals with some clarity that by 1763, the Odawa at Michilimackinac were a very distinct group from the Odawa at Detroit.

The full story can be understood only by facing east and trying to comprehend indigenous actions and motives. Like many other Native Americans across the *pays d'en haut*, most of the Anishinaabeg at the straits wanted to establish a relationship to the British similar to the one they enjoyed with the French. But the Odawa had a unique agenda. Since the British had effectively ignored Michilimackinac following the end of the Seven Years' War, the Odawa had to demonstrate their power. They also needed to prove their widespread influence throughout the region. Only by looking in detail at events at Michilimackinac in the hours and days after the first fighting broke out can we understand the war at the straits as a part of the Odawa's larger strategy of maintaining a hold on power at Michilimackinac. Yet in making this bid, a bid to render themselves as central to British efforts in the Lakes as they had been to the French, the Anishinaabe Odawa at Michilimackinac once again helped change the course of American history.[36]

•

Although much of what happened at Michilimackinac in 1763 will forever be obscure, as French and Anishinaabe participants alike tried to make the best of the situation without fully revealing their designs, we can still piece together the main contours. What is known is that on June 2, almost three weeks after the attack on Detroit commenced, a group of about one hundred Ojibwe initiated a surprise attack on the post at Michilimackinac. They had come to the fort early in the summer "as Customary." Some of them spent their summers on the Island of Michilimackinac, others came from Cheboygan, a few miles southeast of the fort. George Etherington, the British commander at the post later claimed there was nothing suspicious about their presence; they were there with their families.[37]

Under cover of a game of baggataway, or lacrosse, the Ojibwe waited until Etherington and Leslye came outside the gates of the fort to watch. On a signal, they flipped the ball into the fort and rushed after it, just as a group of them seized Etherington and Leslye. Inside the fort, the Ojibwe collected hatchets and "Spears" from "a number of their Women" who had "concealed them under their Blankets." They killed at least sixteen soldiers and a trader named Tracy in the initial attack. Etherington claimed that another two soldiers were wounded, and the rest of the garrison made prisoners, five of whom were killed after the first strike. The Ojibwe took all the English traders captive, too, robbing them of everything they had.[38]

Etherington later noted that the Indians left the French and their property alone. English traders went so far as to claim that the French at the post joined in the plundering. At the very least, some shut their doors to fleeing Englishmen. But overall, the French and Canadian response to the attack was ambivalent. Apart from the Jesuit priest at the post, Father Jaunay, the small French population at Michilimackinac seemed content to simply stand aside and let events take their course. While English traders later fumed that their Gallic counterparts did little to help them, and many British officials suspected that French and Métis habitants were behind the attacks more generally, the events themselves suggest that this was a native affair. The Anishinaabeg were driving the action. The few French on hand at the post could do little under the circumstances.[39]

British officers did seem to have one other ally amid the initial carnage, though. Charles Langlade, who was at the post to trade, ignored the plight of the English traders but moved quickly to save the British officers. In a report written ten days after the attack, Etherington told Gladwin that he and Leslye were seized outside the fort and taken into the woods, "where the Spoil was divided, and a Council held, in what Manner the Officers were to be put to Death." In the midst of the talks, Langlade and the fort interpreter, Jacques-Philippe Farly, arrived and negotiated the release of the officers by giving themselves as security for their return when the Ojibwe demanded them. While Etherington probably understood events only through the eyes of intermediaries such as Langlade himself, the British commander believed the métis trader saved his life. But if Etherington was grateful for his intercession, Langlade—a nephew of one of the more prominent Odawa ogimaag—was likely working on behalf of his Indian kin. Returning to the fort, Langlade immediately sent for his own kin among the Odawa at Waganawkezee. He subsequently left matters— and the British officers—in their hands.[40]

The Odawa, who were some twenty miles from the straits when fighting broke out, later said they had just returned from their winter

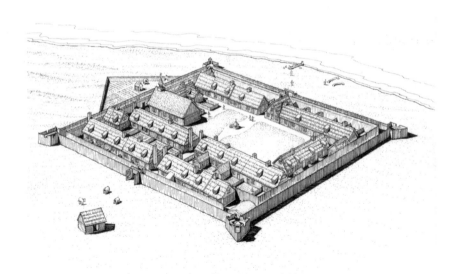

Artist's rendering of Fort Michilimackinac based on Michel Chartier de Lotbinière's drawing and description of 1749. While not wholly accurate in its details, this image is a close approximation of the fort at the time of the attack in 1763. The outbuildings include two bakehouses and a stable belonging to the Langlades. The Ojibwe would have entered the fort from the gates on the land side, near the stable. (Victor Nelhiebel, Mackinac State Historic Parks Collection)

hunt when they heard the "unexpected" news of the taking of the fort. They immediately sent someone on horseback, who found the post in Ojibwe hands. When the messenger brought back this news, most of the Odawa warriors armed themselves and set off immediately in their canoes for Michilimackinac. What seems clear from all accounts is that the Odawa were surprised by the timing of the attack. The exact timing of Pontiac's attack to the south likely took the northern nations by surprise. With little time to spare, the Ojibwe hastily improvised an assault before the British could be apprised of events to the south. The Ojibwe did not tell the local French of their plan, nor did they consult with the Odawa at Waganawkezee.[41]

Within two days, the Odawa arrived at Michilimackinac and held a series of heated councils with the Ojibwe. These lasted about a week. At this early stage, it was not clear which side the Odawa would take. Though they enjoyed close kinship ties with the Ojibwe, the Odawa had more of a stake in protecting the British garrison because of the value of the provisioning trade over which they still presided. Yet they also harbored most of the same grievances as others. Years later, Alexander Henry, a fur trader who wrote an influential memoir of his time in the Lakes, noted that some of the Ojibwe took him and a few others into canoes and headed out for the islands. En route, they came across Odawa warriors on their way up to Michilimackinac, who took them from the Ojibwe and brought them back to the post. The Odawa told him they were friendly and had saved his life. But Henry observed that they had only "changed masters" and "were still prisoners" when they were lodged in the house of the commandant and carefully guarded.[42]

During the ensuing councils, the Odawa asked the Ojibwe why they had attacked the English. The Ojibwe replied that a few days before the attack they had received belts of wampum from Pontiac and other chiefs at Detroit informing them of the rupture with the English there and asking them to cut off Michilimackinac. The Odawa were reportedly "surprised and chagreened" at this news, and "very much displeased at what the [Ojibwe] had done." Yet Henry later said the Odawa were "insulted" that the Ojibwe had attacked the English "without consulting with them on the affair." No doubt they were particularly angry that the Ojibwe had launched the attack at the post, on lands that the

Odawa had long claimed as their own. But the Ojibwe had assumed the Odawa were in general favor of the attack and expected them to approve of what they had done. They were supposedly "confounded at beholding the Odawa espouse a side opposite their own." It is not at all clear whether the Odawa were really helping the British or orchestrating a truly masterful piece of theater for the benefit of British eyes. Whatever they were doing, they were eager to reassert their control over events.[43]

Again, according to English reports by informants who were not privy to any of the Anishinaabe discussion, the Odawa demanded that the Ojibwe deliver them the remaining prisoners. Either out of deference to their brethren or because they had attacked the English on Odawa lands, the Ojibwe complied, despite their superior numbers. By June 10, they had struck a deal, and the Ojibwe handed over all but four captured soldiers and one or two traders. But the Ojibwe managed to extract a concession from the Odawa: they wanted the British removed from the fort. While events elsewhere in the *pays d'en haut* were still uncertain, the Ojibwe wanted to keep their options open. Etherington thought this meant they would plunder any convoys of traders who ventured near. The Odawa agreed to take the British back to Waganawkezee but insisted that Charles Langlade take command of the post in their absence. By June 16, or earlier, the British officers and captured soldiers were refugees at Waganawkezee.[44]

•

Etherington seemed relieved to be in the hands of the Odawa. Yet neither the Odawa's intentions for the British prisoners nor the exact terms of the deal with the Ojibwe were clear. But they had something to do with events at Detroit. Both the Ojibwe and Odawa were clearly anxious to see what had happened at that post. They both sent delegates along with the Jesuit priest, Father Jaunay, to Detroit. The British officers were edgy. Shortly after the Detroit delegation left, news came in that the Ojibwe at Michilimackinac were continuing to plunder canoes in the region. Etherington also heard from ensign James Gorrell at Green Bay. The news was mixed and still murky. Gorrell believed he had uncovered a plot against the fort as early as May 18. He thought some

Odawa might have been involved. Once he heard what happened at Michilimackinac, he left the post and headed for Waganawkezee, even though several chiefs at Green Bay warned him the Odawa could not be trusted. Besides, Gorrell thought he was about to be taken by the nations of Green Bay themselves. By July 1, Gorrell reached Waganawkezee without incident. Everyone now waited anxiously for news from Detroit. Etherington appeared to sense that his fate rested on what had happened there.[45]

Fortunately for the British at Michilimackinac, Father Jaunay and the Odawa and Ojibwe delegation brought back news that the siege of the fort at Detroit had ground to a stalemate, and serious divisions in the aims and objectives of those who attacked the British had emerged. Some were angry that Pontiac seemed to sanction the indiscriminate killing of the British, and that the French there had been plundered. The news from farther afield was also mixed. While many British forts had fallen, most of the Iroquois had apparently held back from joining the attacks. Only the westernmost Seneca had participated in attacks on the British.[46]

In light of the reports from the south and southeast, the Odawa and Green Bay Indians who had come across with Gorrell held a council and called for the Ojibwe to join them. It was clear that negotiations over the fate of the English were not yet finished. They were also further complicated by inter-Indian politics. There was residual hostility between the Ojibwe of Michilimackinac and some of the visiting Menominee over several retaliatory killings between the two. The Odawa had to mediate carefully between them to avoid an open rupture over the fate of the British. There were also rumors that the Sioux had threatened to attack the Ojibwe if they continued hostilities against the British. If war between the Sioux and Ojibwe resumed, the Odawa would invariably find themselves dragged into it.[47]

Nor was there likely consensus among the Odawa. From the evidence before and after June 1763, there was plenty of anti-English sentiment among the Anishinaabe Odawa and some later evidence that at least a few of them had been involved. The narrative of events in June also suggests that the Odawa were equivocating. Annoyed that the Ojibwe had made the first strike, the Odawa quickly moved to capitalize on the opportunity. By positioning themselves as saviors of the British, they also bought themselves some time to see which way the wind was blowing elsewhere. Had the French made a formal move on the colony, or the southern Indians been successful at Detroit, the Odawa might well have acted very differently. Throughout the conflict the Ojibwe hinted as much. A year later, pro-English Ojibwe told the incoming British commander the "Ottawa's were concern'd in the affair here, but had cunning enough not to be seen in it."[48]

In the end, the Odawa decided to move cautiously toward a rapprochement with the British. News of the stalemate at Detroit, the reluctance of the Iroquois to get involved, the lack of formal French help, and the renewed possibility of a Sioux-Ojibwe conflict helped convince wavering Odawa to act as mediators rather than provocateurs. While the Ojibwe were eager to expel the British entirely from the region, and many of the Green Bay Indians were happy to keep them in place, the Odawa saw an opportunity in steering a middle course. The Odawa were long used to Europeans at the straits, but they wanted them there on their own terms. As events unfolded, the Odawa knew that by saving the British officers and remaining troops, they would draw attention not only to their power and influence in the region but also to the importance of Michilimackinac itself. They made a decision not to overtly resist the might of the British Empire, but instead to boldly assert their place within it.

•

That strategy was visible in the final negotiations over the fate of the British prisoners. The Green Bay Indians, but primarily the Menominee, tried to convince the Odawa simply to reinstate the British at Michilimackinac. The Ojibwe, noting that events farther south were not yet settled, opposed such a move. The Odawa, however, insisted they would take the English down to Montreal. Unable to get the British to come to council at Michilimackinac, the Anishinaabe Odawa decided it was time to go to the British. The councils continued until July 7, when, over the continuing objections of the Bay Indians, the Odawa got their demand to take the British to Montreal. Once this was decided, the council delegates moved to Michilimackinac to persuade the Ojibwe there to let them pass through to Montreal and give up their remaining prisoners. Four more days of councils followed, after which the

Green Bay Indians and the "friendly Ottawas" told the British the road was clear.[49]

The Ojibwe had relented. Now, given their part in the negotiations, they expected the British to absolve them. On the thirteenth of July, Gorrell noted that about eight or ten of the principal Indians who were behind the attack came to Etherington and asked him if he would "shake hands with them." It was clear they did not see much difference between the position they had taken, and that of the Odawa who now said they saved them. When Etherington refused, they claimed they had saved him and his garrison. And they did so, they said, on account of the Indians from Green Bay, not the Odawa. They implied that the Odawa were equally guilty. They also reminded him that "though it was the [Ojibwes] that struck, it was the Ottawas that began the war at Detroit, and instigated them to do the same." Further councils followed, until the eighteenth, when the group finally left for Montreal after Etherington gave out presents.[50]

Forty canoes—containing sixty Odawa, a few traders, Etherington, Leslye, Gorrell, and the freed soldiers of both posts—made for Montreal. Still, the British were not out of the woods. The group met a party of allied Anishinaabe Mississauga at the French River. The Mississauga may have conveyed news of developments to the south. On July 31, in an attempt to break Pontiac's siege of Detroit, some 250 British soldiers tried to make a surprise attack on Pontiac's camp. But Pontiac got advance notice of the attack and intercepted the party, killing 20, including Captain James Dalyell, and wounding another 34. The Battle of Bloody Run, as it came to be known, was a serious setback for the British. Perhaps concerned that Pontiac's further success at Detroit might split their ranks again, the Odawa decided to divide their convoy and hurry on Etherington, Leslye, and "all the master traders" to Montreal. Gorrell, the soldiers, and the traders' workers stayed behind to guard the provisons and furs they still had with them. The advance party reached Montreal on August 6. Gorrell and the others arrived a week later. Their ordeal was over.[51]

•

The arrival of the group in Montreal caused a favorable stir—as the Michilimackinac Odawa had no doubt hoped. They arrived while hostilities across the *pays d'en haut* still raged and as bad news continued to pour into Montreal. By the second week of August, the British themselves would have received news of the disastrous Battle of Bloody Run near Detroit, which only confirmed their worst fears about the scale of the conflict and the losses they had incurred. Fresh reports about another skirmish, the Battle of Bushy Run, might just have reached Montreal, too. In that engagement, Colonel Henry Bouquet, at the head of a column of five hundred British troops sent to relieve the besieged Fort Pitt, ran headlong into an ambush set by Delaware, Shawnee, Mingo, and Huron warriors on August 5. Bouquet managed to rout the attackers and bring an end to the siege of Fort Pitt, but only at the cost of the lives of fifty British soldiers. Yet the "victory" was soon followed by a costly defeat. On September 14, some three hundred Seneca Iroquois, together with Odawa and Ojibwe from Detroit and the Ohio, attacked a supply convoy near Niagara Falls and managed to overwhelm a relief force as well. More than seventy soldiers and wagoneers were killed at what became known as the Devil's Hole Massacre, which was one of the deadliest skirmishes of the war for the British.

Native Americans, mostly from the Ohio Valley, also continued their punishing attacks on the colonial frontiers, causing chaos from New York down to North Carolina. Indian attacks had forced as many as four thousand settlers on the Pennsylvania and Virginia frontiers to flee their homes. The British soldiers could do little to shield the colonists they were charged with protecting. By the end of the summer, there were more than four hundred soldiers dead and dozens more captured, and up to two thousand colonists dead or captured.[52]

Under the circumstances, the British were thankful to have found some seemingly powerful friends. Daniel Claus, the Indian agent at Montreal, reported, "The Officers and Traders can not say enough of the good Behaviour of these Ottawas." The Odawa stayed for a week and were entertained lavishly. They also demanded, and got, an audience with General Thomas Gage, the military governor of Montreal who was about to be appointed the commander in chief of North America. Over the course of the council, the Michilimackinac Odawa gave the general a long and pointed geography and history lesson. They described the main trading routes in and out of the *pays d'en haut*, the strategic and commercial importance of Michilimackinac, and the part they played in the trade at the straits. They made a point of noting why neither Detroit nor Montreal was a suitable alternative as a place of trade. The Odawa also spoke of their relationships with other nations in the Lakes, and they explained the similarities and differences between themselves, other Anishinaabeg, and the Odawa at Detroit led by Pontiac.[53]

While distancing themselves from Odawa farther south, the Odawa from Michilimackinac declared their influence over another set of "western nations" that the British would have to take into account. The Odawa said they spoke on behalf of the Menominee, Winnebago, Sauk, Fox, and Illinois Indians, all of whom were willing to take "a fast Hold of your Hand, and declare themselves your firm Friends, and Allies." They even claimed they spoke for the Iowa and the Sioux. Finally, the Michilimackinac Odawa also explained the close relationships they enjoyed with French traders, the terms they enjoyed under the French, the practice of credits and wintering over with their families, and their monopoly on the provisioning trade. They demanded that the British recognize this history and make the same terms the French had if they wanted to maintain a post at Michilimackinac. Significantly, the Michilimackinac Odawa offered little in return, apart from reiterating what risks they had taken to bring the British garrison back to Montreal in the midst of the hostilities. They said nothing about helping the British "chastise" other Indians.[54]

The Odawa eventually left Montreal with presents worth about £600 (or close to $100,000 in today's money), along with promises that they would soon hear from Johnson about the reopening of the trade. Even General Gage seemed to realize what the friendship of the Odawa meant to the British. The day after he held a council with them, he wrote to Johnson that the "whole Behavior of these People, has exceeded any thing that could be expected, from Nations much more polished & refined. It is indeed beyond Belief. They resisted the Menaces of the [Ojibwe] and refused any share in the Plunder." Though the Odawa had stopped short of offering aid against other Indians, Gage was still hopeful they would ally with the British. The Odawa even encouraged Gage to think the tide had turned in the war. With the help of nations such as the Odawa, Gage concluded, "the War upon the Western

Lakes may be soon brought to a happy Issue by a firm & lasting Peace."[55]

Daniel Claus thought the Odawa left Montreal "well contented & satisfied." They had reason to be. Though they did not get all they wanted, the Odawa had orchestrated a diplomatic victory in the midst of the ongoing Anglo-Indian War and begun the process of reeducating the British as to their prominence within *pays d'en haut* politics. Later, they claimed that Gage recognized their influential position at the straits. Unlike Johnson at Detroit, who had been oblivious to their importance, Gage promised that the British would consider them "the largest tree that could be found in all the woods." And while the Anishinaabe Odawa had rescued the British, they had ceded nothing in the process. Indeed, the Odawa's heated discussion with the Ojibwe and Menominee over whether to reinstate the British at Michilimackinac or bring them down to Montreal highlighted the Odawa's ability to broker power and manipulate empires. By bringing the garrison down to Montreal, the Odawa of Michilimackinac symbolically and literally rejected the first British occupation of the straits. The British would have to start again on Anishinaabe terms.[56]

•

Just how much Gage conceded in his treatment of the Odawa became clearer in light of the British war effort more generally. The situation in the *pays d'en haut* looked bleak for the British when the Odawa arrived in Montreal. Native Americans across the region still had the British pinned down and under attack in most of their newly acquired western posts, and Johnson was working feverishly to keep on his side those Iroquois who had not yet joined the war. But British strategy was severely hampered by the bullheadedness of Jeffery Amherst, the commander in chief who presided over the origins and initial months of the war. His disbelief that the Indians would and could surprise them so effectively translated into an obstinate response once the scale of the attacks became apparent. Despite reports noting divisions among the various western nations, Amherst wanted no help from any Indian nation. As news of the losses rolled in, Amherst insisted that the British alone must retaliate, as "our Security must always Depend on our own Superiority & not to their Friendship or Generosity." Several months later, Amherst was still adamant that he did not want the help of well-disposed nations such as the Michilimackinac Odawa even if they offered it. He wanted the English alone to carry out the "Punishment of the Savages" so that the "whole Race of Indians" could see the folly of opposing the British.[57]

In the midst of war, Amherst and some of his officers also laid bare the near-genocidal contempt they had for Indians. On his way from Lancaster, Pennsylvania, to relieve the siege of Fort Pitt, Colonel Bouquet told Amherst he hoped to "extirpate that Vermine from a Country they have forfeited, and with it all Claim to the Rights of Humanity." Amherst, not realizing that the commander at Fort Pitt had already purposely tried to spread disease among the Ohio Indians, told Bouquet when he reached the post he should hand out smallpox-infected blankets to friendly Indians. He hoped they would start a new round of epidemics. "We must Use every Strategem in our Power to Reduce them." Amherst then gave orders to Henry Gladwin at Detroit and other officers that all captured Indians should "immediately be put to death, their extirpation being the only security for our future safety, and their late treacherous proceedings deserving no better treatment at our hands." After hearing that Captain Campbell at Detroit may have been killed, Amherst told Bouquet he wished "there was not an Indian Settlement within a Thousand Miles of our Country; for they are only fit to live with the Inhabitants of the Woods, being more nearly allied with the *Brute* than the *Human* Creation." In their contempt for Native Americans, Amherst and his subordinates only revealed what many nations of the *pays d'en haut* had long suspected.[58]

To make matters worse, Amherst told Johnson to cut Indian expenses even further. He thought the Indians must be punished before any treaties were made; even then, all they should expect was a regulated free trade. They should not expect presents, "for they can never be Considered by Us, as a People to whom We Owe Rewards." "It would be Madness, to the highest Degree," he fumed, "Ever to Bestow Favors on a Race, who have so Treacherously, & without any provocation on our Side, Attacked our Posts." He then betrayed his ignorance of Indian affairs when he noted that as far as the Odawa and Green Bay Indians were concerned, they might be supplied from Montreal, but only after the disturbances were quelled. He did not want any supplies reaching them while the war continued, "for they would most Certainly make a bad Use of it." Amherst could not distinguish between Odawa at Detroit and those at Michilimackinac: "I Can Never think that One Part of a Nation bringing in a few of our People, when the Others are Committing Hostilities . . . should Induce Us to Load them with Presents, which would Serve to Enable their Brethren to prolong the War."[59]

While Amherst blindly stumbled further into a complex war, other British officials were learning a different lesson from the hostilities. Superintendent of Indian Affairs William Johnson, for example, believed the conflict only confirmed his worst fears. He had had enough of Amherst's belligerence. Johnson had begun to learn a thing or two about the politics of the *pays d'en haut* and was livid at Amherst's lack of understanding. He wrote to Amherst in mid-October and gave him a long history lesson in native diplomacy. Repeating some of the arguments he had made in the past year or two, Johnson noted it was much cheaper to conciliate the Indians and cultivate friendly relations than to try to destroy them all: "this certainly none will suppose."[60]

Johnson also undermined Amherst by complaining directly to Whitehall. He first did so as early as July 1. A sense of what he wrote can be gleaned from his letter to Cadwallader Colden, governor of New York, on October 24, 1763. He told Colden in no uncertain terms that if his policies had been followed, there would have been no Indian war. Noting differences of opinion among the Native nations, Johnson said those who joined against them did so because of the "Originall Parsimony" of the British and the fact their friendship was never cultivated with the same attention, expense, and assiduity with which the French obtained their favor. Though it had cost the French a great deal, Johnson believed their system was still much cheaper than keeping a large body of troops at the posts, and certainly much cheaper than war. British troops could never truly protect trade or settlements because of the Indian mastery of the countryside. The French thus chose the "most reasonable & most promiseing Plan, a Plan which has endeared their Memory to most of the Indian Nations."[61]

While Johnson's retrospective view of the problems in the *pays d'en haut* was more than a little self-serving, his ideas did reflect a change in British thinking. Indeed, by the autumn of 1763, Johnson was preaching to the converted. The British press printed news of the start of the Anglo-Indian War as early as July 16, as Amherst himself only awoke to the reality. They kept on printing the bad news. The reports caused a massive stir in London, where they finally put an end to the celebrations of victory in the Seven Years' War. They also threw the Ministry into an uproar. In August, the earl of Egremont gave Amherst his long-sought permission to return to Britain. But by the time Amherst handed Thomas Gage his command in New York in mid-November and sailed for home, he had become a scapegoat. In September, the Lords of Trade had told William Johnson that they and the king's ministers "entirely agree" with him about the causes of the war. They were convinced that reconciliation and good relations with the Indians could be secured only by the "speedy establishment of some well digested and general plan for the regulation of our Commercial and political concerns with them." It was not until Amherst arrived in London that he realized he had been brought home not to be feted as a wartime hero, but to take the blame for a costly, unnecessary, and unsuccessful war.[62]

•

As the historian Fred Anderson has noted, the Second Anglo-Indian War, combined with domestic unrest, also almost brought down the government of Prime Minister George Grenville. Had there been another suitable candidate, the king would almost certainly have replaced him. Instead, the Anglo-Indian War gave the crown an opportunity to reshuffle the ministry and drive home the urgent need for restoring imperial policy and order. The most pressing problem was the need to bring an end to the conflict in North America. Accordingly, the new ministry rushed through plans intended to organize the newly claimed lands in North America and, most important, to create a vast interior Indian preserve. Similar plans had been drafted earlier in the year, but the Anglo-Indian War gave the issue fresh urgency. Ministers pushed through the Proclamation of 1763, as it would come to be called, in less than a month. The king issued it on October 7. The speed with which it traveled through the Board of Trade and the Privy Council reflected a consensus over the need to reassure Native Americans that the British had no designs on their lands.[63]

Simply put, the proclamation decreed that all lands from the Great Lakes down to Florida, and from the Mississippi to the western slopes of the Appalachian Mountains, were reserved for the Indians. No colonial governments could grant lands in this zone, and no one could negotiate the purchase of Indian titles except the king's designated representative. Moreover, no Europeans were allowed beyond the Appalachian ridge, and those already living there would have to leave. The only British subjects allowed in this zone would be British officers and their garrisons at designated posts, representatives of the two Indian superintendents, and traders with licenses from the governor or commander in chief of the colony in which they lived.[64]

Historians are divided about the meaning and impact of the Proclamation of 1763. On one hand, its provisions were hastily drafted, and it was thus vague on a number of a critical points. In particular, it was unlikely to stop English squatters and unlicensed traders from infiltrating Indian country. On the other hand, as the historian Woody Holton has shown, the proclamation did block speculators from procuring clear and secure title to any lands they had purchased west of the mountains. Among these were the likes of George Washington, Thomas Jefferson, Arthur Lee, and Patrick Henry, who were infuriated that the British would now follow the French in frustrating their speculative schemes. Four years after the proclamation, George Washington wrote, "I can never look upon that Proclamation in any other light (but this I may say between ourselves) than as a temporary expedient to quiet the Minds of the Indians & one that must fall of course in a few years." Armed with this belief, but frustrated by British insistence on observing the Line, Washington continued to seek out and claim land in Indian country right up until the start of the American Revolution. Control over these western lands subsequently became a major goal of the newly independent states.[65]

One thing is clear: the Proclamation of 1763 was a declaration of Indian sovereignty, designed to appease the Indians. As the Earl of Egremont explained to a pugnacious Amherst, the king was "much at heart to conciliate the Affection of the Indian Nations, by every Act of strict Justice, and by affording them His Royal Protection from any Incroachment on the Lands they have reserved to themselves, for their hunting Grounds, & for their own Support & Habitation." Another official observed, "Such an Instance of our goodwill to the Indians, would fix them more firmly in our Interest, than all the Talks we can give them, or all the Presents we can bestow on them." The proclamation itself noted the need to convince the Indians of their "Justice" and to "remove all reasonable Cause of Discontent." The British had no choice. The Second Anglo-Indian War convinced men like Johnson that such a move was "essential to our Interest, and the Security of our Colonies." The Ministry recognized Johnson's arguments that "the Indians all know we cannot be a Match for them in the midst of an extensive woody Country." If they were "determined to possess Our Posts, Trade &ca securely, it cannot be done for a Century by any other means than that of purchasing the favour of the numerous Indian inhabitants." As Gage took over from Amherst, he told Johnson, "It is right at all Time to treat the Indians on the Principles of Equity Moderation, and Kindness, [and] to give them occasionally Some small Presents."[66]

•

The Proclamation of 1763 and the new British policy toward Native Americans did have an effect in Indian country, even if it was slow to unfold. Before news of the proclamation reached the *pays d'en haut*, Pontiac lifted the siege of Detroit on October 31, 1763. His influence at Detroit was beginning to wane, and different groups who had joined his coalition had already started to abandon the siege and make their own peace with the British. Many, like the Anishinaabeg at Michilimackinac, believed their point had been made. Pontiac, who had held out for so long in the hope that the French would come to help from the Illinois or Louisiana, left Detroit and took refuge on the Maumee River, where he continued to try to raise warriors to attack the British.[67]

Elsewhere, Native Americans from the Ohio Valley continued to raid the western frontiers of the English colonies into the spring and summer of 1764. Any good feelings the Proclamation of 1763 might have engendered among the Indians involved in these attacks were complicated by a bloody massacre of peaceful Christian Indians at Conestoga (now Millersville, Pennsylvania) in December of the same year. A vigilante group who came to be known as the Paxton Boys from western Pennsylvania murdered six Susquehannock they found there and pursued another group to Lancaster. Local officials put them into protective custody, but the Paxton Boys broke in and brutally murdered and scalped another six unarmed adults and eight children. It was a sign of things to come. One troubling legacy of the Anglo-Indian Wars in America was a deepening rift between many Native Americans, especially to the south of the Lakes, and the English colonists who were invading their lands. Even as British officials in Montreal and London worked toward a peaceable solution to the conflict, the terrible violence of the war—the fury of which has compelled at least one historian to liken it to ethnic cleansing—convinced many participants on both sides that Native Americans and Europeans were inherently different and could not live together.[68]

Faced with these complex and contradictory currents, General Thomas Gage also sent out mixed signals to the Indians still at war with the British in early 1764. While he probably prolonged the war in some quarters by foolishly following the disgraced Amherst's plan to send two punitive expeditions westward to crush any remaining resistance, he also allowed William Johnson to call a major Indian council at Niagara in an effort to bring peace to the region. This was Johnson's big moment to try out the more conciliatory measures he thought were necessary for good relations with the Indians. At Niagara in July 1764, Johnson aimed to awe unfriendly Indians into peace and recruit allies to chastise those who continued to war. The superintendent sent word out across Indian country. He ensured that belts were sent out to friendly nations such as the Odawa at Michilimackinac to head to Niagara, where they would meet a "great English Chief" and "find all they were in need of."[69]

For many northern Anishinaabeg, this was what they were waiting for: an invitation to an important council, and a material first step in the renewal of trade relations. They expected a repeat of the previous year's gift giving. But they also traveled to Niagara with an expectation it would give them an opportunity to dramatize their newfound importance within British councils. High on their agenda was a desire to negotiate the reopening of the post at Michilimackinac. Many important ogimaag made the journey. Mechskima, Nissowaquet (Langlade's uncle), Esguime, and Kisecssam from Waganawkezee led the way. At least another seven others identified by the British as chiefs also traveled southeastward with many of their Ojibwe kin from the straits. At Niagara, they joined as many as two thousand other Indians who attended councils over the month of July.[70]

Johnson boasted that such a gathering was unprecedented. Unfortunately for the British, most of those who turned up, like the Odawa, were those who declared they had never taken part in the hostilities. Only some Detroit Huron and Seneca from New York agreed to make terms of peace with Johnson. Most of the others, Johnson admitted, said they only came to "renew their engagements, not having approved of the War, or engaged in it." Given that few Indians present were interested in peace talks, Johnson quickly made it clear he had other demands. He wanted pledges of continued allegiance, information about who was responsible for the attacks the previous year, and restitution for the losses incurred by British traders. And he wanted warriors to accompany a punitive expedition that Colonel John Bradstreet was busy assembling to move against Detroit. The fur trade could not be opened again until there was peace, Johnson announced. Nor would the British reestablish the trading posts until he had assurances that they would be safe.[71]

But delegations such as those from Michilimackinac pushed their own agenda. They first reminded Johnson that he was in Anishinaabe-claimed territory now by welcoming the superintendent to Niagara. They then moved to demonstrate their influence and authority across the Lakes. In a general council of all the Indians, including the Iroquois, they claimed they spoke on behalf of all the nations present. They reminded Johnson and all those present of their services the previous year. They arrived with certificates from Gladwin and other officers testifying to their fidelity and their actions in protecting the garrisons of Green Bay and Michilimackinac. Now, they came to Niagara in peace. They said they knew nothing about those who attacked the British. Even the accompanying Ojibwe declared they were not the same ones as those residing near Michilimackinac, and they had nothing to do with the attack. The Odawa were in fact uninterested in Johnson's efforts either to end or continue the war against others. They said they were there to trade and collect on their debts from the previous year. What they really wanted was ammunition and supplies for hunting in exchange for the furs they had brought down. Then they wanted to get home to their families as quickly as possible.[72]

The Michilimackinac Anishinaabeg frustrated Johnson. But at Niagara they also educated him. At one crucial point in the proceedings, his secretary minuted that Johnson spent the day in "private Meetings" with several of the northern and western Indians "at which more was done than at the publick ones." Subsequent letters revealed that Johnson learned a fair bit about the internal politics of the Michilimackinac Anishinaabeg and especially about doodemag relations and leadership. Between events at the straits in 1763 and talks at the council, he also gained an appreciation for the differences between the Michilimackinac and Green Bay Indians and those to their south. He realized, too, how important they were to any political settlement with the nations of the *pays d'en haut* and especially any British presence at Michilimackinac. He would not repeat the mistakes he made at Detroit.[73]

Indeed, by this point, Johnson had already realized the British had erred when they occupied the straits in 1761 with virtually no advance diplomacy. This time he came prepared. Johnson formally affirmed British friendship with the Michilimackinac Anishinaabeg and proffered the Covenant Chain to the nations who had allied with the British in 1763. Johnson offered a wampum belt twenty-three rows wide, depicting Johnson holding the hands of all nations between Fort Johnson and the Ojibwe at St. Mary's. The Anishinaabe delegation requested that the "great Belt" be kept at Waganawkezee—"as it is the Centre, where all our People may see it." To confirm the importance of the Anishinaabeg at Michilimackinac, Johnson asked that they show it to all the nations in the region. He then gave out medals to all the headmen gathered. The belt ended up at Waganawkezee, under the care of Nissowaquet.[74]

Yet if Johnson hoped acceptance of the Covenant Chain would guarantee obligations on the part of the Anishinaabeg, he would be disappointed. In return, the Odawa told him what he already knew: some of the Ojibwe near Michilimackinac still held two soldiers and five of the English traders' slaves. But they refused to promise restitution for the traders, since they claimed they had no part in the attack. Near the end of the conference, the Odawa did promise warriors to accompany Colonel John Bradstreet on his punitive expedition to Detroit.

However, only ninety-six warriors from among the seventeen hundred gathered at Niagara offered to accompany Bradstreet. All but ten of these left the expedition after receiving their ammunition and supplies. Alexander Henry said they refused to fight against "their own friends and kinsmen."[75]

In the meantime, Johnson doled out even more presents, spoke of an end to the prohibition on the liquor trade, and promised the British would restore the post and trade at Michilimackinac. In all, Johnson gave out more than £38,000 worth of presents at Niagara. He also spent more than £20,000 on provisions for the assembled delegates. To put this into perspective, at this single council, the British spent almost as much as they initially hoped to raise from the colonies when they passed the Stamp Act the following year. Yet in return for this enormous outlay, the superintendent later admitted all he could secure from the Odawa was an agreement to *let* the British reestablish the post at Michilimackinac—and a promise to protect it "as far as they are able." For the Odawa, the conference at Niagara was a diplomatic success. No wonder the Odawa speaker Mechskima declared they would now be happy to see the British back at Michilimackinac. "We always loved them," he announced, "but we now like them better than ever, as they come for our Good."[76]

•

For many Native nations of the *pays d'en haut*, the royal proclamation, the new attitudes that ushered it in, and William Johnson's conference at Niagara signaled the end of the Second Anglo-Indian War. The conflict dragged on in places over the next year or two, but after the successes of 1763, most Native Americans laid aside the hatchet. After Johnson's conference at Niagara, Bradstreet made it only as far as Presqu'île on Lake Erie before he realized he had insufficient troops to subdue any remaining enemy by force and instead made an unauthorized and embarrassing treaty of peace with the Indians he could find there. He did eventually reach Detroit and reopen the post, though not before he almost reignited the conflict there with some ill-informed diplomatic gestures. General Gage's other punitive expedition, led by Colonel Bouquet, set out only in October 1764 against enemy Indians west of Fort Pitt on the Ohio. Most were ready for peace by then. Though some Native Americans, especially in the Illinois region, continued to agitate for war, even Pontiac wanted an end to the war by 1765. The following year he traveled to New York and came to terms with William Johnson in July 1766.[77]

Though the British were quick to claim victory in the conflict, it is hard to see what they gained. They got back some of the prisoners taken in the war, but few Indians were brought to account for their participation in the conflict. Few Native American antagonists suffered any consequences apart from a verbal rebuke or two. Instead, the British caved in to Native demands. They regained access to the fur trade, but they did so entirely on Indian terms. Effectively, the British had to recognize Indian claims that they had never sold land to the French. The reoccupation of French posts was wholly dependent on the generosity of the Indians. The British would be their tenants. In return, Indians expected compensation. Starting with the Odawa at Montreal, the British began renegotiating the occupation of the western posts on that basis. They distributed extraordinary amounts of presents to different native groups. They promised a quick renewal of trade, and Johnson ended the prohibition on the sale of alcohol. If success were to be measured by the extent to which they removed the British from the *pays d'en haut*, then the Indians obviously did not succeed. But few Native Americans advocated the complete removal of the British. While some may have hoped the war would trigger a return of the French, most rose up against the British to demand respect and more equitable treatment. This they got.[78]

In addition, while the particular details of the new settlement and how they would play out at the posts were still uncertain, the Odawa at Michilimackinac were in a good position to ensure a favorable outcome. Never again would the British fail to take note of Michilimackinac. Nor would they again mistake Detroit for the decision-making center of the "western nations." The Odawa and their Green Bay allies had provided a vivid demonstration of the importance of the straits and the different strategic alliances at work in the *pays d'en haut*. They also earned the gratitude of the British. They and their kinsmen such as Langlade were praised and rewarded for their efforts at the time and seen as key players in the Great Lakes.

Indeed, the British, made aware of the need for their good favor amid a potentially hostile sea of Indian nations, did all they could to cultivate good relations. As late as the mid-nineteenth century, Anishinaabe tradition dated their special relationship with the British from this moment. As Andrew Blackbird wrote, "that was the time the British Government made such extraordinary promises to the Ottawa tribe of Indians . . . She promised them that her long arms will perpetually extend around them from generation to generation, or so long as there should be a rolling sun. They should receive gifts from her sovereign in shape of goods, provisions, firearms, ammunition, and intoxicating liquors." In the years to come, the Anishinaabeg never lost an opportunity to remind the British of these promises.[79]

•

Significantly, the Odawa managed to achieve these gains at the same time that British imperial officials' intransigence toward their own colonists' demands was growing. The two were not unrelated. As the British occupied former French-claimed land in North America, they were still reeling from the staggering costs of the Seven Years' War. It had nearly doubled Britain's national debt. The Second Anglo-Indian War only added to the financial misery, and made officials acutely aware of the potential costs of ongoing conflict with Native Americans. They worked hard to maintain peaceful relations with the numerous Indian nations even as they angered their own colonists with new and more intrusive imperial legislation. The Proclamation of 1763 showed just how far British officials in London were prepared to go to keep the peace.[80]

Indeed, more generally, the Second-Anglo Indian War also gave the British the excuse they needed to maintain a large peacetime army in America. British officials had already decided to keep ten thousand troops in North America to help manage the new Canadian and Indian population and defend against any return of the French. But with opposition MPs in Parliament clamoring for a post–Seven Years' War reduction in troop numbers for economy's sake, the Second Anglo-Indian War helped make it clear that British forces would have to remain in North America. It also convinced many that the colonists ought to pay for them. Since a great deal of the Seven Years' War had been fought in North America, and the Second Anglo-Indian War helped secure peace on colonial frontiers, this now seemed obvious to many British ministers. Yet on the other side of the Atlantic, many colonists in the thirteen mainland provinces along the eastern seaboard were angry about the Proclamation of 1763, which seemed to limit any westward expansion and safeguard the interests of an increasingly detested foe. When Parliament began to pass legislation imposing taxes on the colonists to pay for imperial expenses, the stage was set for a showdown. The Anglo-Indian Wars, then, played a dramatic part in precipitating a different war for independence.[81]

7

REORIENTING EMPIRE

As the Anishinaabeg had agreed at Niagara, they welcomed the British to the straits in 1764. The newly assigned British commander of Michilimackinac, Captain William Howard, and his garrison arrived at the straits in late September. In turn, the British honored their promise to reopen the legal trade market there. This time the British began their tenure with a different mind-set than in 1761. In the wake of the Anglo-Indian Wars, the Board of Trade finalized an extensive "Plan for the Future Management of Indian Affairs." Completed while Johnson was at Niagara, it contained nearly all of the superintendent's previous recommendations. Indian affairs would be governed by specially appointed Indian officers rather than by the army. Trade would be reestablished, at the main posts at least, and would be governed by a detailed schedule of fixed, fair prices. And the custom of giving regular presents to the Indians would be renewed. Johnson's generosity at Niagara was just the beginning. On top of his costs there, the British allocated another £20,000 for presents and other contingencies relating to Indian affairs.[1]

The British believed they knew what this change of plan meant. After his arrival at Detroit, General Bradstreet sent out an agent to the Sault Ste. Marie, Saginaw, Green Bay, and Michilimackinac Indians (including the Odawa at Waganawkezee) with a message that the English king "now wishes to adopt you for his *children* instead of

Brothers as you have hitherto been." The British thought they could step into the position of Onontio, the French father. They would fulfill that fictive kinship role by acting generously and indulgently. News spread quickly among Native communities that British post commanders had been given the green light to give out gifts. As a result, numerous delegations of Anishinaabeg and other Algonquians from the area paid visits to the arriving commander. Then, shortly after Howard's arrival at the post, Major General James Murray issued a declaration on January 24, 1765, noting the cessation of hostilities with the Indians and the official opening of trade in the *pays d'en haut*.[2]

But if the British hoped that peace, stability, and secure alliances with Native Americans would follow this change in their relationship, they were sorely disappointed. Like many subsequent historians, most British officials had idealized the relationship between the French and their Indian so-called allies. Seeing what they thought was a united front, they were quick to conclude that the French better managed their relations with the Indians—that in return for generous gifts and indulgences, the Indians were obliged to the French and happy to do their bidding. But of course this never quite worked for the French the way the British imagined. Gifts and provisions were only the starting point, a minimum requirement in return for the occupation of the posts. Apart from that, nations such as the Anishinaabe Odawa controlled and contained European colonial ambitions from early on. They drove the relationship, threatening, cajoling, and turning against the French when they did not get what they wanted. They proved adept at playing off the European powers against each other. The relationship cost New France dearly—in time, resources, and consequences. The British inherited not the peaceful middle ground of the French empire, but a complex set of Indian-French relations based on uncertainty, realpolitik, and expense. It was the true cost of empire.[3]

Though historians often see the end of the Seven Years' War as the starting point for a downturn in the fortunes of Native Americans, this was true only for those nearer the eastern seaboard and in the Ohio Valley. Savvy nations such as the Iroquois who proved adept at playing off the British against the French suddenly found themselves facing only one major power. They struggled to keep the British in check. More and more Indians also had to face off against a tide of

advancing English colonists. But in the heartland of the *pays d'en
haut*, 1763 marked only a shift in orientation. No British settlers arrived in the upper Lakes, and the British garrisons that occupied the
western posts were no larger, or any more worrying—and just as
needy—as those they replaced. True, British traders swelled the ranks
of those clamoring for trade with the Indians, especially around the
posts of Detroit and Michilimackinac. But French and Métis traders
still had a monopoly on direct trade with the Indians, especially the
important winter trade, and Native Americans had options similar to
those they had had before the war because they could sell to either
the French or the British.

As important, though, the Odawa at Waganawkezee in particular
used their strategic location to keep Michilimackinac as valuable
to the British empire as it was to the French. And they did so even
while they maintained a great deal of leverage over the newcomers.
In effect, they created an important regional triangle of trade and diplomacy with Waganawkezee at its center and themselves as the key
mediators. In their careful maneuvering and their desire to maintain
autonomy, William Johnson thought he could discern "a new system
of Politicks" at work among the nations of the *pays d'en haut*. But for
the Odawa at Waganawkezee, the new system was remarkably similar
to the old one. The most telling difference was that instead of looking
east to balance power in the *pays d'en haut*, the Odawa increasingly
faced west. They drew on their relations with the remaining French
and Métis traders in their midst and their expanding kinship networks
to the west to keep open the possibility of renewed relations with
the French who remained on their western and southern flanks.
By threatening to renew ties with the French, the Odawa got the British to act as the French had and prospered in the years following
the Anglo-Indian Wars. They did so even as the British tightened up
their regulations concerning their own British colonists on the eastern seaboard.[4]

•

When William Johnson sat down in 1767 to sum up Indian affairs in
North America, he began by describing what he thought was a shift
in inter-Indian politics. He thought the nations of the *pays d'en haut*

had repaired and strengthened their relations with one another—particularly those between the Great Lakes Indians, the Catholic Indian villages around Montreal, and the Iroquois. But Johnson also believed that several "confederacies" had formed throughout the region that were trying to create a united front among themselves. "The Nations contained under the several Confederacys," Johnson thought, ". . . endeavoured to draw together their scattered Tribes and reduce themselves to a little more order." He noted efforts to do so among the Illinois nations, the Six Nations, and the Algonquians. Johnson believed the reason for it was clear—they did it with an eye on "their future security." As the superintendent put it, English victory over the French compelled the western nations to "strengthen their mutual Compacts and alliances." "They are in general," he concluded, "not bad politicians."[5]

As far as the Anishinaabeg were concerned, Johnson's comments were probably a reflection of the status quo rather than an assessment of recent developments. His remarks especially need to be considered in light of persistent British efforts to identify more formal political communities and leaders. One commander, for example, believed that Nissowaquet was the head "Chief of the Ottawas at Abercroach [Waganawkezee]." And in general, beginning with events at Michilimackinac at the start of the Anglo-Indian War in 1763, other English officials also began to refer to Nissowaquet as the chief of the Odawa. Yet this was just wishful thinking on the part of the English. Nissowaquet himself was always sure to note the other "principal chiefs" of Waganawkezee. Johnson's comments also need to be read in light of recent ignorance of the links and connections the Anishinaabeg already enjoyed with many nations around the Lakes. And while the Waganawkezee Odawa seemed confident in their relations with others in the region in the 1760s and 1770s, it was only a result of the longer-term evolution of their kin-based alliance building.[6]

To be sure, though, the Waganawkezee Odawa did also make some formal diplomatic moves to secure their position at Michilimackinac. This was most evident in their overtures to the Iroquois, their longtime rivals. Though an uneasy peace between them had held for many decades, the Odawa immediately set to work renewing their engagements with the Iroquois following the Seven Years' War.

Building on long-standing connections between the Huron and the Iroquois, and their own relations with the Catholic Indian villages near Montreal, who in turn lived with Catholic Iroquois who had kin among the Six Nations, the Odawa worked with the Iroquois "and carefully buried (according to custom) all past objects of grievance." The two groups made it clear they had always "manifested a sincere respect" for one another. But now that they faced only the English on their eastern flank, the Anishinaabeg had come to consider the Iroquois "the Door, (as they call it) to their Country, and the channel by which they might receive the surest intelligence concerning the designs of the White people." Under the circumstances, they wished to keep the Iroquois as friends.[7]

But the Waganawkezee Odawa did not have to do much in the way of formal alliance building. By the 1760s, the fruits of decades of intermarriage across the Lakes, and particularly around Lake Michigan, meant that long-established groups such as the Anishinaabeg at Michilimackinac had grown in influence. A thick web of relations now stretched out from Waganawkezee as far west as the Mississippi, and down to St. Joseph's in the southeast corner of Lake Michigan. Secondary webs knitted these communities together with those in Detroit and farther southeast into the Ohio, and also down into the southwestern corner of Lake Michigan and into Illinois country. This was a rich and densely populated network that also connected many French men and women who stayed in the region to the Algonquians. It also included métis families such as the Langlades who were now firmly embedded in these kinship networks. Population growth, migrations, instability among neighboring nations, and exogamous marriages meant these relationships continued to thicken and expand. By these measures, the Anishinaabeg were thriving. By the mid-1760s, if not before, the Anishinaabe Odawa especially enjoyed a commanding influence over the shores all around Lake Michigan. While William Johnson wondered aloud whether the different confederacies were actively organizing through more formal political channels, what he likely glimpsed were the outlines of expanding doodemag relations that helped cohere native policy in the region.

•

This process could be most clearly seen at work in the expansion of the Waganawkezee Odawa down the eastern shore of Lake Michigan. Small groups of Odawa had been slowly drifting southward from Michilimackinac over the past couple of decades or more. They established new settlements on the eastern shores of Lake Michigan at the Manistee, Muskegon, and Grand Rivers. These villages arose from the historic use of those areas as wintering grounds by northern Odawa. Augustin Langlade may have traded in this area over the winter in the 1730s and 1740s; his son Charles Langlade established a more formal trading post in the Grand River area as early as 1755. Both the Langlades simply followed their relations from Michilimackinac to one of their more popular wintering grounds. Given the origins of these villages at Waganawkezee, Langlade's uncle Nissowaquet and other ogimaag were able to knit together a close working relationship with the chiefs of these villages—and particularly a powerful ogimaa named Manétewabe from the Grand River settlements—when dealing with the British in the 1760s.[8]

These relatively new villages were also made possible by—and helped reinforce—the close relations the Odawa from the Michilimackinac region enjoyed with the Potawatomi from the St. Joseph's area. As we have seen, the Odawa and Potawatomi had also long intermarried, though the two communities increasingly acted independently from each other when it came to relations with outsiders. The Potawatomi, particularly at St. Joseph's, for example, took much longer to reconcile themselves to the English in the aftermath of 1763. Still, they enjoyed a mutually beneficial relationship with the Odawa, and each nation could count on the other's support in times of need. In 1771, the Potawatomi, fearing an attack by the Shawnee and Delaware, asked the Odawa at Waganawkezee to shelter their women and children in their village—"as they were all Relations, being intermarry'd with one another."[9]

The Waganawkezee Odawa also capitalized on the creation of new and allied villages along the western shores of Lake Michigan. By the mid-1760s, Ojibwe and Odawa families had established mixed villages there with groups of Potawatomi who had earlier migrated from the east. These stretched from the very northern tip of what is now known as the Door Peninsula down to present-day Chicago, and some

at least were established at the sites of older Sauk and Mesquakie villages. The Potawatomi had interrelationships with the Sauk that
stretched back to the Fox Wars with the French and had obviously
used these relations to move northward from St. Joseph's and southward from an old foothold at Rock Island. In turn, these relationships
helped smooth relations between the Sauk and the Odawa and Ojibwe,
leading to the creation of many new and ethnically mixed villages by
the 1760s.[10]

The tendrils of relations thus stretched across Lake Michigan from
Waganawkezee in a thick and complex weave. Indeed, when George
Croghan attempted to enumerate the nations around Lake Michigan
and its tributary rivers who had relations with the Michlimackinac
post, he had a hard time separating them out. In total, Croghan thought
there might be close to six thousand adult males connected with
Michilimackinac (not counting Ojibwe on Lake Superior). This meant
that as many as twenty-four to thirty thousand Anishinaabeg, Algonquian, and Siouan-speaking Winnebago formed a connected world
across the central Lakes.[11]

This relatively new axis represented a shift westward for the
northern Anishinaabeg, and particularly the Odawa. For much of the
seventeenth and early eighteenth centuries, the Odawa dominated
the shores of Lake Huron and Georgian Bay, with important centers
at Michilimackinac, Manitoulin Island, and Saginaw Bay, and at first
the southern end of Georgian Bay and subsequently around Detroit.
By the middle of the eighteenth century, Odawa summer or winter
villages and mixed Anishinaabe villages dotted the shorelines of most
of Lake Michigan and up into the Fox-Wisconsin waterway. Given
oral traditions that emphasize Anishinaabe origins to the east and
early migrations westward, this relatively new shift may have simply
been a continuation of these older movements. It might also have been
a long-term result of the Fox Wars earlier in the century. By 1734, most
of the Fox had left or been pushed out of the Fox River region. Without
Fox pressure, the Menominee, Winnebago, and Anishinaabeg created
new villages in this area.[12]

Given this expansion and movement, the creation of new axes of
interests and influence, and the recent European geopolitical changes,
the Odawa at Waganawkezee were well placed to continue to play an

active and leading role among the nations of Lake Michigan. Though they did not literally "draw together their scattered Tribes," they did make efforts to use their influence among their many scattered kin throughout the nations of the west to bring the British to heel. The western shift of the Odawa base of operations was originally brought about by earlier intermarriages between the Odawa and others around Lake Michigan. These relationships sometimes led to the creation of new villages. In turn, these settlements and the kinship relations that held them together helped the Odawa at Waganawkezee create a larger (if still loose) pan-Indian confederacy of western nations—one that was distinct from the emerging coalition around the Detroit area (even if the British did not appreciate this emerging distinction until after the Second Anglo-Indian War).

This western orientation and constellation of relations was only reaffirmed by the dramatic events at Michilimackinac and Waganawkezee in June and July 1763. Though the relationships between the Ojibwe, the Odawa, and the Green Bay nations were tested by their differing approaches to the British prisoners, the actions of the Waganawkezee Odawa in the Second Anglo-Indian War reflected their influential position in the region. Their successful mediation earned them further respect. The western nations managed to avoid a major conflict among themselves, and to reap immediate awards for their apparent "loyalty" to the British. Yet the peaceful outcome was possible only because of the new relationships forged between the Odawa and their expanding villages, and their new neighbors and kin.

•

Perhaps most important, this western orientation also allowed the Odawa to keep the road open to alternative sources of diplomatic power at a crucial moment in the geopolitics of North America. For these networks literally and figuratively stretched across the new British imperial borders. It meant that though the British now dominated the entire eastern seaboard of North America, the Anishinaabeg could continue to play off Europeans against one another because of their entwined relations with other native groups in the region as well as with the French. The Odawa used their relations with the French on the edge of new British frontiers to full advantage. Together, their connections to native and Frenchmen alike gave the Odawa a great deal of leverage in their dealings with the British in the years after 1763.[13]

Though officials in Versailles had no plans for recovering Canada (as some English officials dreaded), the French were happy to profit from a continued trade in furs via the Mississippi. When France, by secret treaty, ceded Louisiana to Spain in 1762, they left the door open for trade, which the Spanish abetted and encouraged. When the Spanish extended their authority to the Illinois settlements, for example, they left the French commandant in charge at Fort Chartres—on the east bank of the Mississippi, about forty miles south of present-day St. Louis—with a handful of his soldiers. The British were not able to dislodge them until December 1765.[14]

Yet even after the British occupied Fort Chartres, many French traders simply crossed the river to the Spanish side, and furs continued to roll down the Mississippi. A British report in 1766 noted that French traders had founded the new town of St. Louis just north of Fort Chartres at the junction of the Missouri and Mississippi Rivers. From this base, they had managed to make serious inroads into the fur trade of the Missouri and the northern reaches of the Mississippi as well as that of the nations near Green Bay, Lake Michigan, and St. Joseph's via the Illinois River. When Robert Rogers, a veteran of the Seven Years' War, took charge of Michilimackinac in 1766, he immediately reported that French traders, with and without Spanish passes, were in the region and had come up as close as a hundred miles from the post. After sending out spies to the west, presumably with Indian guides, he learned the French and Spanish had even begun a settlement at Prairie du Chien, on the east side of the Mississippi where the Wisconsin River joined it. The location was a strategic point along the Fox-Wisconsin waterway, which in turn joined the Great Lakes to the Mississippi. According to Rogers, Prairie du Chien was "a thorough fare formerly for great numbers of Indians to Michilimackinac"—and now a place where the French intended to prevent the English from trading. From here, too, Rogers believed the French sent out traders to posts on Lakes Superior and Michigan and into Sioux country.[15]

William Johnson and other British officials believed that these French traders not only were capable of engrossing all the fur trade but also stirred up trouble among the Indians of the region. The French traveled into "the very Towns of our Indians," to whom they often bring "considerable presents." Johnson said these men were known to the Indians and had great influence with them, and were often those who had been "formerly partisans or employed in Indian affairs by the French and have lived for several years in the Indian Country." They were all "Men of Ability & influence," he noted. Johnson worried that they kept up warnings to the Indians to be "upon their guard against the English, and to hold themselves in readiness to fall upon them within a little time."[16]

•

While the British, like the French before them, were always a little too eager to see European influences at work among the Indians of the *pays d'en haut*, Odawa at Waganawkezee and elsewhere were happy to exploit these fears to get what they wanted from the British. At the same time, they drew on their older relations with French and Métis kin to ensure their trade and diplomatic needs were met. They made full use of intermarried families such as the Langlades in the 1760s during the transition in European relations. As one British official complained later, he was forced to let Langlade's nephew accompany a group of Indians because they "declare they cannot do without him, as he speaks their language, and is thoroughly acquainted with their customs, manners, etc." These families played a crucial role in mediating both Odawa-English and Indian-French relations. In turn, not only did these families enjoy a privileged position in Anishinaabe trade networks, but they also helped expand such networks—thus extending the influence of the Waganawkezee Odawa.[17]

Once again the Langlades provide insight into how this worked. Just before the start of the Second Anglo-Indian War of 1763, knowing that British traders would soon swamp the Michilimackinac post, Charles and Augustin Langlade made plans to leave Michilimackinac and live instead at Green Bay. The move suited the Langlades because they had long maintained an interest in the region and were well aware of the importance of the site in attracting trade from all around the Wisconsin area. At Green Bay, Langlade and his relations could capitalize on the presence and trade of the five thousand or more Native Americans who, by 1763, were living in the Fox–Wisconsin River region alone. And when trade at Michilimackinac was suspended or conducted on unfavorable terms, Indians from all around Lake Michigan could and did resort to Green Bay to trade furs to supply their needs. One estimate puts the number of Indians who used Green Bay to supply themselves with trade goods by 1762 at almost twenty thousand.[18]

The British never regarrisoned the post at Green Bay after James Gorrell abandoned it in 1763. Without an official post there, few British traders ventured into the area, at least to stay. It was too dangerous. English traders would struggle to prosper in the region without the kinds of connections with local Indians that the Langlades enjoyed by virtue of their relations with the Odawa. This meant the Langlades were perfectly poised to take advantage of both British trade via Michilimackinac and French trade via the Mississippi. If they could not get cheap goods from English merchants from the east, their long familiarity with the trade routes across Wisconsin meant they could supply themselves from French traders at Prairie du Chien, Fort Chartres, and Louisiana. As important, the Langlades could also capitalize on the higher prices sometimes offered for furs at New Orleans—which were often worth ten pence a pound more than the British were paying. The Mississippi fur trade flourished as savvy traders exploited the key portages from the Lakes to the Mississippi.[19]

Green Bay thus quickly became an important nexus for the western trade—if not one of the most profitable in the region. But the Langlades could capitalize on this trade only because their Anishinaabe kin networks allowed them access—and ensured they could trade in relative safety. Many of the Odawa at Waganawkezee had kin relations throughout the Green Bay region. They had a vested interest not only in protecting Langlade but also in keeping peace in the region. When conflict between an Ojibwe-Cree-Assiniboine alliance and the Dakota Sioux threatened to ignite in 1766–1767, for example, the Odawa stepped in to mediate. The Dakota Sioux were in a loose alliance with different groups of Fox, Sauk, Winnebago, and Menominee mainly along the Fox-Wisconsin waterway. This put the Odawa in a difficult position between the two sets of allies, since they had relations in both camps. The region teetered on the brink of war, but with their extensive kin relations emanating from Michilimackinac, the Waganawkezee Odawa held the key to resolution. Over a series of councils, the ogimaag along the eastern shore of Lake Michigan—including Nissowaquet and Manétewabe—brokered a peace.[20]

The Waganawkezee Odawa claimed they had done so in order to show a willingness in "serving the English," but they had other equally compelling reasons. Peace meant the road to the French remained open, via the Fox-Wisconsin waterway. Good relations with their western neighbors were vital to the Odawa's "new system of Politicks." Indeed, if the Langlades' move to the Bay was good business, it was also good politics for their extended Anishinaabe kin. The Langlades' position at Green Bay not only gave the Odawa especially further access to and influence over the numerous nations on the western side of Lake Michigan, but it also positioned them perfectly between Michilimackinac, French, and Spanish traders at Prairie du Chien and along the Mississippi. The British would come to depend on Charles Langlade to help manage their western affairs, but he also served as a conduit of information and intelligence between the Spanish and French and the Waganawkezee Odawa, as well as between them and the Menominee, Sauk, Fox, and Winnebago of the area. Much as his father, Augustin, had helped keep the road to Montreal and Trois-Rivières open for the Waganawkezee Odawa, Charles Langlade helped keep the western road open for his Odawa kin.[21]

Though the British suspected that men such as Langlade harbored conflicting allegiances, they could not do without them. As suspicious as they were of the French and Métis, the British quickly came to depend on them. Langlade had, of course, been one of the few people in the region the British thought they could trust. When Captain Howard arrived at Michilimackinac in 1764 to regarrison the post, he had orders to remove all the French and Canadians living there. But with few friends at the straits and surrounded by potentially hostile Anishinaabeg, Howard needed help. He was quickly convinced by French arguments that they had nothing to do with the uprising. He could hardly do otherwise. Howard told Campbell he would have to leave the French where they were, as he was desperate for their assistance in repairing the fort.[22]

Yet Howard also realized that at least some of the French and Métis were crucial in helping to manage Indian affairs at the post. Though the British did not trust them completely, there was no alternative. And men such as Langlade, who had shown their worth at moments such as 1763, were particularly indispensable. As successive post commanders moved in at the straits, they counted on Langlade as if he were one of their own. Robert Rogers, for example, who had fought against Langlade and his Indian kin only a few years previously in the Champlain Valley, routinely consulted with him about affairs at the post and Indian relations. Rogers even trusted him with correspondence to other Indian agents and British officers.[23]

•

Langlade's dual role, of course, put his Odawa family in an enviable position. With their French and Métis kin in their midst and the Spanish and French to their west, the Anishinaabeg at Michilimackinac got what they wanted from the British: a full return to the political economy of the *pays d'en haut* that they had enjoyed under the French regime. They alternately bullied, threatened, and cajoled the British even while they protested their fidelity and made themselves indispensable in keeping peace throughout the region. Consequently, they forced the British to adopt French ways of trade and allow French and Canadians to continue to trade. And they were well rewarded for their efforts.

The leverage the Anishinaabe Odawa enjoyed at Michilimackinac can best be seen in their relations with successive British commanders at the post, and particularly in their fight to reestablish the crucial—and very particular—trade practices that had allowed the Odawa to flourish during the French regime. While they were pleased with the arrival of Captain Howard in late 1764 and cheered by seemingly new British attitudes and policies, Odawa celebrations were short-lived. Howard made it clear that the reopening of trade came with two important and related provisions: no longer would traders be allowed to winter over with the Indians, nor could they supply the Indians with goods on credit. William Johnson, mindful of the problems that unlicensed and unregulated traders posed in his own backyard, wanted to keep the trade under strict regulations and to oversee it at the major posts. He believed the only way to maintain a lasting peace with the Indians was to ensure that trade was conducted fairly. To achieve that end, Johnson thought trade had to be conducted under the watchful eyes of the post commanders and Indian agents. The giving of credit, he thought, had precipitated too much conflict. Unscrupulous traders would ply the Indians with alcohol on credit and then give low prices for the pelts and skins they brought in return in the spring. There was too much room for abuse that Johnson thought would inevitably lead to conflict.[24]

Johnson's thinking did arise from Indian complaints about traders, but mainly from those farther to the south who had to deal with the English. Accordingly, these regulations were ill suited to the customs and conditions of the trade at Michilimackinac that had evolved over many decades of exchange with the French. While Johnson was beginning to understand the politics of the *pays d'en haut*, he still seemed in the dark about the nuances of northern trade practices. In the first place, the extending of credit was part of a developed and sophisticated set of practices that arose because of the need to winter away from summer residences. At the start of the long winter, hunters and trappers needed an ample source of provisions to sustain themselves and their families through the coming season. Some may have been happy to accept alcohol, but the large majority took mostly clothing, blankets, and hunting tools. They had come to expect these provisions on credit, to be paid back on their return from their hunts in furs and hides. There were clear advantages for the Anishinaabeg. Having been given credit for their goods in the autumn, Indians returned from their winter hunts in debt to traders, a debt that they usually settled through the exchange of furs. But it also meant they had a guaranteed buyer for their goods. Though Johnson worried this meant the Indians were liable to be swindled, Anishinaabeg and others trading at Michilimackinac well knew where the balance of power lay. Many traders had married into Indian families and so were less likely to try to deceive them. Yet even if they were not so intimately related, in the fluid, connected, and Indian-dominated world of the straits, a trader offered poor prices at his peril.[25]

Yet the issue of credit was also a political one, particularly when it came to admitting incoming British traders into the region. Credit was intimately tied to any new relationship the northern nations might forge with the British. The extension of credit was a sign of great trust and thus a starting point for good relations with newcomers. The Anishinaabeg also saw unpaid debt as an anchor for a continuing reciprocal relationship. In starker terms, everyone knew that a creditor would protect the interests of those in debt to him—especially when there were no real powers to enforce the payment of debts. While in debt to traders and merchants at Michilimackinac, Indians out on their winter hunts would be assured of a safe reception upon their return and would know that their creditors would protect their interests in their absence. The English trader Alexander Henry had to learn this lesson when the Odawa had confronted him on his arrival at Michilimackinac in 1761. Their main demand was that he issue his goods to them on credit. They were testing him. Though Henry failed this first exam, he soon learned what was expected. A couple of years later, when he set out for the unfamiliar waters of Lake Superior, he repeatedly encountered Indians who promised to hunt for him, but only on condition that he advance credit for their necessities to them. Henry extended credit.[26]

•

The practice of traders wintering over with the Anishinaabeg was also a critical issue for the Odawa at Michilimackinac. It, too, had its basis in the reality of the northern winter hunts. Anishinaabeg at places like Waganawkezee traveled far to undertake their winter hunts, usually away from French or British posts and into more remote regions. Wintering with a trader meant immediate access to replacement goods if the necessity arose. Without these replacements, a damaged weapon or lost knife could mean the difference between life and death. It would certainly make the difference between a good and a bad hunt. Moreover, as Robert Rogers noted, accompanying traders acted as a spur to those out on the hunt. Given their still-limited need of European goods, Rogers thought that, on average, Indians would bring in to the posts only about two-thirds of the pelts and skins they now traded to the British if no traders accompanied them.[27]

Other traders agreed with him. Though we often assume Native nations were dependent on Europeans by the middle of the eighteenth century, traders and merchants believed that without a steady supply of consumer goods, the Indians would "not kill a quarter part of the beaver etc. but only hunt for sustenance and a few skins to make themselves cloathing." The Odawa from Waganawkezee got most of their needs supplied through gifts and the provisioning trade at Michilimackinac, so there was little incentive to keep hunting for trade purposes through the winter. Still others far distant from the post would also not bother to amass large quantities of pelts if they did not have accompanying traders. Rogers knew that some Indians complained they had no conveyances with which to bring their furs and pelts to the posts, and many were reluctant in times of war to leave their families behind in the springtime to travel to the posts. Having a trader nearby would not only encourage them to hunt or trap through the winter, but it would also obviate the need for Indians to bring their goods to a post in the spring.[28]

What we often forget is that traders were almost always dependent on the Indians. Food and provisions were scarce at posts such as Michilimackinac over the long winter. And it was expensive to haul enough goods from Montreal or purchase them in advance. British traders quickly learned that the key to staying in the *pays d'en haut* over the harsh months was to winter with an Indian family. Even French post commanders had sometimes taken to wintering over with the Indians because they had a better chance of surviving the winter. In return for their trade goods, their Native family would ensure the trader had enough to eat and enough pelts to stay warm. As many a French trader had learned, the best way to secure a winter refuge was to marry into Native families.[29]

In part because of this dependence of traders on their Indian connections, Johnson, Rogers, and others quickly came to realize there was more than just economics or even survival involved. Under the French regime, traders, and especially those wintering over with Indians, often mediated relations between the Odawa and French officials. French or Métis traders such as Langlade often spent the long winter months among their kin, or their trading partners. The closer the relationship, the more mutually beneficial it was. Traders were privy to discussions among members of different doodemag over the winter. They acted as vital conduits of information.[30]

In theory, at least, traders could also represent official European interests far from the outposts of empire. More often, wintering traders acted in the interest of the relationship they had with the family, or families, with whom they lived or into which they had married. As the British Indian agent George Croghan noted in 1765, the French and Indians had been "bred up together like Children in that Country, & the French have always adopted the Indians Customs & manners, Treated them Civily & supplyed their wants generously." Sometimes, as in the case of Langlade and others like him, General Thomas Gage's observation that the French had become "almost one People with them" was literally true. Yet even traders who were not related by blood had a vested interest in protecting and nurturing the Indians.[31]

Though the British tended to idealize the relationship between French and Indians and to think these kinds of relationships suited imperial interests, French officials themselves of course had constantly complained about the "interior French." Rarely could these traders be counted on to carry out orders from French officials. Most often they acted in the interests of their Indian families. Traders were loath to jeopardize a trust that may have taken years to build for the sake of orders emanating from Versailles or Quebec. The long history of rocky relations between the Anishinaabeg and French officials is testimony to the fact that traders in their midst rarely worked on behalf of imperial interests. On the other hand, however problematic they sometimes were, these close relationships may have been the only thing holding together French and Anishinaabe interests at all. But it was more accurate to say that the Anishinaabeg and other Algonquians in the *pays d'en haut* maintained relations with French traders and not with the French empire.

The politics behind these crucial trading relationships formed at least part of the reason for Johnson's objection to the practice of wintering over. He believed that those most likely to be invited out to winter over with the Indians were the traders most unlikely to keep British imperial interests at heart, whether they be Frenchmen or English. Johnson knew that only those with close connections and ties to the Indians could survive a winter with them. While there were a few new English traders who appeared to adapt quickly to Indian ways of trading and secure their trust, by and large the majority of those who wintered over with Indians were long-established French or Métis traders such as Langlade. They either kept trading themselves or worked for English merchants who knew the French were key to the trade. For merchants, this made good economic sense and made their lives easier even if they sometimes could not trust their agents. But Johnson and Gage believed the practice was bad for the business of empire. They assumed that even those French employed by the English simply represented their own interests with the Indians. Invariably, the British would be blamed for any trouble.[32]

Thus, the finer details of northern trade practices were about much more than trade itself. The practices were a vital part of the diplomatic and political process. Though Johnson and other British officials were often concerned about traders having undue influence over the Indians, the Indians themselves saw traders as crucial in gaining influence over Europeans. As a later British officer complained about Langlade, "he can refuse the Indians nothing they can ask, and they will loose nothing for want of asking." The closer their relations with traders, the more reliable was Indian information about the posts, official policy, and British strategic interests. Winter traders with close relations to the Indians would more likely act in their best interest when dealing with Indian agents or post commanders. At the very least, many Anishinaabeg could and did use these relationships to pass along news—and rumors—to the British, whether welcome or unwelcome, in order to gain political and diplomatic leverage. Indeed, this was precisely how the Anishinaabeg and others manipulated their relations with the French.[33]

•

Anishinaabe strategies to reinstate credit and wintering over help illuminate the new-old politics of the *pays d'en haut*. Johnson simply assumed that European traders provided the main impetus behind efforts to undermine his new trade policies. Subsequent historians have reproduced his faulty assumption. In their eyes, it was another example of the undue influence that traders had over the Indians. But it was the Anishinaabeg and other Indians who traded at the post that called the shots. Traders, French or English, could not and would not have gone out to winter among the Indians if they were not welcome

and encouraged. William Leslye, the British post commander at Michilimackinac, had learned this lesson before the outbreak of the Second
Anglo-Indian War. In a council with Leslye, the Odawa demanded
winter traders and told him it was "always Custommary for the french
to send traders to Winter With them." Leslye, amid swirling rumors of
an imminent attack on the post, conceded.[34]

On the arrival of Captain Howard in 1764, the Anishinaabeg and
other visiting parties of Indians again besieged the new post commander with requests to allow traders among them. Howard quietly
allowed at least one English trader, Edward Chinn, to go out with the
Odawa. He may have secretly allowed other French and English traders to go as well. The following year, the flood of cheap goods from
Albany and Montreal that accompanied the official reopening of the
trade brought hundreds of northern Indians down to Michilimackinac. They, too, added to the demands of the Indians at the straits to
allow traders to go back home with them. Howard had to decide
whether to follow official British policy or not.[35]

The Anishinaabe Odawa gave Howard plenty of reasons to disobey
his orders. As he settled into Michilimackinac, the Odawa alarmed him
with rumors of possible conspiracies. While wintering over with the
Odawa, Edward Chinn, too, heard many wild stories: the St. Joseph's
Potawatomi were reportedly in touch with the French via the Mississippi; fifty canoes of Ojibwe had gone to the Illinois and found plenty
of rum at Chicago; and 50,000 livres' worth of goods had gone out to
the nations in and about Green Bay from French traders now in Spanish territory across the Mississippi. The Odawa ogimaa Manétewabe
even told Howard that while wintering over at the Grand River he
heard talk that the French had retaken Quebec and Trois-Rivières and
would soon come up the Mississippi.[36]

In order to manipulate Howard to their advantage, the Waganawkezee Odawa alternately spread rumors of war and assured him of their
peaceful intentions. The continued uncertainty of British relations
with the nearby Ojibwe and the more distant Potawatomi helped
increase the importance of the Odawa to post commanders such as
Howard. He felt isolated at Michilimackinac, and uneasy about the
sincerity of the Ojibwe. Throughout 1765 he talked to them, but he
did not trust them. Howard's main informant, a Frenchman named

Marsac, kept him on his toes with reports that Indians from the Grand River planned to attack English traders on Lake Erie, and that the Odawa who made peace at Detroit the previous year were plotting another pan-Indian uprising. War belts were in motion again, and the "great Chief of the Chippaweighs [Ojibwe]" intended to strike somewhere as "soon as the *Strawberries are ripe.*" The Odawa also told an English trader wintering over with them that the French from Illinois supplied the Indians as far north as Green Bay with everything they wanted. Amid these troubling reports, Howard sighed with some relief that the "Odawas near me, seem inclinable for Peace," and he loaded them with presents to keep them that way.[37]

Odawa strategy paid dividends during a series of Indian councils throughout June 1765. Eighty canoes of Indians from Lake Superior and its tributaries came in and thirty more were rumored to be on their way. For many of them, it was their very first meeting with the British. They reached the straits just as the Menominee and Winnebago from Green Bay along with all the Odawa and Ojibwe of the Michilimackinac region got there. John Porteous, a trader who had just arrived at the post, thought there were upward of eleven hundred to twelve hundred Indians at Michilimackinac in mid-June. The Odawa used the opportunity to show their influence and power in the region. During the councils, they brought out the covenant belt that Johnson had presented at Niagara for the first time, exhibiting it to the other nations. With the Odawa supporting reconciliation, Howard managed to persuade most nations present to swear their fidelity to the British and criticize the hostile Ojibwe. In return, though, the Odawa took the opportunity to push Howard to send traders out with them over the winter. With his nerves already stretched, Howard consented so as not to "offend them, and perhaps make them change their way of thinking." Without waiting for official sanction, he promised to send a select few traders out (mostly French), distributed a large number of presents, and clung to the hope that with these measures the "Indians will remain in our Interest." Howard told his superiors it was a strategic move: the traders would gather intelligence about the temper of all the Indian nations. Later, though, Howard confessed that he thought if he had not allowed the traders to winter with the Indians, "they would then have declared Warr."[38]

Stuck between the politics of the *pays d'en haut* and the dictates of empire, Howard had to improvise. It would cost him his job as post commander. As early as July 1765, Daniel Claus told Superintendent Johnson that it was whispered about Montreal that Howard had allowed some traders to go, and that he had shown great "partiality" in selecting them. The response from the rest of the trading community was fast and furious, and they effectively accused Howard of accepting bribes in choosing who would go out. But it is most likely that the Anishinaabeg had chosen who would accompany them. Though both Johnson and General Gage believed that Howard acted only with the "prudence" needed in such a delicate situation, and that the complaints arose purely from the "Resentment & Jealousy" of other traders, Howard was eventually forced to return to Montreal to face charges. Though acquitted, he was still reprimanded, and he never returned to Michilimackinac.[39]

Howard's successor at Michilimackinac, Robert Rogers, fared even worse. Within days of his arrival at the post in the summer of 1766, Rogers recorded in a detailed journal that the Odawa summoned him to a council at Waganawkezee. Once there, the Odawa reminded Rogers of their previous fidelity to the British but put him on notice. There were plenty of "bad birds flying from the West side of the Missisipi to this part of the World," they told him. Some were already among the Potawatomi at St. Joseph's. This was a none-too-subtle reminder of the murder of two English traders near the Rouge River thought to be killed by the Potawatomi. Nissowaquet made sure to repeat rumors that the French were assembling a force to come up the Mississippi, through the Great Lakes, and down to Niagara until they met another army landing in New York. He also showed an astute awareness of the colonial crisis sparked by the Stamp Act, which had been passed in Parliament in March 1765. The legislation precipitated public demonstrations, violence, and threats of violence all along the eastern seaboard, as groups calling themselves Sons of Liberty burned court records and attacked the homes of prominent British officials. The Odawa took note of the divisions in the colonies and—perhaps presciently—argued the French could invade "with great ease" because the "English people are divided in America, & more than one half of them will join the French."[40]

Having set the context in an unsubtle manner, Nissowaquet proceeded to business. He pressed Rogers to expand the practice of sending out traders. If he refused, the Odawa reminded Rogers they had alternatives. The French had sent strings of wampum from the Mississippi "inviting all the Indians to go there with thier furs & Peltry to trade with thier old fathers." Though Rogers scoffed at the Odawa for believing lies about a French invasion, he knew that the threat to trade with the French was only too real. So he listened. From the start, he was careful to meet with the Odawa regularly, and he always brought a good supply of presents. Despite the fate of his predecessor and his instructions, Rogers also consented to allowing a limited number of traders out on winter hunts.[41]

The following spring, in May 1767, Nissowaquet and other Odawa ogimaag continued to press their case. After returning from the winter hunt, Nissowaquet again demanded an audience with Rogers. The ogimaa took pains to note how the Odawa had kept the traders with them safe and well fed through the winter and had paid back all their credits. He even brought the traders to Michilimackinac himself to confirm this claim. Then, throughout the summer, Nissowaquet and the other ogimaag from Waganawkezee kept up pressure on Rogers by warning of great unrest in the west. That autumn, Rogers caved in once again on winter traders and effectively opened up the winter trade to all. He granted a total of seventy-seven wintering permits between July and August 1767 and two more in the following month, allowing 121 canoes out on the Lakes. Almost all the men who went out and wintered around Lake Michigan and Green Bay and points farther west were Frenchmen, though at least some were there on behalf of English merchants or traders.[42]

Rogers was convinced that allowing traders to winter over with the Indians would be the key to peace. Justifying his actions, he wrote that the Michilimackinac nations were unanimous on this front: "their principal Request of the Commandant is that Traders may come into their respective Countries, That their Wives, Children, Old Men Friends and Countrymen may be Supplied with such things as / having long been accustomed to the use of / they cannot comfortably and patiently Subsist without." By the time he wrote his defense, Rogers was preaching to the converted. As early as February 1767, while the

Board of Trade in London was again busily trying to work out a formal policy, General Gage had joined the chorus of arguments in favor of permitting traders from the northern districts to winter over with the Indians, admitting that Johnson's policy was not working. When Guy Carleton took over later in the year, he also argued for winter traders. By 1768, just as colonists on the eastern seaboard were coming to terms with a new round of onerous revenue-raising taxes passed by the British, the Odawa at Michilimackinac formally wrested key concessions from the Board of Trade. The Townshend Acts, which placed taxes on a number of essential goods including glass, paper, and tea, were in part designed to control and channel trade within the empire. Yet in that same year, imperial officials also loosened restrictions on the Indian trade. They formally recognized the wintering of traders and the giving of credit as a necessary part of the trade of the *pays d'en haut*.[43]

•

The decision of the Board came too late to save Rogers. In the autumn of 1767 he was arrested at Michilimackinac and taken to Montreal to face charges of treason. He had quarreled with several men at the post, including the new Indian agent, and left himself open to charges of conspiring with the French and Indians to plunder the post and of "retiring with his Booty to the French and Indians." His accusers noted that Nissowaquet was one of his chief co-conspirators. The lavish gifts he bestowed to appease the latter in particular were used as proof of his designs to win the favor of local Indians. Gage believed the expenditures over a few months were fourteen times the usual yearly sum spent at the post for Indian presents. Though acquitted by court-martial, Rogers could not escape the cloud of suspicion and was censured for his actions. He became another casualty of the politics of the *pays d'en haut*.[44]

While British officials in the east believed Rogers conspired with the French and Indians, those at Michilimackinac thought his hands were tied. Most of the traders at the straits backed up his story. The lavish presents given to the Indians were needed to bring stability and peace to the region. Indeed, some traders complained that Rogers had not been generous enough to visiting Indians. Further testimony at the court-martial supported his claims that generous gifts were necessary to prevent an inter-Indian war and to counter threats from the western nations to go over to the French and Spanish. In addition to the Odawa, the Ojibwe, Sauk, Fox, and Sioux had all made it known to him that they had been invited to trade with the Spanish and French along the Mississippi.[45]

Rogers's temporary successor as post commander, Captain Frederick Spiesmacher, thought there was something more afoot. To be sure, local Indians were unhappy about Rogers's arrest. He had been generous in giving out gifts. He had expanded the practice of wintering over in deference to Indian trade expectations. He knew the importance of Indian customs and diplomacy. He was one of the first British officers at Michilimackinac who acted as a good father. But then he had been arrested and confined even while still at Michilimackinac. The British could hardly have sent a more confused message to the Indians. Thus, while Rogers stewed under house arrest in the fort over the winter of 1767–1768, Indians across the region puzzled over how to respond and what they might expect in his absence. Just after his arrest, the Odawa headed for their winter hunting grounds, but not before Nissowaquet and another ogimaa sent out belts to neighboring nations to tell them about Rogers's arrest. Spiesmacher worried that this could trigger another war with the nations of the upper Lakes. The following spring, as the ice was breaking up and the Indians began to return from their winter hunts, Spiesmacher said he had "different informations from Indians of different nations," but the sum of it was that "the whole intending a War against us this Summer, and threatening to release Major Rogers from his Confinement." Initially, it seemed, the Odawa of Waganawkezee were at the center of this conspiracy.[46]

But by the time they returned to Waganawkezee, the Odawa at least appeared to have a change of heart, and instead acted as guardians of the British. Around May 18, Odawa from the Grand River and Waganawkezee came in to the post at Michilimackinac unarmed, headed once again by Nissowaquet and Manétewabe from Grand River. They warned Spiesmacher that "several nations had got giddy headed" and the English should be on guard, but the Odawa were "determined to hold a fast Friendship for us." Two days later, an

armed group of Ojibwe headed by the ogimaag Le Grand Sabre, Mon-
gamik, and Bonnais came in "much discontented" and made their dis-
satisfaction with the English clear. They invited the Odawa to feast
with them and join them in freeing "their Father Rogers" from confinement. The Odawa refused and left for Waganawkezee. Spiesmacher held a council with the Ojibwe, who were now considerably
cooled and, the commandant reported, peaceable. Of course, in his
report to his superiors, Spiesmacher added the inevitable: "These Disturbances have made a small additional Expence, which cou'd not be
prevented." One of Spiesmacher's officers thought this was the whole
point of the theater. He believed the Odawa had sent belts around the
Lakes in order to compel the British to restore not so much Rogers
personally, but someone like him: "We conjecter great presents is expected Nixt Spring," he concluded.[47]

Benjamin Roberts, who had taken up a post as commissary of Indian affairs at Michilimackinac in late March 1767, also struggled
with the demands of the job. Soon after he began his new assignment,
he told his boss, William Johnson, that Nissowaquet's house had
burned down. The ogimaa had come to him and reminded him that
Gage had promised that not even a dog belonging to the Odawa should
ever go hungry. But Roberts, who had accused Rogers of spending too
lavishly on the Indian presents, initially stood firm and told him he was
not authorized to give out provisions. Within a few months, however,
Roberts complained the upper nations continually threatened war
with each other, or spread rumors of possible conspiracies and happily
dropped hints about the possibility of renewed trade with the French
to the west. Roberts soon found himself "continualy in Councills."[48]

Roberts, too, was soon in trouble with British officials in Montreal.
By the middle of 1769, he told Johnson that the Odawa were insistent
in their demands for a commissary, interpreter, and blacksmith, and
he found it "impossible to throw off the Chief" as they continued to
"Visit me, beg so hard in your name for rum, & wheedle so much."
Roberts considered going out to trade with them so as to stop them
from coming to the post. Still, he concluded, "I am sure was I to
Attempt to follow trade they would still expect presents so that I am
at a loss what way of life to try." Roberts concluded with a plea that
would have made Rogers—the man Roberts had helped get censured—

laugh, or perhaps cry: "no person can be a judge of the Expence a Man is at, at this place who has no Kings provision but those that try it." Roberts complained to Johnson that Nissowaquet, or La Force, as he called him—the "Chief of the Ottawas"—was "the richest Indian I ever Saw."[49]

•

Roberts's complaints illuminated the central strategy employed by the Odawa during the early years of the British occupation. They drew on their western and French connections to add weight to their claims that conflict was imminent. Yet even as they circulated rumors of war to the west, the Anishinaabeg continued to preach peace. The Odawa at Waganawkezee especially claimed a privileged place in British councils as peacemakers and protectors of the newcomers. They played the role of good children and compelled the British to take the part of a good father. They also made it clear they had the influence to ensure the other nations would fall in line. When Rogers's permanent replacement, Captain Beamsly Glasier, arrived at Michilimackinac in the summer of 1768, the Odawa, led by Nissowaquet, came to see him. They laid down the rules. Reminding Captain Glasier of their part in the safe delivery of the garrison in 1763, they made it clear that he was there only at the pleasure of the Odawa. Nissowaquet told him that he and his troops could always "Sleep in Safety" because the Odawa would "watch over you." Good relations with the Odawa were vital to British security because they were "a check to all the Nations, whose harts are not True to the English." They had friends in all the villages who would tell them immediately if "any bad news is hered amongst any of the Villages." No one would attempt anything because it would be difficult to do without the Odawa knowing. In return, "as we are your Obedient Children, we expect to be used as Such." They made it very clear they expected Glasier to continue what was now a long European tradition of showering the Odawa with presents. They wanted rum, provisions, pipes, tobacco, and ammunition when they came to see him. They did not expect to be sent away dry or hungry.[50]

The Anishinaabeg stayed well fed. They did so even while the colonial crisis on the eastern seaboard lurched to a climax. The stationing of British troops in Boston in response to the resistance to the

Townshend Acts led to the Boston Massacre in 1770, in which five civilians died when soldiers fired upon them. At times it seemed the British were at war with their own colonists. In this context, as long as the Odawa at Waganawkezee kept the British in a constant state of alarm, they thrived. While enjoying the lavish presents and provisions of the British post commanders, the Odawa made a living, as they had done for many years, feeding the Europeans at the post—despite the best efforts of the British to render themselves independent of Indian supplies. The garrison at Michilimackinac struggled to grow enough on the dry, sandy, and barren soil—"a Mear Sand bank"—that surrounded the post. Indians from around the straits thus made a tidy profit on keeping them alive. Anyone wanting to stay at the post was dependent on the fish, corn, and dried and fresh meats that the Michilimackinac Indians brought to them. These included the many Indian traders who came into the post in the early summer laden with furs. The Odawa would greet both natives and newcomers with furs, skins, maple sugar, grease, and dried meats that they had prepared over the winter. They would trade these essentials with the growing numbers of traders returning from winter hunts or coming up from Montreal, and they kept on trading throughout the summer. Anishinaabe women at Waganawkezee especially took advantage of the "Verey Good Ground" they cultivated thirty miles from the post and grew "Corn Beens and meney articles which thay youse in Part themselves and Bring the Remander to Market." Meanwhile, Anishinaabe men continued to fish and hunt throughout the summer, since the woods were still full of partridges, hares, venison, foxes, raccoons, and wild pigeons, while the lakes and straits still yielded a massive bounty in fish. Traders and soldiers alike complained that the Anishinaabeg charged high prices for their goods. As Michilimackinac renewed its role as the center of a vast trading network—by 1766 even General Gage acknowledged that it was "the greatest Mart of Trade"—the Waganawkezee Odawa were still positioned to take continued advantage of their favorable situation.[51]

With their base once again secure and prospering, the Anishinaabe Odawa also continued to thrive and grow in numbers during this period. A later account of the settlement at Waganawkezee in 1779 referred to three distinct and well-established villages stretching for miles along the shoreline. It also named as many as nineteen different ogimaag in the settlement, including three Ojibwe and one Odawa of mixed French and Anishinaabe parentage. But Odawa growth went beyond the confines of Waganawkezee. Larger populations and the resources available meant that settlements continued to proliferate in this era. Unlike the new towns and cities in Europe, population growth in Anishinaabewaki was dispersed. New Odawa villages continued to spring up all along the eastern shore of Lake Michigan, at least as far south as the mouth of the Grand River. Both Odawa from northern Lake Michigan and Ojibwe from the Bay de Noc region (at the north end of Green Bay) also filtered southward along the Wisconsin shore of the lake, mixing with the Indians already there. Most of the evidence points to continued increase of Native populations in the central, western, and northern Great Lakes regions, and the Odawa were in the middle of that. The leading historical geographer of the region, Helen Hornbeck Tanner, has concluded that the Indian population of the Great Lakes had reached about sixty thousand by 1768, plus another twenty thousand or so who were peripheral to the Lakes but active in them. Tanner argues that across the central and northern Lakes region, the Native nations had achieved, or were in the process of achieving, long-term stability even while the nations of the southern Lakes were on the verge of rapid and violent alterations. At least as many as four thousand Odawa ringed the shores of Lake Michigan, along with another three thousand Potawatomi, while up to another fifteen thousand Ojibwe-Mississauga provided a buffer of sorts between the Odawa and their rivals to the south and northwest.[52]

At the same time, the British were also unable to do much about those they continued to blame the most for their troubled relations with the Indians: the French and Métis. The British constantly railed against the influence that men such as Langlade had over the Indians, but they could get no firm evidence from the Indians with whom they worked that would implicate them in wrongdoing. British frustration culminated in formal arguments for a forced removal of any non-Indians from the region. But the British knew they could not remove the French. The relationship of the French and Métis traders with their Native kin and allies stymied all British efforts. As one official noted, their "Influence over & Connection with the Indians will make it a Work of much difficulty to remove them." The Indians would "hardly consent," and it would likely be "productive of a Quarrel."[53]

Nor could the British afford to remove them, since they were dependent on them. Within a few years of taking over from the French, that dependence was recognized at the highest levels. By 1768, the new British governor of Quebec, Guy Carleton, gave orders to employ Canadians as guides and interpreters in the Indian department, offering lifetime positions, and pensions for widows. Carleton wrote approvingly of the "system pursued by the French government" and believed British success in the *pays d'en haut* and beyond would depend on the help of the French, "who are well acquainted with the country [and] the language and manners of the natives." A few years later, as he was facing an even greater threat in the form of rebellious colonists, Carleton praised the intermediaries who he believed were helpful to the British, but he singled out Langlade in particular. He was "a man I have had reason to be very much satisfied with," Carleton wrote, "and who from his influence amongst the Indians . . . may be [of] very much use to his Majesty's affairs."[54]

French and Métis traders like Langlade were thus able to hold their own in the early years of the British regime in the *pays d'en haut*. Not only did they compete with the British traders who flocked to Michilimackinac, but they also kept traders from the middle colonies at bay in the region south of the Lakes. Gage admitted in late 1766 that the English traders were hard-pressed to keep up with their French competitors because of the "long connections with those Indians and their better knowledge of their languages and customs, must naturally, for a long time give the Canadians an advantage over the English, which it is not improbable they will endeavour to improve, and use every artifice to keep the trade in their hands as long as they can." They did. One historian has argued that French merchants and French and Métis voyageurs, guides, interpreters, and traders dominated the northern fur trade through Michilimackinac for the next sixty years at least.[55]

•

Within a few years, then, the Anishinaabeg at Michilimackinac had brought the British to heel by force and persuasion. Not only had they restored a favorable trade at the straits, the Odawa also made Michilimackinac a central strategic and commercial site for the British. Thus, they made themselves key players within the British Empire.

Despite themselves, the British ended up as presiding over an imperfect imperial system very similar to the one they defeated in 1760. And as they quickly learned, this was not an easy relationship. The Anishinaabeg were more than happy to use any leverage they had to manipulate the relationship in their favor. Of course, this was what the Odawa and others had done to the French for years before—they used the threat of trade or alliance with the English (or indeed, other Indian nations) to get what they wanted from the French. Now the situation was reversed. A continental perspective helps us appreciate that when the British came to Michilimackinac, they, like the French, found themselves enmeshed in and dependent on an Indian world of diplomacy and trade that stretched both east and west from the straits.[56]

William Johnson was one of those who seemed to have learned some hard lessons since the English had inherited French claims in the *pays d'en haut*. The Indians were, Johnson wrote, a "free people who had independent Lands, which were their ancient possessions." They insisted the French occupied their posts only "by favour" and not by conquest, and by ceding Canada had "granted what was not in their power to give." If the Indians conceded any rights to the English, it was to the occupation of those forts only, and on the same terms as the French. They scoffed at English offers of "protection" and replied by saying they feared only each other, not Europeans. And they paid little heed to any terms of "submission"—they called themselves "no more than our friends and Allies." If the British wanted more than these tentative promises from the nations of the *pays d'en haut*, Johnson concluded—as many French officials had previously—they must have a "good army at his back, to protect them from their resentment."[57]

Yet Johnson reasoned that most of the nations of the *pays d'en haut* had little interest in seeing any group of Europeans defeated entirely and one victorious power seizing total control, for as they often said, "the White people were for reducing them to nothing," and both the French and English had the same aim. In that light, most Native nations instead "were desirous to preserve a kind of equilibrium between us, and inclined occasionally to throw their weight into the lightest scale." When the French occupied the posts, the Indians flirted with the English and used threats of going over to them to pursue their interests. Now that the British occupied the posts, the Natives were happy to practice the same manipulative flirtations with the French and Spanish on their flanks and in their midst. Some among them were heartier for one side or another, as Johnson noted, but most wanted to maintain a balance of power. This was little different from what Europeans did, Johnson noted. It was, he concluded, a way of thinking "so exactly correspondent with that of the most Civilized Nations."[58]

Yet while William Johnson fretted that the nations of the *pays d'en haut* wanted to maintain a balance of power, other British officials, already enmeshed in a seemingly intractable colonial crisis along the eastern seaboard, worried that the Indians were up to something much more sinister. General Gage noted that the Indians of the Lakes happily circulated rumors of invitations they had received encouraging them to join the French and Spanish against the English. They spread these rumors not only to gain leverage with the British, he thought, but also to deliberately provoke the British into another war: "I believe the Indians would be glad to embroil us," he noted, "as our Quarrells are generaly the Indian Harvests."[59]

Though ostensibly at peace with the British from 1764 onward, the Anishinaabe Odawa and others showed a great awareness of the tensions between Europeans that they could exploit. They were quick to report all news of Spanish and French intrigues and take advantage of any rumors of war in Europe or America. They were also happy to point out and exploit the divisions between British officials and their colonists. Ultimately, continued Indian agitation helped convince British officials to maintain the western posts to try to keep the Spanish and French from gaining too much influence in the region. They did so even as they abandoned Fort Duquesne and other posts in the Ohio Valley to cut costs.[60]

•

Of course, the spiraling expenses of maintaining the western posts helped keep the pressure on the British to reform their North American empire. The threat of further costly wars with the Native nations of the *pays d'en haut* also helped lead them to pass the Quebec Act in 1774. As well as protecting Catholicism in Quebec, the act defined and expanded the boundaries of the former French colony to include land that is now southern Ontario, Illinois, Indiana, Michigan, Ohio, and Wisconsin. It was designed to create a permanent reserve for Native Americans in the region and to keep English settlers and Indians apart. But to many British colonists, the act appeared again to protect the interests of Native Americans in these areas while permanently voiding the land claims of the colonists, especially to the Ohio region. Militant patriots throughout the thirteen English-speaking colonies quickly labeled it one of the "Intolerable Acts" of 1774 that helped launch the American Revolution. Parliament passed it just as they also imposed several punitive measures on the people of Massachusetts in response to the the Boston Tea Party of 1773. As Gage had predicted, Native Americans in the *pays d'en haut* would soon reap the "harvest" of another European "Quarrell."[61]

8

DEPENDENCE

Most Americans think of their revolution as a contest between Britain and its colonists. If Native Americans feature at all in popular ideas of this era, it is only in the role inscribed for them in the Declaration of Independence: as "merciless Indian Savages whose known rule of warfare, is an undistinguished destruction of all ages, sexes and conditions." Even in this assertion, they do not act independently. They are brought into play by the king, who was charged with endeavoring to unleash his savage allies upon "the inhabitants of our frontiers." With a few exceptions, even more recent historical narratives of the Revolution emphasize a kind of subsidiary role for Native nations on the periphery of the real action taking place along the eastern seaboard. And studies that do encompass the war in the west usually look no further than the contests over the Ohio Valley, and particularly George Rogers Clark's foray into the Illinois country. Scholars of Native American history have seen this period as one in which Indians could only make the best of a bad situation. They were faced with difficult choices about whether to support the colonists or the British, or to somehow stay out of the conflict altogether. Standard narratives emphasize the inevitable drift of most nations toward the British, and the price paid for this decision in the years after the patriot victory at Yorktown.[1]

Yet as we have seen, viewed from Indian country, Native Americans helped set into motion the chain of events that would lead to the Declaration of Independence. From skirmishes and conflicts in the Ohio Valley, to the Seven Years' War and the First Anglo-Indian War, and finally to the Second Anglo-Indian War in 1763, Native Americans in the *pays d'en haut* helped trigger and profoundly shape the contests that would define the geopolitical landscape of North America. As a consequence, too, the enormous costs of the Seven Years' War and the Second Anglo-Indian War, together with the need to placate Native Americans, meant that the British turned to the reformation of their colonial policy starting in 1763 to try to recover some of the costs of keeping peace with the Indians. In turn, many rebellious colonists, now freed from the threat of the French to the north, keen to avenge Native American violence in the recent wars, and eyeing the fertile lands of the Ohio Valley, resisted new imperial legislation and provoked another tragic war that eventually created a new nation.[2]

If viewing events from the perspective of Michilimackinac helps us understand the crucial part Native Americans played in the coming of the Revolution, it also complicates our understanding of their actions during the conflagration itself. For the Anishinaabeg and their extended kin among the nations of the Lakes, the Revolution proved another opportunity. Though we often think of these years as ones of increasing dependence of the Indians on Europeans, the Revolution made it clear that the future of the British Empire in the upper Lakes was dependent on the Indians. With the war in the east preoccupying the British, imperial outposts like Michilimackinac suddenly found themselves even more isolated, vulnerable, and reliant on their neighbors than they had been before the war. Moreover, while early in the conflict the British spent enormous sums to try to bring the western nations into an alliance, from about 1778 onward they had to spend that same money simply to keep the Indians from turning against them. By the end of the war, British officials believed the Indians were interested only in prolonging the conflict, and by any means necessary. But they could do little about it. While war raged in the east, Native Americans at the straits of Michilimackinac continued to hold the upper hand in the west. In doing so, they not only helped shape the contours of the conflict to their east, but they also ensured a place for themselves in the new nations that would result.

•

For many Native Americans, their own war for independence began in 1768. In that year, only five years after the Proclamation of 1763, William Johnson—in direct violation of orders from London— arranged for the Iroquois to cede lands south of the Ohio River for European settlement at the Treaty of Fort Stanwix. The Iroquois walked away from the treaty with £10,000. But the Shawnee and other Ohio Indians who contested Iroquois claims to that territory refused to recognize the treaty. As settlers poured over the mountains, many Native Americans prepared for war. By 1774, simmering tensions between settlers and Indians had exploded into frontier violence, which included an attack on a group of colonists led by Daniel Boone and the unprovoked killing of the relatives of the Mingo leader Logan. Once fighting had broken out, Lord Dunmore, the governor of Virginia, saw an opportunity to claim the region for his colony and the many speculators in it, as well as to quell colonial agitation against imperial legislation with a popular war. Dunmore led an infamous punitive expedition across the Ohio River in a conflict that would become known as Dunmore's War. The conflict was one-sided and short-lived, culminating in the Battle of Point Pleasant in which more than a thousand Virginia militia faced off against some three hundred warriors under the Shawnee chief Cornstalk. Though the English lost some 75, and had another 140 wounded, against 40 Indian warriors killed, Dunmore managed to force a peace on the Ohio nations. It would not last long.[3]

Though far removed from events on the Ohio, Anishinaabeg at Michilimackinac watched the conflict unfold with some concern. William Johnson's part in negotiating the treaty was especially worrying. Even as talk of heated divisions between Britain and its colonists reached the *pays d'en haut*, new settlements and Dunmore's War were an ominous sign of growing British power and their willingness to use it once again against the Indians. On the other hand, while many Anishinaabeg north of Detroit were suspicious of broken British promises, it was not immediately apparent whether it would be worse to have English colonists or even more ancient enemies such as the Catawba living south of the Ohio River. The presence of British squatters might prove a salutary buffer between the northern Anishinaabeg and their southern rivals.

Nor was it entirely clear that the Anishinaabeg needed to do anything for the moment. Even before Dunmore's War started, reports swirled through Indian country that British warriors might soon be put to use against their own settlers. The Anishinaabeg were well apprised of the growing rift between Britain and its colonies. In May 1772, an Ojibwe reported that the only reason the nations of the *pays d'en haut* had not yet thrown out the British was that there was no hurry. They could bide their time and take advantage of colonial unrest to the east. Anishinaabe informants along the St. Lawrence Valley told them they should all wait a year or two in peace. Then there would be war. At the very least, the Odawa at Michilimackinac well knew that British dependence would only increase during another conflict between Europeans. In that case, the rent the British paid for maintaining posts in the Lakes could go up as well. As Gage had noted, war between Europeans could be profitable for Native Americans.[4]

The Odawa at Waganawkezee made their position clearer immediately upon the arrival of the latest British post commander, Arent Schuyler De Peyster, in July 1774. A few days after he reached the straits, Nissowaquet and several other ogimaag paid him a visit. Though they reaffirmed their commitment to peace with the British, Nissowaquet also reminded De Peyster of the cost of peace. The ogimaa showed De Peyster a belt he had received. Deliberately vague, Nissowaquet said he thought it came from the Mohawk and represented harmful plans against the British. Nissowaquet reminded De Peyster of his obligations to nations such as the Odawa who maintained the peace. But he also pointed out that it was not easy to do so. Pro-British ogimaag could maintain their influence over their warriors and kin—and other doodemag—only with generous presents. Those presents were arguments in favor of good relations with the British. And with war threatening on the Ohio and in the eastern settlements, there were risks involved in allowing the British to maintain the post at Michilimackinac. The Anishinaabeg needed more insurance. Later that same day, a courier brought an oral message from Louis

Chevalier at Fort St. Joseph to say the Potawatomi had received belts from the Delaware. They were looking for allies in their conflict with the Virginians. With the Ohio alight with news of Dunmore's War against the Shawnee and Delaware, De Peyster quickly realized—like many others before him—that he was in a precarious position at Michilimackinac.[5]

Nissowaquet and the other ogimaag and warriors who visited the post made an impression on De Peyster. The new commander was well aware that colonial resistance on the eastern seaboard had reached a boiling point with the Boston Tea Party in 1773. As he arrived at the post, colonists were just facing up to a raft of retaliatory measures against the port of Boston and the colony of Massachusetts. De Peyster also knew that Governor Dunmore was mobilizing for war on the Ohio. He could not afford to make any more enemies. The new commandant set about mastering the politics of the *pays d'en haut* with a vigor not seen since Robert Rogers had taken charge. He held numerous councils with the Indians, and he was generous with presents. He quickly realized the importance of key figures at Michilimackinac and their connections across the Lakes. He especially acknowledged the importance of those who had married into Indian families, and he tried to co-opt them. Taking advantage of Quebec governor Guy Carleton's 1768 recommendation that Canadians be employed as guides and interpreters in the Indian Department, and his offer of lifetime positions and pensions for widows, De Peyster expanded the Indian Department at the straits. Then, as war between the British and the colonists broke out in Massachusetts in April 1775, De Peyster recruited Langlade as an agent in the British Indian Department, believing he had great influence with the Indians in the region.[6]

•

De Peyster's efforts seemed to pay off in the early years of the war. Indeed, the Anishinaabeg and other Algonquians in the region gave the British some reason to hope they could count on their native neighbors as allies. Shortly after fighting broke out at Lexington and Concord, some of the newly formed Continental Army had headed north to invade Canada. They hoped to gain control over the strategic St. Lawrence River and persuade French colonists to join them. They took Montreal in November 1775 and then made for Quebec City. Charles Langlade, his nephew Charles Gautier, and the fort interpreter, Joseph-Louis Ainsse, went out to "beat up for Indian Volunteers" to aid the desperate British. Odawa and Ojibwe warriors headed toward the Ottawa River on their return from their winter hunts and were soon followed by a group of Green Bay Indians traveling with Langlade. But by the time they arrived in Montreal in the late summer of 1776, the siege of Quebec had ended dramatically with the death of Major General Richard Montgomery, and the patriot army was in full retreat back through the Champlain Valley.[7]

The British—who of course had never had much success in mobilizing Indian allies—were buoyed by the initial reaction of some of the ogimaag and warriors of Michilimackinac and Green Bay. They had had little success in bringing the Iroquois into the war against the Americans, so they were even more grateful for the support of the Odawa and their kin. As the Anishinaabeg traveled through Montreal, the British laid on generous presents and hosted numerous councils and lavish feasts. The Odawa also extracted promises from Carleton to send up more presents to the posts and requested a belt be made up for the occasion. In return, the commander invited Langlade and some of his kinsmen to ally with him in pursuit of the retreating rebels. In early October, Langlade joined Carleton on board the ship *Maria* just before the naval battle of Valcour Bay on Lake Champlain, where the British inflicted heavy damage to the fledgling American fleet newly assembled under General Benedict Arnold. Though a "large Detachment" of western Indians in birch bark canoes accompanied the British during the skirmishing, Langlade—perhaps ailing—departed before the battle. Still, he and his native allies obviously impressed Carleton, who wrote several letters of recommendation for Langlade.[8]

Under the circumstances, the British were pleased and more than a little relieved by this first test of the allegiances of the nations of the northern *pays d'en haut*. By the end of 1776, skirmishing with rebel militia had given way to a full-blown war with the former colonies, who had declared independence in July. The British then retaliated for getting ousted from Boston earlier in the year by taking New York City in the autumn. Given their relative success in recruiting Indians for the 1776 campaign, British officials confidently predicted

Habit of an Ottawa, an Indian Nation of N. America, c. 1772. From *A collection of the dresses of different nations, ancient and modern, particularly old English dresses*, Vol 4: Plate 197 (Art and Architecture Collection, Miriam and Ira D. Wallach Division of Art, Prints, and Photographs, New York Public Library, Astor, Lenox, and Tilden Foundations)

that more Indians would join them the following year. But flushed with new expectations, they made the mistake of counting on it. Carleton told De Peyster he had authorized Langlade to bring down two hundred "chosen" Indians from the upper Lakes, and ordered the commandant at Niagara to ready all the Indians of his neighborhood to take the field early in the spring. The superintendent of Indian affairs at Detroit, Lieutenant Governor Henry Hamilton, also wrote with some relief that a large council of Indians there had decided against joining the rebels and would likely launch attacks on the frontier. Finally, De Peyster wrote early in the spring of 1777 that he had seen many Indians over the winter at the post at the straits and all were well inclined. He thought the biggest problem they would face in the coming months would be stopping too many Indians from joining the campaign. "Such as are prevented," he warned, "will take it ill."[9]

•

Reading these reports in London, Lord George Germain—the secretary of state for America—concurred with Carleton's suggested plans for the new year and ordered the "most Vigorous efforts" against the colonists in March 1777. In an attempt to take advantage of what seemed like Indian promises to help, these plans included outfitting war parties at Detroit to attack and alarm the colonial frontiers. But when General John Burgoyne took command of the war effort in Quebec in the spring of 1777, the British increased their reliance on their Native allies even further. Burgoyne hatched a plan for a major expedition through the Champlain Valley–Hudson River corridor in the hope of driving a wedge between the New England colonies, who the British thought were the primary agitators in the conflict, and the rest of the colonies. Burgoyne's plans depended on a thousand Indian warriors to act as scouts and advance raiding parties to cow the inhabitants into submission. In making his plans, Burgoyne may have recalled French success along the same route in the Seven Years' War that had culminated in the fall of Fort William Henry in 1757. Significantly, Germain in London believed that Burgoyne's plan "cannot be advantageously executed without the assistance of Canadians and Indians."[10]

But Burgoyne and the British high command overestimated their ability to mobilize their allies. Even as British officials in the east planned their coming campaign around an expectation of native support, the Anishinaabeg and others were still weighing their own options. They had already made their ambivalence clear to officials in the *pays d'en haut*, including De Peyster. As the post commander sent out agents to drum up support for the campaign along the St. Lawrence in 1775 and 1776, he also fortified the post to prevent an attack by Indian neighbors. And at least part of the reason he acted so quickly to mobilize the Indians at Michilimackinac in late 1775 was that he feared the initial bad news about the fall of Montreal would push many Indians into the rebel camp. He wanted to involve them before they turned on the British.[11]

Yet while the British were impressed by the response of the nations from Michilimackinac and Green Bay, that response was mixed given the number of warriors in the *pays d'en haut*. The interpreter at the post, Joseph Ainsse, managed to cobble together only a small force. Langlade's numbers were not large, either. Not all Indians were eager to go to Montreal. A group passing through Sault Ste. Marie on their way to Michilimackinac had stopped short of the post, "being afraid that application would be made to them to join the others who are going to Montreal." Nor were the loyalties of those who went beyond suspicion, either. At least some among the party were as curious to know more about this new civil conflict between the British as they were to fight against the rebels. They left Michilimackinac believing Montreal was still in rebel hands, and Quebec had likely been taken, too. Many wanted to see for themselves what was going on in the St. Lawrence Valley. It was a reconnaissance mission. Some reports noted that those who had returned from Montreal had spent time with kin at the Lake of Two Mountains gathering intelligence and ignoring rebel war parties.[12]

After the initial foray in 1776, most Native Americans in the *pays d'en haut* spent the winter further debating their options. British success in repelling the rebel attack on Quebec the previous year gave succor to some of the pro-English *ogimaag* in their ranks but worried others. Though few likely favored an alliance with the hated colonists, many—with memories of the Anglo-Indian wars still fresh—would have worried about an all-too-powerful English father. The situation was further complicated by a renewed Spanish effort to exploit the conflict in the British colonies. Spanish officials had begun to circulate belts and agents among the nations of the *pays d'en haut* calling for increased trade and more formal alliances. With the nearest British troops now at Detroit and Michilimackinac and officials preoccupied with events to the east, the Spanish saw this as a good chance to test the waters with the Indians. By 1777, they had made inroads among the Sauk and Fox, and thought they could yet win over the Odawa, Ojibwe, and Menominee of the Lakes. Under the circumstances, many Anishinaabeg believed the best policy was to sit on their mats for the ensuing summer. Some wanted to wait and attend a council called by the Iroquois in the spring of 1777. An outbreak of smallpox in the Michilimackinac area over the winter confirmed many in their decision to wait and see.[13]

Even well-connected go-betweens such as Langlade struggled to recruit warriors in these circumstances. Langlade had finally made it back to Michilimackinac in February 1777 after a brief winter sojourn with the Odawa on the Grand River. Upon Langlade's return, De Peyster asked him to start recruiting warriors for the coming campaign. British plans now depended on large numbers of Indian allies joining them, and though De Peyster was initially confident the warriors could be raised, he had grown concerned when Langlade and other recruiters were slow in coming back to the post. On April 18, 1777, he sent eighty pounds of tobacco and two barrels of whisky to Green Bay to help Langlade recruit there, and he warned that if the Indians were to help Burgoyne, they had to move immediately.[14]

But few of the nations of Green Bay or Michilimackinac were in the mood to help. It simply was not clear the campaign was in their best interests. Langlade only got back from Green Bay in early June, accompanied by a mere sixty warriors. He was hopeful there were more coming, since Gautier (his nephew) was recruiting farther west among the Fox and Sauk. Yet De Peyster fretted they would arrive far too late to be effective in that summer's campaign. Instead, he "completed" Langlade's contingent with a small group of Anishinaabeg from Michilimackinac and readied them to leave by June 4. But even these warriors threatened to leave before De Peyster could send them on. The Waganawkezee Odawa had news that Spanish agents had been among their neighbors, which De Peyster feared would make them "rather more difficult to move than I expected." His worries were realized when a large group of Menominee left without saying a word shortly after Langlade departed.[15]

De Peyster grew frantic. Under the circumstances, he had to forget past transgressions and accept any help offered, even that of a group of St. Joseph's Potawatomi who had still not made reparations for killing two British traders. He also had to rely on help from Charles Gautier. Though Carleton warned De Peyster to watch Gautier because his loyalties were suspect, the commander could not hide his relief when Gautier arrived at the post accompanied by a war party of Sauk and Fox, along with a group of traders who sang his praises. Even Gautier's enemies admitted that in the very face of Spanish agents and rebel belts he was the only person who could have recruited warriors for the British. De Peyster sent him to Carleton and noted he should be forgiven for any past indiscretions. But the British had no choice, really. De Peyster confided to Carleton that "in so doing, I comply with the earnest request of the Indians, who declare they cannot do without him, as he speaks their language, and is thoroughly acquainted with their customs, manners, &c."[16]

Despite the enormous sums expended by the British to recruit Indians, and despite the cheery promises of the previous autumn, Langlade and only a few pro-British ogimaag and curious warriors straggled into Montreal in July 1777. There they joined a combined Indian force under fellow French veteran Luc de La Corne. The sixty-six-year-old La Corne had commanded at Michilimackinac during the French regime and he and Langlade had served together at the siege of Fort William Henry in 1757. Yet in stark contrast to that earlier campaign, Langlade and La Corne together managed to bring only about a hundred Odawa and other western Indian warriors with them. While British officials in Montreal and London remained optimistic that the alliances of their western neighbors would prove the making of their campaign in 1777, those on the ground were relieved they could send as many warriors as they did.[17]

•

During Burgoyne's ill-fated expedition along the Champlain Valley–Hudson River corridor in 1777, British officials in London learned just how dependent they were on Indian help. Langlade's group managed to catch up to Burgoyne at Skenesborough, a small village located at the southern end of Lake Champlain. The general had set out in mid-June and by the end of the month had reached the patriot-held post of Ticonderoga (formerly the French Fort Carillon). Within a few days, the rebels abandoned the fort and fell back to Fort Edward (about twenty miles southeast of Fort William Henry). Burgoyne moved to Skenesborough, twenty-three miles away, and waited for reinforcements. When Langlade and La Corne joined him there on July 12, Burgoyne had perhaps another four hundred Indian warriors with him, including a diverse mix of Iroquois, Algonquians, Abnaki, and some Odawa and Huron from Detroit. For the British, whose relations with Native Americans had never been easy, it was a good turnout. But it fell far short of expectations. Most Native Americans from the Lakes were content to watch events unfold. Instead, they got on with the business of hunting and trading.[18]

They would have been glad they did. The British mismanaged their native allies from the start. At Montreal, Langlade and his kin learned that British commissary officers—not those accompanying Indians from the Lakes—had been put in charge of the distribution of provisions. Neither the Anishinaabeg nor their accompanying officers were happy about this arrangement; it rendered them too dependent on the British officers. Then, as soon as Langlade's group joined Burgoyne, the temperamental general held a council with them and tried to lay down some rules. Though pleased with their presence, he urged them to act with restraint. He asked them to bring in prisoners alive, and to scalp only those who had fallen in battle.[19]

Yet while Burgoyne preached restraint to the Indians, he was quick to exploit their presence to terrorize wavering rebels. He had issued a proclamation as early as June 20 warning colonial inhabitants that he had "Thousands" of Indians waiting for his word to attack. Once Langlade joined him, he told the loyalist governor of New York, Philip Skene, to spread the word among rebel sympathizers specifically that Langlade and the Odawa had come to fight. He wanted Skene to announce that "Five Hundred Savages from the upper nations are arrived under Langlade and St. Luc the two most famous officers of the last war." Burgoyne had heard the rumors of Langlade's participation in the Seven Years' War; perhaps Langlade had boasted of it himself.

Burgoyne told Skene to make it clear that Langlade was "the very man who projected and executed with these very nations the defeat of General Braddock." The general announced he would use his native allies "to prevent, if possible, by their terror" the retreating rebels from destroying roads and burning supplies in their wake.[20]

Burgoyne was playing a dangerous game with his Native allies. Warriors accompanying the expedition at first did exactly what Burgoyne intended, spreading panic in front of the advancing British expedition. They also seemed to abide by European rules. Shortly after Langlade's arrival, the Odawa took part in a skirmish with the rebels and brought back prisoners unharmed. But a little later, Burgoyne heard of the murder of Jane McCrea. Though the details of this event are still murky, what is known is that on July 27 a Huron party seized Jane McCrea, a colonial woman engaged to an officer in Burgoyne's army, as she was being escorted back to British lines. By the time they got to the British camp, she had been killed and scalped. The Huron claimed the rebels had shot her while they were bringing her back, and they had scalped her only after her death. Other reports said that two warriors fought over who would bring her in as a prisoner; unable to resolve the conflict, one of them had killed her.[21]

Whatever the truth behind McCrea's murder, Burgoyne was furious with his Native allies. Later testimony claimed he immediately went to the Indian camp and called a council. There he threatened the suspected murderer with death and insisted the Indians deliver him up. The Huron protested that the rebels had shot her. There were heated exchanges. Burgoyne finally had to concede; "policy" meant he had to pardon the Huron. British dependence on their Native allies meant they could do little to calm the waters stirred by McCrea's death. The Earl of Harrington, with others, believed that had the British insisted on bringing those responsible to justice, the result would have been the "total defection of the Indians" with "dreadful" consequences on their return through Canada. They feared the Indians would simply side with the rebels and start attacking the British.[22]

Though Burgoyne had to back down, he made some critical errors that compromised the expedition. His Native allies, already chafing under the provisioning restrictions, were offended by Burgoyne's accusations and expressed "great resentment" at the council. But they

were appalled at Burgoyne's next move: he announced that British officers would have to accompany any future Indian patrols or scouts.
He made this announcement in spite of his promise that his allies
would be allowed to join him under their own captains and fight "in
their own way." Burgoyne now believed the Canadian officers were
behind the troubles, and he did not trust them, because they knew
the Native languages of his allies. Burgoyne missed the mark. His
Native allies were angry that the general tried to treat them as subordinates. In their eyes, they were not answerable to Burgoyne. They
had had enough. Some left the night of the council, others the following morning. Those who remained chafed at the new restrictions on
their movements. "From this time there was an apparent change in their
tempers," wrote one officer, "their ill humor and mutinous disposition
strongly manifested itself."[23]

To make matters worse, within a week or two of McCrea's murder,
reports of ferocious fighting at the Battle of Oriskany, near Fort Stanwix, began to reach Burgoyne's camp. Since the start of the war, both
the British and the patriots had tried to woo the Iroquois out of their
neutrality. By early 1777, the patriots had made some inroads, among
the Oneida especially, while the influential Mohawk leader Joseph
Brant helped bring most of the rest of the Iroquois into the war on the
British side. Burgoyne hoped to capitalize on this diplomatic success by
sending a diversionary force under Brigadier General Barry St. Leger to
the Mohawk River Valley to impress the Iroquois, clear out the rebels,
and join him at Albany. Some four hundred Iroquois (mostly Seneca,
Cayuga, and Mohawk) warriors joined him. As they laid siege to Fort
Stanwix, the combined force ambushed a rebel relief force, resulting in
one of the bloodiest battles of the Revolution. But for the Iroquois, the
result was even worse, as Oneida warriors were among the rebel troops
who had killed some thirty or more Seneca warriors. Though General
Burgoyne was interested only in the progress of St. Leger, his Indian
allies at Saratoga were perturbed to learn that less than one hundred
miles away, Iroquois warriors faced off against each other for the first
time in their history.[24]

Burgoyne's diplomatic bungling with his Native allies only made a
difficult situation worse. The story of Jane McCrea's murder was pre-
dictably exploited in the patriot press, helping to inspire the turnout of

thousands of New York and New England militia against Burgoyne in the midst of his campaign. In the face of this gathering storm, Burgoyne again miscalculated in the ill-conceived Battle of Bennington on August 16. On his slow march to Fort Edward, the general heard there were badly needed horses and supplies at Bennington. He sent 1,400 men, including 150 Indians under La Corne, to bring back what they could. But this party was surprised by an American counterattack. It was a disaster. The British lost almost a thousand men dead, captured, or wounded. Indian casualties were also high. Some reports put the number of Indian dead and wounded as high as eighty. La Corne simply said "many" were killed, along with a "Great Chief." Despite these losses, a desperate Burgoyne accused them and La Corne of deserting the field soon after the fighting began.[25]

The remaining Indian warriors and their leaders were fed up. After the battle, La Corne reported greater "discontents" among the Indians and called another council with Burgoyne. La Corne and Langlade and their Indian allies were angry at the way they had been deployed in the battle and wanted Burgoyne to cover their dead. La Corne accused Burgoyne of sending the Indians out too late and mismanaging them. In return, Burgoyne allegedly told them their losses were "trifling" and ignored their complaints. On August 19, the Odawa met with La Corne and Langlade and left, probably with Langlade. There is no further mention of Langlade or the Odawa in Burgoyne's records after the council. Fewer than a hundred Indian scouts remained with Burgoyne.[26]

The general would pay for the loss of his allies. Two months later, Burgoyne famously surrendered at Saratoga, and shortly after, the French entered the war on the rebel side. They had been waiting for some sign of patriot success before joining the conflict. It was the beginning of the end for the British. Yet it might not have been so. Most historians blame poor British coordination for the loss of Burgoyne's army, because he did not receive reinforcements from New York. But there were also other reasons for the surrender. The campaign against Fort William Henry in 1757 (only twenty-five miles from Saratoga) had shown how Native Americans could make a difference to the success of a military campaign. If the British had the support of as many Indians as the French enjoyed in 1757—and as many as Germain and

Burgoyne hoped would turn out when they planned the campaign—there might have been a different outcome to the British campaign of 1777. In turn, that would have changed the course of the Revolutionary War.

•

At the same time General George Washington settled into Valley Forge and took stock of the war at the end of 1777, the Anishinaabe Odawa also reassessed their situation over winter campfires in the *pays d'en haut*. Those few who had gone out in support of the British had been roughly treated. The dead had not been covered. They had not avenged their losses in the campaign, nor had the British given them adequate compensation. Now the traders talked of impending shortages, so the dead would likely remain uncovered. On top of that, the British had suffered a major loss, and they were already calling for more help in the spring. Few Native Americans had much confidence in their new allies at this stage. While some were concerned that the rebels might now have the upper hand against the British, rumors swirled that the French were about to return to America—on the patriot side. Such rumors intensified over the winter and looked more credible as the Anishinaabeg headed back to their summer residences. Opinion in Indian country once again hung in the balance.

Pro-British advocates had few arguments left to support an active alliance with the English. Continued trade with the British was attractive enough, but at what cost? Some were preoccupied by inter-Indian conflicts that were far more worrisome than the British civil war. The Iroquois had already begun fighting among themselves. Close to Michilimackinac, the Ojibwe had killed two Menominee ogimaag, and the two nations again stood on the brink of war. Farther west, the Winnebago were threatening to ally with the Sioux against the Ojibwe. Though it is not clear what the cause of those renewed conflicts was, it may have been related to questions over whether to support the British or the looming French-Spanish-rebel alliance. Certainly word of the bloody divisions among the Iroquois would have alerted many to the possibility of further inter- and intratribal war if they did not tread carefully.[27]

But there also seemed to be a renewed push in Indian country for ridding the *pays d'en haut* of Europeans altogether. Reports reached the British that the Sauk and Fox were frustrated with all Europeans and accused them of wanting to destroy them "by Drink and by war." They even threatened to kill Langlade's nephew, Gautier, and other Frenchmen in the region. Farther south, Hamilton at Detroit was relieved to find that many ogimaag and warriors there were ready to go on the warpath against the rebels. But they made it clear they would do so for their own reasons. The Huron told Hamilton early in 1778 they would send war parties again to the frontiers, but "they expected what Lands they should drive the Rebels from should be vested in them as by right of conquest."[28]

At Michilimackinac, De Peyster also grew worried about the intentions of the nearby Anishinaabeg. As they returned from their winter hunts, De Peyster found himself running low on presents and provisions. As expectant Odawa from around the straits milled about the post, De Peyster felt he was under siege. Though visiting Indians professed their willingness to ally with the British, De Peyster believed they were only awaiting more news about the French entry into the war. As he equipped Indians to campaign in the east, he secretly prepared to defend Michilimackinac. When more Odawa gathered in Michilimackinac, he told Carleton they needed an armed vessel to winter over at the post to protect it from a land-based attack by neighboring Indians. It was, he said, "dangerous" to leave the post any longer without an armed ship. As it looked increasingly likely that the French would enter the war on the side of the rebels, De Peyster made secret plans to keep both Frenchmen and Indians out of the fort altogether.[29]

Native indifference to the British plight was only exacerbated through 1778 by a run of bad news. The few warriors and ogimaag who made their way to Montreal in the summer were decidedly unimpressed when the British finally called off their offensive plans for the year. While in Montreal, they learned of the details of Burgoyne's humiliation at Saratoga. They heard stories of the British evacuation of Philadelphia in June 1778, and of the Battle of Monmouth Courthouse, New Jersey, on June 28, where the rebels claimed victory over a retreating British force. On top of these reports, Anishinaabeg visited Montreal in August just as the British received confirmation of the entry of

France into the war. There were now rumors about French forces returning to North America.

•

Such rumors resonated powerfully when the war finally moved westward in the summer of 1778. Eyeing western lands and stung by the intensity and success of early Indian war parties on colonial frontiers, rebellious colonists sent George Rogers Clark on the offense. Clark, born near Monticello, Thomas Jefferson's home in Charlottesville, Virginia, had spent much of his adult life in western Virginia, surveying lands in the contested Ohio region. He had also served as a militia captain in Dunmore's War in 1774. During the Revolutionary War, Clark continued to fight against Indians in the area who had launched raids on Kentucky settlers to regain lands south of the Ohio River. Clark thought the sources of these raids were the British posts north of the Ohio and wanted to take them out to neutralize the threat. Once the French entered the war on their side, Clark persuaded Governor Patrick Henry of Virginia that the time was right for a western campaign. Henry commissioned him as a lieutenant colonel in the Virginia militia and authorized him to raise troops. Initially, the plan worked astonishingly well. Clark left Lousiville, Kentucky, on June 24 with about 175 men. By July 4, he had taken Kaskaskia, along the eastern banks of the Mississippi about eighty miles north of where the Ohio River joins it. Within six weeks, he also moved up the Mississippi and took control of both Cahokia (across the Mississippi from modern St. Louis, Missouri) and Vincennes (in Illinois, along the lower Wabash River) and was threatening Detroit. Clark did all this with no bloodshed. The French, Métis, and Native population of the area simply stood aside.[30]

Most Indian nations in the region were still uncertain of the rebels' intentions. Like many other Native Americans of the upper Lakes, the Odawa sent delegates down to the Illinois as soon as they heard Clark was on the move. Clark later claimed to have met with "an Amazeing number" of Indians who flocked into the town of Cahokia after he had taken it in July "to treat for peace, and to hear what the Big Knives had to say." Many of them, he noted, had come from as far as five hundred miles away, and they included Ojibwe, Odawa, Potawatomi,

Mississauga, Winnebago, Sauk, Fox, Miami, and several other nations living east of the Mississippi, many of whom were "at War against us." They wanted to sound Clark out but also to confer with the French living there. Some wanted confirmation of rumors that the French themselves would return to the region. Over several bumpy weeks, Clark claimed to have hammered out a peace with ten or twelve different nations. He thought he helped extend the rebels' influence "even to the Border of the Lakes." To encourage this, he sent agents "into every quarter." He met with particular success among the Winnebago, mixed groups near Milwaukee, and the Potawatomi at St. Joseph's. A later British report from Michilimackinac also claimed that Nissowaquet's Odawa ally at the Grand River, Manétewabe, had accepted a "rebel commission" along with others "in our neighbourhood."[31]

It is unclear whether representatives of the Odawa at Michilimackinac agreed to make peace with Clark, but what is more certain is that when they returned to the straits, they hiked up the rent they charged the British for the continued occupation of the post in their land. When returning warriors and ogimaag from Montreal and Cahokia arrived back in Michilimackinac with news of the French alliance and new rebel offensive, they pressed De Peyster severely. The post commander complained that those who went east had made away with almost everything that Frederick Haldimand, the new British governor of the Province of Quebec, had given them in Montreal before they got to the post. Despite Haldimand's orders to economise, De Peyster had to provision them all again with winter clothing, food, ammunition, tobacco, and rum. This included 120 new shirts and 30 "bed gowns," 87 blankets of varying sizes, 96 knives, 30 pounds of paint pigment, and 4 barrels of gunpowder. He also had to repair their guns and furnish them with replacement canoes in order to keep them on the British side. The Odawa even demanded payment for their own canoes—they said they had not been paid for them as promised in Montreal—and they put in a claim for the provisions they had taken along themselves. Finally, they compelled De Peyster to cover their dead by providing presents. De Peyster felt "obliged" to appease them or "run the risk of forfeiting all that we have ever done."[32]

De Peyster worried about a domino effect that would engulf Michilimackinac if the nearby nations chose to side with the rebels. The post at Michilimackinac, he warned, was so badly constructed and situated that it could not be defended. The fort was merely square in shape with twelve-foot-high palisaded walls and sentry posts at each corner, enclosing a virtual village of little rowhouses and barracks. De Peyster called it "a patched picketed fort at best much incumbered with wooden houses & commanded by small arms." It sat exposed on the sandy southern shore of the straits, with few natural defenses to protect it. Little had changed since the Ojibwe had taken it during the Second Anglo-Indian War in 1763, and what effort and money had been spent by the British to patch it up was just as quickly worn away by the ice, snow, and incessant winds that blew across the straits. Whereas previously it was not necessary to shore up the fort because the British thought they could rely on the Indians to help protect them, it was now clear that "the friendships with the Indians may be depended upon [only] till a greater force appear against us, and I fear no longer some few excepted." A month later, De Peyster fretted about the few numbers of men at Michilimackinac, which he feared would "in all probability soon become the scene of action if the Rebels are not routed from the Illinois." When he wrote this, he likely had Louis Chevalier's recent report in hand. In mid-September, Chevalier, a French trader, had written from St. Joseph's to say his sources made it clear that "the rebels intend to go to your fort for breakfast this spring."[33]

Knowing that the eyes of the Indians were upon them, the British began preparations to move against Clark in mid-August. Governor Hamilton at Detroit led the way. Hamilton thought he had no choice but to go on the offensive. If the rebels attacked Detroit, he believed that only one in twenty of the Frenchmen residing there would stay loyal to the British, and that the Indians would join them in a heartbeat. The governor worried that Clark would exploit this weakness to take the post. He thus recalled traders heading for the Mississippi and hastily organized an expedition against Clark. He planned to leave Detroit in late September, head for the Maumee River, portage to the Wabash, and take Vincennes. Before he left, he asked De Peyster to send Indians to help him via the Illinois River. He also asked Chevalier at St. Joseph's to get the Potawatomi to send reinforcements.[34]

•

Governor Hamilton would get little help. When De Peyster only be-
latedly learned of Hamilton's movements in mid-October, he asked
Gautier and Langlade—who had just returned from Montreal—to
head out to the Grand River and to St. Joseph's to mobilize warriors
and gather intelligence. De Peyster thought the presence of the two
men "amongst the Indians will do more good than I could have expected by sending my Belts by the hands of Indians." But even the two
veterans of Indian relations could do little in these circumstances.
Most of the Odawa balked at De Peyster's new initiatives. Delayed by
winds, Langlade did not reach the mouth of the Grand River until
November 13. He spoke with various Odawa ogimaag, most of whom
refused to join the expedition, he said, because they did not have
enough notice. They wanted to finish their winter hunts and wait until
spring. They were eager to see what would develop over the coming
months. Still, Langlade managed to raise about eighty warriors, likely
from among his own kinsmen. When they arrived at St. Joseph's, how-

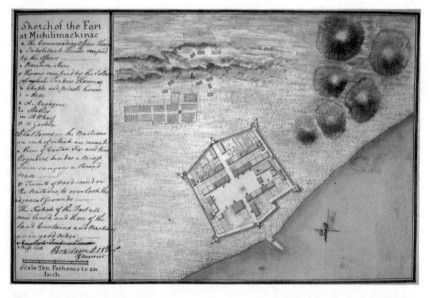

Perkins Magra, *Sketch of the Fort at Michilimackinac*, c. 1765, watercolor, pen
and ink. Note that the defenses of the fort were improved shortly after the Anglo-
Indian War of 1763. (Thomas Gage Papers, Map Division, Maps 6-N-8, Clements Library,
University of Michigan)

ever, they found that Hamilton was already beyond reach. The Odawa called off their advance and instead rejoined their nearby winter camps at Grand River.[35]

In the meantime, Hamilton took back Vincennes from a detachment of Clark's force and settled down there for the rest of the winter. Ignoring De Peyster, Hamilton then wrote directly to Langlade at Green Bay and asked him and Gautier to join him early in the spring via the Illinois River. Langlade and Gautier complied, but they could make little headway in a divided Indian country. They were now also up against old friends such as Daniel-Maurice Godefroy de Linctot. Linctot had been an Indian agent with the French and had served alongside Langlade at the Battle of the Plains of Abraham. He went to France for a year after the fall of Quebec but returned to trade along the Mississippi River at Prairie du Chien and Cahokia. In early June 1778, he met with Langlade and Gautier at Green Bay and talked about Spanish intrigues among the Indians. But when Clark invaded the Illinois, like many other Frenchmen in the area, Linctot joined him, welcoming Clark to Cahokia on July 6. Clark eventually made him Indian agent for the Illinois.[36]

Once close friends, Linctot and Langlade now found themselves on opposite sides of the conflict. When Linctot established himself at Fort Le Pee (Peoria, Illinois), he competed fiercely with British-allied officers like Langlade for the loyalty of the Indians. Linctot immediately headed up the Illinois River, and along the western shores of Lake Michigan, with twenty horsemen. They also sent belts up the Mississippi. They spread word of Clark's exploits and announced there would be many more attacking Detroit in the spring. While near present-day Milwaukee, Linctot ran headlong into Langlade, who was trying to recruit for the British among the mixed villages of Potawatomi, Odawa, Ojibwe, and Sauk in the area. What transpired between the two old friends will likely never be known. But Langlade told De Peyster that he could not capture Linctot and his party since the "Indians were so much divided."[37]

Gautier also ran into problems on the Mississippi. He had gathered some two hundred Fox, Winnebago, Menominee, Odawa, and Ojibwe and led them down the river, but they ran into a party of pro-rebel Sauk at Rock River on April 4. The Sauk mocked British threats to stop trade, forced Gautier to "release" 120 of his men, and even tried to seize the man himself. Carrying on, Gautier hoped to rendezvous with Langlade's Ojibwe and Sauks from Wisconsin. But he only ran into more pro-rebel Sauk, who also rejected his message. Gautier and his Indian allies were forced to make a hasty retreat to Green Bay. Though the Menominee and Winnebago continued to profess loyalty to the British, Gautier suspected several of their chiefs had turned their young warriors against him. He was back in Green Bay before the end of the month.[38]

The difficulties Langlade and Gautier experienced in carrying out British orders reflected the divided loyalites at work in the *pays d'en haut*. Though intermediaries such as Gautier and Langlade were seen by the British as their most valuable allies, their influence was limited when there was either opposition or little consensus among their kin. They could act only as Anishinaabe ogimaag: they might still have some influence among their own extended families, but they could only try to persuade others. In light of the feeble British war effort, their history of conflict with Native Americans, and the entry of the French into the war, their arguments would hold only so much weight.

Those arguments only got weaker. At least part of the reason Gautier and his allies beat such a hasty retreat back to Green Bay was that they got word that Hamilton had surrendered. The lieutenant governor, thinking it was safe to stay put at Vincennes over the winter, had sent home the few Indian allies who had joined him. He awaited reinforcements from men such as Gautier and Langlade early in the spring. But Clark launched a surprise winter attack with only a handful of troops, and on February 25, 1779, wrongly believing he was outnumbered, Hamilton surrendered.[39]

Hamilton, furious at this humiliation, lashed out at his supposed allies. He blamed his Canadian volunteers, and the numerous French inhabitants of Vincennes. But he also accused Langlade and Gautier of deceiving him. Shortly after his capture, he talked to Linctot. After this discussion, Hamilton concluded that he had "reason to think that Lang—e and Gaut—r were either false to their trust, or imposed on." Hamilton thought that if Langlade had followed orders and launched a diversion from Michilimackinac as Hamilton had intended, it might have kept Clark at Kaskaskia until reinforcements arrived. Whoever was to blame, the British were in deep trouble.[40]

•

Hamilton's capture at Vincennes marked another turning point in Indian-British relations in the *pays d'en haut*. Whereas prior to the loss many Native communities still contemplated the possibility of joining the British in their fight against their own colonists, after the surrender they began to consider joining the war against empire. In Indian eyes, there was little point in supporting the British further. They were weak and had failed again. Farther afield, the British seemed little interested in the war in the northeast since they had shifted strategy toward regaining the southern colonies late in 1778. Indian country was also alight with rumors that the rebels would soon launch an attack against Detroit or Michilimackinac. The rumors were given credibility by reports that the Americans were amassing a four-thousand-strong army at Easton, Pennsylvania, under Major General John Sullivan and Brigadier General James Clinton. Only in July was it clear they were heading north against the Iroquois rather than west to reinforce George Rogers Clark. Under the circumstances, although British trade was useful, the entry of the French into the war suggested that the French might return to the posts. Reports also swirled over the winter months that the Spanish would soon enter the war on the rebel side, opening the possibility of a joint Spanish-French attack up the Mississippi. Odawa wintering over at the Grand River delayed their departure for Michilimackinac to await more news. De Peyster believed the rebels had sent belts to the Odawa and Ojibwe at Grand River to induce them to stay put until they or the French attacked Michilimackinac. The post commander thought the Odawa and Ojibwe would not wait if Detroit was taken in the meantime. If that post fell, De Peyster warned, "it must be expected that their friendship will fall with it."[41]

All across the *pays d'en haut*, the entry of the French to the war changed the mood of native communities. De Peyster confirmed that Michilimackinac was no exception: "the Indians are growing very importunate since they hear that the French are assisting the rebels." The Odawa reportedly even hosted a rebel spy at Waganawkezee, under the noses of the British. From there, he traveled along Odawa kin networks across to Green Bay and down to Cahokia. The spy said he received nothing but "the kindest treatment from the Indians who seam Intirely disposd. in our [the Americans'] favor." Anishinaabeg around Michilimackinac eventually came to the post in late spring of 1779 to gather intelligence and extract promises and provisions from the now vulnerable British. De Peyster complained he was being "pulled to pieces" by them. Under the circumstances, neither the Odawa nor their French and Métis contacts were giving much away. The anxious De Peyster began to suspect the loyalties of everyone. He thought they were conspiring against the British, but he could find out nothing. The Odawa and Ojibwe were "perfect Free Masons when entrusted with a secret by a Canadian," he concluded, particularly since "most of them" were "much connected by marriage."[42]

As they had done through the 1760s and 1770s, the Anishinaabeg used their French contacts and the presence of the French and Spanish along the Mississippi to put more pressure on the British. Early in the summer, many slipped off to a council in Detroit. There, they discussed the situation in the Lakes. A Delaware embassy later told the rebels they had been at an Indian council at Detroit with the Wyandot, Ojibwe, Odawa, Potawatomi, "& all those Nations over the Lake." After the council, they had gone to Captain Richard Lernoult at Detroit and told him they did not want his hatchet. Instead, they were "going to our brothers the Virginians, with whom we will make peace & receive that which is good." Even if the specifics of these reports were untrue, De Peyster was well aware that the Odawa and other nations of the *pays d'en haut* were in constant communication with the rebels. His intelligence was so good because his Indian informants happily made matters clear to him. De Peyster thought the visits he knew about were only the tip of the iceberg—"such is the traffic carried on by many nations at present."[43]

Eventually, Indian agitation in the upper Lakes pushed De Peyster into action. By the end of June, he wrote that the situation of the upper posts was critical: "our existence almost entirely depends upon the dispositions of the Indians." De Peyster became convinced that if the British did not act decisively and prove they were committed to defending the region, they would lose any remaining Indian support they had. Yet De Peyster was so worried about the safety of the post that he thought he could spare no one from the garrison for an attack. General Haldimand at Quebec wanted to help. He well knew the value of their Indian allies at places like Michilimackinac. He took pains to send up extra supplies and provisions for presents to both Detroit and Michilimackinac, but crucially, he promised no new troops.[44]

De Peyster decided to try to raise Indian warriors for an offensive. He attempted to mobilize the Indians via the kinship networks of the region. On July 1, he ordered Langlade to set out and "do your best to levy the people of la fourche, Milwaukee, the puants and others along the shore of Lake Michigan." De Peyster thought that Linctot would advance on Detroit, so he sent an officer, Lieutenant Thomas Bennett, down to St. Joseph's along with sixty "Canoe Indians" and twenty soldiers. De Peyster was relieved he could finally take action. He hoped the numbers of Indians accompanying the expedition would "daily increase" once the expedition became known. He also thought that even if the reports of Linctot's movements were false, the sortie would have a good effect. It would show the rebels that not all Indians would remain neutral. Moreover, it would encourage the inhabitants of Detroit and "secure the wavering Indians."[45]

Knowing what was at stake, De Peyster accompanied Langlade to Waganawkezee to address the Odawa directly. Though no contemporary record of his speech is extant, De Peyster composed a rhymed version of it for his own amusement afterward. The speech may have been fanciful, but it reflected the state of Indian affairs at the time. In it, De Peyster warned that he knew the Odawa and others had been in touch with Clark and the rebels and had been swayed by French and Spanish entry to the war. De Peyster played on Indian fears of losing leverage. Addressing each of the ogimaag in the villages of Waganawkezee, he asked what would become of the Indians at the hands of the "big knives" if the British left. He reached back in history to remind Indians of the "black legend" and the cruelty of Spanish relations with nations to the south when they faced Europeans alone. Finally, and perhaps crucially, he also warned that the French were not interested in returning to the *pays d'en haut*, despite Clark's assertions. Rather, the Indians would face the rebels alone, and they were interested only in their land. It was now time to act, De Peyster concluded. Returning to Michilimackinac, De Peyster was hopeful. He thought Langlade might be able to bring as many as three hundred warriors to aid Bennett. The commander believed that Langlade and the Odawa could call upon extended kin and bring Menominee and Winnebago warriors, too. In turn, these recruits would set a good example for kin among the Potawatomi at St. Joseph's, who could "change the law of affairs there."[46]

But De Peyster was whistling in the dark. Few Native Americans in the upper Lakes felt they needed to help the British at this uncertain moment. Indeed, most of the Indians accompanying Bennett treated the expedition as a reconnaissance, and a chance to meet with their kin among the Potawatomi, who made it clear they blamed the British for disturbing the peace and creating divisions among them. They were happy to wait for the reappearance of the French. The Potawatomi then excluded the British from their councils with the Odawa and Ojibwe from Michilimackinac. Bennett was left in the dark until he realized that most of the Anishinaabeg were leaving. He thought there were not twenty Indians at St. Joseph's who would accompany him to Detroit. Apparently the Waganawkezee ogimaa Kewishishgum told the Potawatomi that "the Ottawa were forced much against their Inclinations to join the English on the present occasion, that upon their leaving L'Arbre Croche they were determined not to go farther than St. Joseph's and seemed to coincide with him in his opinion, should the French take a part in the War." Bennett soon learned that "the Ottawas want[ed] much to return." Even the arrival of Langlade could not stop them. Bennett headed home in disgust.[47]

In the face of wavering Potawatomi support, most Odawa and Ojibwe were reluctant to risk civil war with their kin. Even had the Potawatomi joined them, they would all still have had to negotiate relations with the numerous Native peoples of Detroit, who were also divided in opinion. Several groups of Indians cited the possibility of a French war as an excuse not to get involved. But more were reluctant to face the chance of squaring off against French kin and relations who had joined the rebels. The three Anishinaabe nations might also have wanted to wait to get more news about the fate of the American campaign against the Iroquois. By early August, Sullivan and Clinton had reached Tioga (near present-day Athens, Pennsylvania), on the southern edge of Iroquoia. Conflict looked inevitable. Finally, the warriors who came with Bennett may already have learned that the rebel offensive in their own region had stalled. Though Linctot had reached Ouiatenon on the Wabash River by August, Clark called off the attack on Detroit for want of reinforcements. Linctot, with only a ragtag group of cavalry and uncertain Indian allies, waited in vain for reinforcements from the French at Vincennes. Linctot was as unsuccessful as Bennett in raising either Indian or French allies to war against their northern brethren.[48]

The British were furious. De Peyster said he held a council with the Odawa and made them "most heartily ashamed of their impatience." But the Odawa were happy with the outcome. They professed some regret, but Kewishishgum insisted they left because the enemy had stopped advancing and they were running out of provisions. They then went off to their wintering grounds early, "apparently well disposed." As they left, they told De Peyster, perhaps with tongue in cheek, they were aware of the cost of the campaign to the British, and under the circumstances asked for little for the coming campaign. They only wanted, he said, three or four parcels of powder and ball and some spare guns.[49]

•

While the upper nations went to their wintering grounds pleased they had avoided an inter-Indian conflict, the British prepared for war with their former Native allies. By the time the Odawa left the straits, news had spread throughout the *pays d'en haut* of the devastation wrought by Sullivan and Clinton in Iroquoia. In late August, some three to four thousand rebel troops had marched into Iroquois territory and on August 29 had faced off against about six hundred Iroquois warriors at the Battle of Newtown (near Elmira, New York) and routed them. They then destroyed some forty towns, along with the Iroquois' late-summer harvest-ready crops of corn, beans, squash, and fruit trees. British officials worried that the rebel victory, combined with the recent turn in sentiment among the Anishinaabeg, would push the Indians of the *pays d'en haut* to turn on the British.[50]

Governor Haldimand had worried all year about reducing the trade in ammunition and firearms to the Indians of the *pays d'en haut*, lest it fall into the wrong hands or be used against them. Though De Peyster believed restricting this trade would be disastrous for their relations with the Indians at this critical juncture, he continued to take measures to fortify Michilimackinac. He tore down two houses just outside the walls of the fort so they could not be used by attackers, then replaced all the rotten pickets in the palisade. He also built a stockade around the barracks and a platform around the inside of the fort walls so that his soldiers could fire through loopholes. He even had his troops level the sand dunes that had blown in around the fort. De Peyster's main aim was to be "protected from surprise from the Indians." He also continued to plead with Haldimand to send him more troops to render the post "independent" of the Indians even as he repeatedly asked for a reposting because he was thoroughly tired of the efforts he had to make to keep the peace.[51]

De Peyster got his wish for a change in scenery, but no troops. Consequently, his successor at Michilimackinac, Lieutenant Governor Patrick Sinclair, continued to fret when he took over in October 1779. Believing the post indefensible where it was, Sinclair immediately began planning to move it to the island of Mackinac, where it could be more easily defended—from rebels and Indians alike (see map on page x). Sinclair believed that at least some of the Indians in the neighborhood, including Nissowaquet's Grand River ally Manétewabe, carried rebel commissions. He then sent Gautier (now the post interpreter) and Samuel Robertson around Lake Michigan to purchase all the grain, grease, and provisions in the country on the credit of the merchants and traders at the post. He did not want to depend on the Michilimackinac Odawa for supplies for the garrison. Finally, he planned to administer the oath of allegiance to everyone in the region. With the Spanish now in the war against them, Sinclair believed he could trust no one.[52]

Spain had actively supported the American colonies with secret funding since at least 1776. Allied with France, both powers saw the Revolutionary War as an opportunity to avenge their losses from the Seven Years' War. But whereas France formally allied with the rebels in 1778, Spain waited another year before declaring war on Britain, in April 1779. Spanish forces immediately launched plans to take back Gibraltar and Minorca from the Spanish, and they also took several British forts in the Mississippi Valley, including Fort Bute at Manchac, Baton Rouge, Natchez, and Mobile in 1779 and early 1780. They also made plans to take British West Florida. The Spanish took advantage of a particularly low ebb in British fortunes. Since they had turned their attention southward to try to regain the southern colonies, the British had managed to take only Savannah, Georgia, from the rebels, in December 1778. Much of the early part of 1779 was spent bogged down in skirmishing around Augusta, Georgia. And with the formal entry of France into the war, Britain, with once again a global war to fight, spent much time and energy defending its possessions in Europe, the Caribbean, and India.

As the winter closed in on Michilimackinac, Sinclair's suspicions grew—perhaps as he also realized how dependent he was on just a few key people. Though he had only a couple of months' experience dealing with Gautier and Langlade, he began using his own officers to try to circumvent Langlade's influence over the Indians. To Governor Haldimand, he complained the two agents were "men of no understanding, application or steadiness." But Sinclair was not so stupid as to think he could do without them. The quarrelsome commandant, never one to back down from a public dispute, only quietly complained to Haldimand, acknowledging they were too important to anger outright.[53]

Sinclair needed help. Like De Peyster, he continued to think that the only way to keep the Anishinaabeg and other Algonquians from siding with the rebels was to force them into action against them. Gautier and Robertson's Lake Michigan expedition was designed to impress the "wavering" Indians. But Sinclair wanted more. Believing that a "Doctrine of neutrality" and "Canadian Creed" had become Indian policy, he wanted the Indians to act offensively. Sinclair told Gautier to try to taunt the Indians he encountered into action. Counting on the two chiefs most in favor of the British, he told Gautier to tell the Indian warriors that if they were brave enough to go to war, they could accompany Odawa ogimaa Amiable and Ojibwe chief Matchiquewish. They were going to take a select group of warriors to act in concert with the Sioux, Sauk, and Fox against the rebels on the Illinois River in the early spring. Sinclair believed if he could embroil the Indians in a skirmish with the rebels or pro-American Indians, they would have to stay with the British.[54]

Sinclair's plan for the Indians was part of his scheme to mount an expedition against the Spanish at St. Louis. Because of the threat they posed in the region, he had arrived at the post with secret orders to act in concert against the Spanish on the Mississippi. The main thrust of the plan was an assault on New Orleans. The British would then move up the Mississippi to Natchez. There they would join with a force from the upper Lakes coming down the Mississippi and Illinois Rivers. This group would clear the western Illinois region of any remaining rebels and take St. Louis. They also hoped to secure help from Detroit. The British hoped that by specifically targeting the Spanish and rebels, they would avoid putting Indian loyalty to the French to the test. They would also eliminate an important base from which wavering Indians and rebels alike drew succor.[55]

Sinclair first tried to circumvent Langlade and ordered another trader, Emmanuel Hesse, and a Dakota interpreter, Joseph La Roque, out to Green Bay and the Mississippi to try to recruit warriors from the Menominee, Sauk, Winnebago, and Sioux. From there, they were to head down the Misssissippi and attack St. Louis. Eventually, however, Sinclair realized he would need Langlade's help. When expected reinforcements from Detroit failed to materialize, Sinclair asked Langlade and the Waganawkezee Odawa to join the expedition. Only a few pro-British warriors were interested. At the end of May, Langlade managed to persuade a "chosen Band" of Indians and Canadians to join him in traveling to Chicago and from there down the Illinois River to St. Louis. Another group said they would be happy going to "watch the Plains" between the Wabash and the Illinois. But Sinclair got bogged down in negotiations with the bulk of the Odawa at a council of more than three hundred Indians. Sinclair wanted them to cut off the rebels at Vincennes but had "met with Difficulties in bringing it about." He blamed their leaders. Frustrated, he noted "they are under the management of two Chiefs, the one a drunkard and the other an avaricious trader." But he also thought they had been influenced by the "Rebels, & French Emissaries." Sinclair understood it was vital to win them over. The expenses were "enormous." Eventually, Nissowaquet and at least some of the Odawa agreed to head for St. Joseph's to join the Potawatomi in the attack on Vincennes.[56]

At first, it looked as if Sinclair's plans would pay off. By the time he sent off Langlade, Sinclair reported that there were as many as 750 Indians, Canadians, traders, and servants gathered at Prairie du Chien.

But despite the promising start, the offensive stalled, then failed. Nissowaquet's group ran into three Potawatomi war parties returning from the Illinois, where they said some Miami had ambushed them. This kind of skirmishing threatened a general Indian war. The Algonquians of the *pays d'en haut* had not warred against each other for close to three generations. The Odawa and Ojibwe hesitated. Though the Potawatomi claimed to be able to assemble three hundred warriors, they looked to Sinclair and the Odawa and Ojibwe for more assistance. They would not venture toward Vincennes without it. Nissowaquet said he would go back to Michilimackinac for supplies, instructions, and reinforcements from Sinclair. But by the time he got there, on July 8, it was clear there were bigger problems. The attack on St. Louis had failed and the warriors and traders were retreating in droves back to Michilimackinac.[57]

The British had not anticipated any problems taking St. Louis. They were told only fifty men held the town. But in the divided world of the *pays d'en haut*, it was inevitable that the Spanish got word of the British offensive. Hesse's attack on the town was a disaster. The Spaniards had thrown up more entrenchments than the British expected and brought in reinforcements from nearby towns. Sinclair later said they had heard about the attack as early as March. Langlade's force met the retreating attackers partway up the Illinois River. There was some discussion about whether they should regather and head back to St. Louis, but the Indians accompanying him decided against it. They joined the retreat.[58]

•

Though Sinclair tried to put a positive spin on the outcome, British officials to the east were livid. Over the past few years, expenses in the western Indian department had grown enormously. In 1779, one officer at Niagara, looking back at expenditures over the war, concluded that the cost of keeping the Indians "in a good temper (as it is called), has cost old England much more than all the Posts are worth." In early 1780, Haldimand ordered a full accounting of the money spent by De Peyster, who was now at Detroit, and—echoing French officials' complaints years before—chafed about the "vast Treasure lavished upon these People." When reports of the failed attack on St. Louis came in,

Haldimand had had enough. He told De Peyster that the Indians had become too accustomed to receiving gifts, so "that now their demands are quite unlimited." But what angered Haldimand most was the return on those demands. The Indians had continuously raised objections to British campaigns. They made excuses for not going to war. They professed loyalty but practiced deception. In short, Haldimand complained, "no dependance can be had on them." But the general—like Gage before him—also began to suspect that something more sinister was afoot. "This conduct," he lamented, "has been uniformly their system." Haldimand could conclude only that they were purposefully holding back. "It evidently appears that the Indians in general, wish to protract the War," he lamented.[59]

But the British could do little in response. While Haldimand fumed about the expenses, he knew that if they stopped provisioning the Indians and handing out presents, the Spanish would simply move in and supply their needs. As De Peyster reminded him, "The Indians are now come to such a pitch . . . that the refusal of a triffle, if not done with caution, may turn a whole war party." And at this stage of the war, the British could ill afford to anger any remaining supporters. Though they had managed to take Charleston, South Carolina, in May 1780, the British had their hands full with the now global war with France and Spain. Even the Dutch were threatening to enter the war against Britain. Their hold on the *pays d'en haut* hung by a slender thread. Haldimand knew they were in a bind. "Retaining the Indians in our Interests has been attended with a very heavy expense to Government," he told officials at Whitehall, "but their attachment, has, alone, hitherto preserved the Upper Country." Haldimand told Sinclair at Michilimackinac to give out the accustomed presents or withhold them for cause. Whatever he did, though, "in these critical Times, you should be extremely careful to avoid giving any grounds of offence to the Indians."[60]

•

Though Haldimand moaned about the "infidelity" of the Anishinaabeg and other Native nations in the *pays d'en haut*, they had greater concerns than simply serving British strategic interests. Direct campaigns against the Spanish made little sense to nations such as the Odawa.

The Spanish posed no threat to the Indians of the *pays d'en haut* and instead provided a good counterbalance to British designs. Nor was the squabble between the British and their former colonists on the eastern seaboard of particular interest. But they did grow more concerned about the war in the wake of Sullivan and Clinton's destructive campaign in Iroquoia and Clark's victories in the west. The latter especially made two things clear to the Odawa and other Indian nations. The first was that the French were unlikely to take advantage of the situation and formally reoccupy the Lakes. Neither the French inhabitants in the area nor any forces from the metropole moved to reestablish French control over the region. Simultaneously, Clark's exploits garnered much attention in the former British colonies along the eastern seaboard. Though little came of his occupation of the Illinois, word of his victories opened the floodgates for a wave of new settlers and squatters to pour over the mountains and into the Ohio Valley. These two developments worried many Indians across the *pays d'en haut*. In addition, Sullivan's campaign against the Iroquois and the new movements of settlers into the Ohio Valley only confirmed British warnings that the Indians would end up facing off against the Americans alone if they lost their hold on the western posts.[61]

Thus, at the moment the British tried unsuccessfully to mobilize the Indians against the Spanish to their west, more and more Indians were worried about the east. In late October 1779, delegates from the Mingo, Huron, Delaware, and Shawnee nations at the Upper Shawnee village asked for help from Detroit. They claimed there was a large body of Virginians approaching the Ohio Valley from Fort Pitt. Since the Detroit commander had made various promises to help, they now called on that help, noting "we can't doubt your complying at this critical juncture" since "your failing will entirely destroy our hopes hereafter." But they also reminded the newly arrived De Peyster of his vulnerable position. They were the last buffer between Detroit and the rebels. The British needed them. De Peyster initially balked at the request, saying he could only send some supplies. But the Detroit nations grew more insistent after they learned of the rebel success against the Iroquois. They called De Peyster to council and demanded that he support them in joining with the Ohio Indians against the rebels. They insisted that he send at least a few soldiers until a larger body could be spared.

De Peyster gave in and sent soldiers, Indian officers, and as many volunteers as he could gather to help keep up the spirits of the Indians until Haldimand gave further orders. De Peyster hoped that at the very least, the expedition up the Ohio Valley would help Sinclair by diverting the attention of the rebels.[62]

Just as the ill-fated British-led attack on St. Louis stuttered and failed, at least a thousand Indians launched an attack on settlers in the Ohio Valley, and many more sent further war parties to the region. As De Peyster told Haldimand in June of that year, the Indians well knew they were in a good position "as to make their own demands." While on campaign in the Ohio Valley, Native Americans effectively ignored the British officers who accompanied them and who wanted to target the American fort at the Forks of the Ohio, and they went after the smaller forts and settler stations instead. They managed to return to Detroit with more than three hundred prisoners. Though some British officers fumed about the plunder and indiscriminate killings by the Indians, even Haldimand had to admit that the Indians had played an important role in pinning the rebels down in the Ohio Valley. In this context, while the war raged between the British and the colonists, Native Americans could count on British support to hold back illegal settlers. Drawing out the war, then, made for good policy in Indian country.[63]

In retrospect, at least, at the same time the "European" war was winding down along the eastern seaboard, it was becoming increasingly deadly in the Ohio Valley especially. Still smarting from the Indian campaign against settlers in Kentucky in 1780, George Rogers Clark managed to persuade Thomas Jefferson, who was then governor of Virginia, to support a campaign to attack Detroit, despite the fact that his state was struggling to keep the British from its own borders. Under the circumstances, Clark could raise only four hundred men instead of the two thousand he had hoped to mobilize and only managed to leave Fort Pitt in August 1781. Thus, as General George Washington rushed to pen Cornwallis in at Yorktown with French help, De Peyster once again exhorted his erstwhile Indian allies to fight for their land and independence. He told his officers to urge the Indians against Clark with promises of regaining their land. He told them to tell the Indians that if they beat Clark, "which they certainly will do . . . they will recover their Hunting Grounds, and their descendants will bless their memory." As it turned out, a detachment of Clark's force was ambushed and decisively beaten by an Indian group headed by the Mohawk leader Joseph Brant, who happened to be in Detroit when news came of Clark's approach. Clark, who narrowly avoided being killed himself, called off the expedition and returned east. But unlike Washington's famous victory over Cornwallis at Yorktown just two months later, which effectively ended the American war for independence against the British, this Indian victory led only to further violence and bloodshed, not Native independence.[64]

If there was any doubt that American independence would bring further threats to Indian country, it was dispelled in 1782. Early that year, as news began to reach the western posts of the surrender of Yorktown, word also reached the *pays d'en haut* of the Gnadenhutten massacre in Ohio, on the Tuscarawas River. Here a raiding party of about 160 Pennsylvania militia attacked a small group of peaceful Moravian Lenape (Delaware) Indians. The Lenape had tried to steer a neutral course during the Revolutionary War, but the Pennsylvania militia accused them of taking part in raids into their state. The militia took the Lenape captive, then voted to kill them. After giving them a night to prepare, during which the captured Indians prayed and sang hymns, the militia took them into two "killing houses" where they were clubbed, scalped, killed, then burned. Some sixty-eight women and children perished, along with twenty-eight men. Shortly after the massacre, hundreds of Indians met at Sandusky to oppose an expedition of almost five hundred Pennsylvania militia under Colonel William Crawford deep into Indian country in May and June 1782. An indecisive battle turned vicious when the American force found themselves surrounded and tried to retreat. More than seventy militiamen were killed, while the Indians lost few. In retaliation for the Gnadenhutten massacre, some of the Indians tortured the captured William Crawford and eventually burned him at the stake. The proximity of the Americans to Detroit and the victory over Crawford's forces only emboldened other Native nations to launch further attacks on illegal settlements west of the Appalachians. While American history books often end the Revolutionary War story with the victory at Yorktown in 1781, in the Ohio country, 1782 is remembered as the "Bloody Year."[65]

Among those raiding the new colonial settlements were the Anishinaabe Odawa from Waganawkezee. In the early summer of 1782,
Nissowaquet and Kewishishgum assembled an Odawa war party on
Mackinac Island. In late June, Lieutenants Charles Langlade Jr. (son
of Charles Langlade and now also in the British service) and Antoine
Ignace accompanied them to Detroit, where De Peyster ordered them
to join Captain William Caldwell, Alexander McKee, and Simon
Girty at Pickawillany. The British were preparing to block a rumored
advance by George Rogers Clark and a gang of militia on the warpath.
When it became clear that Clark was not advancing toward Pickawillany, a force of about three hundred "Hurons and Lake Indians," along
with perhaps fifty British rangers, moved into Kentucky, where they set
up a trap. They first attacked a small fort at Bryan's Station, five miles
north of Lexington, but were sure to let several people flee to Lexington.
They then burned the settlers' crops, killed their cattle, and withdrew,
moving slowly toward Blue Licks on the Licking River. When news of
the attack spread, volunteers still incensed by Crawford's torture poured
into Bryan's Station, among them Daniel Boone in the Fayette County
militia. One hundred eighty riflemen set out, but they quickly fell into an
ambush. After a brief skirmish, the Americans panicked and fled. Seventy of the volunteers, including Boone's son, died before they could
reach the ford on the Licking River. The Anishinaabeg and Huron
retreated, with minimal casualties.[66]

•

As it turned out, Blue Licks was the last major battle of the American
war for independence. Soon after this rout, and to the astonishment of
most Native Americans, word reached Indian country of a peace treaty
between Britain and the rebellious colonists. The British defeat at
Yorktown in October 1781 had helped trigger a crisis in London that
led to negotiations for peace. These began in April 1782, and a preliminary peace treaty was signed in November. News of the start of
negotiations reached the *pays d'en haut* shortly after the battle at Blue
Licks. British officers in the region immediately canceled further
expeditions.[67]

Many Native Americans were stunned by the news. Just as they
had started to make some real headway against the most important

threat to them, the British called a halt to the war. But as details of the peace treaty began to filter through, they were more shocked to find that with no consultation with the Indians, the British had ceded their claims to the entire *pays d'en haut*. They simply transferred control to the newly independent United States of all the lands east of the Mississippi River (see map on page 214). Native Americans were not even mentioned in the peace treaty. In their haste to put an end to another costly and bloody war both the British and Americans had simply ignored Native Americans. It would be a costly mistake. The Treaty of Paris of 1783 ensured that while one war for American independence came to an end, many other contests for Native American independence would continue.[68]

CONCLUSION: PERSISTENCE IN AN ERA OF REMOVAL

When the British suddenly ended their war with the colonists, it looked as though the Anishinaabeg would pay a heavy price for their continued attempts to keep empire at bay. While they had remained largely aloof from the fighting between the British and the colonists in the east, Native Americans in the *pays d'en haut* had secured some important victories late in the war in the west. They met with considerable success against rebel forces in the Ohio Valley in particular. Yet when the British signed the Treaty of Paris in 1783, they ceded to the victorious rebels all lands south of the Great Lakes. Native Americans in the region were taken aback. The British had promised to preserve their lands in the Proclamation of 1763. They had confirmed that promise with the Quebec Act of 1774. Now they ignored these agreements and the interests of Native Americans. Though they had suffered no major losses to the Americans in the preceding years, the Indian inhabitants of the *pays d'en haut* were now faced with a triumphant new nation bent on making good on its claims to western lands.

Further conflict was inevitable. Most Native Americans simply ignored the official peace treaty. While the violence at Blue Licks may have been the last major battle of the American Revolution, it was not the last major offensive in the war for North America. For many Native nations, the conflict over the Ohio Valley and what became known as the Old Northwest continued for decades. This long contest, and the story of the fate of Indians in the new republic, has now become a woefully familiar one. Forced land cessions followed the violent conflicts and were in turn followed by halfhearted attempts on the part of Americans to assimilate Indians. Eventually, concluding that Indians and whites were unable to live peacefully together in the new nation, policy makers including President Jefferson fell back on the expedient of "Removal"—the relocation of Indians west of the Mississippi River and out of the way of American settlers. The Native nations of the *pays d'en haut*—who had long shaped the geopolitics of early America—were pushed from their homelands and faced with an uncertain and doubtful future.[1]

At first glance, the Anishinaabe Odawa at Waganawkezee seemed destined to share this fate. By 1796, the Americans had occupied the British fort, which had been moved to Mackinac Island during the Revolution, and Anishinaabe lands had been severed by new international borders. Within a year, the Odawa lost one of their most important leaders, Nissowaquet. Four years later, another powerful ogimaa, Charles Langlade, also died. A newly arrived Catholic priest, Father Gabriel Richard, declared that the previously thriving villages at Waganawkezee were in a state of decline. Once mighty warriors were dead, or lay drunk in the streets. Faced with a new and rampant imperial nation, it seemed only a matter of time before the Odawa lost their land and were also removed. Yet somehow the Odawa persisted. Using age-old strategies of incorporating newcomers, exploiting kinship relations, playing off external rivals, and protecting their economic interests, most of the Waganawkezee Odawa managed to stay where they were. A brief look at the history of the Odawa in this era can help overturn one more myth of American history. The Indians of the Old Northwest were not all pushed beyond the Mississippi. And they certainly did not vanish.[2]

•

As American settlers poured into the Ohio Valley in the wake of the Revolutionary War in overwhelming numbers, the disparate Native nations of the region tried unsuccessfully to band together to hold back the onrushing tide. With barely a pause between the end of the war for independence and the start of what would become known as the Northwest Indian War (1785–1795), skirmishing continued between newly arrived illegal settlers who were moving to the north side of the Ohio and the Native nations who came together in a "Western Confederacy" centered on the Huron village of Upper Sandusky, south of Detroit. The confederacy included leaders and warriors from a broad coalition of nations who had an interest in the lands north of the Ohio River, including the Iroquois, Huron, Shawnee, and Miami, along with the Ojibwe, Potawatomi, and Odawa from Detroit and villages farther south and east. They drew supplies from and continued to trade with British officials and traders who refused to give up their posts and forts in the northwest under the pretense that the Americans had not fulfilled all their obligations, either, under the Treaty of Paris.[3]

Yet there is little evidence to suggest that the Odawa from Waganawkezee and other Anishinaabeg around Michilimackinac were much involved in this new war. While many of their kin who had moved south over the past century were involved, the Odawa at Michilimackinac were only distantly concerned with the outcome in the Ohio Valley. Nor had American warriors yet impressed much with their fighting abilities. But even if they were concerned, the Odawa had more pressing problems to contend with at the end of the formal hostilities between Britain and the colonies. While we tend to focus on European-Indian relations in this period, conflicts between Native Americans could still preoccupy Anishinaabe diplomacy, even if we have not been privy to some of the consequences. A complex war between the Western Ojibwe and the Sioux had simmered since at least the middle of the Revolutionary War. By 1784, it threatened to shatter the relatively long period of peace among the northern nations. This time, for some reason, the Sauk and Menominee appeared to take opposing sides. With the Fox and Winnebago threatening to join with the Menominee despite the Ojibwe-Sauk alliance, the Odawa had to tread carefully once more. This was all the more imperative since the Odawa were also again at war with the Osage.[4]

Even as the Northwest Indian War heated up, the Odawa generally kept their distance. Raids and counterraids in the Ohio Valley in the mid to late 1780s meant the death toll kept mounting. At first, it seemed the new nation was unable to protect its settlers from Native

American attacks. But the federal constitution that came into force in 1789 gave the new president, George Washington, power to marshal the weight of federal forces against the Western Confederacy. Still, it took three major campaigns to bring the Indians to terms. One of these, led by Major General Arthur St. Clair in November 1791, ended in the biggest victory Native Americans ever won, and on the other side, the greatest military disaster the United States ever suffered in proportionate terms. Near where Fort Recovery, Ohio, is now, on the Wabash River, two thousand Native American warriors attacked St. Clair's poorly trained recruits and killed some 630 soldiers and another 200 camp followers.[5]

In response to the shocking disaster, Washington ordered General "Mad" Anthony Wayne, a former Revolutionary War officer, to put together a well-trained legion of two thousand men. Together with Choctaw and Chickasaw scouts, the force met about fifteen hundred warriors from the Western Confederacy at the Battle of Fallen Timbers on the Maumee River (in present-day Toledo, Ohio). Though casualties on both sides were relatively light, Wayne did manage to rout the Indians from their defensive position. More significantly, when some of the fleeing Indians tried to find refuge with the British at nearby Fort Miami, the commander closed the gates on his former allies, unwilling to start a new war with the United States. Faced with the loss of British support and supplies, most nations of the Western Confederacy ended up signing the Treaty of Greenville in 1795, which ceded much of present-day Ohio to the United States (see map on page 214).[6]

While there is evidence that at least some Odawa and Ojibwe from Michilimackinac participated in these battles, they seemed to do so only because of kinship obligations with their relations farther south. For example, in early 1791, at least some Odawa from Michilimackinac joined members of the Western Confederacy and "danced the war dance" with them before joining parties going to war. And there may have been a sizable contingent of Odawa and Ojibwe at St. Clair's defeat in 1791. But the evidence is sketchy because the incoming Americans, like the British before them, initially found it hard to distinguish between Odawa and Ojibwe from the upper Lakes and those from Detroit, the Wabash, and the Ohio Valley.[7]

Instead, British sources suggest that inter-Indian politics continued to shape the Michilimackinac Odawa's policy toward the Americans.

As late as the spring of 1793, the British believed the Odawa were re-luctant to send warriors south to join their kin against the Americans because some of them were warring with the Sioux. There were also rumors that they were unhappy with the increasingly militant leadership of the Western Confederacy. The following year, large par-ties of Odawa and other Anishinaabe warriors did travel south to meet Anthony Wayne's expedition on the Maumee. But most were only there to observe. After the fifteen-hundred-strong multination force skir-mished with two hundred of Wayne's troops near Fort Recovery, many of the northern Anishinaabeg returned home, apparently unconcerned with the results. The British at Mackinac Island could not persuade them to return. Even a late offer to help by an aging Charles Langlade at Green Bay and his son at Mackinac Island to help mobilize warriors failed to have any direct result. Subsequently, at least some Odawa ogimaag from Waganawkezee supported the efforts of peace advo-cates who ended up bringing the war to a close with the Treaty of Greenville.[8]

·

Anthony Wayne's success on the Maumee River had a profound effect on relations between the southern nations and the new empire be-cause the Treaty of Greenville turned over to the Americans a signifi-cant amount of Indian land north of the Ohio River, including lands around Detroit and Chicago. But it was the near-simultaneous signing of what has become known as Jay's Treaty—ratified in 1796—that concerned the Odawa at Michilimackinac more. Since the end of the war for independence in the east, the Anishinaabeg and others in the *pays d'en haut* had put enough pressure on the British to compel them to maintain their posts in the region. Subsequently they forced the British to continue to give gifts and provisions generously by oc-casionally threatening them. The British believed that if they did not maintain the posts, the Indians might turn on them. Consequently, they almost embroiled themselves in further conflict with the new American republic. But Jay's Treaty, along with the Treaty of Greenville, finally put an end to the British garrisoning of forts such as Detroit and Michilimackinac and saw the beginning of a new era of American occupation.[9]

Still, little changed—at least in the short run—when a small

American force arrived at Mackinac Island in 1796. It was the last British post in American territory to be surrendered. The Odawa at Michilimackinac had seen it all before. They immediately made it clear to the Americans they were there at their sufferance. The Anishinaabeg expected the Americans to continue the custom of giving gifts and provisions in return for their safety at the post. They also reminded the new commander that the Odawa still had leverage. The British had only removed across the straits to St. Joseph's Island. Odawa command over the waters around Michilimackinac meant they could still rely on British support to harass the Americans, or entirely remove to British-held territory.[10]

The Americans knew that such threats were not idle because the British were desperate to cultivate continued good relations with the nations of the Lakes for at least two important reasons. In the first place, the British wanted to hold on to the fur trade. The Jay Treaty stipulated that Native Americans, Americans, and British subjects could freely move across the new international boundaries to carry on trade and commerce. This meant that both the Americans and the British had to woo Native Americans with favorable terms of trade. The British had a significant advantage because they had several decades of connections to build upon, but there was much at stake. One estimate has put the worth of the fur trade outside Hudson's Bay to the British at £200,000 per year after the Revolution (or more than $20,000,000 in today's money), with a majority of the most valuable furs still moving through Michilimackinac. Good relations with the Odawa were critical for the maintenance of this trade, not just because extended kinship continued to be vital to the movement of furs but also because the Odawa still held the key to peace in the region. With war among nations to the west always a threat to the fur trade, the British believed it necessary to cultivate the best relations with the Odawa, since they were "a Nation much respected by all the others." One prominent British Indian agent, Robert Dickson, put it another way: "The Ottawas" of Michilimackinac, he said, "are a political and dangerous set and have much influence with the other tribes."[11]

As Dickson's assessment hints, perhaps even more vitally the British depended on nations such as the Odawa for their continued survival in North America. Without effective alliances with the Indians around both Detroit and Michilimackinac, new British settlements in upper Canada were vulnerable to Americans moving northward. The British quickly came to see the nations of the *pays d'en haut* as a buffer between them and the new republic and courted them accordingly. This was particularly imperative at the end of two costly wars in America and in the midst of continued turmoil in Europe. Indeed, despite the costs of Indian presents and provisions during the Revolutionary War, even Haldimand had to argue that they could not afford to retrench expenses and alienate their former allies at the end of the conflict. As new wars in Europe increasingly preoccupied the British in the 1790s, this imperative grew stronger. The British were more dependent than ever on their indigenous allies not just in North America but also across their new holdings in Asia and Africa. The Odawa and others in the *pays d'en haut* would play an important role in British foreign policy until well into the nineteenth century.[12]

Because of this continued leverage, the new American tenants of the post at Michilimackinac came to feel their dependence on the Anishinaabeg as vividly as the British. Once again a relatively small garrison found themselves in the midst of a dense network of thousands of Native Americans who thrived in the marginal climate and who had long ago mastered the waterways that controlled access to the post. The Anishinaabeg repeatedly journeyed across the straits to pick up provisions and gifts from the British post at St. Joseph's Island and entertain talk of alliances. Then they returned to the American post and demanded the same. Cooped up at Fort Mackinac in the middle of the straits, the post commandants could perhaps have made the same lament that Beaucours did in 1747: that they were in the midst of a vast alien country and still very much dependent on neighboring Indians whom they could not entirely trust.[13]

If the Americans had not understood the precarious position they occupied on the island in the opening years of the nineteenth century, they did so at the outset of the War of 1812. In July of that year, hundreds of Anishinaabe warriors—including Charles Langlade's grandson—spurred on a much smaller British force from St. Joseph's Island and forced the surrender of the entire American garrison at Fort Mackinac without a shot being fired—forty-nine years and a month after the taking of the British fort in 1763. The terrified American commander, Lieutenant Porter Hanks—who had been reared on colonial stories of the ferocity of the nations of the north—feared that the small garrison and inhabitants would be massacred if they tried to defend the post. Hanks died a month later, at the battle for Fort Detroit. Otherwise he might have been hanged for cowardice. Hanks was yet another European victim of the politics of the *pays d'en haut*.[14]

•

The War of 1812, long ignored by American historians especially, has more recently been brought back to life amid bicentennial celebrations. The critical part Native peoples played in initiating and shaping this conflict has also been highlighted, particularly that of Tecumseh and Tenskwatawa, who helped lead another pan-Indian coalition against illegal land cessions in the northwest and eventually into another conflict with the Americans, most notably at the Battle of Tippecanoe in November 1811. Shortly afterward, Tecumseh and many other Native Americans joined with the British in the War of 1812 and made important contributions to the war effort, particularly in defending the borders of what would become Canada. But scholars have tended to see the War of 1812 as the last gasp of Native independence and influence on events in the Old Northwest. While the conflict between Britain and the United States effectively ended in a stalemate, many Native Americans at war's end found themselves on the wrong side of the border and bereft of any support from the British, who were increasingly less interested in entangling relations with Indians in the United States. Native Americans were thus left to face the influx of a rapidly growing number of vengeful settlers on their own.[15]

In the face of this pressure, some migrated west on their own. Others were compelled to go. President Thomas Jefferson had first proposed the idea of exchanging Indian lands in the Old Northwest for similar amounts of territory west of the Mississippi as early as 1803. Starting in 1817, this idea of Removal was steadily incorporated into many treaties made with Native Americans. In legal and illegal treaties, most Native American nations of the Old Northwest lost their land, and their livelihoods. In 1819, for example, under duress from land-hungry settlers, Anishinaabeg to the south ceded thousands of acres of land to the north and east of Detroit all the way to the northern reaches of Saginaw Bay. At the Treaty of Chicago in 1821, the Potawatomi at St. Joseph's and some Odawa ceded lands in the western part of what was becoming the state of Michigan north to the Grand River. American officials then plotted the removal of the landless Anishinaabeg to territory far west—to the prairies of Kansas or the headwaters of the Mississippi.[16]

Yet throughout this seemingly momentous era of change in the geopolitics of North America—and in the lives of many Native Americans to the south—there is little evidence of dramatic disruptions and discontinuities for the Odawa at Waganawkezee until well into the nineteenth century. To be sure, the Odawa at Waganawkezee did lose some important leaders at the end of the eighteenth century, such as Nissowaquet and Langlade. Yet they were both succeeded by relations who appeared to take up simliar responsibilities. Langlade's son and grandson served with the British Army as officers and interpreters, among other positions. His extended family sprawled across the Lakes from Montreal to Green Bay. And they carried on trading with and living among the Anishinaabeg and other Algonquian peoples, with whom they continued to intermarry. Nor were Charles Langlade and Nissowaquet the only leaders of the Odawa, of course. A document from 1835 appointing Augustin Hamlin as an Odawa representative to treat with the Americans was signed by more than fifty-three ogimaag from northern Michigan, including thirty-one from the Waganawkezee area alone. Most left a pictograph of their doodemag. The first signer was an ogimaa called Nisawakwat.[17]

Nor did the Odawa succumb to the deleterious effects of alcohol, despite the comments of Father Richard in 1799. While much has been made of the impact of the trade in liquor among Native Americans, there is little evidence of sustained alcohol abuse among the Anishinaabe Odawa for most of the early history of North America. Though anxious European officials and moralistic priests often condemned the trade in liquor, the evidence suggests that alcohol was only a minor item in the panoply of trade goods brought up to Michilimackinac, where clothing and hunting tools were by far the most common items exchanged for furs. As the historian Peter Mancall has

Unknown artist, attributed to Sir Joshua Jebb, *Two Ottawa Chiefs Who with Others Lately Came Down from Michillimachinac Lake Huron to Have a Talk with Their Great Father The King or His Representative*, c. 1813–1820. (David Ives Bushnell collection of Canadiana, Acc. No 1981-55-41, Library and Archives Canada)

shown, stereotypes about Indian drinking derived from the Euro-Americans' own insecurities and views of Indians as inferior. It is likely that colonial Americans drank far more per capita than Native Americans.[18]

Instead, Andrew Blackbird, the Anishinaabe Odawa writer from Waganawkezee, called the period from 1812 to 1836 a "golden age" in the history of the Odawa. Taking advantage of the fierce competition between rival fur trade companies in the region, the Anishinaabeg continued to thrive at Michilimackinac. Blackbird, who was born around 1814 and wrote his history of the Odawa in 1887, recalled a childhood amid abundance. He thought his people never wanted for anything in terms of food and clothing. There was plenty of wild meat, the Odawa continued to grow corn and vegetables, and the lakes and rivers still teemed with fish. Blackbird also recalled the same seasonal rhythms of life that his ancestors had enjoyed for generations. After the late summer harvest, families would set off to hunt and trap southward. Some went as far south as Chicago, but most went to the St. Joseph's, Black, or Grand Rivers south of Waganawkezee. His own extended family hunted and trapped muskrats, beavers, and other fur-bearing mammals above the Big Rapids on the Muskegon River before making sugar in the early spring. Shortly after, loaded with sugar, furs, deerskins, venison, honey, and bear oil, they would meet other families at the mouth of the river and celebrate the Feast of the Dead.[19]

Blackbird's perhaps overly rose-tinted view of his childhood years is corroborated by other accounts—most notably by the famous geographer Jedidiah Morse. The federal secretary of war commissioned Morse in 1820 to gather intelligence about Native Americans on the borders of new American settlements. Tired of costly and often ineffective warfare with these still powerful nations, many in Washington began hoping that Christianizing and supposedly civilizing the Indians might be the most effective way to neutralize the threat they posed to Americans. During his visit to Waganawkezee in 1822, Morse noted with some surprise that the Odawa were an important and thickly woven nation that stretched across most of present-day Michigan. Contrary to what he had been led to believe by his contemporaries, the Odawa at Michilimackinac were a very different nation from those around Detroit.[20]

Around the time of Morse's visit, the Odawa and Ojibwe population was about 4,700 in the Michilimackinac area in as many as fifty-two villages and towns. There were a further 1,200 merchants, traders, military personnel, and families of Indian heritage living on Mackinac Island and at St. Ignace, and another 980 at the Sault. Visiting Indians continued to inflate those numbers to 6,000 or more at Michilimackinac and 3,000 at the Sault. The principal Odawa base was still Waganawkezee, where at least five major villages now dotted the shoreline from above Cross Village down to at least present-day Petoskey. There were also significant outlying Odawa communities located on Beaver Island, near the mouth of the Manistique River on the Upper Peninsula, and on Little Detroit Island in present-day Wisconsin at the northern

end of Green Bay, south of Big Bay de Noc. The Grand River settlements also continued to be an important center for numerous and related Odawa communities. Here, orchards and cleared lands supported
more than three thousand apple trees and close to twenty-five hundred acres of corn and vegetable crops. South of the Grand River
more mixed groups of Odawa and Potawatomi flourished in the Ka-
lamazoo River valley.[21]

Of all the Indians he had visited, the Odawa at Waganawkezee impressed Jedidiah Morse the most. He noted they had long cultivated
corn, potatoes, and pumpkins and sold their surpluses at the Mackinac
market. In 1819 alone, they sent a thousand bushels of corn to the island; often they had three thousand or more. His account of the Waganawkezee Odawa stood in marked contrast to Father Richard's account
from 1799, a point that Morse himself noted with surprise. There was
only one problem he could see: the Waganawkezee Odawa were little
interested in his proposals to civilize them with his education and missionary program. Though they politely heard him out, Morse believed
they were still too much under the "medicine influence," as he called
it, which expressed itself in their hostility to schools and Christianity.
Indeed, the Odawa listened to Morse in council and replied that they
"knew about his purpose and were not prepared to accept the proposals." "They were," Morse concluded, "contented and happy in their present situation."[22]

•

However content the Odawa were, they were foresighted enough to
begin preparing for changes and forestall American efforts to interfere
with their lives. Shortly after Morse's visit, for example, some Odawa
families began seeking out their own missionaries before any were
imposed on them. According to Blackbird, around 1824, a former
Waganawkezee resident, Andowish, returned to the Odawa settlements
from a sojourn among the Stockbridge Indians to the east. Blackbird
claimed that Andowish had become a Catholic while away and had
come back to teach some of his family the same. Many Odawa said they
wanted a priest of their own. Some petitioned the president of the
United States. Eventually several families went to see some Métis kin
still living on Mackinac Island and asked them to procure a priest.

Others began teaching Catholic doctrine themselves. Significantly, Blackbird stated that when the Reverend Father Baden arrived in 1825 and began baptizing the Odawa, this was the "first" time European religion had been introduced to the nation. Blackbird was at pains to distinguish the adoption of Catholicism in the nineteenth century from the Odawa tolerance of Catholic missionaries in previous centuries, and he made a point of noting it was not introduced by whites.[23]

Around the same time, Blackbird noted that his family stopped traveling southward for the winter. Though he implied it had something to do with the coming of Catholicism to Waganawkezee, it likely resulted from the final decline of the fur trade in the Michigan region. As stocks of furs and skins began to decline throughout the Lakes, changes in the operation of the fur trade helped convince many Indians to abandon it altogether. In 1822, John Jacob Astor succeeded in his efforts to lobby Congress to eliminate government-operated stores (often called factories) at places such as Michilimackinac, thereby reducing competition and raising prices for supplies. He even succeeded in putting the Langlade family out of business at Green Bay. By 1830, the American Fur Company held a nearly complete monopoly on the fur trade and imposed new traders and regulations on Indians who wished to continue trading. Few were interested in the new arrangements. While some families continued to bring their pelts to British merchants at Drummond Island for several years, the long journey to the southern shores of Georgian Bay combined with the aggressive new measures of the American Fur Company may have limited incentive.[24]

Yet faced with an uncertain future that included the decline of the fur trade and the loss of wintering lands, the Anishinaabeg continued to adapt. When their needs could not be met with the profits from the fur trade, the Odawa did what they had done in times past and simply relied more on fishing and farming. Within a few years, some Odawa around Lake Michigan and northern Green Bay turned these skills to profit when they allied themselves with trading firms who had already established commercial fishing operations for dried and smoked fish. Together, they helped create a new market for the sale of fresh fish to the rapidly expanding American settler populations around Detroit and the lower Great Lakes.[25]

•

Eventually, however, the Odawa at Waganawkezee were faced with the serious and twin threat of dispossession and removal. Their response to those threats would chart one more innovation in European-Indian relations in this era. In the face of dwindling fur trade profits, the Odawa wanted to sell a small portion of their more marginal lands to the government in 1835. But the U.S. Indian agent for northern Michigan, Henry Rowe Schoolcraft, saw an opportunity to exploit the situation. Schoolcraft, a member of the Michigan Territory legislature from 1828 to 1832, and now ostensibly charged with protecting Indian interests, did not seem too worried about the conflict of interest inherent in his roles. With one eye on impending statehood, Schoolcraft called for treaty negotiations in Washington that included all the Anishinaabeg of Michigan. The Indian agent was bent on securing all remaining lands in the Territory.[26]

Representatives who went to Washington to negotiate what would be called the Treaty of 1836 were in a tough position. Since most Waganawkezee Odawa were opposed to further land sales, almost all were set against leaving their homelands. They were well aware of the Indian Removal Act of 1830, which authorized the president of the United States to negotiate with the southern Indian nations for their removal to lands west of the Mississippi. Anishinaabeg in Michigan had already seen the policy in practice among some of their kin to their south. Odawa ogimaag in Washington made their position clear. They made sure to reserve for themselves territory surrounding their major villages in the northern part of the lower peninsula of Michigan, which were outside the direct line of American settlement. They also stipulated that the proceeds from the sale of other lands should be used for the economic development of the reserved territories. The first draft of the 1836 treaty reserved 142,000 acres in five tracts to be held in common and gave the Anishinaabeg the right to stay on several large islands in Lakes Michigan and Huron. The treaty also provided for annuities, mission stations and schools, farmers, blacksmiths and gunsmiths in the ceded areas, a residence for Anishinaabeg visiting Mackinac Island, and salt and fish barrels for those involved in the developing commercial lake-fishing industry. Finally, the delegates got the U.S. representatives to agree that the Odawa and Ojibwe could even use the ceded areas as well, at least until they were surveyed, sold, and settled. Nothing was said about removal west of the Mississippi.[27]

Subsequent senatorial tinkering with the treaty saw the inclusion of a clause that abolished the creation of permanent reservations and instead compelled the surrender of the reserved land at the end of five years. In return, the Odawa were promised a cash payment of $200,000 and land west of the Mississippi if they wanted to move. While unhappy with this new clause, Odawa representatives accepted it because they believed American farmers were uninterested in the ceded lands. They were aware that much of the land ceded by other nations in southern and eastern Michigan in earlier treaties still remained unsold. They thought they would be able to use those lands indefinitely. Odawa familiarity with agriculture, of course, also in turn made it easier to convince state and federal authorities that the Odawa were well on their way to becoming civilized through assimilation. Significantly, the Odawa were at pains to note that the lands they laid claim to were not as fertile as those that settlers most coveted, and yet they had managed to make them productive for many generations. In making such arguments, of course, they also turned on its head the traditional view that only Europeans could make the land "productive."

•

The Odawa position at the edge of two empires also helped give them leverage in this difficult position, as it often had. Since at least 1796, the Odawa had traveled back and forth across the imaginary international boundary between the United States and Canada and courted both the British and the Americans. Some had even gone back to form more permanent villages on Manitoulin Island, one of their ancient sites of settlement. Under pressure from returning Anishinaabeg, the British established a reserve for Native Americans and welcomed and encouraged any new arrivals with promises of gifts and generous annuities. Those unhappy with the Treaty of 1836 could and did move across to Manitoulin Island and other British-claimed territory after the details of the agreement became clear. Most chose to stay but used the threat of relocating eastward as leverage against American arguments to move west.[28]

Still, there was significant pressure put on the Anishinaabeg to remove westward. The Odawa at Waganawkezee countered these efforts by petitioning for land at the headwaters of the Mississippi rather than on the prairies of Kansas, buying themselves some time. They knew full well that the United States would not remove them to this region while there was still conflict between the Ojibwe and Sioux, and while British fur traders continued to influence the nations in that area. But perhaps more important, the Odawa at Waganawkezee also followed the example of many of their Grand River kin by buying up land at government land offices and thus becoming property owners and taxpayers. To do so, they often enlisted the aid of missionaries. Promising to remain near the Protestant missions instead of moving to Catholic missions in Ontario, many groups of Odawa were able to mobilize fund-raising campaigns on the east coast to buy them land in Michigan. Despite the best coercive efforts of Henry Schoolcraft, the Odawa steadfastly refused to entertain the idea of western removal to Kansas. When pushed, they again threatened to remove eastward, to Manitoulin Island, where Schoolcraft worried they would augment a growing number of Anishinaabeg hostile to Michigan.[29]

When a new Whig government came to power in 1841, Schoolcraft lost his position as superintendent of the Michigan Indian agency and the Odawa eventually won their battle over removal. With a former fur-trading agent from Mackinac installed in Schoolcraft's place, the Odawa from Waganawkezee again threatened to move to Canada at the same time they formally requested American citizenship. This was a deliberate strategy. They believed that as citizens, they could hold on to any lands they had acquired. The Michigan legislature countered that the Odawa could take up citizenship, but only if they renounced their so-called tribal ties. The Odawa were happy to comply. As the historian James McClurken has shrewdly noted, the "Ottawa" and "Chippewa" of the state could easily renounce their tribal affiliation because they had no formal tribal government. The ruling had no impact on the culture, kinship networks, and day-to-day governance of the Anishinaabeg.[30]

Throughout these negotiations, the Anishinaabeg also continued to use their extended kin relations to add weight to their arguments. With their Métis kin and neighbors pushing the Michigan legislature,

that body in turn pressed the federal government to secure Anishinaabe rights to permanent settlement in the state. The result was the
Treaty of 1855. The treaty called for the retention of former reservations
as communal holdings for a further five years, after which time the
land would be divided into privately held allotments for familial own-
ership. While many of their kin to the south, along with so many other
nations of the Ohio Valley, the Maumee and Wabash watershed, and
the Detroit area were forcibly removed from the main line of American
settlement, the Anishinaabeg of northern Michigan, along with the
Menominee and many Winnebago of Wisconsin, managed to stay
where they were.[31]

•

Of course, the Odawa would face—and still face—many more, and
even greater, challenges in their dealings with Euro-Americans. But in
confronting these challenges, the Odawa of Waganawkezee especially
could look back on a long and rich history of conflict and cooperation
with both other Native groups in the *pays d'en haut* and more recent
European newcomers. From their central and strategic position at the
straits of Michilimackinac, the Odawa together with their Anishinaabe
kin helped stabilize the region in the face of a threat from the Iroquois
and shape new French imperial efforts in North America. Drawing on
important if difficult-to-discern kinship networks that grew steadily
throughout the seventeenth and eighteenth centuries, the Odawa were
able to hold their own against ancient rivals and new European threats.
The actions of the Odawa often changed the course of North American events and perhaps even shaped world history, embroiling first
the French and then the English in conflicts with other Native nations and also with each other. It seems no exaggeration to say that
the Odawa helped spark one of the first global conflicts in the Seven
Years' War and in turn contributed to the genesis of the American
Revolution.

They did all this while seemingly remaining invisible. Though a
virtual parade of famous and not-so-famous Europeans walked the
sandy shores at the straits of Michilimackinac, or were fed around fires
at Waganawkezee—including Pierre-Esprit Radisson, Father Jacques
Marquette, Antoine de La Mothe Cadillac, Robert Rogers, John Askin,

Jedidiah Morse, and Henry Schoolcraft—few grasped the significance of the long history of the peoples they met there. And despite the Odawa's key role in so many important events and turning points in North American history—often talked about and noted in the dispatches of colonial officials and European monarchs and their ministers—few Europeans fully understood who or what was behind it all. The French were initially puzzled by what they encountered, and only dimly understood the politics of the *pays d'en haut*. The British also blundered in and made some tragic mistakes before they comprehended the significance of the Odawa at Waganawkezee. In turn, the Americans also struggled, and American historians have largely followed suit in underestimating the importance of the peoples at Michilimackinac. They have remained largely invisible. While the Anishinaabeg have long passed this rich history from generation to generation, it is only recently that scholars have begun to take note of the extraordinary and entwined stories of the peoples of the Lakes.[32]

That invisibility and lack of understanding were sometimes great strengths of the Anishinaabe Odawa at Michilimackinac. They were rarely targeted as a threat to Europeans. Indeed, ironically perhaps, the same reasons that helped the Odawa evade removal also contributed to the vanishing of the Odawa even while they remained where they were. Kinship relations in particular meant the Odawa were quietly embedded into and across the existing community rather than living outside it. That web of relations helped sustain them in the new state even while it made them less visible. For while those extensive threads of kinship were central to the Anishinaabeg, they made the Odawa seem much less a threat to American settlers and officials than the more formally organized and politically autonomous nations farther to the south. Moreover, as property-owning or wage-earning citizens of the new state, the Anishinaabeg more often than not simply became "white" to outsiders looking in, and thus they were left alone.[33]

Yet over the past few decades, the Odawa of the Michilimackinac region have reemerged from what one historian has called "hiding in plain sight" to claim long-overdue treaty rights and to shape a future for themselves within and across the two modern nation-states of Canada and the United States. More than four thousand people claim membership today in the Little Traverse Bay Bands of Odawa alone, the group most closely descended from the Waganawkezee community. Though there was a movement of substantial numbers to urban centers in search of work starting in the 1930s, many of these Odawa still live near Waganawkezee, in and around a reservation encompassing some 336 square miles of land in present-day Charlevoix and Emmet Counties. Together, the community fought for and won federal recognition of the United States' political relationship with the Little Traverse Bay Odawa in 1994.[34]

Yet the real strength of the Anishinaabe Odawa at Little Traverse Bay still lies in their links to so many others across the Great Lakes. As one of the foremost historians of the Odawa from Michigan in particular notes, kinship and kin networks remain one of the most vital features of cultural autonomy among the Anishinaabeg today. In particular, James McClurken writes that "kinship is perhaps the Wawgaw-nawkezee Odawa's most important unifying cultural force in modern society." The continued and expansive growth of the tendrils of kinship across the *pays d'en haut* even in some trying times over the course of the nineteenth and twentieth centuries has also meant the Odawa today are connected to peoples all across the Great Lakes, and to nations with reservations in Michigan, Wisconsin, Minnesota, North Dakota, Quebec, Ontario, and Manitoba. The Anishinaabeg, long a powerful presence in the *pays d'en haut*, are today one of the largest indigenous ethnic groups in North America. They have shaped the history of the continent in profound and diverse and creative ways. One way or another, they will continue to shape it yet.[35]

NOTES

·

NOTE ON FRENCH TRANSLATIONS AND ENGLISH SOURCES
Where possible, I have used and cited the available published English translations of
French colonial documents in the interests of pointing readers toward the most accessible version of the sources. For some of the more important documents used, I have
also cited the original French source. Many of the official French colonial records
pertaining to New France have been digitized and are now available in searchable
form on the Library and Archives Canada website. Translations are my own, though
I have to thank Briony Neilson—whose French-language skills are far superior to
mine—for her research assistance and patience when correcting these.

ABBREVIATIONS

Amherst Papers:	Jeffery Amherst Papers. National Archives, UK
Ayer MS:	Edward E. Ayer Collection, Newberry Library, Chicago
BL:	British Library, London
Clements Library:	William L. Clements Library, University of Michigan, Ann Arbor
CTG:	Clarence Edwin Carter, ed., *The Correspondence of Thomas Gage.* 2 vols. Hamden, Conn.: Archon Books, 1969–
DCB:	*Dictionary of Canadian Biography.* Toronto: University of Toronto Press, 1966–. www.biographi.ca
Gage Papers:	Thomas Gage Papers, Clements Library
IHC:	*Collections of the Illinois State Historical Library.* 38 vols. Springfield, Ill.: Illinois State Historical Library, 1903–1978
JP:	James Sullivan, et al., eds., *The Papers of Sir William Johnson.* 14 vols. Albany: University of the State of New York, 1921–1962
JR:	Reuben Gold Thwaites, ed., *The Jesuit Relations and Allied*

       Documents. 73 vols. Cleveland: The Burrows Brothers Company, 1896–1901

LAC: Library and Archives Canada

MG 1, Série C11A: Archives des colonies, Correspondance générale, Canada. Online at Library and Archives Canada

MPA: Dunbar Rowland, A. G. Sanders, and Patricia Kay Galloway, eds., *Mississippi Provincial Archives [1701]–1763: French Dominion*. 2 vols. Jackson: Press of the Mississippi Department of Archives and History, 1927–

MPHC: *Michigan Pioneer and Historical Collections*. 40 vols. Lansing: Michigan Pioneer and Historical Society, 1874–1929

NA: National Archives, UK

NYCD: E. B. O'Callaghan, ed., *Documents Relating to the Colonial History of the State of New-York*. 15 vols. Albany: Weed, Parsons, 1853–1857

Pa Archives: Samuel Hazard et al., eds., *Pennsylvania Archives*. 1st series. 12 vols. Philadelphia: Joseph Severns & Co., 1852–1856

Penn Col Recs: Samuel Hazard, ed., *Colonial Records of Pennsylvania*. 16 vols. Harrisburg: T. Fenn, 1851–1853

PRDH: Le Programme de recherché en démographie historique (The Research Program in Historical Demography). Online at www .genealogie.umontreal.ca/en/home

RAPQ: *Rapport de L'Archiviste de la Province de Québec*

SHSW: State Historical Society of Wisconsin, Madison

WHC: Reuben Gold Thwaites, ed., *Collections of the State Historical Society of Wisconsin*. 20 vols. Madison: State Historical Society of Wisconsin, 1855–1911

WMQ: *William and Mary Quarterly*

INTRODUCTION: OLD STORIES AND NEW

1. Journal of William Trent and related papers, in Alfred T. Goodman, ed., *Journal of Captain William Trent . . .* (1781, repr., New York: Arno Press, 1971), 87–89; Robert Callender to Governor Hamilton, Aug. 30, 1752, The Twightwees to Governor Dinwiddie, June 21, 1752, in Charles A. Hanna, *The Wilderness Trail*, 2 vols. (New York: G. P. Putnam's Sons, 1911), II:289–90, 298–99; Longueuil to Rouillé, Aug. 18, 1752, Macarty to Vaudreuil, Sept. 2, 1752, Deposition of English Traders, Feb. 2, 1753, *IHC* XXIX:652–53, 680–81, 811–12; Duquesne to the Minister, Oct. 25, 1752, *WHC* XVIII:128–31; R. Douglas Hurt, *The Ohio Frontier: Crucible of the Old Northwest, 1720–1830* (Bloomington: Indiana University Press, 1996), 35; Fred Anderson, *Crucible of War: The Seven Years' War and the Fate of Empire in British North America, 1754–1766* (London: Faber and Faber, 2000), 28–32.

2. This brief biography is drawn from the nineteenth-century memoirs left by Langlade's grandson, Augustin Grignon, "Seventy-Two Years' Recollections of Wisconsin," *WHC* III:195–295, as well as the work of Paul Trap, who generously shared his unpublished and undated manuscript "Charles Langlade" (a copy of

which is also lodged at the Mackinac State Historic Park). Cf. "Charles-Michel Mouet de Langlade," *DCB*; Michael A. McDonnell, "Charles-Michel Mouet de Langlade: Warrior, Soldier and Intercultural 'Window' on the Sixty Years' War for the Great Lakes," in David C. Skaggs and Larry Nelson, eds., *The Sixty Years' War for the Great Lakes, 1754–1816* (East Lansing: Michigan State University Press, 2001), 79–104.

3. "Charles-Michel Mouet de Langlade," DCB; Robert M. Dessureau, *History of Langlade County, Wisconsin* (Antigo, WI: Berner Bros. Publishing Co., 1922), 5; Reuben Gold Thwaites, *The Story of Wisconsin* (Boston: D. Lothrop Company, 1890), 85, 372; M. M. Quaife, "Langlade, Father of Wisconsin," *Milwaukee Journal,* July 25, 1920.

4. Trap, "Charles Langlade," Appendix A; *RAPQ* 1932–1933, 307–308; chapter 6, below.

5. For naming problems, see especially, Michael J. Witgen, "The Rituals of Possession: Native Identity and the Invention of Empire in Seventeenth-Century Western North America," *Ethnohistory* 54, no. 4 (2007): 639–68. And for a rich, illuminating, and detailed study of the Anishinaabeg, particularly western Ojibwe in the Mississippi and Lake Superior region, see Michael J. Witgen, *An Infinity of Nations: How the Native New World Shaped Early North America* (Philadelphia: University of Pennsylvania Press, 2012).

6. In this respect, Richard White's magisterial work *The Middle Ground: Indians, Empires, and Republics in the Great Lakes Region, 1650–1815* (New York: Cambridge University Press, 1991), has had a decidedly mixed effect on our understanding of this world. While he has drawn attention to the Indian communities of the *pays d'en haut*, he has also alienated them from their own historical context. In his reading, they are "shattered peoples"—refugees and remnant groups—who needed an "imported imperial glue" to reconstruct their world in the *pays d'en haut* (see White, *Middle Ground*, ix–xv, and Richard White, "Creative Misunderstandings and New Understandings," *WMQ* 3rd ser., LXIII, no. 1 [January 2006]: 9–11). For another explicit argument that overplays the role of French imperialism in the region, see Gilles Havard, *Empire et Métissages: Indiens et Français dans le Pays d'en Haut, 1660–1715* (Paris: PU Paris-Sorbonne, 2003). For a more in-depth discussion of White's legacy and its more recent critics, see Michael A. McDonnell, "Rethinking the Middle Ground: French Colonialism and Indigenous Identities in the *Pays d'en Haut*," in Gregory D. Smithers and Brooke N. Newman, eds., *Native Diasporas: Indigenous Identities and Settler Colonialism in North America* (Lincoln: University of Nebraska Press, 2014), 79–108.

7. White's mixed legacy on the history of the Anishinaabeg and Odawa in particular has been exacerbated by further historiographical elisions. Native Americans in the central and upper Great Lakes saw colonial powers redraw the boundary lines between them several times over the course of the seventeenth and eighteenth centuries. These historical boundary-marking exercises subsequently precipitated new, artificial boundaries between different camps of French and English historians. English-speaking historians of colonial America have tended to focus their attention on the regions that were eventually incorporated into the new United States. We know a great deal more now about Iroquoia, the Ohio Valley, the trans-Mississippi southwest, and even—more recently—the Detroit and lower Great

Lakes areas. In this, historians have tended to follow in the footsteps of westward-moving English officials and settlers. English-speaking historians have by and large left the histories of Native Americans to the north of these regions to the French-speaking historians. Yet this latter group has, with a few important exceptions, been mostly focused on the St. Lawrence Valley between Montreal and the Gaspé Peninsula. Few have studied the broader history of French North America, and fewer still the history of French-Indian relations in the heart of North America. Native Americans in historically central places such as Michilimackinac have until very recently been virtually ignored. For the most recent review of the literature available and an insightful critique of its limits, see the Introduction to Robert Englebert and Guillaume Teasdale, eds., *French and Indians in the Heart of North America, 1630–1815* (East Lansing: Michigan State University Press, 2013), xi–xxxiii.The one exception to the general indifference shown to the Odawa in this period in particular was William James Newbigging, "The History of the French-Ottawa Alliance: 1613–1763" (PhD dissertation, University of Toronto, 1995). Written shortly after White's *Middle Ground* was published, Newbigging offered a trenchant criticism of that work and a new perspective on the Odawa. While Newbigging's interpretation is difficult to sustain in many of its particulars, his orientation and findings have been influential in my own work. I am particularly indebted to his study for many of the insights raised in chapters 1 and 2. James M. McClurken has also done a great deal of important research on the Odawa, though the bulk of it has dealt with the nineteenth and twentieth centuries. But see James A. Clifton, George L. Cornell, and James M. McClurken, *Peoples of the Three Fires: The Ottawa, Potawatomi, and Ojibway of Michigan* (Grand Rapids: Michigan Indian Press, 1986); James M. McClurken, "We Wish to Be Civilized: Ottawa/American Political Contests on the Michigan Frontier" (PhD dissertation, Michigan State University, 1988), 1–70; James M. McClurken, *Gah-Baeh-Jhagwah-Buk, the Way It Happened: A Visual Culture History of the Little Traverse Bay Bands of Odawa* (East Lansing: Michigan State University Museum, 1991). Several scholars have also focused on the importance of the Michilimackinac region to early American history. Even while their main focus was not the Odawa, their work has uncovered much about the native population of the area and has been essential to this work. These include the enormously helpful collation of documents by Timothy J. Kent, *Rendezvous at the Straits: The Trade and Military Activities at Fort de Buade and Fort Michilimackinac, 1669–1781*, 2 vols. (Ossineke, MI: Silver Fox Enterprises, 2004), and the work of Keith R. Widder, David A. Armour, and Brian Leigh Dunnigan—see especially Keith R. Widder, *Beyond Pontiac's Shadow: Michilimackinac and the Anglo-Indian War of 1763* (East Lansing: Michigan State University Press, 2013); David A. Armour and Keith R. Widder, *At the Crossroads: Michilimackinac During the American Revolution* (Mackinac Island, MI: Mackinac State Park Commission, 1978); Brian Leigh Dunnigan, *A Picturesque Situation: Mackinac Before Photography, 1615–1860* (Detroit: Wayne State University Press, 2008). Mackinac State Historic Parks at Mackinaw City has also amassed a rich collection of original and copied materials dealing with the straits and its history.

8. For more general works detailing these divisions and the broader contours of Anishinaabe history, see especially Clifton et al., *Peoples of the Three Fires*; Phil

Bellfy, *Three Fires Unity: The Anishinaabeg of the Lake Huron Borderlands* (Lincoln: University of Nebraska Press, 2011); Newbigging, "French-Ottawa Alliance"; Heidi Bohaker, "*Nindoodemag*: The Significance of Algonquian Kinship Networks in the Eastern Great Lakes Region, 1600–1701," *WMQ* 63, no. 1 (Jan. 2006): 23–52; Heidi Bohaker, "*Nindoodemag*: Anishinaabe Identities in the Eastern Great Lakes Region, 1600 to 1900" (PhD dissertation, University of Toronto, 2006); R. David Edmunds, *The Potawatomies: Keepers of the Fire* (Norman: University of Oklahoma Press, 1978); Donald L. Fixico, "The Alliance of the Three Fires in Trade and War, 1630–1812," *Michigan Historical Review* 20 (Fall 1994): 1–23; Charles E. Cleland, *Rites of Conquest: The History and Culture of Michigan's Native Americans* (Ann Arbor: University of Michigan Press, 1992); Theresa M. Schenck, *The Voice of the Crane Echoes Afar: The Sociopolitical Organization of the Lake Superior Ojibwa, 1640–1855* (New York: Garland, 1997); McClurken, "We Wish to Be Civilized," 1–70; Witgen, *Infinity of Nations*; Heidi Kiiwetinepinesiik Stark, "Marked by Fire: Anishinaabe Articulations of Nationhood in Treaty-Making with the United States and Canada," in *Tribal Worlds: Critical Studies in American Indian Nation Building*, ed. by Brian Hosmer and Larry Nesper (Albany: State University of New York Press, 2013), 111–40.

9. Contemporary Ottawa often use the term Odawa, and the group descended from the Michilimackinac Odawa refer to themselves as the Waganawkezee Odawa, or the Little Traverse Bay Band of Odawa Indians. See James M. McClurken, "Augustin Hamlin, Jr.: Ottawa Identity and the Politics of Persistence," in James A. Clifton, ed., *Being and Becoming Indian: Biographical Studies of North American Frontiers* (Chicago: Dorsey Press, 1989), 83; Little Traverse Bay Band of Odawa Indians' website history, www.ltbbodawa-nsn.gov; Little Traverse Bay Band of Odawa Indians, *Our Land and Culture: A 200 Year History of Our Land Use* (2005); Newbigging, "French-Ottawa Alliance," 26–82; McClurken, "We Wish to Be Civilized," 1–70.

10. Michael A. McDonnell, "'Il a Epousé une Sauvagesse': Indian and Métis Persistence Across Imperial and National Borders," in Tony Ballantyne and Antoinette Burton, eds., *Moving Subjects: Gender, Mobility, and Intimacy in an Age of Global Empire* (Urbana: University of Illinois Press, 2008), 149–71; Newbigging, "French-Ottawa Alliance," 26–82; McClurken, "We Wish to Be Civilized," 15–16. Throughout, I use the term "nation" rather than "tribe" to denote the Anishinaabeg and the Odawa. For an extended discussion of these terms, especially in relation to kinship, see Christina Gish Hill, "Kinship as an Assertion of Sovereign Native Nationhood," in Hosmer and Nesper, *Tribal Worlds*, 65–109.

11. Witgen, "Rituals of Possession," 647–48; Bohaker, "*Nindoodemag*," 23–52.

12. White, *Middle Ground*, 1–9; Witgen, "Rituals of Possession," 648; Witgen, *Infinity of Nations*, 29–115; Bohaker, "*Nindoodemag*," 23–52.

13. Bohaker, "*Nindoodemag*," esp. 25–26; Raymond J. DeMallie, "Kinship: The Foundation for Native American Society," in *Studying Native America: Problems and Prospects*, edited by Russell Thornton (Madison: University of Wisconsin Press, 1998), 306–56; Jacqueline Louise Peterson, "The People In Between: Indian-White Marriages and the Genesis of a Métis Society and Culture in the Great Lakes Region, 1680–1830" (PhD dissertation, University of Illinois at Chicago, 1981), 200–201; McClurken, "We Wish to Be Civilized," 16–28, quote on 28.

14. Bohaker, "*Nindoodemag*," 25–26, 34–35, 47–48; Peterson, "People In Between," 200–201; Laura Peers and Jennifer S. H. Brown, "'There Is No End to Relationships Among the Indians': Ojibwa Families and Kinship in Historical Perspective," *History of the Family* 4, no. 4 (1999): 532–35; Gary A. Wright, "Some Aspects of Early and Mid-Seventeenth Century Exchange Networks in the Western Great Lakes," *Michigan Archaeologist* 13 (1967): 181–97; McClurken, "We Wish to Be Civilized," 16–28.

15. Clifton, Cornell, and McClurken, *Peoples of the Three Fires*, 11.

16. Cary Miller, *Ogimaag: Anishinaabeg Leadership, 1760–1845* (Lincoln: University of Nebraska Press, 2010), 10; Witgen, *Infinity of Nations*, 52; McClurken, "We Wish to Be Civilized," 25–28; Clifton, Cornell, and McClurken, *Peoples of the Three Fires*, 4–7; Francis Assikinack, "Legends and Traditions of the Odahwah Indians," *Canadian Journal of Industry, Science, and Arts*, new series, III (1858): 119–20; Account of Governor de Courcelles, 1671, Narrative of Occurrences, 1694–1695, *NYCD* IX:78, 612.

17. Proceedings of an Indian Conference, Dec. 3–5, 1760, *JP* X:202; Bohaker, "*Nindoodemag*," 47–48; Witgen, *Infinity*, 31–34, 42, 372.

18. Witgen, "Rituals of Possession," 645–47; Witgen, *Infinity*, 69–107. In this respect, we need not exoticize these kinship relations. European officials had only to look at the social organization of their own communities, or indeed of the new European settlements on the east coast of North America. While there were often formal structures of governance in place, these were overlaid upon a much more informal—and often more important—network of allegiances, obligations, and resource sharing that was often tied to the relations among nuclear and extended families. For a discussion of some of the kinds of networks, see Melissah J. Pawlikowski, "The Plight and the Bounty: Squatters, War Profiteers & the Transforming Hand of Sovereignty in Indian Country, 1750–1774 (PhD dissertation, Ohio State University, 2014), esp. chapter 3.

19. *JR* 55:155–59.

20. White, *Middle Ground*, 50–93; Jeremy Adelman and Stephen Aaron, "From Borderlands to Borders: Empires, Nation-States, and the Peoples in Between in North American History," *American Historical Review* 104, no. 3 (June 1999): 817–23; Michael A. McDonnell, "Facing Empire: Indigenous Histories in Comparative Perspective," in Kate Fullagar, ed., *The Atlantic World in the Antipodes: Effects and Transformations since the Eighteenth Century* (Newcastle Upon Tyne: Cambridge Scholars Publishing, 2012), 220–36.

21. Daniel K. Richter, *Facing East from Indian Country: A Native History of Early America* (Cambridge, MA: Harvard University Press, 2001), 1–10; Colin G. Calloway, *One Vast Winter Count: The Native American West Before Lewis and Clark* (Lincoln: University of Nebraska Press, 2003), 1–21; D. Peter MacLeod, "The Anishinabeg Point of View: The History of the Great Lakes Region to 1800 in Nineteenth-Century Mississauga, Odawa, and Ojibwa Historiography," *Canadian Historical Review* 73, no. 2 (June 1992): 194–210; Andrew J. Blackbird, *History of the Ottawa and Chippewa Indians of Michigan: A Grammar of their Language, and Personal and Family History of the Author* (Ypsilanti, MI: Ypsilantian Job Printing House, 1887).

22. Some of the best examples of the new Indian histories were inspired by James H.

Merrell, *The Indians' New World: Catawbas and Their Neighbors from European Contact Through the Era of Removal* (Chapel Hill: University of North Carolina Press, 1989), and Daniel K. Richter, *The Ordeal of the Longhouse: The Peoples of the Iroquois League in the Era of European Colonization* (Chapel Hill: University of North Carolina Press, 1992), and include Joshua Aaron Piker, *Okfuskee: A Creek Indian Town in Colonial America* (Cambridge, MA: Harvard University Press, 2004); Kathleen DuVal, *The Native Ground: Indians and Colonists in the Heart of the Continent* (Philadelphia: University of Pennsylvania Press, 2006); Ned Blackhawk, *Violence over the Land: Indians and Empires in the Early American West* (Cambridge, MA: Harvard University Press, 2006); Pekka Hämäläinen, *The Comanche Empire* (New Haven, CT: Yale University Press, 2008); Andrew Sturtevant, "Jealous Neighbors: Rivalry and Alliance among the Native Communities of Detroit, 1701–1766" (PhD dissertation, College of William and Mary, 2011); Claudio Saunt, *West of the Revolution: An Uncommon History of 1776* (New York: W. W. Norton, 2014); Elizabeth A. Fenn, *Encounters at the Heart of the World: A History of the Mandan People* (New York: Hill and Wang, 2014).

23. As the governor of Montreal lamented as late as 1747, after over one hundred years of relations with the nations of the *pays d'en haut*, even the French along the St. Lawrence still felt they were in the middle of a vast forest, surrounded by people they barely knew, and who had no real love for them. Mémoire de Canada de 1747, par Beaucours, gouverneur de Montréal, C11A, vol. 87, fol. 16; Joseph L. Peyser, ed., *Letters from New France: The Upper Country, 1686–1783* (Urbana: University of Illinois Press, 1992), 184–85. This book joins a more recent but growing scholarly chorus of those moving out from under the shadow of Richard White's work to test the limits and even the premises of the middle ground more generally. While scholars such as Kathleen DuVal and Alan Taylor have shown that the idea of middle ground may have had limited applicability in areas outside the *pays d'en haut* and a narrow moment in time, others who have "faced east" have begun to show that even the heart of the Great Lakes remained very much a native ground for most of the seventeenth and eighteenth centuries (DuVal, *Native Ground*; Taylor, *The Divided Ground: Indians, Settlers, and the Northern Borderland of the American Revolution* [New York: Alfred A. Knopf, 2006]). Rushforth's work on Indian slavery and the Fox Wars, for example, has shown us how much French officials were at the mercy of Indian politics (see especially Brett Rushforth, "Slavery, the Fox Wars, and the Limits of Alliance," *WMQ*, 3rd ser., LXIII, no. 1 (January 2006): 53–59, and Rushforth, *Bonds of Alliance: Indigenous and Atlantic Slaveries in New France* (Chapel Hill: University of North Carolina Press, 2012). This is a theme raised earlier, in the work of D. Peter MacLeod, William Newbigging, and taken up more vigorously by George Ironstack, Andrew Sturtevant, Kathyrn Magee Labelle, Heidi Bohaker, and Michael Witgen (MacLeod, "Anishinabeg Point of View"; Newbigging, "French-Ottawa Alliance"; George Ironstack, "From the Ashes: One Story of the Village of Pinkwi Mihtohseeniaki" (MA thesis, Miami University, 2006); Andrew Sturtevant, "'Inseparable Companions' and Irreconcilable Enemies: The Hurons and Odawas of French Detroit, 1701–1738," *Ethnohistory* 60, no. 2 (2013): 219–43; Sturtevant, "Jealous Neighbors"; Kathryn Magee Labelle, *Dispersed but not Destroyed: A History of the Seventeenth-Century Wendat People* (Vancouver, BC:

UBC Press, 2013); Witgen, *Infinity of Nations*; Bohaker, *"Nindoodemag."* All of these scholars have paid careful attention to the specifics of local interactions between French and Indians in the *pays d'en haut* and come to two important conclusions: that Native American communities existed independently of the French empire, and that the French were almost always dependent on them for their very existence.

24. James H. Merrell, *Into the American Woods: Negotiations on the Pennsylvania Frontier* (New York: W. W. Norton, 2000); Eric Hinderaker, "Translation and Cultural Brokerage," in Philip Deloria and Neal Salisbury, eds., *A Companion to American Indian History* (Malden, MA: Blackwell, 2002), 357–76.

25. Langlade's story is thus still important as a narrative anchor and a window on to the world of the Anishinaabe Odawa at Michilimackinac. To understand how he came to live and have even a little influence in this complex milieu forces us to stay focused on one place and take seriously the rich history of the Odawa at the straits, to reexamine kinship politics, the economy of the *pays d'en haut,* and the complex politics of inter-Indian relations as well as those between Europeans and Indians. Langlade's story forces us to face east and focus equally on the motives, activities, and experiences of mixed communities in the Great Lakes as they sought to negotiate their way through an uncertain world of shifting alliances and seemingly local conflicts that were at the heart of imperial and new national contests. At times, these negotiations were directly related to the imperial story; at other times, though, they were not. Yet to understand the full picture, *all* of these negotiations need to be understood. In an important sense, then, using Langlade as a metaphoric window allows us to recount the story of the Odawa from more than just the traditional perspective of empire.

26. Peterson, "People in Between," 59–60.

27. Blackbird, *History of the Ottawa,* 95.

28. As the pioneering ethnohistorian Bruce G. Trigger put it some time ago, "if Europeans had gained a toehold in Canada, it was because a substantial number of native peoples wished them to do so." Trigger, *Natives and Newcomers: Canada's "Heroic Age" Reconsidered* (Montreal: McGill-Queen's University Press, 1985), 289.

1. RECENTERING MICHILIMACKINAC

1. Tracy Neal Leavelle, *The Catholic Calumet: Colonial Conversions in French and Indian North America* (Philadelphia: University of Pennsylvania Press, 2012), 22, 26–28, 40; *JR* 54:199–203, 55:157–61; 67:153–61; Emma Helen Blair, ed., *The Indian Tribes of the Upper Mississippi Valley and Region of the Great Lakes . . .*, 2 vols. (Lincoln: University of Nebraska Press, 1996), I:283–88; W. Vernon Kinietz, *Indians of the Western Great Lakes, 1615–1760* (Ann Arbor: University of Michigan Press, 1965), 379; Blackbird, *History of the Ottawa,* 19–20; Newbigging, "French-Ottawa Alliance," 28–38; William W. Warren, *History of the Ojibway People,* 2nd ed. (St. Paul: Minnesota Historical Society, 2009), 46–47.

2. "Relation of Sieur de Lamothe Cadillac," 1718, *WHC* XVI (1902): 350; Helen Hornbeck Tanner, ed., *Atlas of Great Lakes Indian History* (Norman: University of Oklahoma Press, 1987), 14–15, 19–21; *JR* 55:135–67; Peterson, "People In Between," 38.

3. Newbigging, "French-Ottawa Alliance," 41, 46–82.

4. Tanner, *Atlas*, 2, 22–23; Newbigging, "French-Ottawa Alliance," 64–78, 81–82; White, *Middle Ground*, 43–44; Charles E. Cleland, "The Inland Shore Fishery of the Northern Great Lakes: Its Development and Importance in Prehistory," *American Antiquity* 47, no. 4 (Oct. 1982): 761, 764; *JR* 55:155–61.

5. Newbigging, "French-Ottawa Alliance," 64–70.

6. Gabriel Sagard-Théodat, *Long Journey to the Country of the Hurons*, ed. George M. Wrong (Toronto: Champlain Society, 1939), 66–67; Newbigging, "French-Ottawa Alliance," 78–80.

7. W. J. Eccles, *France in America* (New York: Harper and Row, 1972), 1–10.

8. Eccles, *France in America*, 10–12; W. J. Eccles, *The Canadian Frontier, 1534–1760* (Albuquerque: University of New Mexico Press, 1974), 19–20.

9. Eccles, *France in America*, 12–18; Eccles, *Canadian Frontier*, 23–24; David Hackett Fischer, *Champlain's Dream* (New York: Simon & Schuster, 2008), 227–53.

10. Newbigging, "French-Ottawa Alliance," 98–101; Bohaker, "*Nindoodemag*," 41–42; Trigger, *Natives and Newcomers*, 149–163, 233–34; Labelle, *Dispersed but Not Destroyed*, 1–3, 84–85; Sturtevant, "Jealous Neighbors," 26, 40–41, 141.

11. Sagard, *Long Journey*, 66–67.

12. Eccles, *Canadian Frontier*, 23–24.

13. Eccles, *Canadian Frontier*, 24–25; Trigger, *Natives and Newcomers*, 175–76; Eccles, *France in America*, 20–21; Fischer, *Champlain's Dream*, 254–80.

14. Trigger, *Natives and Newcomers*, 176–83; Fischer, *Champlain's Dream*, 324–37; Samuel de Champlain, *Voyages and Discoveries* (Toronto: Champlain Society, 1929), III:43–44.

15. Pierre François Xavier de Charlevoix, *Journal of a Voyage to North America*, edited by Louise Phelps Kellogg, 2 vols. (Chicago: Caxton Club, 1923), I:288–93.

16. Richter, *Ordeal of the Longhouse*, 50–74, quote on 57.

17. There were few Europeans to record any casualties among the Anishinaabeg, though their dispersed settlements across the Lakes may have helped them to avoid the kind of devastating population losses suffered by groups such as the Huron. Tanner, *Atlas*, 29, 169–72; White, *Middle Ground*, 41; *JR* 50:287, 55:117–31, 57:223, 61:69–70.

18. Richter, *Ordeal of the Longhouse* 58–61, 65–66; Dulhut, Apr. 12, 1684, *WHC* XVI:119; Edward P. Hamilton, ed., *Adventure in the Wilderness: The American Journals of Louis Antoine de Bougainville, 1756–1760* (Norman: University of Oklahoma Press, 1964), 170–74, 175, 197, 204; Bougainville to Paulmy, Aug. 19, 1757, Montcalm to Paulmy, Apr. 18, 1758, *NYCD* X:616–19, 700; White, *Middle Ground*, 76–82.

19. Richter, *Ordeal of the Longhouse* 58–61, 65–66, 74, quote on 61; J. A. Brandão, "'Your fyre shall burn no more': Iroquois Policy Towards New France and Her Native Allies to 1701" (PhD dissertation, York University, 1994), chapter 6.

20. Richter, *Ordeal of the Longhouse*, 60–62; Peterson, "People In Between," 22–23; Newbigging, "French-Ottawa Alliance," 121–123.

21. White, *Middle Ground*, 1–9.

22. *JR* 45:161, 193–201; 49:237–39; Richter, *Ordeal of the Longhouse*, 64; Eccles, *France in America*, 37; Marie de L'Incarnation, *Word from New France: The Selected*

Letters of Marie de L'Incarnation, ed., Joyce Marshall (Toronto: Oxford University Press, 1967), 209, 255, 265; "Pierre Boucher," *DCB;* Fischer, *Champlain's Dream,* 495–96; Rushforth, *Bonds of Alliance,* 139–40; W. J. Eccles, *Canada Under Louis XIV: 1663–1701* (Toronto: McClelland and Stewart, 1978), 3–4.

23. Marshall, ed., *Word from New France,* 181–82, 255, 265; Eccles, *France in America,* 34, 37, 51; Fischer, *Champlain's Dream,* 395, 405, 465; Marcel Trudel, *La Population du Canada en 1663* (Montreal: Fides, 1973), 11, 23, 26, 150–51; Leslie Choquette, *Frenchmen into Peasants: Modernity and Tradition in the Peopling of French Canada* (Cambridge, MA: Harvard University Press, 1997), 249–53; Census of Canada, 1666, *NYCD* IX:57–58; Gilles Havard and Cécile Vidal, *Histoire de l'Amérique français* (Paris: Flammarion, 2003), esp. 207–208.

24. Eccles, *France in America,* 56, 60.

25. Marshall, ed., *Word from New France,* 311–12, 314; Instructions to Talon, March 27, 1665, Talon to Colbert, October 4, 1665, *NYCD* IX:26, 32; Jack Verney, *The Good Regiment: The Carignan-Salières Regiment in Canada, 1665–1668* (Montreal: McGill-Queen's University Press, 1991), 3, 6–7, 16–17, 28–29.

26. Leroy V. Eid, "The Ojibwa-Iroquois War: The War the Five Nations Did Not Win," *Ethnohistory* 26, no. 4 (Fall 1979): 297–324. But see also J. A. Brandão and William A. Starna, "The Treaties of 1701: A Triumph of Iroquois Diplomacy," *Ethnohistory* 43, no. 2 (Spring 1996): 209–44, and Brandão, "'Your fyre shall burn no more.'"

27. Charlevoix, *Journal,* II:22; Newbigging, "French-Ottawa Alliance," 125–58; Bohaker, "Nindoodemag," 43.

28. Louis Armand de Lom d'Arce, Baron de Lahontan, *New Voyages to North-America . . . ,* 2 vols. (London: H. Bonwicke, 1703), I:82, 88; *JR* 41:77–79, 44:205; Newbigging, "French-Ottawa Alliance," 126, 132–37, 160–65; Ralph Flenley, ed. and trans., *A History of Montreal, 1640–1672: From the French of Dollier de Casson* (London: J. M. Dent & Sons, Ltd., 1928), 207; Newbigging, "French-Ottawa Alliance," 136–37; Tanner, *Atlas,* 31.

29. Bohaker, "Nindoodemag," 47–48; Witgen, *Infinity of Nations,* 42.

30. Richter, *Ordeal of the Longhouse,* 62; Jon Parmenter, *The Edge of the Woods: Iroquoia, 1534–1701* (East Lansing: Michigan State University Press, 2010), 88; Newbigging, "French-Ottawa Alliance," 126, 130–35; *JR* 38:179–81, 40:211–13, 41:77–79, 44:205; Witgen, *Infinity of Nations,* 29–31, 59–64; Blair, ed., *Indian Tribes,* I:178–81.

31. *JR* 40:211–13, 41:77–79, 49:245–49; Marshall, ed., *Word from New France,* 254; Kent, *Rendezvous,* 34.

32. Blair, ed., *Indian Tribes,* I:173–74; Duchesneau's Memoir on the Western Indians, Nov. 13, 1681, *NYCD* IX:161.

33. *JR* 50:266–67, 51:20–21; Instructions for Sieur Gaudais, May 1, 1663, *NYCD* IX:11; Kent, *Rendezvous,* 18–19; Marshall, ed., *Word from New France,* 342; Newbigging, "French-Ottawa Alliance," 173–75; Warren, *History of the Ojibway,* 46–47; Clifton et al., *Peoples of the Three Fires,* 11.

34. *JR* 50:266–67, 54:165–67, 191; Kent, *Rendezvous,* 18; Rushforth, *Bonds of Alliance,* 143.

35. Gilles Havard, *The Great Peace of Montreal of 1701: French-Native Diplomacy in the Seventeeth Century* (Montreal: McGill-Queen's University Press, 2001), 89;

José António Brandão, *"Your fyre shall burn no more": Iroquois Policy Toward New France and Its Native Allies to 1701* (Lincoln: University of Nebraska Press, 1997), 114–18; Parmenter, *Edge of the Woods*, 111, 115–16; Richter, *Ordeal of the Long-house*, 98–102; Verney, *Good Regiment*, 44–53, 71–84; Marshall, ed., *Word from New France*, 321–28.

36. *JR* 44:205, 54:197–99, 55:99–101, 133, 141–47, 159–61, 171, 57:248–51, 60:210–11; Kent, *Rendezvous*, 22–23, 26–33, 39–41.

37. "Lettre de Frontenac au minister . . . ," Oct. 9, 1679, MG 1, Série C11A, vol. 5, fol. 5–7v; Lahontan, *New Voyages*, I:271; "Lettre du roi à Frontenac . . . ," Apr. 30, 1681, MG 1, Série C11A, vol. 5, fol. 349–358v; "'Opinion' de l'intendant Jacques de Meulles . . . ," 1686, MG 1, Série C11A, vol. 121/1, fol. 4–6.

38. Blair, ed., *Indian Tribes*, I:188–190; Newbigging, "French-Ottawa Alliance," 159–223.

39. Eccles, *Canada Under Louis XIV*, 24, 47–55; Eccles, *France in America*, 75–77. For currency conversions and today's equivalents, see John J. McCusker, *How Much Is That in Real Money?: A Historical Commodity Price Index for Use as a Deflator of Money Values in the Economy of the United States*, 2nd ed. (Worcester, MA: American Antiquarian Society, 2001), and John J. McCusker, *Money and Exchange in Europe and America, 1600–1775: A Handbook* (Chapel Hill: University of North Carolina Press, 1978).

40. Eccles, *Canada Under Louis XIV*, 24, 47–55; Eccles, *France in America*, 75–77; Talon to Colbert, Oct. 27, 1667, *NYCD* IX:60; Hubert Charbonneau et al., *The First French Canadians: Pioneers in the St. Lawrence Valley*, translated by Paola Colozzo (Newark: University of Delaware Press, 1993), 28–29; Instructions to M. Talon, Mar. 27, 1665, *NYCD* IX:24–25; Colbert to Talon, April 5, 1666, *NYCD* IX:43; Colbert to Talon, Feb. 20, 1668, MG 1, Série C11A, Correspondance gé-nérale, Canada; Talon to Colbert, Oct. 27, 1667, *NYCD* IX:60.

41. Verney, *Good Regiment*, 110–15, 126; Eccles, *Canada Under Louis XIV*, 48; *Censuses of Canada, 1665–1871*, 5 vols. (Ottawa, 1876), vol. 4; Peterson, "People In Between," 18–19.

42. Benjamin Sulte, *Histoire des Canadiens-Français, 1608–1880: Origine, Histoire, Religion, Guerres, Découvertes, Colonisation, Coutumes, Vie Domestique, Soci-ale et Politique, Développement, Avenir*, 8 vols. (Montreal: Wilson & Cie, 1882), 5:75.

43. *JR* 40:214–15, 41:77–83, 42:218–25; Kent, *Rendezvous*, 16–17; "Groseilliers," *DCB*.

44. Ibid.

45. MacLeod, "Anishinabeg Point of View," 206–207; "Ménard," *DCB*; Blair, ed., *Indian Tribes*, I:172; Michael J. Witgen, "An Infinity of Nations: How Indians, Empires, and Western Migration Shaped National Identity in North America" (PhD dissertation, University of Washington, 2004), 172.

46. Kent, *Rendezvous*, 48, 90; Eccles, *Canadian Frontier*, 104–106; "Lettre de Duch-esneau au ministre . . . ," Nov. 13, 1680, MG 1, Série C11A, vol. 5, fol. 161–81; Colbert to Talon, April 5, 1666, *NYCD* IX:40.

47. Frontenac to the King, Nov. 6, 1679, *NYCD* IX:130; Kent, *Rendezvous*, 47; "Lettre de Frontenac au ministre . . . ," Oct. 9, 1679, MG 1, Série C11A, vol. 5, fol. 5–7v; "Lettre de Duchesneau au ministre . . . ," Nov. 10, 1679, MG 1, Série C11A, vol. 5, fol. 32–70.

48. Kent, *Rendezvous*, 48, 90; Newbigging, "French-Ottawa Alliance," 169; Duchesneau to Seignelay, Nov. 10, 1679, *NYCD* IX:131–33; Frontenac to the Minister, Nov. 6, 1679, *NYCD* IX:129–30; Peterson, "People In Between," 32–38; Eccles, *Canadian Frontier*, 104–106, 110.

49. Witgen, *Infinity of Nations*, chapter 3.

50. Tanner, *Atlas*, 30–35; "Lettre de Talon au ministre . . . ," Sept. 20, 1670, MG 1, Série C11A, vol. 3, fol. 72–73; Parmenter, *Edge of the Woods*, 128.

51. "An Account of what occurred during the Voyage of Monsieur de Courcelles, Governor of New France, to Lake Ontario, 1671," *NYCD* IX:84–85; Marshall, ed., *Word from New France*, 373–74; Frontenac to Colbert, Nov. 2, 1672, *NYCD* IX:91; Frontenac to the King, Nov. 6, 1679, *NYCD* IX:129; Eccles, *Canada Under Louis XIV*, 199–201; Kent, *Rendezvous*, 29–30; Parmenter, *Edge of the Woods*, 138–40.

52. "An Account of what occurred during the Voyage of Monsieur de Courcelles, Governor of New France, to Lake Ontario, 1671," *NYCD* IX:84–85; Kent, *Rendezvous*, 34–37.

53. "Lettre de Frontenac au ministre . . . ," Nov. 2, 1672, MG 1, Série C11A, vol. 3, fol. 233–51; Journal of Count de Frontenac's Voyage to Lake Ontario in 1673, *NYCD* IX:95–114; Newbigging, "French-Ottawa Alliance," 224, 228–29.

54. Richter, *Ordeal of the Longhouse*, 134–40; Duchesneau, Memoire, 1681, *NYCD* IX:165; "Lettre du gouverneur général La Barre au ministre . . . ," 1682, MG 1, Série C11A, vol. 6, fol. 59–65.

55. Council at Montreal, 1682, *NYCD* IX:176–83; La Barre to Seignelay, Nov. 4, 1683, *NYCD* IX:201–202, 208.

56. La Barre to Seignelay, Nov. 4, 1683, *NYCD* IX:201–202, 208; Newbigging, "French-Ottawa Alliance," 165–66; "Dulhut," *DCB*; Kent, *Rendezvous*, 49–50, 65–66, 106–107.

57. Duchesneau's Memoir on the Western Indians, Nov. 13, 1681, *NYCD* IX:161.

58. Duchesneau au ministre, Nov. 10, 1679, AN C11A 5:32–70; Frontenac to the Ministry, Nov. 6, 1679; *NYCD* IX:129–30; Newbigging, "French-Ottawa Alliance," 170–72; "Lettre du roi à Frontenac . . . ," Apr. 30, 1681, MG 1, Série C11A, vol. 5, fol. 349–358v; "Observations on the State of Affairs in Canada," Nov. 18, 1689, *NYCD* IX:434.

59. Blair, ed., *Indian Tribes*, I:281.

60. *JR* 55:157, 66:283; Lahontan, *New Voyages*, I:87–90, 216; Milo Milton Quaife, ed., *The Western Country in the 17th Century: The Memoirs of Lamothe Cadillac and Pierre Liette* (Chicago: Lakeside Press, 1947), 4–5; Peterson, "People In Between," 38; Relation of Sieur Cadillac, *WHC* XVI (1902), 350; Cadillac to Unknown, August 3, 1695, in E. M. Sheldon, *The Early History of Michigan from the First Settlement to 1815* (New York: A. S. Barnes and Company, 1874), 73–74.

61. White, *Middle Ground*, 29–33; Newbigging, "French-Ottawa Alliance," 188–89; Lahontan, *New Voyages*, I:88; Sheldon, *Early History*, 73–74.

62. "Expense Account of La Durantaye, 1683, 1684," *IHC* 23 (1934), 60–67; *JR* 65:205–207; Daniel K. Richter and Troy L. Thompson, "Severed Connections: American Indigenous Peoples and the Atlantic World in an Era of Imperial Transformation," in Nicholas Canny and Philip Morgan, eds., *The Oxford Handbook of*

the Atlantic World, c. 1450–c. 1850 (New York: Oxford University Press, 2011), 501; Catherine M. Desbarats, "The Cost of Early Canada's Native Alliances: Reality and Scarcity's Rhetoric," *WMQ*, 3rd ser. 52, no. 4 (Oct. 1995): esp. 612–14.

63. Eccles, *Canadian Frontier*, 55; *JR* 54:169–77. Leavelle, *Catholic Calumet*, esp. 144–53, discusses the limited success the Jesuits did have among the Odawa and other Indians.

64. Marshall, ed., *Word from New France*, 331; *JR* 50:249–309, 51:23–25, 71–73, 261–66, 332, 52:199–213, 55:99–101, 133, 141–47, 157–61, 171–73, 66:283–85; Newbigging, "French-Ottawa Alliance," 140–48, 153; Lahontan, *New Voyages*, I:88; Louise Phelps Kellogg, *The French Régime in Wisconsin and the Northwest* (Madison: State Historical Society of Wisconsin, 1925), 172; Father Nau to Father Bonin, from Sault St. Louis, Oct. 2, 1735, in Rev. Arthur E. Jones, *The Aulneau Collection, 1734–1745* (Rare or Unpublished Documents, II; Montreal: Archives of St. Mary's College, 1893), 67; Kent, *Rendezvous*, 151–52; Charlevoix, *Journal*, II:39–40; Leavelle, *Catholic Calumet*, 194–96; James Axtell, *The Invasion Within: The Contest of Cultures in Colonial North America* (New York: Oxford University Press, 1985).

65. "Relation of Sieur de Lamothe Cadillac, 1718," *WHC* XVI (1902): 356–57; Kent, *Rendezvous*, 39.

66. Tanner, *Atlas*, 36; Blair, ed., *Indian Tribes*, I:276, 281–88; Kent, *Rendezvous*, 66, 186, 230; "Relation of Cadillac, 1718," *WHC* XVI:363–76; White, *Middle Ground*, 130–32; Lahontan, *New Voyages*, I:90; Kinietz, *Western Indians*, 380–81.

67. Narrative of Occurrences, 1695, 1696, *NYCD* IX:647; "Relation of Cadillac, 1718," *WHC* XVI (1902): 354–55; Blair, ed., *Indian Tribes*, I:282; White, *Middle Ground*, 42.

68. Brandão and Starna, "Treaties of 1701," 229–30.

69. Clifton et al., *Peoples of the Three Fires*, 4–7; "An Account of what occurred during the Voyage of Monsieur de Courcelles, Governor of New France, to Lake Ontario, 1671," *NYCD* IX:78; Cadillac to Unknown, Aug. 3, 1695, in Sheldon, *Early History*, 72; "Relation d'évènements survenus en 1694 et 1695 . . . ," [1695], MG 1, Série C11A, vol. 14, fol. 65–99v.

70. Dulhut, Apr. 12, 1684, *WHC* XVI:114–25; Sheldon, *Early History*, 43–59; White, *Middle Ground*, 77–82.

71. Dulhut, Apr. 12, 1684, *WHC* XVI:119.

72. *JR* 55:155–59; D'Aigremont, Report, Nov. 14, 1708, *MPHC* 33:424–52, esp. 441–42, 446–52; Kent, *Rendezvous*, 226; Blackbird, *History of the Ottawas*, 95; Sturtevant, "Jealous Neighbors," 156–57; Denys Delâge, "L'Alliance franco-amérindienne, 1660–1700," *Recherches Amérindiennes au Québec* XIX, no. 1 (1990): 13; Havard, *Empire et Métissages*, 223.

73. "Relation d'évènements . . ." [1695], MG 1, Série C11A, vol. 14, fol. 65–99v; Narrative of Occurrences, 1694, 1695, *NYCD* IX:605; Narrative of Occurrences, 1697, 1698, *NYCD* IX:683–84; Havard, *Great Peace*, 87–88; "Copy of a Representation of the Lords' Commissioners for Trade and Plantations to the King, upon the State of His Majesty's Colonies and Plantations on the Continent of North America," Sept. 8, 1721, *MPHC* 19:7; Kinietz, *Western Indians*, 231–32, 380; White, *Middle Ground*, 1–49.

2. DEFENDING ANISHINAABEWAKI

1. *JR* 50:249–71.
2. Memorial of Intendant Bégon, Sept. 20, 1713, *WHC* XVI:298; Blair, *Indian Tribes*, II:78.
3. "Lettre de Talon au ministre . . . ," Sept. 20, 1670, MG 1, Série C11A, vol. 3, fol. 72–73; Newbigging, "French-Ottawa Alliance," 178–87.
4. Witgen, *Infinity of Nations*, 121; Boisguillot to La Barre, May 5, 1684, in Kent, *Rendezvous*, 72.
5. Enjalran to La Barre, May 7, 1684, in Kent, *Rendezvous*, 73; "Lettre de M. de Meulles à La Barre . . . ," Aug. 14, 1684, MG 1, Série C11A, vol. 6, fol. 293–94v.
6. Boisguillot to La Barre, May 5, 1684, Enjalran to La Barre, May 7, 1684, in Kent, *Rendezvous*, 72, 73.
7. Blair, *Indian Tribes*, I:232–43; De Meulles to Seignelay, July 8, 1684, *NYCD* IX:231; Presents of the Onondaga, Sept. 5, 1684, *NYCD* IX:236–39.
8. Meulles to Seignelay, Oct. 10, 1684, *NYCD* IX:248; Newbigging, "French-Ottawa Alliance," 193–202; Blair, *Indian Tribes*, I:250–52; "Lettre de Denonville au ministre . . . ," June 8, 1687, MG 1, Série C11A, vol. 9, fol. 20–31; Denonville to Seignelay, Nov. 8, 1686, *NYCD* IX:297; Denonville, Memoir, 1687, *NYCD* IX:363; "Lettre de Denonville au ministre . . . ," Aug. 25, 1687, MG 1, Série C11A, vol. 9, fol. 61–77v; "Copie d'une lettre de Denonville à Dongan . . . ," Aug. 22, 1687, MG 1, Série C11A, vol. 9, fol. 54–57; Kent, *Rendezvous*, 97–100; Kellogg, *French Régime*, 230–31.
9. Denonville to Seignelay, June 12, 1686, *NYCD* IX:293–95; Denonville to Seignelay, Nov. 8, 1686, *NYCD* IX:296; "Mémoire adressé à Seignelay . . . ," Jan. 1687, MG 1, Série C11A, vol. 9, fol. 249–50v.
10. Denonville to Seignelay, Aug. 25, 1687, *NYCD* IX:336–40; Denonville, Memoir, 1687, *NYCD* IX:358–69; "Mémoire de Denonville au ministre . . . ," 1688, MG 1, Série C11A, vol. 10, fol. 100–111; "Kondiarank," *DCB*; Kent, *Rendezvous*, 108–12; Havard, *Great Peace*, 81; "Lettre de Frontenac au ministre . . . ," Nov. 15, 1689, MG 1, Série C11A, vol. 10, fol. 217–224v; "Parole qui doit être dite (par M. de Frontenac) . . . ," June 1690, MG 8, A1 series 1, vol. 4, 223–30, transcription; Narrative of Occurrences, 1690, *NYCD* IX:463, 480–81.
11. *JR* 64:26–39, 57:129–31; Blair, ed., *Indian Tribes*, II:183–86; Charlevoix, *Journal*, I:304–305; Rushforth, *Bonds of Alliance*, 30–35; White, *Middle Ground*, 21–23.
12. *JR* 64:26–39; Blair, ed., *Indian Tribes*, II:44–45.
13. *JR* 64:26–39; Blair, ed., *Indian Tribes*, II:44–49; Havard, *Great Peace*, 81; Narrative of Occurrences, 1690, *NYCD* IX:463; Kellogg, *French Régime*, 244–45; Newbigging, "French-Ottawa Alliance," 212–13; "'Extrait du mémoire de M. de Denonville . . . ," [1689], MG 1, Série C11A, vol. 10, fol. 200–205; Parole qui doit être dite (par M. de Frontenac) . . . ," June 1690, MG 8, A1 series 1, vol. 4, 223–30, transcription; "Mémoire du roi à MM. de Frontenac et Champigny . . . ," July 14, 1690, MG 1, Series B, vol. 15, fol. 121–26; "Relation par Charles de Monseignat de ce qui s'est passé . . . ," Nov. 1690, MG 1, Série C11A, vol. 11, fol. 5–40.
14. Blair, *Indian Tribes*, II:44–54; Narrative of Occurrences, 1689, 1690, *NYCD* IX:463–64; Eid, "Ojibwa-Iroquois War," 297–324.
15. Eid, "Ojibwa-Iroquois War," 297–324; Tanner, *Atlas*, 31, 34; Narrative of Military

Operations, 1691, 1692, *NYCD* IX:534–37; *JR* 64:37–39; Blair, *Indian Tribes*, I:262; "Relation par Charles de Monseignat de ce qui s'est passé . . . ," Nov. 1690, MG 1, Série C11A, vol. 11, fol. 5–40.

16. "Mémoire de Denonville à Seignelay . . . ," Aug. 10, 1688, MG 1, Série C11A, vol. 10, fol. 63–71v; Observations, Nov. 18, 1689, *NYCD* IX:434; Havard, *Great Peace*, 88.

17. Narrative of Occurrences, 1690, 1691, *NYCD* IX:524; "Observations sur les dépêches de Frontenac . . . ," [1691], MG 1, Série C11A, vol. 125, fol. 232–233v; Kent, *Rendezvous*, 123, 130–31; Eccles, *Canadian Frontier*, 124–25; Havard, *Great Peace*, 81–82; "Lettre de Callière au ministre . . . ," Oct. 19, 1694, MG 1, Série C11A, vol. 13, fol. 104–109v; "Résumé de dépêches du Canada (Frontenac, Champigny) . . . ," 1695, MG 1, Série C11A, vol. 13, fol. 251–52v; "Lettre de Callière au ministre . . . ," Oct. 27, 1695, MG 1, Série C11A, vol. 13, fol. 376–88; "Lettre de Frontenac au ministre . . . ," Nov. 4, 1695, MG 1, Série C11A, vol. 13, fol. 283–95v; "Extrait général des dépêches reçues du Canada en 1695 . . . ," 1695, MG 1, Série C11A, vol. 13, fol. 259–272v, 276v; "Relation d'évènements survenus en 1694 et 1695 . . . " [1695], MG 1, Série C11A, vol. 14, fol. 65–99v.

18. Havard, *Great Peace*, 81–90, quote on 90; "Lettre de Callière au ministre . . . ," Oct. 20, 1696, MG 1, Série C11A, vol. 14, fol. 216–36; "Lettre de Frontenac et Champigny au ministre . . . ," Oct. 26, 1696, MG 1, Série C11A, vol. 14, fol. 119–29; Eccles, *Canadian Frontier*, 124–25; Narrative of Occurrences, 1697, *NYCD* IX:672; "Lettre de Champigny au ministre . . . ," Aug. 18, 1696, MG 1, Série C11A, vol. 14, fol. 182–92; "Lettre de Callière au ministre . . . ," Oct. 15, 1698, MG 1, Série C11A, vol. 16, fol. 164–70v; "Relation de ce qui s'est passé de plus remarquable . . . ," Oct. 20, 1698, MG 1, Série C11A, vol. 15, fol. 22–37; "Paroles des députés iroquois adressées à Callière . . . ," July 1700, MG 1, Série C11A, vol. 18, fol. 81–83; "Discours des Iroquois qui sont venus à Montréal . . . ," Sept. 3, 1700, MG 1, Série C11A, vol. 18, fol. 84–88v; Ratification de la paix conclue entre les Français, leurs alliés . . . ," Aug.-Sept. 1701, MG 1, Série C11A, vol. 19, fol. 41–44v; "Lettre de Callière au ministre . . . ," Oct. 4, 1701, MG 1, Série C11A, vol. 19, fol. 114–22v.

19. Bohaker, "*Nindoodemag*," 24–25; "Ratification de la paix conclue entre les Français, leurs alliés . . . ," Aug.–Sept. 1701, MG 1, Série C11A, vol. 19, fol. 41–44v; Havard, *Great Peace*, 109–83.

20. "Déclaration du roi . . . ," May 21, 1696, MG 1, Série C11A, vol. 125, fol. 195–99; "Mémoire du roi pour MM. de Frontenac et de Champigny . . . ," May 26, 1696, MG 1, Series B, vol. 19, fol. 84–96v; "Lettre de Frontenac et Champigny au ministre . . . ," Oct. 15, 1698, MG 1, Série C11A, vol. 16, fol. 2–22v; Havard, *Great Peace*, 85; Eccles, *France in America*, 99.

21. Richard Weyhing, "'Gascon Exaggerations': The Rise of Antoine Laumet (dit de LaMothe, Sieur de Cadillac), the Foundation of Colonial Detroit, and the Origins of the Fox Wars," in Englebert and Teasdale, eds., *French and Indians*, 77–112; "Lettre de Callière au ministre . . . ," Oct. 16, 1700, MG 1, Série C11A, vol. 18, fol. 63–71v; "Résumé d'une lettre de Lamothe Cadillac . . . ," Sept. 25, [1702], MG 1, Série C11A, vol. 20, fol. 130–36.

22. Newbigging, "French-Ottawa Alliance," 202–203; "Conference Between M. de

Longueuil, Commandant at Detroit, and the Indians, 1700," *NYCD* IX:704–705; Denonville to Seignelay, Nov. 8, 1686, *NYCD* IX:296–300; Kent, *Rendezvous*, 99.

23. Newbigging, "French-Ottawa Alliance," 235; Brandão and Sarna, "Treaties of 1701," 216–17; Havard, *Great Peace*, 31, 42, 85; "Lettre de Callière au ministre . . . ," Oct. 27, 1695, MG 1, Série C11A, vol. 13, fol. 376–88; "Mémoire sur le Canada . . . ," [1696], MG 1, Série C11A, vol. 14, fol. 177–80v; Rushforth, "Limits of Alliance," 57; R. David Edmunds and Joseph L. Peyser, *The Fox Wars: The Mesquakie Challenge to New France* (Norman: University of Oklahoma Press, 1993), 26–28.

24. Weyhing, "'Gascon Exaggerations': Rise of Antoine Laumet," 96–97.

25. Edmunds and Peyser, *Fox Wars*, 29–30; Rushforth, "Limits of Alliance," 58.

26. Tanner, *Atlas*, 32–33; "Relation d'évènements . . . ," [1695], MG 1, Série C11A, vol. 14, fol. 65–99v; "Lettre de Callière au ministre . . . ," Oct. 27, 1695, MG 1, Série C11A, vol. 13, fol. 376–88; Witgen, *Infinity of Nations*, 229–30; "Lettre de Callière au ministre . . . ," Oct. 20, 1699, MG 1, Série C11A, vol. 17, fol. 36–41.

27. "Extrait d'une lettre de Louis-Hector de Callière . . . ," Oct. 20, 1699, MG 1, Série C11A, vol. 120/1, fol. 67–69v; "Lettre de Callière au ministre . . . ," Oct. 20, 1699, MG 1, Série C11A, vol. 17, fol. 36–41; "Réponse de Callière aux discours des chefs Mekawa et Miscouaky . . . ," June 27, 1700, MG 1, Série C11A, vol. 18, fol. 79–80; Sheldon, *Early History,* 124–25.

28. Narrative of Occurrences, 1696, 1697, *NYCD* IX:672, 673; Narrative of Occurrences, 1698, *NYCD* IX:683–84.

29. Rushforth, "Limits of Alliance," 59; Edmunds and Peyser, *Fox Wars*, 59–60.

30. Rushforth, "Limits of Alliance," 56; Newbigging, "French-Ottawa Alliance," 235–36; "Conference Between M. de Longueuil, Commandant at Detroit, and the Indians, 1700," *NYCD* IX:704–705.

31. *JR* 65:189–253, quote at 253; "Kondiaronk," *DCB*; Narrative of Occurrences, 1694, 1695, *NYCD* IX:605; Havard, *Great Peace*, 159.

32. Sturtevant, "Jealous Neighbors," chapter 1; D'Aigremont, Report, Nov. 14, 1708, *MPHC* 33:447; Denonville to Seignelay, June 12, 1686, *NYCD* IX:293–95; Council at Montreal, 1682, *NYCD* IX:176–83; "Lettre de Frontenac au ministre . . . ," Nov. 4, 1695, MG 1, Série C11A, vol. 13, fol. 283–295v; "Relation de ce qui s'est passé de plus remarquable . . . ," 1696, MG 1, Série C11A, vol. 14, fol. 35–64; "Relation de ce qui s'est passé de plus remarquable . . . ," 1697, MG 1, Série C11A, vol. 15, fol. 3–21.

33. Sturtevant, "Jealous Neighbors," 42, 57–59; D'Aigremont, "Report," Nov. 14, 1708, *MPHC* 33:446–52; "Relation de ce qui s'est passé de plus remarquable . . . ," 1697, MG 1, Série C11A, vol. 15, fol. 3–21.

34. Rushforth, "Limits of Alliance," 59; Newbigging, "French-Ottawa Alliance," 258–66; Sheldon, *Early History*, 103, 104–105; "Réponse de Vaudreuil—déplore que les Indiens de Michillimakinac . . . ," Aug. 4, 1705, MG 1, Série C11A, vol. 22, fol. 257–59v.

35. Sturtevant, "Jealous Neighbors," 57–59.

36. Cadillac to Unknown, Sept. 25, 1702, *MPHC* 33:138; *JR* 65:189–253; Marest to Cadillac, May 30, 1702, *MPHC* 33:121–22; Carheil to Cadillac, July 25, 1701, *MPHC* 33:102; Marest to Cadillac, July 28, 1701, *MPHC* 33:103; Marest to Cadillac, May 12, 1703, *MPHC* 33:159–60; Cadillac to Pontchartrain, Aug. 31, 1703, *MPHC* 33:162–63.

37. Marest to Vaudreuil, June 21, 1712, *MPHC* 33:557; "Réponse de Vaudreuil—déplore que les Indiens de Michillimakinac . . . ," Aug. 4, 1705, MG 1, Série C11A, vol. 22, fol. 257–59v.

38. Vaudreuil to Pontchartrain, Nov. 4, 1706, *NYCD* IX:780–81; "Résumé de lettres de Vaudreuil . . . ," 1706, MG 1, Série C11A, vol. 24, fol. 103–20; "Lettre de Vaudreuil et des intendants Raudot au minister . . . ," Apr. 30, 1706, MG 1, Série C11A, vol. 24, fol. 8–19; "Réponse de Vaudreuil aux Onontagués . . . ," Aug. 17, 1707, MG 1, Série C11A, vol. 26, fol. 87v–93v; Rushforth, "Limits of Alliance," 156 and note 33; Sturtevant, "Jealous Neighbors," 118; Newbigging, "French-Ottawa Alliance," 267–69; "Paroles des Tsonnontouans . . . ," Sept. 12, 1704, MG 1, Série C11A, vol. 22, fol. 57–57v; "Paroles de La Grande Terre . . . ," Oct. 18, 1704, MG 1, Série C11A, vol. 22, fol. 52–52v; "Lettre de Vaudreuil au ministre . . . ," Nov. 16, 1704, MG 1, Série C11A, vol. 22, fol. 34–40; Havard, *Great Peace*, 168; "Réponse de Vaudreuil . . . ," Aug. 16 & 17, 1705, MG 1, Série C11A, vol. 22, fol. 268–271v; "Lettre de Vaudreuil au ministre . . . ," Oct. 19, 1705, MG 1, Série C11A, vol. 22, fol. 235–54; "Observations de Vaudreuil sur la lettre de M. de Lamothe . . . ," [1707], MG 1, Série C11A, vol. 26, fol. 94–105v; *JR* 65:251–53.

39. D'Aigremont, Report, Nov. 14, 1708, *MPHC* 33:431–32; Vaudreuil to the Minister, May 5, 1705, *MPHC* 33:242; "Lettre de Vaudreuil au ministre . . . ," Nov. 14, 1703, MG 1, Série C11A, vol. 21, fol. 50–59; Words of the Ottawas, June 18, 1707, *MPHC* 33:323; Sturtevant, "Jealous Neighbors," 60, 61–65; "Réponse de Vaudreuil—déplore que les Indiens de Michillimakinac . . . ," Aug. 4, 1705, MG 1, Série C11A, vol. 22, fol. 257–59v.

40. White, *Middle Ground*, 82–90; Sturtevant, "Jealous Neighbors," chapter 1, esp. 65–70; Newbigging, "French-Ottawa Alliance," 258–66; "Résumé de lettres de Vaudreuil . . . ," 1706, MG 1, Série C11A, vol. 24, fol. 103–20; "Copie d'une lettre de Lamothe Cadillac à Vaudreuil . . . ," Aug. 27, 1706, MG 1, Série C11A, vol. 24, fol. 275–87; "Résumé d'une lettre de Bourgmond . . . ," Aug. 27, 1706, MG 1, Série C11A, vol. 24, fol. 207v; D'Aigremont, Report, Nov. 14, 1708, *MPHC* 33:424–52; Speech of Jean la Blanc, June 18, 1707, *MPHC* 33:238.

41. Marest to the Governor, Aug. 14, 1706, *MPHC* 33:262–69; "Lettre de Vaudreuil au ministre . . . ," Nov. 4, 1706, MG 1, Série C11A, vol. 24, fol. 214–37; Sturtevant, "Jealous Neigbors," 71–72; "Copie d'une lettre de Lamothe Cadillac à Vaudreuil . . . ," Aug. 27, 1706, MG 1, Série C11A, vol. 24, fol. 275–87.

42. Vaudreuil to Pontchartrain, Nov. 4, 1706, *NYCD* IX:780–81; "MM. de Vaudreuil et Raudot au ministre . . . ," Nov. 1706, MG 1, Série C11G, vol. 3, fol. 54v–74v.

43. "Le Pesant," *DCB*; "Lettre des sieurs Vaudreuil et Raudot au ministre . . . ," July 16, 1707, MG 1, Série C11A, vol. 26, fol. 3–6; "Lettre de Vaudreuil au ministre . . . ," July 24, 1707, MG 1, Série C11A, vol. 26, fol. 54–61v; "Observations de Vaudreuil . . . ," [1707], MG 1, Série C11A, vol. 26, fol. 94–105v; Sturtevant, "Jealous Neigbors," 71–72, 120; "Le ministre à M. de Vaudreuil . . . ," June 30, 1707, MG 1, Series B, vol. 29, fol. 55v–65v.

44. Sturtevant, "Jealous Neighbors," 70; Newbigging, "French-Ottawa Alliance," 266–68, 272–76, 293–94; Speech of the Outtavois of Michilimakina," July 23, 1708, *MPHC* 33:388–89.

45. Newbigging, "French-Ottawa Alliance," 246.

46. "Instructions pour servir au Sieur d'Aigremont . . . ," June 30, 1707, MG 1, Series

B, vol. 29, fol. 89v–94v; "Clairambault," *DCB*; Newbigging, "French-Ottawa Alliance," 273–75, 281–87, 310–15.

47. D'Aigremont, Report, Nov. 14, 1708, *MPHC* 33:424–52.

48. Ibid., 33:445–51.

49. D'Aigremont, Report, Nov. 14, 1708, *MPHC* 33:445–51; Kent, *Rendezvous*, 178–79.

50. D'Aigremont, Report, Nov. 14, 1708, *MPHC* 33:445–51; Kent, *Rendezvous*, 175–76.

51. Kent, *Rendezvous*, 174; Vaudreuil and Raudot Report, Nov. 14, 1708, Vaudreuil and Raudot to the Minister, Nov. 14, 1709, *MPHC* 33:402–16, 441, 453–55; "Lettre de Raudot fils au ministre . . . ," Nov. 1, 1709, MG 1, Série C11A, vol. 30, fol. 229–58v.

52. Kent, *Rendezvous*, 174; Vaudreuil and Raudot Report, Nov. 14, 1708, Vaudreuil and Raudot to the Minister, Nov. 14, 1709, *MPHC* 33:402–16, 441, 453–55; "Mémoire de la marquise de Vaudreuil au ministre Pontchartrain . . . ," [1710], MG 1, Série C11A, vol. 31, fol. 67–70v; Vaudreuil to the Minister, Sept. 3, 1710, *MPHC* 33:480; Clairambault to the Minister, Oct. 18, 1710, *MPHC* 33:488.

53. Rushforth, "Limits of Alliance," 59–61; Newbigging, "French-Ottawa Alliance," 304–305; "Extraits d'une lettre de François Dauphin de La Forest . . . ," 1711, MG 1, Série C11A, vol. 120/1, fol. 123v–126.

54. Marest to Vaudreuil, June 21, 1712, *MPHC* 33:557; "Paroles adressées à Vaudreuil par les Indiens descendus avec d'Argenteuil . . . ," July 29, 1710, MG 1, Série C11A, vol. 31, fol. 114–120v; "Lettre de Pierre d'Ailleboust d'Argenteuil au ministre . . . ," Oct. 10, 1710, MG 1, Série C11A, vol. 31, fol. 185–188v; "Lettre du père Marest à Vaudreuil . . . ," July 2, 1712, MG 1, Série C11A, vol. 33, fol. 77–80v.

55. Sturtevant, "Jealous Neighbors," 97–101.

56. "Paroles de Makisabi, chef potéouatami . . . ," Aug. 17, 1712, MG 1, Série C11A, vol. 33, fol. 85–90v; Vaudreuil to Pontchartrain, Nov. 6, 1712, *NYCD* IX:863; White, *Middle Ground*, 154–58; "Lettre de Dubuisson à Vaudreuil . . . ," June 15, 1712, MG 1, Série C11A, vol. 33, fol. 160–178v; De Lery, Account of the siege of the Fox, 1712, *WHC* XVI:293–95; Rushforth, "Limits of Alliance," 59–63; Edmunds and Peyser, *Fox Wars*, 64–75; Newbigging, "French-Ottawa Alliance," 321–22, 336–37.

57. Rushforth, *Bonds of Alliance*, 197–221; Rushforth, "Limits of Alliance," 54–57; Newbigging, "French-Ottawa Alliance," 323.

58. Newbigging, "French-Ottawa Alliance," 302–303, 323–24, 326–28; Kent, *Rendezvous*, 178–87, 216.

59. Marest to Vaudreuil, June 21, 1712, *MPHC* 33:553–56; "Lettre de Dubuisson à Vaudreuil . . . ," June 15, 1712, MG 1, Série C11A, vol. 33, fol. 160–178v.

60. Newbigging, "French-Ottawa Alliance," 329–30; Kent, *Rendezvous*, 206–207, 208–14.

61. Beauharnois to the French Minister, July 21, 1729, *WHC* XVII:63–64.

62. Edmunds and Peyser, *Fox Wars*, 128–29, 244n20; Beauharnois to the French Minister, Oct. 25, 1729, enclosing La Corne to Beauharnois, October 12, 1729, *WHC* XVII:80–81; Marin to Beauharnois, May 11, 1730, *WHC* XVII:88–100.

63. Rushforth, *Bonds of Alliance*, 197–221; Edmunds and Peyser, *Fox Wars*, 136–57, quote on 156.

64. Edmunds and Peyser, *Fox Wars*, 176–79, 189–91; Beauharnois and Hocquart to the French Minister, Nov. 11, 1733, *WHC* XVIII:188–91; Beauharnois to the French Minister, Oct. 5, 1734, *WHC* XVII:202; Beauharnois and Hocquart to the French Minister, Oct. 7, 1734, *WHC* XVII:206–13; Beauharnois to the Minister, Oct. 17, 1736, *WHC* XVII:255–60; Beauharnois to the King, 1737, *WHC* XVII:263.

65. Beauharnois to the Minister, Oct. 17, 1736, *WHC* XVII:256.

66. Beauharnois and Hocquart, Oct. 7, 1734, *WHC* XVII:206–13; Beauharnois to the Minister, Oct. 9, 1735, *WHC* XVII:217; Edmunds and Peyser, *Fox Wars*, 182–83, 188, 189–91; "Résumé de lettres de Beauharnois et Bienville . . . ," Jan. 1736, MG1, Série C11A, vol. 66, fol. 148–54; Beauharnois to the Minister, Oct. 17, 1736, *WHC* XVII:255–60; Beauharnois to the King, 1737, *WHC* XVII:263; Beauharnois to the French Minister, Oct. 16, 1737, *WHC* XVII:275–76; "Lettre de Charles de Beauharnois au ministre . . . ," Oct. 15, 1740, MG 1, Série C11A, vol. 114, fol. 139–139v.

67. Rushforth, "Limits of Alliance," 54; Edmunds and Peyser, *Fox Wars*, 157.

68. David R. Farrell, "Anchors of Empire: Detroit, Montreal and the Continental Interior, 1760–1775," *American Review of Canadian Studies* 7 (1977): 45; Skinner, *Upper Country*, 139–42. But see also Karen Marrero, "Founding Families: Power and Authority of Mixed French and Native Lineages in Eighteenth-Century Detroit" (PhD dissertation, Yale University, 2011).

3. EXPANSION

1. Blackbird, *History of the Ottawa*, 82–83, 95–97; Bellfy, *Three Fires Unity*, xxxiii–xxxvii; Schenck, *Voice of the Crane*, 104–33; Warren, *History of the Ojibway*, 42–57.

2. Blackbird, *History of the Ottawa*, 79–80, 95–97; Witgen, *Infinity of Nations*, 29–68; Bohaker, "*Nindoodemag*," 38; Newbigging, "French-Ottawa Alliance," 95n28; Trigger, *Natives and Newcomers*, 159–63; Sturtevant, "Jealous Neighbors," 124–29.

3. Witgen, *Infinity of Nations*, 31; Blackbird, *History of the Ottawa*, 82–83, 95–97; Rushforth, "Limits of Alliance," 61–62.

4. Witgen, *Infinity of Nations*, 31, 34; Harold Hickerson, "The Feast of the Dead Among the Seventeenth-Century Algonkians of the Upper Great Lakes," *American Anthropologist* 62 (1960): 88–92; Blackbird, *History of the Ottawa*, 46–47.

5. White, *Middle Ground*, 84–85.

6. Peers and Brown, "No End to Relationships," 532–35; McClurken, "We Wish to Be Civilized," 16–28; Bohaker, "*Nindoodemag*," 34–35, 47.

7. Blair, ed., *Indian Tribes*, I:187–90; Bohaker, "*Nindoodemag*," 47–48; Marest to Vaudreuil, June 21, 1712, *MPHC* 33:553, 556; Dulhut, Apr. 12, 1684, *WHC* XVI:115.

8. Newbigging, "French-Ottawa Alliance," 91; Sturtevant, "Jealous Neigbors," 48–51; Rushforth, "Limits of Alliance," 61–62.

9. Witgen, *Infinity of Nations*, 52; McClurken, "We Wish to Be Civilized," 25–28; Bouganville, *Journals*, 134.

10. Miller, *Ogimaag*, 10; Witgen, *Infinity of Nations*, 52; McClurken, "We Wish to Be Civilized," 25–28; Bougainville, *Journals*, 134.

11. Clifton, et al., *Peoples of the Three Fires*, 4–7; Assikinack, "Legends and Traditions," 119–20; "An Account of what occurred during the Voyage of Monsieur de Courcelles," 1671, *NYCD* IX:78; "Extrait général des dépêches reçues du Canada en 1695," 1695, MG 1, Série C11A, vol. 13, fol. 259–272v, 276v.

12. Narrative of Occurrences, 1696, 1696, *NYCD* IX:644–46.

13. Jon Parmenter, "At the Wood's Edge: Iroquois Foreign Relations, 1727–1768" (PhD dissertation, University of Michigan, 1999), 7–8; Marest to Cadillac, Oct. 8, 1701, *MPHC* 33:113–14; Witgen, *Infinity of Nations*, 42; McClurken, "We Wish to Be Civilized," 310, 327–28.

14. James A. Clifton, *The Prairie People: Continuity and Change in Potawatomi Indian Culture, 1665–1965* (Iowa City: University of Iowa Press, 1998), 9–10, 14; *JR* 18:231; Relation of Cadillac, *WHC* XVI:353; "Discours des Iroquois . . . ," Sept. 3, 1700, MG 1, Série C11A, vol. 18, fol. 84–88v; Havard, *Great Peace*, 118, 121–22; Kinietz, *Western Indians*, 380–81; "Nissowaquet," *DCB*; "Ratification de la paix . . . ," Aug.–Sept. 1701, MG 1, Série C11A, vol. 19, fol. 41–44v.

15. Blair, ed., *Indian Tribes*, I:281, II:22, 93, 107–108; Johanna E. Feest and Christian F. Feest, "Ottawa," in William C. Sturtevant, *Handbook of North American Indians*, vol. 15, *Northeast*, edited by Bruce G. Trigger (Washington, DC: Smithsonian Institution, 1978), 776; News from the Outawais, 1695, 1697, *WHC* XVI:164–65, 166–72; Narrative of Occurrences, 1694, 1695," *NYCD* 9:621–27; Speech of Ottawa Katabouile, 1700, *NYCD* 9:719.

16. Blair, ed., *Indian Tribes*, II:108; Narrative of Occurrences, 1694, 1695, *NYCD* 9:621–27; *WHC* XVI:164–65, 166–72; "Words of the Outavois," June 18, 1707, *MPHC* 33:319; "Copie d'une lettre du père Chardon . . . ," May 6, 1708, MG 1, Série C11A, vol. 28, fol. 161–164v.

17. "Copie d'une lettre du père Chardon . . . ," May 6, 1708, MG 1, Série C11A, vol. 28, fol. 161–164v; "Ounanguissé," *DCB*; Clifton, et al., *Peoples of the Three Fires*, iv–v.

18. Narrative of Occurrences, 1696, *NYCD* IX:647; Kent, *Rendezvous*, I:68, 85; White, *Middle Ground*, 128–32; Richter and Thompson, "Severed Connections," 501, 508; *JR* 65:205–207.

19. Callieré and Champigny, Oct. 5, 1701, *MPHC* 33:108; Peterson, "People In Between," 39–40.

20. *JR* 65:237–39; White, *Middle Ground*, 66–68; Jacqueline Peterson, "Many Roads to Red River: Métis Genesis in the Great Lakes Region, 1680–1815," in Jacqueline Peterson and Jennifer S. H. Brown, eds., *The New Peoples: Being and Becoming Métis in North America* (Winnipeg: University of Manitoba Press, 1985), 42–48.

21. *JR* 65:189–253; White, *Middle Ground*, 60, 64; Blair, ed., *Indian Tribes*, I:68–70; Kinietz, *Western Indians*, 272–74.

22. Bruce M. White, "The Woman Who Married a Beaver: Trade Patterns and Gender Roles in the Ojibwa Fur Trade," *Ethnohistory* 46, no. 1 (Winter 1999): 112, 120–38; Peterson, "People In Between," 47, 71, 88; White, "A Skilled Game of Exchange: Ojibway Fur Trade Protocol," *Minnesota History* 50 (Summer 1987): 229–40; Dean L. Anderson, "The Flow of European Trade Goods into the Western Great Lakes Region, 1715–1760," in Susan Sleeper-Smith, ed., *Rethinking the*

Fur Trade: Cultures of Exchange in an Atlantic World (Lincoln: University of Nebraska Press, 2009), 385–410; Kent, *Rendezvous*, II:506.

23. Susan Sleeper-Smith, "Women, Kin, and Catholicism: New Perspectives on the Fur Trade," *Ethnohistory* 47, no. 2 (Spring 2000): 424–25, 440–41.

24. White, "Woman Who Married a Beaver," 120–38; White, "Skilled Game of Exchange," 229–40.

25. Kent, *Rendezvous*, 226.

26. Father Marest to Vaudreuil, Aug. 14, 1708 [1706], *WHC* XVI:234–35; Talk Between Vaudreuil and Onaskin, Chief of the Outavois, Aug. 1, 1706, *MPHC* 33:258–62.

27. *JR* 65:189–253; Peterson, "People in Between," 59–60; Susan Sleeper-Smith, "Furs and Female Kin Networks: The World of Marie Madeleine Réaume L'archevêque Chevalier," in Jo-Anne Fiske, Susan Sleeper-Smith, and William Wicken, eds., *New Faces of the Fur Trade: Selected Papers of the Seventh North American Fur Trade Conference Halifax, Nova Scotia, 1995* (East Lansing: Michigan State University Press, 1998), 53–63.

28. "Charles Amiot," "Henri Nouvel," *DCB*.

29. Engagement of Amiot to Boisrondel, May 8, 1690, Memoir of De Gannes, *IHC* XXIII:207–10, 328; PRDH, 956, 957, 47991; "Memoir of Pierre Liette," in Quaife, ed., *Western Country*, 111.

30. PRDH 75002, 47991, 956, 73837; "Mackinac Baptisms," *WHC* XIX:1–2; "Nissowaquet," *DCB*; Kinietz, *Western Indians*, 270–73, 278; Marest to Vaudreuil, June 21, 1712, *MPHC* 33:553–55.

31. McDonnell, "Indian and Métis Persistence," 149–71.

32. Father Nau to Father Bonin, Oct. 2, 1735, Pierre du Jaunay to Madame Aulneau, May 25, 1741, in Jones, *The Aulneau Collection,* 67, 137–38; Charlevoix, *Journal*, II:39–40; Leavelle, *Catholic Calumet,* 194–96; *JR* 66:283–85; Marest to Vaudreuil, June 21, 1712, *MPHC* 33:553–55.

33. Peterson, "Many Roads," 41–52; Claiborne A. Skinner, *The Upper Country: French Enterprise in the Colonial Great Lakes* (Baltimore: Johns Hopkins University Press, 2008), 122; Memorial, Sept. 20, 1713, *WHC* XVI:295; Helen Hornbeck Tanner, "The Career of Joseph La France, *Coureurs de Bois* in the Upper Great Lakes," in Jennifer S. H. Brown, W. J. Eccles, and Donald P. Helderman, eds., *The Fur Trade Revisited: Selected Papers of the Sixth North American Fur Trade Conference, Mackinac Island, Michigan, 1991* (East Lansing: Michigan State University Press, 1994), 171–88.

34. "Mackinac Baptisms," *WHC* XIX:1–2; Kinietz, *Western Indians*, 270–73; Sleeper-Smith, "Women, Kin, and Catholicism," 440, 452n99; Peterson, "People In Between," 156–58.

35. Trap, "Charles Langlade," 1:8; PRDH 88401.

36. PRDH 88286, 89216, 89830, 88350, 88935, 68544, 88994, 180356, 180382, 180498, 146508; "Jacques-Charles Renaud Dubuisson," *DCB*; Trap, "Charles Langlade," 1:8–10; Pass for Langlais to escort Madame Dubuisson, Montreal, Apr. 18, 1726, Congés et Permis Déposés ou enregistrés a Montréal sous le régime français, *RAPQ* 1921–1922 (Ls-A. Proulx: Imprimeur de sa Majesté le Roi, 1922), 211; PRDH 88822, 88831; "Memoir of Charles Langlade," *WHC* VII:124n.

37. Edmunds and Peyser, *Fox Wars*, 111–17; *WHC* XVII:31–35, 36–56; Grignon, "Recollections," *WHC* III:197–98; "Louvigny," *DCB*; PRDH 73837; Mackinac Baptisms, *WHC* XIX:2; Mackinac Marriages, *WHC* XVIII:469.
38. "Nissowaquet," *DCB*; "Charles Langlade," *DCB*; McDonnell, "Charles-Michel Mouet de Langlade," 79–105.
39. "Mackinac Baptisms," *WHC* XIX:1–8.
40. "Mackinac Baptisms," WHC XIX:2–3, 33; Grignon, "Recollections," 260–61; Trap, "Charles Langlade," 2:11–12; Du Jaunay, *DCB*; Kent, *Rendezvous*, II:592–606; Rushforth, *Bonds of Alliance*, 253–98.
41. McDonnell, "Indian and Métis Persistence," 149–71; Mackinac Marriages, *WHC* XVIII:472, 475; Mackinac Baptisms, *WHC* XIX:13, 32; Sleeper-Smith, "Women, Kin, and Catholicism," 423–52.
42. Mackinac Baptisms, *WHC* XIX:23–24, 28, 33–34, 38–39; Mackinac Marriages, *WHC* XVIII:472, 480; Sleeper-Smith, "Women, Kin, and Catholicism," 426, 440–41.
43. Skinner, *Upper Country*, 147–48; R. Cole Harris, ed., *Historical Atlas of Canada*, 3 vols. (Toronto: University of Toronto Press, 1987–1993), I:Plate 41; Marie Gérin-Lejoie, ed., "Fort Michilimackinac in 1749: Lotbinière's Plan and Description," *Mackinac History* 2, no. 5 (1976): 9; Widder, *Beyond Pontiac's Shadow*, 31–54.
44. Treaty of the New Sioux Company, June 6, 1731, *WHC* XVII:135–39; Peter L. Scanlon, *Prairie du Chien: French, British, American* (Menasha, WI, 1937), 26–27; Beauharnois to the Ministry, Oct. 15, 1732, *WHC* XVII:169.
45. Scanlon, *Prairie du Chien*, 26–27; Beauharnois to the Ministry, Oct. 15, 1732, *WHC* XVII:169; Grignon, "Recollections," *WHC* III:241–43; Peterson, "People In Between," 131; Edmunds and Peyser, *Fox Wars*, 176–79; Beauharnois and Hocquart to the French Minister, Nov. 11, 1733, *WHC* XVIII:188–91; Beauharnois to the French Minister, Oct. 5, 1734, *WHC* XVII:202; Mackinac Baptisms, *WHC* XIX:4, 8–9; Trap, "Charles Langlade," 2:8–9.
46. Trap, "Charles Langlade," 2:9; Mackinac Baptisms, *WHC* XIX:8–10; Herbin to Langlade, 15 Oct. 1755, *WHC* VIII:211–12; Kellogg, *French Regime*, 376; Grignon, "Recollections," *WHC* III:199–201; Memos on Supplies, Feb. 22, 1745, May 12, 1742, June 18, 1743, Sept. 19, 1743, Sept. 4, 1744, MG 1, Série C11A, 83:319–23, 80:198, 81:375, 83:319, 320, 322, 323.
47. Grignon, "Recollections," 198–99.
48. McClurken, "We Wish to Be Civilized," 50.
49. Beauharnois to the French Minister, *WHC* XVII:466–69; Bougainville, *Journals*, July 15, 1757, 126.
50. D'Aigremont, Report, Nov. 14, 1708, *MPHC* 33:446–52; Sleeper-Smith, "Women, Kin, and Catholicism," 423–52; Gérin-Lajoie, ed., "Fort Michilimackinac," 4–9.
51. Tanner, *Atlas*, maps 6, 9, and 13; Sturtevant, "Jealous Neighbors," 101–107, 109–114, 128–29; Havard, *Empire et Métissages*, 206–209.
52. Sheldon, *Early History*, 307–309.
53. Vaudreuil and Raudot to the Minister, Nov. 14, 1709, *MPHC* 33:453–54; Ramezay to the Minister, Sept. 18, 1714, *WHC* XVI:303; Beauharnois to the Minister, Oct. 16, 1737, *WHC* XVII:274–75; De Noyan to the Minister, Aug. 24, 1741, *WHC* XVII:358.

4. THE BALANCE OF POWER

1. "Lettre de Vaudreuil au Conseil de Marine . . . ," Oct. 12, 1717, MG 1, Série C11A, vol. 38, fol. 109–116v; "Lettre de Vaudreuil et Bégon au Conseil de Marine . . . ," Oct. 26, 1719, MG 1, Série C11A, vol. 40, fol. 50–67v; "Lettre de Vaudreuil au ministre . . . ," May 22, 1725, MG 1, Série C11A, vol. 47, fol. 165–73; "Lettre de Longueuil et Bégon au ministre . . . ," Oct. 31, 1725, MG 1, Série C11A, vol. 47, fol. 121–135v; White, *Middle Ground*, 119–21; Govenor Burnet to the Lords of Trade, May 29, 1723, and Nov. 21, 1724, *NYCD* V:684–85, 739; "Lettre de Beauharnois au ministre . . . ," Oct. 15, 1736, MG 1, Série C11A, vol. 65, fol. 134–137v; De Noyan to the French Minister, August 24, 1741, *WHC* XVII:358; Vaudreuil to the Ministry, May 22, 1725, C11A, vol. 47:169v–170; Kent, *Rendezvous*, 221–22.

2. Gilles Havard, "'Protection' and 'Unequal Alliance': The French Conception of Sovereignty over Indians in New France," in Englebert and Teasdale, eds., *French and Indians*, 115, 122, quote on 126; Beauharnois to the Court, Oct. 17, 1736, *WHC* XVII:256; La Galissonière, Memoir, Dec. 1752, *NYCD* X:223.

3. Beauharnois to the Minister, Oct. 17, 1736, AN C11A, vol. 65, fol. 142–49; Witgen, *Infinity of Nations*, 306–12; Beauharnois to the French Minister, Oct. 14, 1737, *WHC* XVII:268; St. Pierre's to Beauharnois, Oct. 14, 1737, La Ronde to Beauharnois, June 28, 1738, and July 22, 1738, *WHC* XVII:269–74, 277–78; Beauharnois to the King, 1737, *WHC* XVII:264; D. Peter MacLeod, "'Une Conspiration Générale': The Exercise of Power by the Amerindians of the Great Lakes During the War of the Austrian Succession, 1744–1748" (PhD dissertation, University of Ottawa, 1992), 19–20; Warren, *History of the Ojibway*, 90–93; "Paroles des Sakis et des Renards à Beauharnois . . . ," June 20, 1740, MG 1, Série C11A, vol. 74, fol. 86–87v; "Lettre de Beauharnois au ministre . . . ," Oct. 1, 1740, MG 1, Série C11A, vol. 74, fol. 80–84; "Paroles des Sioux, Sakis, Renards, Puants . . . ," July 1742, MG 1, Série C11A, vol. 77, fol. 213–24.

4. Sturtevant, "Jealous Neighbors," 139; Beauharnois to the Minister, Oct. 6, 1738, *MPHC* 34:151–53; White, *Middle Ground*, 193.

5. Michael N. McConnell, *A Country Between: The Upper Ohio Valley and Its Peoples, 1724–1774* (Lincoln: University of Nebraska Press, 1992), 44–45; Sturtevant, "Jealous Neighbors," 167–69.

6. Beauharnois to the Minister, Oct. 6, 1738, *MPHC* 34:151–53; Sturtevant, "Jealous Neighbors," 139–41.

7. Noyan to the Minister, Oct. 5, 1738, *MPHC* 34:150; "Lettre de Beauharnois au ministre . . . ," Oct. 1, 1738, MG 1, Série C11A, vol. 69, fol. 133–135v; Beauharnois to the Minister, Oct. 6, 1738, *MPHC* 34:151–53; "Lettre de Hocquart au ministre . . . ," Oct. 22, 1738, MG 1, Série C11A, vol. 70, fol. 116–119v; Noyelle to Beauharnois, Feb. 1, 1739, *MPHC* 34:163–64; Memorandum, Aug. 12, 1738–June 12, 1741, *WHC* XVII:279–88; Tanner, *Atlas*, 44; Sturtevant, "Jealous Neighbors," 168–71.

8. Skinner, *Upper Country*, 114–15, 123–25; Lettre de Beauharnois au ministre . . . ," Sept. 22, 1738, MG 1, Série C11A, vol. 69, fol. 96–97v; "Lettre de Hocquart au ministre . . . ," Oct. 22, 1738, MG 1, Série C11A, vol. 70, fol. 116–119v; Arrell M. Gibson, *The Chickasaws* (Norman: University of Oklahoma Press, 1971), 47–50.

9. Daniel H. Usner, Jr., *Indians, Settlers, and Slaves in a Frontier Exchange Economy: The Lower Mississippi Valley Before 1783* (Chapel Hill: University of North Carolina Press, 1992), 82–83; Gibson, *Chickasaws*, 52–53; Michael J. Foret, "War or Peace? Louisiana, the Choctaws, and the Chickasaws, 1733–1735," *Louisiana History* XXXI (1990): 273–92; Skinner, *Upper Country*, 131.

10. Skinner, *Upper Country*, 131–33; Bienville and Salmon to Maurepas, June 1736, *MPA* I:314–15.

11. Louboey to Maurepas, May 7, 1738, *MPA* I:365–66; Report to the King, recd. Jan. 1, 1739, *MPA* I:386–87; Bienville to Maurepas, May 20, 1739, *MPA* I:397; Norman W. Caldwell, "Chickasaw Threat to French Control of the Mississippi in the 1740s," *Chronicles of Oklahoma* 16, no. 4 (1938): 468–69; Beauharnois to the Minister, Sept. 22, 1738, C11A 69:96–97; Beauharnois to the Minister, June 30, 1739, C11A 71:36–36v; Louboey to Maurepas, Oct. 12, 1739, *MPA* I:404; Usner, *Indians, Settlers, and Slaves*, 83–84; Gibson, *Chickasaws*, 55; Salmon to Maurepas, Jan. 29, 1740, *MPA* I:418–19; Grignon, "Recollections," *WHC* III:199; Beauchamp to Maurepas, Mar. 19, 1740, *MPA* I:438–41.

12. Beauchamp to Maurepas, Mar. 12, 1740, *MPA* I:436; Caldwell, "Chickasaw Threat," 475; *WHC* XVII:335–36; Salmon to the Minister, May 4, 1740, *MPA* I:444–45; Bienville to Maurepas, Sept. 30, 1741, *MPA* III:751–52; "Memoir on the Indians and their Relations," 1740–1741, *WHC* XVII:337; Caldwell, "Chickasaw Threat," 477; Michael J. Foret, "The Failure of Administration: The Chickasaw Campaign of 1739–1740," *Revue de Louisiane / Louisiana Review* XI (1982): 49–60. Cf. Jacob Lee, "Rivers of Power: Indians and Colonists in the North American Midcontinent" (PhD dissertation, University of California, Davis, 2014), especially chapter 3.

13. Beauharnois to the Outaouacs of Missilimakinac, July 8, 1741, *NYCD* IX:1072–73; Céloron to Beauharnois, Sept. 2, 1741, *WHC* XVII:359–60; Beauharnois to the Minister, Oct. 5, 1741, *WHC* XVII:367–69.

14. Céloron to Beauharnois, Sept. 2, 1741, *WHC* XVII:359–60; "Lettre de Beauharnois au ministre . . . ," Oct. 18, 1741, MG 1, Série C11A, vol. 75, fol. 226–227v.

15. "Mémoire d'une fourniture . . . ," May 12, 1742, MG 1, Série C11A, vol. 76, fol. 221 (this was just one of many certificates given out to traders in 1742 for providing supplies to the Odawa for the resettlement); Speech of the Outaouacs of Missilimakinac, of the band of La Fourche, Sinagos and Kiskakons to Beauharnois, June 16, 1742, Response of Beauharnois to the Speech of the Outaouacs of Missilimakinac, of the band of La Fourche, Sinagos and Kiskakons, June 23, 1742, *WHC* XVII:374–75; Céloron to Beauharnois, Sept. 2, 1741, *WHC* XVII:359–60; Beauharnois to the Minister, Sept. 5, 1742, *WHC* XVII:410; Beauharnois and Hocquart to the French Minister, Sept. 24, 1742, *WHC* XVII:419; Beauharnois to the Minister, Oct. 1, 1742, *WHC* XVII:423–24; "Mémoire concernant diverses nations indiennes . . . ," 1742, MG 1, Série C11A, vol. 78, fol. 388–92; "Lettre de Hocquart au ministre . . . ," Oct. 31, 1742, MG 1, Série C11A, vol. 78, fol. 116–120v.

16. *WHC* XVII:396–97; Speech of the Odawa of Detroit to Beauharnois, July 14, 1742, *WHC* XVII:387–90, 390–91, 393; Beauharnois to the Minister, Sept. 5, 1742, *WHC*

NOTES TO PAGES 135–140

XVII:410–11; Speech of the Outaouacs of Saguinan, June 18, 1742, *WHC* XVII:373–74; Response of Beauharnois to the Speech of the Outaouacs of Saguinan, *WHC* XVII:376–77; Father de la Richardie to Father St. Pé, Aug. 26, 1740, *WHC* XVII:328; Response of Beauharnois to the Speech of the Outaouacs of Missilimakinac, of the band of La Fourche, Sinagos and Kiskakons, June 23, 1742, *WHC* XVII:374–75; *MPHC* 34:73–74; Minister to Beauharnois and Hocquart, May 2, 1730, *MPHC* 34:85–87; Beauharnois to the Minister, Sept. 5, 1742, *WHC* XVII:409–11; Kent, *Rendezvous*, 283–84.

17. Beauharnois to the Minister, Oct. 28, 1745, Sept. 22, 1746, *WHC* XVII:447–49, 450–51; La Galissonière and Hocquart to the French Minister, Oct. 7, 1747, *WHC* XVII:470–72; Kent, *Rendezvous*, 290–94; MacLeod, "Une Conspiration Générale," 57–67.

18. Beauharnois to the Minister, Oct. 28, 1745, Sept. 22, 1746, *WHC* XVII:447–49, 450–51; La Galissonière and Hocquart to the French Minister, Oct. 7, 1747, *WHC* XVII:470–72; Eccles, *Canadian Frontier*, 151–52; Skinner, *Upper Country*, 163–72.

19. Longueuil to Beauharnois, July 28, 1745, *WHC* XVII:446–47; MacLeod, "Une Conspiration Générale," 67–70.

20. Newbigging, "French-Ottawa Alliance," 358–59; Beauharnois to the Minister, Oct. 28, 1745, C11A 83:102–107v; Beauharnois to the Minister, Nov. 7, 1744, C11A 81:126–133v; "Rapport . . . ," 1746, MG 1, Série C11A, vol. 86, fol. 302–307v; "Extrait de la dépense . . . ," Dec. 31 1746, MG 1, Série C11A, vol. 86, fol. 178–236; MacLeod, "'Une Conspiration Générale,'" 38–39.

21. Beauharnois to the French Minister, 1747, *WHC* XVII:457–58; *NYCD* X:99–130; MacLeod, "'Une Conspiration Générale,'" chapter 3.

22. Beauharnois to the French Minister, 1747, *WHC* XVII:457–58, 462–63, 467–68; *NYCD* X:99–130; La Galissonière to the Minister, Oct. 23, 1748, *WHC* XVII:506; Journal of Occurrences in Canada During the year 1747–1748, *NYCD* X:142; MacLeod, "'Une Conspiration Générale,'" 107–108; Raymond to the French Minister, Nov. 2, 1747, *WHC* XVII:475–76; Skinner, *Upper Country*, 171.

23. Beauharnois to the French Minister, 1747, *WHC* XVII:462–63, 466–69; La Galissonière to the French Minister, Oct. 23, 1748, *WHC* XVII:506; Journal of Occurrences in Canada During the Year 1747–1748, *NYCD* X:142; MacLeod, "'Une Conspiration Générale,'" 90.

24. Beauharnois to the French Minister, 1747, *WHC* XVII:466–69; Bougainville, *Journals*, July 15, 1757, 126.

25. Beauharnois to the French Minister, 1747, *WHC* XVII:466–69; Governor and Intendant to the French Minister, 1747–1748, *WHC* XVII:478–92.

26. La Galissonière to the French Minister, Quebec, Oct. 23, 1748, *WHC* XVII:506, 510–12; Abstract of despatch from Galissonière, Apr. 5, 1748, *WHC* XVII:492–93; Journal of Occurrences in Canada During the Year 1747–1748, *NYCD* X:140; Extracts from the diary of events for the year 1747–1748, sent by the Governor and Intendant to the French Minister, *WHC* XVII:478–92.

27. La Galissonière to the Minister, Oct. 23, 1748, *WHC* XVII:506, 510–12; Extracts from the diary of events for the year 1747–1748, sent by the Governor and Intendant to the French Minister, *WHC* XVII:489–91; Abstract of despatch from Galissonière, Apr. 5, 1748, *WHC* XVII:492–93; Journal of Occurrences in Canada

During the Year 1747–1748, *NYCD* X:140, 151; MacLeod, "'Une Conspiration Générale,'" chapter 4.

28. Beauharnois to the French Minister, *WHC* XVII:462–63, 467–68; La Galissonière to the French Minister, Quebec, Oct. 23, 1748, *WHC* XVII:506; Journal of Occurrences in Canada During the Year 1747–1748, *NYCD* X:142; Skinner, *Upper Country,* 171. Cf. Journal of Occurrences in Canada During the Year 1747–1748, *NYCD* X:151.

29. La Galissonière to the Minister, Oct. 23, 1748, *WHC* XVII:506, 510–12; Abstract of despatch from Galissonière, Apr. 5, 1748, *WHC* XVII:492–93; Journal of Occurrences in Canada During the Year 1747–1748, *NYCD* X:140.

30. Mémoire de Canada de 1747, par Beaucours, gouverneur de Montréal, Série C11A, vol. 87, fol. 16; Peyser, *Letters from New France* 184–85; "Beaucours," *DCB.*

31. Kent, *Rendezvous,* 317; La Jonquière to the French Minister, Sept. 17, 1751, *WHC* XVIII:83.

32. Ironstack, "From the Ashes," 15.

33. Ironstack, "From the Ashes," 24–28; White, *Middle Ground,* 216–22.

34. White, *Middle Ground,* 216–22; Eric Hinderaker, *Elusive Empires: Constructing Colonialism in the Ohio Valley, 1673–1800* (Cambridge: Cambridge University Press, 1997), 41–42.

35. Hinderaker, *Elusive Empires,* 41–42; Ian K. Steele, *Warpaths: Invasions of North America* (Oxford: Oxford University Press, 1994), 182; Tanner, *Atlas,* 44; Matthew C. Ward, *Breaking the Backcountry: The Seven Years' War in Virginia and Pennsylvania, 1754–1765* (Pittsburgh: University of Pittsburgh Press, 2003); R. David Edmunds, "Pickawillany: French Military Power versus British Economics," *Western Pennsylvania Historical Magazine* 58 (April 1975): 172–73.

36. White, *Middle Ground,* 211–12.

37. Tanner, *Atlas,* 44; "Lettre de La Jonquière au ministre . . . ," Sept. 20, 1750, MG 1, Série C11A, vol. 95, fol. 237–240v; "Lettre de La Jonquière au ministre . . . ," Sept. 17, 1751, MG 1, Série C11A, vol. 115, fol. 69–73v.

38. Sturtevant, "Jealous Neighbors," passim; White, *Middle Ground,* 211–12.

39. "Detail of Indian Affairs," *Pa Archives,* ser. 1, 2:238; Extracts from the diary of events for the year 1747 sent by the governor and intendant of New France to the Minister, Nov. 10, 1747, *WHC* XVII:482, 488–89; La Galissonière to the Minister, Oct. 23, 1748, *WHC* XVII:506; Emily J. Blasingham, "The Miami Prior to the French and Indian War," *Ethnohistory* 2, no. 1 (Winter 1955): 1–10.

40. White, *Middle Ground,* 222; MacLeod, "'Une Conspiration Générale,'" 43–48; Tanner, *Atlas,* 40–41; Céloron's Journal of the Expedition of 1749, *WHC* XVIII:36–58, quote on 45; *JR* 69:149–97; George A. Wood, "Céloron de Blainville and French Expansion in the Ohio Valley," *Mississippi Valley Historical Review* 9 (March 1932): 302–19.

41. Céloron's Journal of the Expedition of 1749, *WHC* XVIII:36–58; *JR* 69:149–97; Wood, "Céloron de Blainville," 302–19; Edmunds, "Pickawillany," 174–75; White, *Middle Ground,* 221–22; La Jonquière to the French Minister, Quebec, Sept. 17, 1751, *WHC* XVIII:84.

42. Charles de Raymond to the Commander at Fort Ouiatanon, Jan. 5, 1750, *Oui-*

atanon Documents, translated and edited by Frances Krauskopf (Indianapolis: Indiana Historical Society, 1955), 214; Raymond to the Governor, Feb. 11, 1750, *WHC* XVIII:58–60; White, *Middle Ground*, 221; Ironstack, "From the Ashes," 28.

43. Jonquière to the Minister, Sept. 20, 1750, *WHC* XVIII:67–68; Jonquière and Bigot to the Minister, Oct. 20, 1750, *WHC* XVIII:78; Jonquière to the Minister, Sept. 17, 1751, *WHC* XVIII:81; Conference between Jonquière and the Onondagas, July 11, 1751, *NYCD* X:232–36; Paroles addressées à la Jonquière par les Kiskakons, juillet 1751, C11A 97:38–39; Christopher Gist, Journal, in Lois Mulkearn, ed., *George Mercer Papers: Relating to the Ohio Company of Virginia* (Pittsburgh: University of Pittsburgh Press, 1954), 109; Le Pian, Report to Raymond, May 1750, *IHC* XXIX:197–200.

44. Paroles échangées entre La Jonquière et des Indiens de Michillimakinac . . . ," July 1750, MG 1, Série C11A, vol. 95, fol. 241–44; Jonquière to the Minister, Sept. 17, 1751, *WHC* XVIII:83; La Jonquière to the French Minister, Sept. 17, 1751, *WHC* XVIII:67–68; White, *Middle Ground*, 209–210; Le Pian, Report to Raymond, May 1750, *IHC* XVIII:215.

45. White, *Middle Ground*, 227–28; Edmunds, "Pickawillany," 179–80; Longueuil to the Minister, Apr. 21, 1752, *WHC* XVIII:104–116; Jonquière to Céloron, Oct. 1, 1751, C11A 97:177ff; Wood, "Céloron de Blainville," 317–18; *IHC* 29:417, 420–21; Tanner, *Atlas*, 44; Benjamin Stoddart at Fort Oswego to William Johnson, July 19, 1751, Captain Thomas Cresap to Governor Dinwiddie Nov. 20, 1751–Jan. 23, 1752, in Hanna, *The Wilderness Trail*, II:281–85; Jonquière to Rouillé, Aug. 26, 1751, Oct. 29, 1751, *IHC* 29:324–25, 417–22; De Ligneris to Vaudreuil, Oct. 25, 1751, *IHC* 29:414–17.

46. White, *Middle Ground*, 229; Longueuil to the Minister, Apr. 21, 1752, *WHC* XVIII:104–105, 108–109; Ligneris to Vaudreuil, Oct. 3, 1752, *IHC* 29:730–33; Minsterial Minute on the English Encroachments on the Ohio, 1752, *NYCD* X:240–41; Edmunds, "Pickawillany," 180–81; Wood, "Céloron de Blainville," 317.

47. Longueuil to the Minister, Apr. 21, 1752, *WHC* XVIII:104–105, 108–109; Céloron's Journal of the Expedition of 1749, *WHC* XVIII:36–58; Conference between Jonquière and the Onondagas, July 11, 1751, in the presence of the Iroquois of Sault St. Louis and Lake of Two Mountains, the Abenaki of Saint Francis, and the Odawa Sinago and Kiskakon of Michilimackinac, *NYCD* X:232–36.

48. Longueuil to the French Minister, Apr. 21, 1752, *WHC* XVIII:108–109, 177; Vaudreuil to Rouillé, Apr. 8, 1752, *IHC* 29:578; Longueuil to the French Minister, Aug. 18, 1752, in Hanna, *Wilderness Trail*, II:290; Minute of Instructions to be given to M. Duquesne, Approved, April 1752, *NYCD* X:243–44; Instructions Regarding the Indians—letter from the French Minister to Duquesne, May 15, 1752, *WHC* XVIII:118–19; Wood, "Céloron de Blainville," 318–19.

49. Ironstack, "From the Ashes," 14–17.

50. Ironstack, "From the Ashes," 14–17, 28; Gist, Journal, 20–23; *WHC* XVIII:104–108; Hanna, *Wilderness Trail*, II:282–85; Edmunds, "Pickawillany," 167–78; Nicholas B. Wainwright, *George Croghan: Wilderness Diplomat* (Chapel Hill: University of North Carolina Press, 1959), 30–39.

51. June 15, 1751, Report of John Lindesay, May 24–June 25, 1751, *JP* IX:81; Conference between Jonquière and the Onondagas, July 11, 1751, in the presence of the Iroquois of Sault St. Louis and Lake of Two Mountains, the Abenaki of Saint Francis, and the Odawa Sinago and Kiskakon of Michilimackinac, *NYCD* X:232–36; Minute of Instructions to be given to M. Duquesne, Approved, April 1752, *NYCD* X:243–44; Instructions Regarding the Indians—letter from the French Minister to Duquesne, May 15, 1752, *WHC* XVIII:118–19, 121–22; Jonquière to the Minister, Sept. 17, 1751, *WHC* XVIII:80–81; "Lettre de La Jonquière au minister . . . ," Sept. 17, 1751, MG 1, Série C11A, vol. 115, fol. 69–73v.

52. White, *Middle Ground*, 230–31, 233–34; Edmunds, "Pickawillany," 182–83; Trap, "Charles Langlade," 4:8–10; Bigot to the Minister, Oct. 26, 1752, C11A 18:175–86; "Lettre de Duquesne au ministre," Oct. 10, 1754, MG 1, Série C11A, vol. 99, fol. 273–81.

53. Trent, *Journal*, 87–89; Robert Callender to Governor Hamilton, Aug. 30, 1752, The Twightwees to Governor Dinwiddie, June 21, 1752, in Hanna, *Wilderness Trail*, II:289–90; 298–99; Longueuil to Rouillé, Aug. 18, 1752, Macarty to Vaudreuil, Sept. 2, 1752, Deposition of English Traders, Feb. 2, 1753, *IHC* XXIX:652–53, 680–81, 811–12; Duquesne to the Minister, Oct. 25, 1752, *WHC* XVIII:128–31.

54. White, *Middle Ground*, 231; Twightwees to the Governor, *Penn Col Recs* V:600–601; Du Guyenne to Vaudreuil, Sept. 10, 1752, *IHC* XXIX:712–25; *Pennsylvania Gazette*, Nov. 23, 1752; David Dixon, *Never Come to Peace Again: Pontiac's Uprising and the Fate of the British Empire in North America* (Norman: University of Oklahoma Press, 2005), 114; Gordon M. Sayre, *Les Sauvages Américains: Representations of Native Americans in French and English Colonial Literature* (Chapel Hill: University of North Carolina Press, 1997), 296–98; Deposition of English Traders, Feb. 2, 1753, *IHC* 29:811–12; De Cosné to Amyand, Feb. 7, 1753, *IHC* XXIX:812–13; Trent, *Journal*, 87–89. Cf. Blair, ed., *Indian Tribes*, I:188, for an early report of Odawa cannibalism.

55. Ligneris to Vaudreuil, Oct. 3, 1752, *IHC* 29:733–34; *Pennsylvania Gazette*, Nov. 23, 1752; Trent, *Journal*, 74, 84–85; The Twightwees to Governor Dinwiddie, June 21, 1752, in Hanna, *Wilderness Trail*, II:289, 298–99.

56. Trent, *Journal*, 85, 87–90; Twightwees to Governor Dinwiddie, June 21, 1752, in Hanna, *Wilderness Trail*, 298–99.

57. White, *Middle Ground*, 233–34, 236; Trent, *Journal*, 89–90; Twightwee to Governor Dinwiddie, June 21, 1752, in Hanna, *Wilderness Trail*, II:298–99; *Penn Col Recs* V:1745–1754, 601.

58. Edmunds, "Pickawillany," 183–84; Trent, *Journal*, 90–93; Ligneris to Vaudreuil, Oct. 3, 1752, *IHC* 29:733–34; White, *Middle Ground*, 231–33, 236.

59. Du Guyenne to Vaudreuil, Sept. 10, 1752, *IHC* 29:715–16; Macarty to Vaudreuil, Sept. 2, 1752, *IHC* 29:684–85.

60. Anderson, *Crucible of War*, 38–40; McConnell, *Country Between*, 106–107.

61. Beauharnois to the Court, Oct. 17, 1736, *WHC* XVII:256; La Galissonière, Memoir on the French Colonies in North America, Dec. 1752, *NYCD* X:223.

5. THE FIRST ANGLO-INDIAN WAR

1. George Chalmers, *An Introduction to the History of the Revolt of the American Colonies . . .* , 2 vols. (Boston: James Munroe and Company, 1845), II:263–64; Hurt, *Ohio Frontier*, 35; Anderson, *Crucible of War*, 28–32.

2. Edmunds, "Pickawillany," 184; Anderson, *Crucible of War*, passim; Steele, *Warpaths*, 179–233; White, *Middle Ground*, 240–68.

3. Eccles, *Canadian Frontier*, 160–62; Anderson, *Crucible of War*, 32.

4. Anderson, *Crucible of War*, 37–45.

5. Ward, *Breaking the Backcountry*, 30–31; Abstract of Despatches from Canada, *NYCD* X:423; White, *Middle Ground*, 243.

6. Secret Conference, Oct. 23, 1754, *NYCD* X:269.

7. McConnell, *Country Between*, 103; Francis Jennings, *The Invasion of America: Indians, Colonialism, and the Cant of Conquest* (Chapel Hill: University of North Carolina Press, 1975), 289–90; Eccles, *Canadian Frontier*, 160–62; White, *Middle Ground*, 243; Ian K. Steele, "The Shawnees and the English: Captives and War, 1753–1765," in Daniel P. Barr, ed., *The Boundaries Between Us: Natives and Newcomers along the Frontiers of the Old Northwest Territory, 1750–1850* (Kent, OH: Kent State University Press, 2006), 1–24; *Maryland Gazette*, Mar. 7, 1754; Donald Jackson, ed., *The Diaries of George Washington*, 6 vols. (Charlottesville: University of Virginia Press, 1976–1979), Dec. 14, 1753, I:150–51, 156; Trent, *Journal*, Aug. 4, 6, 9, 1753, CO 5, 1328; *Journal of Major George Washington* (Williamsburg, VA: William Hunter, 1754), 11, 22.

8. Washington to Horatio Sharpe, Apr. 24, 1754, in W. W. Abbot, ed., *Papers of George Washington*, Colonial Series, I:86; Steele, *Warpaths* 183–85; Anderson, *Crucible of War*, 51–65.

9. Sylvester K. Stevens, Donald H. Kent, and Emma Edith Woods, eds., *Travels in New France by J. C. B.* (Harrisburg: Pennsylvania Historical Commission, 1941), 39–41.

10. Stevens et al., *Travels*, 39–41.

11. Ibid.

12. An Account of the Battle of Monongahela, 9 July 1755, *NYCD* X:303–304; Journal of the Operations of the Army from 22nd July to 30th September, 1755, *NYCD* X:337–38; Anderson, *Crucible of War*, 94–107; D. Peter MacLeod, *The Canadian Iroquois and the Seven Years' War* (Toronto: Dundurn/Press, 2012), 51–59. Cf. David L. Preston, *Braddock's Defeat: The Battle of the Monongahela and the Road to Revolution* (New York: Oxford University Press, 2015).

13. "Lettre de Duquesne au ministre . . . ," Oct. 10, 1754, MG 1, Série C11A, vol. 99, fol. 273–81; Trap, "Charles Langlade," Appendix A; *RAPQ* 1932–1933, 307–308; M. Pouchot, *Memoir upon the Late War in North America . . .* , edited by Franklin B. Hough, 2 vols. (Roxbury, MA: W. Elliot Woodward, 1866), I:39–42. The British records that give credit to Langlade were all written after he had joined the British Indian Service during the Revolutionary War.

14. Anderson, *Crucible of War*, 94–107; Johnson to Braddock, June 27, 1755, *JP* I:663; Steele, *Warpaths*, 188–90.

15. Abstract of M. de Vaudreuil's Despatches, Dec. 1755, *NYCD* X:380; Anderson, *Crucible of War*, 108–109.

16. Vaudreuil to the French Minister, Oct. 20, 1755, *WHC* XVIII:157; Extract of a

letter from Detroit, Oct. 18, 1755, *WHC* XVIII:157; Vaudreuil to Machault, Oct. 30, 1755, *NYCD* X:376; Ward, *Breaking the Backcountry*, 60–70.

17. Abstract of Despatches from Canada, *NYCD* X:423; Montcalm to Count d'Argenson, June 12, 1756, *NYCD* X:416; Extract of a letter, Apr. 5, 1756, *NYCD* X:396; Abstract of Occurrences in Canada, June 1755–May 1, 1756, *NYCD* X:398; The Journal of Occurrences in Canada from October 1755 to June 1756, *NYCD* X:401–402.

18. Orders to Douville, Fort Duquesne, Mar. 23, 1756, *NYCD* X:396; *Pa Archives*, ser. 1, II:620; Orders to Langlade, Fort Du Quesne, Aug. 9, 1756, "Langlade Papers, 1737–1800," *WHC* VIII:213; Abstract of Despatches from Canada, *NYCD* X:423–25; *WHC* XVIII:163; Vaudreuil to Machault, June 8, 1756, *NYCD* X:413; Vaudreuil to Machault, Aug. 8, 1756, *NYCD* X:436–38; Ian K. Steele, *Betrayals: Fort William Henry and the Massacre* (New York: Oxford University Press, 1990), 78–79; *JR* 70:90–91; Abstract of Occurrences in Canada, June 1755–May 1, 1756, *NYCD* X:398; The Journal of Occurrences in Canada from October 1755 to June 1756, *NYCD* X:401; Anderson, *Crucible of War*, 158–65.

19. Machault to Duquesne, Feb. 17, 1755, *NYCD* X:277; La Galissonière, Memoir on the French Colonies in North America, December 1752 [dated December 1750], *NYCD* X:223; "Lettre de Vaudreuil de Cavagnial au ministre . . . ," Oct. 30, 1755, MG 1, Série C11A, vol. 100, fol. 132–33.

20. Memorandum from the King to serve as instructions to the Sieur de Vaudreuil de Cavagnial, Mar. 22, 1755, *WHC* XVIII:150–53; Orders, Michilimackinac, Oct. 15, 1755, "Langlade Papers," *WHC* VIII:211–12; Trap, "Charles Langlade," 4:15–16, 17; Vaudreuil to the Minister, Oct. 20, 1755, *WHC* XVIII:157; Extract of a letter from Detroit, Oct. 18, 1755, *WHC* XVIII:157; Vaudreuil to Machault, Oct. 30, 1755, *NYCD* X:376.

21. Vaudreuil to Machault, Aug. 8, 1756, *NYCD* X:436–37.

22. Vaudreuil to Machault, July 24, 1755, Sept. 25, 1755, *NYCD* X:308–309, 319–27; Steele, *Betrayals*, chapter 4; Bougainville, *Journals*, 5, 8–10; Anderson, *Crucible of War*, 150–57; MacLeod, *Canadian Iroquois*, 87; D. Peter MacLeod, "Microbes and Muskets: Smallpox and the Participation of the Amerindian Allies of New France in the Seven Years' War," *Ethnohistory* 39, no. 1 (Winter 1992): 470–78; Six Nations Answer to William Johnson, Nov. 19, 1756, *NYCD* VII:233.

23. Journal of the Siege of Oswego, 11 Aug.–14 Aug., 1756, *NYCD* X:440–41; Journal of the Siege of Oswego, *NYCD* X:457–61; Vaudreuil to the French Minister, Oct. 20, 1755, *WHC* XVIII:157; Extract of a letter from Detroit, Oct. 18, 1755, *WHC* XVIII:157; Vaudreuil to Machault, Oct. 30, 1755, *NYCD* X:376; Bougainville, *Journals*, 26, 59; Steele, *Warpaths*, 199–200; Anderson, *Crucible of War*, 150–57; Pouchot, *Memoir*, 70–71; Steele, *Betrayals*, 78–79.

24. Anderson, *Crucible of War*, 150–57; Journal of the Siege of Oswego, Aug. 11–14, 1756, *NYCD* X:440–44; Journal of the Siege of Oswego, *NYCD* X:457–61; Letter from an officer Dated Camp at Oswego, Aug. 22, 1756, *NYCD* X:456; Pouchot, *Memoir*, 70–71; Montcalm to D'Argenson, Apr. 24, 1757, *NYCD* X:548.

25. Account of the Embassy of the Five Nations, *NYCD* X:563.

26. Vaudreuil to Machault, Oct. 31, 1755, *NYCD* X:377–78; Accounts of the Conference, *NYCD* X:500–512, 548–63; Jon Parmenter, "L'Arbre de Paix: Eighteenth-Century Franco-Iroquois Relations," *French Colonial History* 4 (2003): 63–80, esp. 72.

27. Steele, *Betrayals*, 79, 84–85; Bougainville, *Journals*, 80–82, 116; Anderson, *Crucible of War*, 185–201; Montcalm to D'Argenson, Apr. 24, 1757, *NYCD* X:548; Account of Two Expeditions in Canada, undated, *NYCD* X:569–70, 571–72; An Account of the Attack on Fort William Henry, undated, but should be Fort George, *NYCD* X:543–46; Vaudreuil to Moras, June 1, 1757, *NYCD* X:567; Malartic to Count d'Argenson, June 16, 1757, *NYCD* X:568–69; Vaudreuil to Moras, July 12, 1757, *NYCD* X:579.

28. Bougainville, *Journals*, 126, 132, 142–43.

29. Pouchot, *Memoir*, 79, 81–82, 85–86; Bougainville, *Journals*, 113–17; Steele, *Betrayals*, chapter 4; Vaudreuil to the Ministry, Feb. 13, 1758, in Sylvester K. Stevens and Donald H. Kent, eds., *Wilderness Chronicles of Northwestern Pennsylvania* (Harrisburg: Pennsylvania Historical Commission, 1941), 109–10.

30. *JR* 70:90–91.

31. Montcalm to de Paulmy, Montreal, July 11, 1757, *NYCD* X:574–75; Vaudreuil to Moras, June 1, 1757, *NYCD* X:567; Vaudreuil to Moras, July 12, 1757, *NYCD* X:584–86; Bougainville, *Journals*, 60.

32. *JR* 70:110–11; Bougainville, *Journals*, 132–43; Steele, *Betrayals*, 87–88; Montcalm to Vaudreuil, July 27, 1757, *NYCD* X:591–92.

33. Steele, *Betrayals*, 91; Montcalm to Vaudreuil, July 27, 1757, *NYCD* X:591–92.

34. *JR* 70:124–26, 129; Bougainville, *Journals*, 142–43, 144, 150; Steele, *Betrayals*, 85, 91; Dixon, *Never Come to Peace Again*, 114.

35. Bougainville, *Journals*, 144, 152; Steele, *Betrayals*, 91; Bougainville to Paulmy, Aug. 19, 1757, *NYCD* X:609–10; Journal of the Expedition against Fort William Henry, from 12 July to 16 August, 1757, *NYCD* X:599.

36. Bougainville, *Journals*, 149, 150–51, 163–64, 165; Bougainville to Paulmy, Aug. 19, 1757, *NYCD* X:609–10, 611, 613.

37. Bougainville, *Journals*, 150–51; Steele, *Betrayals*, 80.

38. *JR* 70:112–13; Bougainville to Paulmy, Aug. 19, 1757, *NYCD* X:606–608; Bougainville, *Journals*, 150–51; Steele, *Betrayals*, 80.

39. Anderson, *Crucible of War*, 192–96.

40. Bougainville, *Journals*, 169, 170, 170–71; Bougainville to Paulmy, Aug. 19, 1757, *NYCD* X:614–15.

41. Bougainville to Paulmy, Aug. 19, 1757, *NYCD* X:609–13; Steele, *Betrayals*, 81; *JR* 70:151–52; Bougainvlle to Madame Herault, June 30, 1757, Bougainville, *Journals*, 331.

42. Bougainville, *Journals*, 169, 170, 170–71; *JR* 70:177; Bougainville to Paulmy, Aug. 19, 1757, *NYCD* X:614–15.

43. Bougainville, *Journals*, 172–73; Steele, *Betrayals*, 109–28; *JR* 70:176–82; Bougainville to Paulmy, Aug. 19, 1757, *NYCD* X:616–19; Detail of the Campaign of 1757, from July 30 to Sept. 4, 1757, *NYCD* X:629.

44. Bougainville, *Journals*, 172–73.

45. Bougainville, *Journals*, 172–73; *JR* 70:179–83, 195; Return of the State of the Following Corps that were at Fort William Henry, from Daniel Webb, Aug. 25, 1757, Daniel Webb to Lord Barrington, Aug. 17, 1757, George Munro to Loudoun, Aug. 30, 1757, Daniel Webb, Remarks upon the Capitulation of Fort William Henry according to the intelligence received from Col. Munro, 30 August 1757, Loudoun Papers, Huntington Library.

46. Bougainville, *Journals*, 174; Bougainville to Paulmy, Aug. 19, 1757, *NYCD* X:616–19; Steele, *Betrayals*, 129–30.

47. Bougainville, *Journals*, 170–74, 175; Bougainville to Paulmy, Aug. 19, 1757, *NYCD* X:616–19; Orders, Montreal, Sept. 1757, "Langlade Papers," *WHC* VIII:213.

48. Bougainville, *Journals*, 170–74, 175, 178–79; Bougainville to Paulmy, Aug. 19, 1757, *NYCD* X:616–19; Steele, *Betrayals*, 129–30, 139, table 2; Vaudreuil to Moras, Sept. 1757, *NYCD* X:631–34; Spenser Wilkinson, *The French Army Before Napoleon* (Oxford: Clarendon Press, 1915), 85.

49. Montcalm to de Paulmy, Aug. 15, 1757, Sept. 18, 1757, *NYCD* X:597–98, 638; White, *Middle Ground*, 246.

50. Pouchot, *Memoir*, 85–86, 89–92; Steele, *Betrayals*, chapter 4.

51. Anderson, *Crucible of War*, 202–204; Vaudreuil to the Ministry, Feb. 13, 1758, in Stevens and Kent, eds., *Wilderness Chronicles*, 109–10.

52. Vaudreuil to Machault, Sept. 7, 1755, Aug. 8, 1756, *NYCD* X:324, 438; Vaudreuil au Ministre, June 15, 1756, AN, C11A, vol. 101, fol. 28; Vaudreuil, Mémoire, Nov. 3, 1758, AN, C11A, vol. 103; Bougainville, *Journals*, 152, 180.

53. Vaudreuil to Moras, July 12, 1757, *NYCD* X:579; Doreil to Paulmy, Oct. 25, 1757, *NYCD* X:653; Bougainville, *Journals*, 193, 197, 201, 204; Pouchot, *Memoir*, 92; Journal of Occurrences in Canada, Oct. 20, 1757, to Oct. 20, 1758, *NYCD* X:840; Trap, "Charles Langlade," 5:22, 28–29; Blackbird, *History of the Ottawa*, 9–10; Widder, *Beyond Pontiac's Shadow*, 34–36.

54. Bougainville, *Journals*, 193, 197; Blackbird, *History of the Ottawa*, 9–10; Montcalm to Paulmy, Apr. 18, 1758, *NYCD* X:700; Pouchot, *Memoir*, 92.

55. Blackbird, *History of the Ottawa*, 9–10; Bougainville, *Journals*, 197, 204; Montcalm to Paulmy, Apr. 18, 1758, *NYCD* X:700; Pouchot, *Memoir*, 92.

56. Anderson, *Crucible of War*, 200; Doreil to Marshal Belle Isle, June 16, 1758, *NYCD* X:718; Journal of Occurrences, 1757, 1758, *NYCD* X:840; Bougainville, *Journals*, 204.

57. Jaunay to Langlade, Sept. 24, 1758, "Langlade Papers," *WHC* VIII:214.

58. Bougainville, *Journals*, 204; Pouchot, *Memoir*, 104; Montcalm, Journal, Aug. 13, 1758, *WHC* XVIII:203–204; White, *Middle Ground*, 246–47; Journal of Occurrences, 1757, 1758, *NYCD* X:840.

59. Ward, *Breaking the Backcountry*, 178–82; Anderson, *Crucible of War*, 275–79; Steele, *Warpaths*, 214–15; McConnell, *Country Between*, 133–34.

60. Forbes to Governor Denny, Nov. 26, 1758, *NYCD* X:905–906; Anderson, *Crucible of War*, 282–83; Albert T. Volwiler, *George Croghan and the Westward Movement, 1741–1782* (Cleveland, OH: Arthur H. Clark Company, 1926), 147; Colonel Mercer to Governor Denny, Jan. 8, 1759, Aug. 6, 1759, *Penn Col Recs* VIII:292–93, 391–92; Bougainville, *Journals*, 242–60; Vaudreuil to Massiac, Aug. 4, 1758, *NYCD* X:780–83, 788–89, 805–806.

61. Colonel Mercer to Governor Denny, Aug. 6, 1759, *Penn Col Recs* VIII:391–92; Johnson's Proceedings with Deputies, Fort Johnson, Feb. 13–14, 1760, *JP* III:188–89; Conference at Fort Pitt, Apr. 7, 1760, *JP* III:211; Pouchot, *Memoir*, I:261, 266, II:5–6.

62. Anderson, *Crucible of War*, 208–96, 309–10; Steele, *Warpaths*, 215; Eccles, *Canadian Frontier*, 177–78.

63. Montcalm to Moras, Feb. 19, 1758, *NYCD* X:686; Journal of the Military opera-

tions before Ticonderoga, June 30th to July 10th, 1758, *NYCD* X:721–24; Montcalm to Marshal de Belle Isle, July 12, 1758, *NYCD* X:732, 734; Montcalm to Marshal de Belle Isle, July 20, 1758, *NYCD* X:737; Doreil to Moras, July 28, 1758, *NYCD* X:746.

64. Anderson, *Crucible of War*, 250–66; News from St. Joseph's River, Oct. 1, 1758, *WHC* XVIII:205; Montcalm to Cremille, Nov. 21, 1758, *NYCD* X:901–902.

65. Vaudreuil to Massiac, Aug. 4, 1758, *NYCD* X:780–83, 788–89, 805–806; White, *Middle Ground*, 246; Vaudreuil's answer to Montcalm's note on Fort Carillon, Sept. 12, 1758, *NYCD* X:874; Memoir of Péan on the Condition of Canada, Nov. 15, 1758, *NYCD* X:898–99.

66. Marshal de Belle Isle to Montcalm, Feb. 19, 1759, *NYCD* X:943–44; French Minister to Vaudreuil and Bigot, Sept. 23, 1758, *WHC* XVIII:204–205; Montcalm's Journal, Dec. 10, 1758, *WHC* XVIII:206; James C. Riley, *The Seven Years' War and the Old Regime in France: The Economic and Financial Toil* (Princeton: Princeton University Press, 1986), 85–86.

67. Marshal de Belle Isle to Montcalm, Feb. 19, 1759, *NYCD* X:943–44; French Minister to Vaudreuil and Bigot, Sept. 23, 1758, *WHC* XVIII:204–205; Berryer to Bigot, Jan. 19, 1759, *NYCD* X:937–38.

68. Extract of a letter from Montcalm to Bourlamaque, March 12 and 15, 1759, *WHC* XVIII:209; Extract of Montcalm's Journal, dated May 11, 1759, *WHC* XVIII:209–10; Steele, *Warpaths*, 219; MacLeod, "Microbes and Muskets," 52; D. Peter MacLeod, *Northern Armageddon: The Battle of the Plains of Abraham* (Vancouver: Douglas & McIntyre, 2008), 72–73.

69. MacLeod, *Canadian Iroquois*, 131–32, 150–52; Journal of the Siege of Quebec, undated, *NYCD* X:1000; Extract of Montcalm's Journal of the siege of Quebec, *NYCD* X:1028, 1031, 1039; "Dialogues of the Dead—Montcalm and Wolfe—a Narrative of the siege operations before Quebec in 1759—attributed to the Chevalier Johnstone, A.D.C. to General Levi," *Manuscripts Relating to the Early History of Canada,* 2nd ser. (Literary and Historical Society of Quebec, 1868), 12–15; MacLeod, *Northern Armageddon*, 163–67, 194–95; Bigot to Marshal de Belle Isle, Oct. 25, 1759, *NYCD* X:1051–52; Trap, "Langlade," 6:6–7, 8.

70. Promotion, from Louis, at Versailles, Feb. 1, 1760, registered at the comptroller's office of the Marine, of New France, at Montreal, June 16, 1760; "Langlade Papers," *WHC* VIII:214–15; Vaudreuil to Chevalier de Lévis, to serve as Instructions, no date, *NYCD* X:1070; Vaudreuil to Berryer, May 3, 1760, *NYCD* X:1075–76; Extract from a letter of Vaudreuil, Aug. 17, 1760, *WHC* XVIII:219; Trap, "Langlade," 6:6–14; Vaudreuil's orders, 1760, "Langlade Papers," *WHC* VIII:215; Extract from a letter of D'Abbadie, Aug. 9, 1764, *WHC* XVIII:221–22.

71. Vaudreuil's orders, Sept. 3, 1760, Vaudreuil to Langlade, Sept. 9, 1760, "Langlade Papers," *WHC* VIII:215, 216–17; Levi to Marshal de Belle Isle, Aug. 7, 1760, *NYCD* X:1102; Articles for the Surrender of Canada, Sept. 8, 1760, *NYCD* X:1105–1108, 1117–18.

6. THE SECOND ANGLO-INDIAN WAR

1. George Croghan to William Johnson, Jan. 25, 1760, *JP* X:134.

2. Gregory Evans Dowd, *War Under Heaven: Pontiac, the Indian Nations & the British*

Empire (Baltimore: Johns Hopkins University Press, 2002); William Nester, *"Haughty Conquerors": Amherst and the Great Indian Uprising of 1763* (Westport, CT: Praeger, 2000); Dixon, *Never Come to Peace Again.*

3. Nicholas B. Wainwright, ed., "George Croghan's Journal, 1759–1763," *Pennsylvania Magazine of History and Biography* 71, no. 4 (Oct. 1947): 332.

4. Governor Vaudreuil's orders, dated Montreal, Sept. 3, 1760, Vaudreuil to Langlade, Sept. 9, 1760, "Langlade Papers," *WHC* VIII:215, 216–17; Anderson, *Crucible of War,* 330–33; Croghan, "Journal," 371; Sturtevant, "Jealous Neighbors," 270–71.

5. Sturtevant, "Jealous Neighbors," 250–51.

6. *JP* X:200; Robert Rogers, *Journals of Major Robert Rogers . . .* (London, 1765), 145–71; Robert Rogers, *Concise Account of North America* (London, 1765), 240–43; Croghan, "Journal of 1760–1761," in Reuben Gold Thwaites, ed., *Early Western Travels, 1748–1846*, 32 vols. (Cleveland: A. H. Clark Co., 1904–1907), I:100–106; Donald Campbell to Henry Bouquet, Dec. 2, 1760, Dec. 23, 1760, *MPHC* 19:44–45, 50; Richard Shuckburgh to Johnson, Feb. 2, 1761, *JP* III:323; Amherst to Johnson, Feb. 1, 1761, *JP* III:316–17; Jaunay to St. Pé, May 7, 1761, *JP* III:412–16.

7. Memoranda of Points of Inquiry, Detroit, Sept. 6, 1761, *JP* III:501–502, 523.

8. Sturtevant, "Jealous Neighbors," 268–71, 287–90; *JP* X:200–202.

9. *JP* X:202.

10. Sturtevant, "Jealous Neighbors," 269.

11. Campbell to Bouquet, Nov. 2, 1760, Dec. 11, 1760, Dec. 23, 1760, *MPHC* 19:44–45, 46–47, 49–50; Jaunay to St. Pé, May 7, 1761, *JP* III:412–16; Richard Shuckburgh to Johnson, Feb. 2, 1761, *JP* III:323; Amherst to Johnson, Feb. 1, 1761, *JP* III:316–17.

12. Jaunay to St. Pé, May 7, 1761, *JP* III:412–16.

13. Croghan to Johnson, May 10, 1762, *JP* III:733.

14. Campbell to Bouquet, June 16, 1761, June 21, 1761, *MPHC* 19:76–77, 78–79; *JP* III:448–53; Parmenter, "At the Wood's Edge," 446.

15. Amherst to Johnson, June 24, 1761, *JP* III:421, 422–23; Campbell to Bouquet, Dec. 11, 1760, *MPHC* 19:46–47; Monckton to Campbell, Oct. 19, 1760, *MPHC* 19:41–42, 43–44.

16. Niagara and Detroit Proceedings, July-September 1761, *JP* III:428–55; Widder, *Beyond Pontiac's Shadow*, 69–72.

17. Niagara and Detroit Proceedings, July-September 1761, *JP* III:455, 468–78, 483, 486–87, 491–92.

18. *JP* III:494.

19. Niagara and Detroit Proceedings, July-September, 1761, *JP* III:494–99; Johnson to Amherst, Nov. 5, 1761, *JP* III:559.

20. Henry Balfour's Conference with Indians, Sept. 29, 1761, *JP* III:537–45.

21. Milo Milton Quaife, ed., *Alexander Henry's Travels and Adventures in the Years 1760–1776* (Chicago: Lakeside Press, 1921), 39–53; Henry Balfour's Conference with Indians, Sept. 29, 1761, *JP* III:537–45.

22. Henry Balfour's Conference with Indians, Sept. 29, 1761, *JP* III:537–45; Bruce M. White, "Give us a Little Milk: The Social and Cultural Meanings of Gift Giving in the Lake Superior Fur Trade," *Minnesota History* 48, no. 2 (Summer 1982): 62, 65–67, 70–71.

23. Henry, *Travels*, 44; Henry Balfour's Conference with Indians, Sept. 29, 1761, *JP* III:537–45; Amherst to Johnson, Mar. 13, 1762, *JP* III:645.

24. James Gorrell, "Lieut. James Gorrell's Journal," *WHC* I:26–27.

25. Croghan to Johnson, May 10, 1762, *JP* III:733; Johnson to Croghan, Oct. 24, 1762, *JP* III:914; "Journal of Ensign Thomas Hutchins, April 3, 1762–Sept. 24, 1762," in Hanna, *Wilderness Trail*, II:361–67.

26. Hutchins, "Journal," 361–67; Croghan to Johnson, May 10, 1762, *JP* III:733.

27. Johnson to the Lords of Trade, Aug. 20, 1762, *JP* III:865–69.

28. Anderson, *Crucible of War*, 472–75, 518–34; Croghan to Johnson, January 13, 1761, *JP* III:302.

29. Amherst to Johnson, Aug. 11, 1761, *JP* III:517.

30. Johnson Diary, Sept. 4, 1761, *WHC* XVIII:231; Sturtevant, "Jealous Neighbors," 253; Claus to Johnson, Dec. 3, 1761, Johnson to Claus, Feb. 9, 1762, *JP* III:576, 629.

31. Thomas Baugh to Amherst, July 20, 1762, *JP* III:831; Johnson to Robert Monckton, Aug. 1, 1762, *JP* III:853; Hugh Wallace to Alexander Duncan, Aug. 27, 1762, *JP* III:870; Johnson to Alexander Duncan, Sept. 21, 1762, *JP* III:882–83; Campbell to Bouquet, July 3, 1762, *MPHC* 19:153–54; Leslye to Amherst, Sept. 16, 1762, Amherst Papers, W.O. 34/49:116–17; Copy of Indian Intelligence, from Croghan to Amherst and Johnson, Sept. 28, 176[2], and Sept. 30, 176[2], *JP* X:534–35.

32. Anderson, *Crucible of War*, 535–46; McConnell, *Country Between*, 183; Amherst to Bouquet, Jan. 21, 1763, *MPHC* 19:176; Croghan to Johnson, March 12, 1763, *JP* IV:62; George Croghan to Amherst, Apr. 30, 1763, *MPHC* 19:183–84; Croghan to Johnson, Apr. 24, 1763, *JP* X:659–60.

33. Anderson, *Crucible of War*, 535–46; Amherst, *Journal*, 301–26; James McDonald to George Croghan, July 12, 1763, *JP* X:736–45; James McDonald to Bouquet from Detroit, July 12, 1763, *MPHC* 19:217.

34. Gorrell, "Journal," 39–44; Richard Middleton, *Pontiac's War: Its Causes, Course and Consequences* (New York: Routledge, 2007), 83–99; Dowd, *War Under Heaven*, 114–47.

35. Anderson, *Crucible of War*, 541; Gary B. Nash, *Red, White, and Black: The Peoples of Early America* (Englewood Cliffs, NJ: Prentice-Hall, 1974), 232–33.

36. For a detailed view of events at Michilimackinac in 1763, but one that differs in emphasis to my interpretation of French and Métis influences on events, see Widder, *Beyond Pontiac's Shadow*.

37. Etherington to Gladwin, June 12, 1763, *WHC* VII:162–63; Claus to Johnson, Aug. 6, 1763, *WHC* XVIII:256–58; James McDonald to Bouquet from Detroit, July 12, 1763, *MPHC* 19:217.

38. Etherington to Gladwin, June 12, 1763, *WHC* VII:162–63; Claus to Johnson, Aug. 6, 1763, *WHC* XVIII:256–58; James McDonald to Bouquet from Detroit, July 12, 1763, *MPHC* 19:217.

39. *JR* 70:251–53; Etherington to Gladwin, June 12, 1763, *WHC* VII:162–63; Testimony of Henry Bostwick, Aug. 13, 1763, *MPHC* 27:666–71; Henry, *Travels*, 80–95.

40. Etherington to Gladwin, June 12, 1763, *WHC* VII:162–63; Kent, *Rendezvous*, II:351; Claus to Johnson, Aug. 6, 1763, *WHC* XVIII:256–58; Speech of Feubleu, or Beendanoa, at the Indian Conference, Montreal, Aug. 9–11, 1763, *JP* X:779–86;

Henry, *Travels*, 95–97; Louis B. Porlier, "Capture of Mackinaw, 1763," *WHC* VIII:230; Grignon, "Recollections," *WHC* III:225.

41. John Porteous, "Schenectady to Michilimackinac, 1765 & 1766," *Ontario Historical Society Papers and Records* XXXIII (1939): 91–98; Speech of Feubleu, *JP* X:779–86; Henry, *Travels*, 95–97.

42. Etherington to Gladwin, June 12, 1763, *WHC* VII:162–63; Claus to Johnson, Aug. 6, 1763, *WHC* XVIII:256–58.

43. Etherington to Gladwin, June 12, 1763, *WHC* VII:162–63; Claus to Johnson, Aug. 6, 1763, *WHC* XVIII:256–58; Henry, *Travels*, 95–97.

44. Etherington to Gladwin, June 12, 1763, *WHC* VII:162–63; Claus to Johnson, Aug. 6, 1763, *WHC* XVIII:256–58; Henry, *Travels*, 95–97; James McDonald to Bouquet, July 12, 1763, *MPHC* 19:217.

45. Mary Agnes Burton, ed., *Journal of Pontiac's Conspiracy 1763* (Detroit: Clarence Monroe Burton, 1912), 170–76, 178, 180, 186; James McDonald to Bouquet, July 12, 1763, *MPHC* 19:217; Etherington to Langlade, July 1, 1763, *WHC* XVIII:254, 254n49; Etherington to Gorrell, from Michilimackinac, June 11, 1763, in Gorrell, "Journal," 38–39; Gorrell, "Journal," 38–44; Etherington to Langlade, June 16, 1763, June 18, 1763, Ayer MS 277; Etherington to Gorrell, June 28, 1763, Gorrell, "Journal," 44–45; Etherington to Langlade, July 1, 1763, *WHC* XVIII:254.

46. Burton, ed., *Journal of Pontiac's Conspiracy*, 170–76, 178, 180, 186; James McDonald to Bouquet, July 12, 1763, *MPHC* 19:217; Etherington to Langlade, July 1, 1763, *WHC* XVIII:254, 254n49.

47. Hutchins, "Journal," 363; Gorrell, "Journal," 46; Howard to Bradstreet, Oct. 15, 1764, Gage Papers.

48. *JP* XI:302; Howard to Bradstreet, Oct. 15, 1764, Gladwin to Gage, Jan. 9, 1764, Gage Papers.

49. Gorrell, "Journal," 43–46.

50. Ibid., 45–47.

51. Etherington to Gladwin, July 18, 1763, *WHC* XVIII:255–56; Gorrell, "Journal," 47; Middleton, *Pontiac's War*, 106–107; Claus to Johnson, Aug. 6, 1763, *WHC* XVIII:256–58.

52. Lords of Trade to William Johnson, Sept. 29, 1763, *NYCD* 7:567; Dowd, *War Under Heaven*, 137–38, 142, 145–46, 274–75.

53. Speech of Feubleu, *JP* X:779–86; Affidavit from Daniel Claus, Sept. 18, 1766, *JP* V:377–78.

54. Speech of Feubleu, *JP* X:779–86.

55. Etherington to Gladwin, June 12, 1763, *WHC* VII:162–63; Claus to Johnson, Aug. 6, 1763, *WHC* XVIII:256–58; Gorrell, "Journal," 46–47, 48; Gage to Johnson, on Aug. 12, 1763, *JP* X:787–88.

56. Claus to Johnson, Aug. 29, 1763, *JP* X:806–807; Speech of Feubleu, *JP* X:779–80; Major Rogers speech to the Several Chiefs of Ottawas at Michilimackinac, Aug. 18, 1766, National Library of Canada, MG 19, F 35—Superintendent of Indian Affairs in the Northern District of North America, Original n.d. 1762–1829, Photocopy, n.d. 1753–1795, series 1, lot 646, 1–7, 11.

57. Bouquet to Amherst, June 25, 1763, *MPHC* 19:201; Amherst to Johnson, June 22, 1763, *JP* IV:151; Amherst to Bouquet, June 29, 1763, *MPHC* 19:203; Amherst to

Bouquet, Aug. 7, 1763, *MPHC* 19:224; Amherst to Bouquet, Sept. 25, 1763, *MPHC* 19:233–34; Anderson, *Crucible of War*, 542–44.

58. Anderson, *Crucible of War*, 542–43; Amherst to Bouquet, June 29, 1763, *MPHC* 19:203; Amherst to Bouquet, Aug. 7, 1763, *MPHC* 19:224; Amherst to Bouquet, Sept. 25, 1763, *MPHC* 19:233–34; Bouquet to Amherst, June 25, 1763, *MPHC* 19:201; Amherst to Johnson, Sept. 30, 1763, *JP* X:856–58; Elizabeth A. Fenn, "Biological Warfare in Eighteenth-Century North America: Beyond Jeffery Amherst," *Journal of American History* 86 (March 2000): 1552–80.

59. Amherst to Johnson Sept. 30, 1763, *JP* X:856–58.

60. Johnson to Amherst, Oct. 13, 1763, *JP* X:876–82.

61. Johnson to Cadwallader Colden, Oct. 24, 1763, *JP* IV:273–77.

62. Lords of Trade to William Johnson, Sept. 29, 1763, *NYCD* VII:567; Anderson, *Crucible of War*, 553.

63. Anderson, *Crucible of War*, 557–59, 560–66.

64. Anderson, *Crucible of War*, 557–59, 560–66; Colin G. Calloway, *The Scratch of a Pen: 1763 and the Transformation of North America* (New York: Oxford University Press, 2006), 91.

65. Woody Holton, *Forced Founders: Indians, Debtors, Slaves, and the Making of the American Revolution in Virginia* (Chapel Hill: University of North Carolina Press, 1999), 3–38; Anderson, *Crucible of War*, 740; Calloway, *Scratch of a Pen*, 91–100.

66. Calloway, *Scratch of a Pen*, 93–94; Royal Proclamation, Oct. 7, 1763, *JP* X:977–85; Bruce Clark, *Native Liberty, Crown Sovereignty: The Existing Aboriginal Right of Self-Government in Canada* (Montreal: McGill-Queen's University Press, 1990), 81; Gage to Johnson, Dec. 12, 1763, *JP* X:953–54.

67. White, *Middle Ground*, 295–96; Dixon, *Never Come to Peace Again*, 221–24; Anderson, *Crucible of War*, 617–32.

68. Anderson, *Crucible of War*, 617–32; McConnell, *Country Between*, 190–91; Richter, *Facing East*, 190–91, 208; Dixon, *Never Come to Peace Again*, xiii; Peter R. Silver, *Our Savage Neighbors: How Indian War Transformed Early America* (New York: W. W. Norton, 2009).

69. Anderson, *Crucible of War*, 617–32; *JP* V:426.

70. Jaunay to Ralph Burton, June 6, 1764, enclosed in Burton to Gage, July 13, 1764, Gage Papers; Proceedings with the Indians, July 9–Aug. 2, 1764, *JP* IV:466–68, XI:262–312.

71. Johnson to the Lords of Trade, Aug. 30, 1764, *NYCD* VII:648; Jon Parmenter, "Forging New Links in the Anglo-Iroquois Covenant Chain, 1758–1766," *Ethnohistory* 44, no. 4 (Autumn 1997): 631–32; Proceedings with the Indians, July 9–14, 1764, *JP* XI:262–312.

72. Proceedings with the Indians, July 9–14, 1764, *JP* IV:466–81.

73. Proceedings with the Indians, *JP* XI:289; Johnson to the Lords of Trade, Oct. 8, 1764, *IHC* X:331–32.

74. General Meeting with all the western Indians in their Camp, July 31, 1764, *JP* XI:309–12; Bradstreet to Gage, Aug. 4, 1764, Gage Papers; Michilimackinac, Aug. 19, 1766, The Odawas answer to the Speech made to them the day Before, MS/Rogers, Robert, 1:1 Correspondence, 1760–1771, Burton Historical Collection, Detroit Public Library; Widder, *Beyond Pontiac's Shadow*, 200–201.

75. Parmenter, "Anglo-Iroquois Covenant Chain," 631–32; Johnson to the Lords of Trade, Aug. 30, 1764, *NYCD* VII:648; Bradstreet to Gage, Aug. 4, 1764, Gage Papers; Gage to Halifax, Sept. 21, 1764, *CTG* I:57; Henry, *Travels*, 175–76; Proceedings with the Indians, July 9–Aug. 2, 1764, *JP* XI:262–312.

76. Nations at Indian Congress at Niagara, July 1764, *JP* XI:276; Johnson to the Lords of Trade, Aug. 30, 1764, *NYCD* VII:648; Bradstreet to Gage, Aug. 4, 1764, Gage Papers; Gage to Halifax, Sept. 21, 1764, *CTG* I:57; Anderson, *Crucible of War*, 620; Parmenter, "Anglo-Iroquois Covenant Chain," 631–32; Calloway, *Scratch of a Pen*, 96–98. The British hoped to raise somewhere between £60,000 and £100,000 from the Stamp Act (see P.D.G. Thomas, *British Politics and the Stamp Act Crisis: The First Phase of the American Revolution, 1763–1767* [Oxford: Clarendon Press, 1975], 69–90).

77. Gage to Bradstreet, Apr. 2, 1764, Gage Papers; Parmenter, "Anglo-Iroquois Covenant Chain," 633–34; Peter Marshall, "Imperial Policy and the Government of Detroit: Projects and Problems, 1760–1774," *Journal of Imperial and Commonwealth History* 2, no. 2 (1974): 163–64; Anderson, *Crucible of War*, 617–32; *WHC* XVIII:269n, 270–71; Bradstreet to Howard, Aug. 31, 1764, Gage Papers; Howard to Bradstreet, Oct. 15, 1764, Gage Papers.

78. Anderson, *Crucible of War*, 620, 631; Parmenter, "Anglo-Iroquois Covenant Chain," 637–38; White, *Middle Ground*, 310; Johnson to Lords of Trade, Aug. 30, 1764, *NYCD* 7:649; Board of Trade, "Plan for the Future Management of Indian Affairs," July 10, 1764, *NYCD* 7:634–41; Parmenter, "Anglo-Iroquois Covenant Chain," 634; Farrell, "Anchors of Empire," 40–41.

79. Blackbird, *History of the Ottawa*, 8.

80. Anderson, *Crucible of War*, 560–71.

81. Anderson, *Crucible of War*, 560–63; John Shy, *Toward Lexington: The Role of the British Army in the Coming of the American Revolution* (Princeton: Princeton University Press, 1965), esp. 53–62, 113–24; Michael N. McConnell, *Army and Empire: British Soldiers on the American Frontier, 1758–1775* (Lincoln: University of Nebraska Press, 2004); Calloway, *Scratch of a Pen*, 91; John L. Bullion, "'The Ten Thousand in America': More Light on the Decision on the American Army, 1762–1763," *WMQ*, 3rd ser. 43, no. 4 (Oct. 1986): 646–57.

7. REORIENTING EMPIRE

1. While the plan was never fully implemented because of further cost-saving measures at Whitehall, it did guide British thinking in the initial years of their occupation of Michilimackinac. Johnson to William Howard, Apr. 25, 1765, *JP* V:724–25; *WHC* XVIII:269n, 270–71; Parmenter, "Anglo-Iroquois Covenant Chain," 634, 653n136; Farrell, "Anchors of Empire," 40–41.

2. Marsac to John Campbell, July 29, 1765, *JP* IV:803–808; Relations of M. Marsac, July 29, 1765, Ayer MS 565; Kent, *Rendezvous*, 429.

3. For one example of British expectations, see J. Simcoe to Lord Barrington, June 1, 1755 [1758?], Add. Mss. 59236, 28ff., Dropmore Papers, BL.

4. William Johnson, "Review of the Trade and Affairs of the Indians in the Northern District of America," *NYCD* VII:957.

5. William Johnson, "Review of the Trade," *NYCD* VII:955, 957–58, 966–67.

6. Clements, ed., *Journal of Rogers*, 27–37; Relation of the Proceedings of Mons. Marsac, July 29, 1765, *JP* V:807; Brown to Gage, draft, Oct. 16, 1770, Brown to Johnson, Oct. 17, 1770, Claus to Johnson, Sept. 12, 1770, Johnson to Gage, Jan. 31, 1771, *JP* VII:942, 943, 898, 947, 1118; Account of an Indian Conference, Aug. 9–11, 1763, *JP* X:779–87; Proceedings with the Indians, July 9–14, 1764, *JP* IV:469–70, 476–77; *JP* XI:273, 274–75, 278–90, 309–13; Account of goods . . . purchased of Stephen Grosbeck by order of Robert Rogers, Feb. 1–May 23, 1767, in David Armour file on Nissowaquet, Mackinac State Historic Parks Archives; Johnson to the Lords of Trade, Oct. 8, 1764, *IHC* X:331–32.

7. Johnson, "Review of the Trade," *NYCD* VII:958.

8. Tanner, *Atlas,* Map 13; McClurken, "We Wish to Be Civilized," 54.

9. George Turnbull to Gage, May 29, 1771, *JP* VIII:117–18; Gage to Johnson, Sept. 10, 1771, *JP* VIII:251–52.

10. Tanner, *Atlas*, 32–33, 40–41, 58–59.

11. "A List of the Different Nations and Tribes of Indians in the Northern District of North America, with the number of their Fighting Men," Thwaites, ed., *Early Western Travels* I:167–69; Kent, *Rendezvous*, II:436.

12. Tanner, *Atlas*, 32–33, 40–41, 58–59, 61–62, 80, 85; MacLeod, "The Anishinabeg Point of View," 194–210; Jeanne Kay, "The Land of La Baye: The Ecological Impact of the Green Bay Fur Trade, 1634–1836" (PhD dissertation, University of Wisconsin, Madison, 1977), 157–60, 164–65, 170, 382–418; Jeanne Kay, "The Fur Trade and Native American Population Growth," *Ethnohistory* 31 (1984): 265–87.

13. Jay Gitlin, "On the Boundaries of Empire: Connecting the West to Its Imperial Past," in William Cronon, George Miles, and Jay Gitlin, eds., *Under an Open Sky: Rethinking America's Western Past* (New York: W. W. Norton, 1992), 71–89.

14. Marjorie G. Reid, "The Quebec Fur-traders and Western Policy, 1763–1774," *Canadian Historical Review* VI, no. 1 (March 1925): 17–18; Marshall, "Imperial Policy and the Government of Detroit," 171; Stephen Aron, *American Confluence: The Missouri Frontier from Borderland to Border State* (Bloomington: Indiana University Press, 2006), 39–68.

15. Reid, "Quebec Fur-traders," 21–22; Journal of Captain H. Gordon, 1766, *IHC* XI:299–301; Croghan to Benjamin Franklin, Jan. 27, 1767, *IHC* XI:502–503; Rogers to Thomas Gage, Aug. 24, 1766, Clements Library; William L. Clements, ed., *Journal of Major Robert Rogers* (Worcester, MA, 1918), 50; Marshall, "Imperial Policy," 157; Colden to the Earl of Halifax, Dec. 22, 1763, *NYCD* VII:594; Johnson, "Review of the Trade," *NYCD* VII:965; Lucy Eldersveld Murphy, *Great Lakes Creoles: A French-Indian Community on the Northern Borderlands, Prairie Du Chien, 1750–1860* (New York: Cambridge University Press, 2014), 24–39; Jay Gitlin, *The Bourgeois Frontier: French Towns, French Traders, and American Expansion* (New Haven: Yale University Press, 2010), 26–35.

16. Johnson, "Review of the Trade," *NYCD* VII:965; Gage to Shelburne, Nov. 11, 1766, Gage to Hillsborough, Aug. 17, 1768, *CTG* I:114, 185.

17. De Peyster to Carleton, June 17, 1777, *MPHC* 10:278.

18. Grignon, "Recollections," 224, 241; Mr. Parent to the Governor of Montreal, June 5, 1764, enclosed in Burton to Gage, July 13, 1764, Gage Papers; Trap, "Charles Langlade," 7:22–25; Testimony of William Bruce in September 1763, Testimony

of Roseboom, Fischer, Shields, and Bruce, July 4, 1764, *MPHC* 27:668–70; Letter from Cardin to Augustin Langlade, Aug. 16, 1767, *WHC* XVIII:287–88; Kay, "Land of La Baye," 58–59, 151–54, 161–63, 188–201, 392–98; Lucy Eldersveld Murphy, *A Gathering of Rivers: Indians, Métis, and Mining in the Western Great Lakes, 1737–1832* (Lincoln: University of Nebraska Press, 2000), 21, 30–35, 47–51; Clements, ed., *Journal of Rogers*, 17–18.

19. Johnson to the Lords of Trade, Mar. 22, 1766, *WHC* XVIII:274; Memoir to the Board of Trade, *WHC* XVIII:286–87; Reid, "Quebec Fur-traders," 30; Kay, "Land of La Baye," 153–54; Journal of Captain H. Gordon, 1766, *IHC* XI:299–301; Croghan to Benjamin Franklin, Jan. 27, 1767, *IHC* XI:502–503; Gage to Hillsborough, Nov. 10, 1770, *CTG* I:279.

20. Reid, "Quebec Fur-traders," 21–22, 27; Clements, ed., *Journal of Rogers*, 27–37; "News from Wisconsin," *WHC* XVIII:261–62; Johnson to the Earl of Hillsborough, Aug. 17, 1768, *NYCD* VIII:94.

21. Clements, ed., *Journal of Rogers*, 27–37.

22. Instructions to Capt. Howard, Aug. 31, 1764, Ayer MS 104; Howard to Bradstreet, Oct. 15, 1764, Campbell to Bradstreet, Nov. 10, 1764, Howard to Bradstreet, Jan. 6, 1765, enclosed in Bradstreet to Gage, Apr. 22, 1765, Gage Papers; William Leslye to Amherst, Sept. 16, 1762, Amherst Papers, W.O. 34/49, 116–17, microfilm copy, Reel 40 (Sept. 1760–Oct. 1763), NA.

23. Rogers to Lieut. Langlade, Oct. 15, 1766, *WHC* XVIII:278–79.

24. Kent, *Rendezvous*, II:434; Marjorie G. Jackson, "The Beginning of British Trade at Michilimackinac," *Minnesota History* II, no. 3 (Sept. 1930): 244; Johnson to the Lords of Trade, Oct. 8, 1766, *NYCD* VII:871–72; Johnson to Gage, Aug. 28, 1765, Gage to Johnon, Sept. 8, 1765, *JP* IV:833–35, V:838–40.

25. White, "Skilled Game of Exchange," 236–40; Anderson, "Flow of European Goods," 385–410.

26. Parmenter, "Anglo-Iroquois Covenant Chain," 622; White, "Skilled Game of Exchange," 236–40; Henry, *Travels*, 39–52, 183–88.

27. Clements, ed., *Journal of Rogers*, 42–43.

28. Kent, *Rendezvous*, II:434; Jackson, "Trade at Michilimackinac," 249–52; Clements, ed., *Journal of Rogers*, 42–43. On dependence, see White, *Middle Ground*, 479–85. But see also Kent, *Rendezvous*, passim, for a detailed sense of the trade goods exchange at Michilimackinac and the operation of the trade.

29. Kent, *Rendezvous*, II:410–11, 434; Jackson, "Trade at Michilimackinac," 249–52; Rogers, *Concise Account*, 250–51.

30. Johnson to Gage, Aug. 28, 1765, *JP* XI:915–17.

31. Croghan to Johnson, Nov. 1765, *IHC* XI:53–54; Gage to Hillsborough, Nov. 10, 1770, *CTG* 1:275; White, *Middle Ground*, 316–17.

32. Johnson to the Lords of Trade, Oct. 8, 1766, *NYCD* VII:871–72; John Lottridge to Johnson, Dec. 12, 1762, Johnson to Gage, Aug. 28, 1765, Gage to Johnson, Sept. 8, 1765, *JP* III:969, IV:833–35, V:838–40; *JP* XI:879–80, 902–904, 915–17, 926–27; Jackson, "Trade at Michilimackinac," 240–41. Kent, *Rendezvous*, II:408–409, maintains that the French and Métis remained central to the trade at the straits for another sixty years at least, until about 1820.

33. De Peyster to Carleton, June 6, 1777, *MPHC* 10:275–76.

34. William Leslye to Amherst, Sept. 16, 1762, Amherst Papers, W.O. 34/49, 116–17, microfilm copy, Reel 40 (Sept. 1760–Oct. 1763), NA.

35. Journal of William Howard, [Nov. 3, 1764–April 16, 1765], *JP* XI:698; Daniel Claus to Johnson, July 11, 1765, *JP* IV:789–90; Johnson to Gage, Aug. 9, 1765, *JP* IV:815; Kent, *Rendezvous*, II:434–35; Johnson to Howard, July 2, 1765, *JP* IV:781.

36. Journal of William Howard, [Nov. 3, 1764–April 16, 1765], *JP* XI:696–98.

37. Howard to Johnson, May 17, 1765, Campbell to Johnson, June 3, 1765, *JP* XI:739–40, 764–65.

38. John Porteous, "Schenectady to Michilimackinac, 1765 & 1766," *Ontario Historical Society Papers and Records* XXXIII (1939): 91; William Howard to William Johnson, June 24, 1765, *JP* XI:804–809, 816–17; Howard to Burton, Sept. 24, 1765, Howard to Eyre Massey, June 16, 1766, enclosed in Massey to Gage, July 10, 1766, Gage Papers.

39. Daniel Claus to Johnson, July 11, 1765, *JP* IV:789–90; Jackson, "Trade at Michilimackinac," 244–45, 247–49; *JP* IV:870–72, 883; Gage to Conway, June 24, 1766, *CTG* I:96–97.

40. Clements, ed., *Journal of Rogers*, 11–12, 27; Johnson to Gage, Dec. 12, 1766, *JP* XII:227–29; Susan Sleeper-Smith, *Indian Women and French Men: Rethinking Cultural Encounter in the Western Great Lakes* (Amherst: University of Massachusetts Press, 2001), 62–63.

41. Clements, ed., *Journal of Rogers*, 28, 48.

42. Clements, ed., *Journal of Rogers*, 27–37, 48; Kent, *Rendezvous*, 457–61; Charles E. Lart, ed., "Fur-trade Returns, 1767," *Canadian Historical Review* 3, no. 4 (Dec. 1922): 351–58.

43. Clements, ed., *Journal of Rogers*, 28, 48; Jackson, "Trade at Michilimackinac," 253–54, 256–57; Sleeper-Smith, *Indian Women and French Men*, 62–64; Lart, "Fur-trade Returns," 351–58; "Orders and Regulations," [1767], *JP* XII:246–47; "Regulations for the Indian Trade, Jan. 15, 1768," *JP* XII:409–13.

44. David A. Armour, *Treason? At Michilimackinac: The Proceedings of the Court Martial Trial Held at Montreal in October 1768 for the Trial of Major Robert Rogers* (Mackinac Island, MI: Mackinac State Historic Parks, 1972), passim; Gage to Shelburne, Jan. 27, 1768, Gage to Hillsborough, Aug. 17, 1768 and Sept. 9, 1769, Gage to Barrington, Mar. 12, 1768, Gage to Grey Cooper, Sept. 8, 1770, *CTG* I:161, 184, 237, II:454, 558–59.

45. Kent, *Rendezvous*, 454–55; Armour, *Treason?* 63, 76–79, 87.

46. John Christie to William Johnson, Oct. 28, 1767, *JP* V:764; Spiesmacher to Johnson, May 6, 1768, *JP* XII:491–92; Spiesmacher Journal, Dec. 6, 1767–June 17, 1768, Gage Papers, Supplementary Accounts; Gage to Guy Johnson, July 18, 1768, *JP* VI:275.

47. Spiesmacher to Johnson, May 6, 1768, *JP* XII:491–92; Spiesmacher to Gage, May 26, 1768, Gage Papers; Gage to Guy Johnson, July 18, 1768, *JP* VI:275; Lieut. John Christie to William Johnson, Oct. 28, 1767, *JP* V:764.

48. Benjamin Roberts to William Johnson, Sept. 31 [Oct. 1], 1767, *JP* V:710–17; Guy Johnson to Thomas Gage, May 20, 1768, *JP* XII:508.

49. Benjamin Roberts to William Johnson, Aug. 29, 1769, *JP* VII:146–47; Account of William Johnson, Oct. 7, 1769, *JP* VII:207–208; Kent, *Rendezvous*, II:429, 496; Benjamin Roberts to William Johnson, Sept. 31 [Oct. 1], 1767, *JP* V:710–17; Gage to Hillsborough, March 5, 1769, *CTG* I:223.

50. Gage to Hillsborough, Jan. 5, 1769, *CTG* I:209–10; B. Glasier, "Speech of La

Force, and all the Ottaway Chiefs delivered at Michimackina, Aug. 30, 1768," *JP* VI:348–49; John Vattas to Thomas Gage, May 16, 1773, *MPHC* 19:299.

51. Gage to Johnson, Mar. 23, 1766, *JP* V:95; "Journal of Peter Pond, 1740–1775," *WHC* XVIII:327–28, 329, 341; Robert Rogers, *A Concise Account of North America . . .* (Dublin: J. Potts, 1770), 250–52; Daniel Ingram, *Indians and British Outposts in Eighteenth-Century America* (Gainesville: University Press of Florida, 2012), chapter 3; Kent, *Rendezvous*, II:429, 446, 448; Henry, *Travels*, 47, 54–56; William Leslye to Amherst, Sept. 16, 1762, Amherst Papers, W.O. 34/49, pp. 116–17, microfilm copy, Reel 40 (Sept. 1760–Oct. 1763), NA.

52. De Peyster's speech at L'Arbre Croche, July 4, 1779, *WHC* XVIII:377–90; Arent Schuyler De Peyster, *Miscellanies by an Officer* (Dumfries, Scotland: C. Munro, 1813), 5–15; Tanner, *Atlas*, 62–63, 65–66; Kay, "Fur Trade," 265–87; Kay, "Land of La Baye," 166–67.

53. Clements, ed., *Journal of Rogers*, 19, 49–50; Johnson to Gage, July 25, 1765, *JP* XI:869; Croghan to Johnson, Nov. 1765, *NYCD* VII:788; Jackson, "Trade at Michilimackinac," 247–49; Gage to Halifax, Aug. 10, 1765, *CTG* I:65; *JP* V:331, 339; Johnson to the Lords of Trade, Jan. 20, 1764, *NYCD* VII:600; Johnson to the Earl of Shelburne, Dec. 3, 1767, *NYCD* VII:1002; Bouquet to Gage, Nov. 30, 1764, *MPHC* 19:284–85; Robert Rogers to Thomas Gage, Feb. 12, 1767, Clements Library; Gage to Carleton, Oct. 5, 1767, Gage Papers; Marshall, "Imperial Policy," 170–71; Guy Johnson to Thomas Gage, May 20, 1768, *JP* XII:509.

54. Carleton to Shelburne, March 2, 1768, *WHC* XVIII:288–92; Carleton to John Caldwell, Oct. 6, 1776, 270, *MPHC* 10:270.

55. Reid, "Quebec Fur-traders," 26–27; Sleeper-Smith, *Indian Women and French Men*, 62–64; Kent, *Rendezvous*, II:408–409.

56. Parmenter, "Anglo-Iroquois Covenant Chain," 639; Gitlin, "Connecting the West," 81–82; Jackson, "Trade at Michilimackinac," 258–67, 269–70; White, *Middle Ground*, 311–12.

57. Johnson, "Review of the Trade," 1767, *NYCD* VII:958–59; Carleton to Shelburne, March 2, 1768, *WHC* XVIII:288–92.

58. Johnson, "Review of the Trade," 1767, *NYCD* VII:958–59.

59. Gage to Hillsborough, Jan. 5, 1769, *CTG* I:210.

60. Anderson, *Crucible of War*, 633–37; Patrick Griffin, *American Leviathan: Empire, Nation, and Revolutionary Frontier* (New York: Hill and Wang, 2007), 92–94.

61. Marshall, "Imperial Policy," 177–78.

8. DEPENDENCE

1. For important exceptions that put Native Americans front and center of their narratives of the Revolutionary era, see especially Griffin, *American Leviathan*, Woody Holton, *Forced Founders*, and Hinderaker, *Elusive Empires*.

2. The man who originally put forward the idea of the Stamp Act in November 1764, Henry McCulloh, specifically stated that the revenue from it would "provide presents for cultivating the friendship of the Indians [and] to pay Rangers for the support and protection of the frontiers." By the time it was passed in 1765, most ministers in Parliament believed it was solely for the maintenance of the ten thousand British troops that the Ministry wanted to keep in North America (Thomas, *British Politics*, 71–72, 86–87).

3. Colin G. Calloway, *Pen and Ink Witchcraft: Treaties and Treaty Making in American Indian History* (Oxford: Oxford University Press, 2013), 49–95; Eric Hinderaker and Peter C. Mancall, *At the Edge of Empire: The Backcountry in British North America* (Baltimore: Johns Hopkins University Press, 2003), 159; Holton, *Forced Founders*, chapter 1.

4. Turnbull to Gage, May 28, 1772, *JP* VIII:501–502; Gage to Hillsborough, Jan. 5, 1769, *CTG* I:210.

5. Armour and Widder, *Crossroads*, 20; De Peyster to Gage, July 16, 1774, Gage to de Peyster, Oct. 5, 1774, Gage Papers.

6. Carleton to Shelburne, March 2, 1768, *WHC* XVIII:288–92; Trap, "Charles Langlade," 8:1–8; De Peyster, *Miscellanies*, 7.

7. De Peyster's orders to Langlade, *WHC* XVIII:355–56; De Peyster to Charles Langlade, July 4, 1776, *Miscellanies*, lxix; Armour and Widder, *Crossroads*, 52–55; Kent, *Rendezvous*, II:536–37; Carleton to De Peyster, June 25, 1776, *MPHC* 10:261.

8. Carleton to De Peyster, June 25, 1776, *WHC* XI:174; *WHC* XVIII:355n; Unknown to De Peyster, Aug. 21, 1776, *MPHC* 10:262–63; Unknown to De Peyster, Aug. 24, 1776, *MPHC* 10:264; Unknown to De Peyster, July 19, 1776, *MPHC* 10:263; Kent, *Rendezvous*, II:537; Unknown to Hamilton, July 19, 1776, *MPHC* 10:262; Grignon, "Recollections," 229; De Peyster to Carleton, June 6, 1777, *WHC* VII:406–407; De Peyster to Carleton, Feb. 1777, *MPHC* 10:271; Unknown to De Peyster, Oct. 6, 1776, *MPHC* 10:270; Carleton to Caldwell, Oct. 6, 1776, *MPHC* 10:270; Kent, *Rendezvous*, II:537; Walter Butler to Langlade, Nov. 16, 1776, *WHC* XVIII:356; James M. Hadden, *Hadden's Journal and Orderly Books: A Journal Kept in Canada and Upon Burgoyne's Campaign in 1776 and 1777, by Lieut. James M. Hadden, Roy. Art.*, edited by Horatio Rogers (Albany: Joel Munsell's Sons, 1884), 18–21.

9. Unknown to De Peyster, Oct. 6, 1776, *MPHC* 10:270; Unknown to Col. Caldwell, Oct. 6, 1776, *MPHC* 10:270; De Peyster to Carleton, April 12, 1777, *MPHC* 10:271; Lt Gov. Henry Hamilton to the Earl of Dartmouth, Aug. 29, 1776–Sept. 2, 1776, *MPHC* 10:265–69.

10. Armour and Widder, *Crossroads*, 58–59; Germain to Carleton, Mar. 26, 1777, John Burgoyne, *A State of the Expedition* (London: J. Almon, 1780), Appendix, vii–viii; Germain to Carleton, Mar. 26, 1777, *MPHC* 9:347.

11. De Peyster, *Miscellanies*, 3–4; Lt Gov. Henry Hamilton to the Earl of Dartmouth, Aug. 29, 1776–Sept. 2, 1776, *MPHC* 10:265; De Peyster to Carleton, Feb. 1777, *MPHC* 10:271; Armour and Widder, *Crossroads*, 58.

12. Carleton to Hamilton, July 19, 1776, *MPHC* 10:262; Kent, *Rendezvous*, II:537; De Peyster, *Miscellanies*, 11; Carleton to De Peyster, Oct. 6, 1776, *MPHC* 10:270.

13. Armour and Widder, *Crossroads*, 59, 61; Summary of the Indian Tribes, *WHC* XVIII:358–68; De Peyster to Carleton, Feb. 1777, *MPHC* 10:271.

14. De Peyster to Carleton, Feb. 1777, De Peyster to Carleton, Apr. 12, 1777, *MPHC* 10:271; De Peyster to Unknown, Apr. 18, 1777, "Langlade Papers," *WHC* VIII:220–21; To the officer commanding at Michilimackinac, from HQ at Quebec, May 18, 1777, *MPHC* 10:274–75.

15. De Peyster to Carleton, June 4, 1777, *WHC* VII:405; *MPHC* 10:275; Armour and Widder, *Crossroads*, 62; De Peyster to Carleton, June 6, 1777, *WHC* VII:406–407; *MPHC* 10:275–76.

16. De Peyster to Carleton, June 13, 1777, *MPHC* 10:276–77; De Peyster to Carleton, June 17, 1777, *WHC* VII:407–408.

17. Carleton to De Peyster, July 14, 1777, *WHC* XI:177; Testimony of the Earl of Harrington, 1779, in Burgoyne, *State of the Expedition*, 48–50.

18. Burgoyne, *State of the Expedition*, 7–8, 48–50; Barbara Graymont, *The Iroquois and the American Revolution* (Syracuse: Syracuse University Press, 1972), 150–56; Hadden, *Journal*, lx.

19. Burgoyne, *State of the Expedition*, 48–50.

20. Burgoyne, *State of the Expedition*, Appendix, xii–xiv, xx–xxi; De Peyster to [Burgoyne?], June 4, 1777, *WHC* VII:405; Burgoyne's Proclamation, June 20, 1777, in Hadden, *Journal*, 61–62; Burgoyne to Skene, July 15, 1777, in John Pell, ed., "Philip Skene of Skenesborough," *New York State Historical Association, Quarterly Journal* 9, no. 1 (Jan. 1928): 34.

21. Burgoyne, *State of the Expedition*, 48–50; Rupert Furneaux, *Saratoga: The Decisive Battle* (London: Allen and Unwin, 1971), 97–99; Burgoyne to Gates, Sept. 6, 1777, in Henry Steele Commager and Richard B. Morris, eds., *The Spirit of Seventy-Six: The Story of the American Revolution as Told by Participants* (New York: Harper and Row, 1967), 560–61; Thomas Anburey, *Travels through the Interior Parts of America* (London: William Lane, 1789), 369–72.

22. Burgoyne, *State of the Expedition*, 48–50; Burgoyne to Gates, Sept. 6, 1777, in Commager and Morris, eds., *Spirit of Seventy-Six*, 560–61.

23. Letter of Colonel John Peters, Dec. 9, 1779, in Thomas Jones, *History of New York during the Revolutionary War* (New York, 1879), 683–85; Burgoyne, *State of the Expedition*, 99–101; Anburey, *Travels*, 371–72.

24. Taylor, *Divided Ground*, 92–93; Ray Raphael, *A People's History of the American Revolution: How Common People Shaped the Fight for Independence* (New York: New Press, 2001), 194–201.

25. Brian Burns, "Massacre or Muster? Burgoyne's Indians and the Militia at Bennington," *Vermont History* 45, no. 3 (Summer 1977): 133–44; Burgoyne, *State of the Expedition*, 160–63; Hadden, *Journal*, 134–35, Appendix 17, 529–32; William Digby, Journal, in *The British Invasion from the North . . .* , ed. James Phinney Baxter (1887; repr., New York: Da Capo, 1970), 252–55.

26. Hadden, *Journal*, lx, Appendix 17, 529–32; Digby, Journal, 254–55; Graymont, *Iroquois*, 150–56; Anburey, *Travels*, 371–75, 425–26; Burgoyne, *State of the Expedition*, 48–40, 48–50, 56, 99–101, Appendix, xxii, xlvii–xlv; Trap, "Charles Langlade," 8:12–17; Armour and Widder, *Crossroads*, 63; Ray W. Pettengill, trans., *Letters from America, 1776–1779: Being Letters of Brunswick, Hessian, and Waldeck Officers with the British Armies During the Revolution* (Boston: Houghton Mifflin, 1924), 81–82.

27. De Peyster to the Traders, May 10, 1778, *WHC* XVIII:368–69; Gautier's Journal and De Peyster's letters, *WHC* XI:97–112.

28. De Peyster to Carleton, May 30, 1778, *MPHC* 9:365–66; Gautier's Journal, *WHC* XI:100, 105–11; De Peyster to Carleton, June 29, 1778, *MPHC* 9:366; Hamilton to Captain McKee, Apr. 23, 1778, *MPHC* 10:285; Hamilton to Carleton, Apr. 25 [prob.], 1778, *MPHC* 9:437; Haldimand to Lt Gov Hamilton, Aug. 2, 1778, *MPHC* 9:400; Council minutes held at Detroit June 14–20, 1778, *MPHC* 9:442–52; Hamilton to Lt Gov Cramahe, Aug. 12, 1778, *MPHC* 9:462.

29. De Peyster to Haldimand, July 20, 1778, July 24, 1778, De Peyster to Carleton, May 30, 1778, *MPHC* 12:311–12, 9:365–67; Askin to Sterling, Apr. 28, 1778, in Quaife, ed., *Askin Papers* 1:70–72; [Edward] Foy to Carleton, Mar. 10, 1778, *MPHC* 10:282.

30. Griffin, *American Leviathan*, 142–49; Jack M. Sosin, *The Revolutionary Frontier, 1763–1783* (New York: Holt, Rinehart and Winston, 1967), 117–18.

31. De Peyster to Haldimand, Aug. 15, 1778, *MPHC* 9:368; Hamilton to Lt Gov Cramahe, Aug. 12, 1778, *MPHC* 9:462; Kent, *Rendezvous*, 564; Clark to Mason, Nov. 19, 1779, *IHC* 8:125–29; Louis Chevalier to De Peyster, July 20, 1778, *MPHC* 10:286; De Peyster to Haldimand, Aug. 31, 1778, *MPHC* 9:369–70; Louis Chevalier to De Peyster, Sept. 15, 1778, *MPHC* 19:352–53; Sinclair to Brehm, Oct. 29, 1779, *MPHC* 9:531–32.

32. De Peyster to Haldimand, Sept. 16, 1778, Sept. 21, 1778, Oct. 7, 1778, *MPHC* 9:370, 371–74; Capt Edward Foy to De Peyster, Aug. 28, 1778, *MPHC* 19:350; *MPHC* 9:650–58; Kent, *Rendezvous*, II:564–65.

33. Dunnigan, *Picturesque Situation,* 32–40, quote on 58; Widder, *Beyond Pontiac's Shadow*, 8–9; De Peyster to Haldimand, Sept. 21, 1778, Oct. 24, 1778, *MPHC* 9:371–74, 11:121; Kent, *Rendezvous*, II:565; Louis Chevalier to De Peyster, Sept. 15, 1778, *MPHC* 19:352–53; "List of Indian Licences," *WHC* XI:99.

34. Armour and Widder, *Crossroads*, 88; Account of the Expedition of Lieut. Gov. Hamilton, *MPHC* 9:489–516.

35. De Peyster to Haldimand, Oct. 24, 1778, *WHC* XI:118–21; De Peyster to Haldimand, Oct. 27, 1778, *WHC* XI:121–22; De Peyster to Langlade and Gautier, Oct. 26, 1778, *WHC* XVIII:371–73. Lt Col. Mason Bolton to Haldimand, Nov. 13, 1778, *MPHC* 19:365–66; De Peyster to Haldimand, Jan. 29, 1779, *WHC* XI:122–23; De Peyster to Haldimand, Jan. 29, 1779, *MPHC* 9:377–78; Louis Chevalier to Haldimand, Feb. 28, 1779, *MPHC* 19:375–76.

36. De Peyster to Haldimand, Mar. 29, 1779, May 13, 1779, *MPHC* 9:378–79, 381; Trap, "Langlade," 9:1–8; Gautier, Journal, *WHC* XI:110; "Daniel-Maurice Linctot," *DCB*; George A. Brennan, "De Linctot, Guardian of the Frontier," *Journal of the Illinois State Historical Society* X, no. 3 (Oct. 1917): 323–66.

37. De Peyster to Haldimand, May 13, 1779, *MPHC* 9:381; Trap, "Charles Langlade," 9:7–9.

38. Gautier to De Peyster, Apr. 19, 1779, *WHC* XI:126–27.

39. Griffin, *American Leviathan,* 143–44.

40. John D. Barnhart, ed., *Henry Hamilton and George Rogers Clark in the American Revolution with the Unpublished Journal of Lieut. Gov. Henry Hamilton* (Crawfordsville, IN: R. E. Banta, 1951), 190.

41. De Peyster to Haldimand, May 2, 1779, *MPHC* 9:379.

42. De Peyster to Haldimand, May 13, 1779, June 1, 1779, June 14, 1779, June 27, 1779, *MPHC* 9:380–81, 382, 384–85, 388–89; Capt D. Brehm to Haldimand, May 28, 1779, *MPHC* 9:410–12; Haldimand to De Peyster, July 3, 1779, *MPHC* 9:362; Joseph Bowman to George Rogers Clark, June 3, 1779, *WHC* XVIII:373–74; De Peyster to John Campbell, May 13, 1779, *MPHC* 19:411.

43. De Peyster to Haldimand, May 13, 1779, June 1, 1779, June 14, 1779, June 27, 1779, July 21, 1779, *MPHC* 9:380–81, 382, 384–85, 388–89, 391; Armour and

Widder, *Crossroads*, 106; *WHC* XXIII:363; Alexander Mckee to Haldimand, July 16, 1779, *MPHC* 10:341–42.

44. De Peyster to John Campbell, May 13, 1779, *MPHC* 19:411; De Peyster to Haldimand, June 1, 1779, June 14, 1779, June 27, 1779, *MPHC* 9:382, 385, 388–89; Haldimand to De Peyster, May 20, 1779, June 12, 1779, July 3, 1779, *MPHC* 9:359, 360, 362; Haldimand to Mason Bolton, Apr. 18, 1779, *MPHC* 19:396; Haldimand to De Peyster, May 6, 1779, *MPHC* 19:402.

45. De Peyster to Haldimand, June 27, July 9, 1779, *MPHC* 9:388, 390; Instructions from De Peyster to Langlade, July 1, 1779, *WHC* XVIII:375–76; De Peyster to Major Nairne, July 9, 1779, *MPHC* 9:390.

46. De Peyster's speech at L'Arbre Croche, July 4, 1779, *WHC* XVIII:377–90; De Peyster, *Miscellanies*, 5–15; De Peyster to Haldimand, Aug. 9, 1779, Aug. 13, 1779, *MPHC* 9:392.

47. De Peyster to Haldimand, July 21, 1779, *MPHC* 9:391; Extract of a Council held by Mr Bennett with the Potawatomis at St. Joseph, Aug. 3, 1779, *MPHC* 10:349–50, 352–53; Thomas Bennett to De Peyster, Aug. 9, 1779, *MPHC* 9:392–93; Bennett's Report, Sept. 1, 1779, *MPHC* 9:395–96; De Peyster to Haldimand, Aug. 23, 1779, *WHC* XVIII:396–97; De Peyster to Haldimand, Sept. 4, 1779, *WHC* XVIII:397–98.

48. *WHC* XVIII:376n6; De Peyster, *Miscellanies*, 16–17.

49. De Peyster to Haldimand, Sept. 4, 1779, *WHC* XVIII:397–98; De Peyster to Haldimand, Sept. 24, 1779, *WHC* XVIII 401–402; De Peyster, *Miscellanies*, 16–17.

50. Taylor, *Divided Ground*, 98–99; Raphael, *People's History*, 202–203; Graymont, *Iroquois in the American Revolution*, 212–13.

51. Haldimand to Hamilton, Dec. 25, 1778, *MPHC* 9:405–406; De Peyster to Haldimand, June 14, 1779, Aug. 9, 1779, Aug. 13, 1779, *MPHC* 9:384, 392; De Peyster to Capt Brehm, June 20, 1779, *MPHC* 9:387; Armour and Widder, *Crossroads*, 104; Haldimand to De Peyster, May 6, 1779, *MPHC* 19:402.

52. Armour and Widder, *Crossroads*, 117–22; Instructions for Captain Patrick Sinclair, *MPHC* 9:516–23; Kent, *Rendezvous*, II:570–71; De Peyster to Haldimand, June 29, 1779, Oct. 5, 1779, *MPHC* 9:389, 398; Haldimand to De Peyster, Aug. 28, 1779, *MPHC* 9:364–65; Sinclair to Brehm, Oct. 7, 1779, Oct. 29, 1779, July 8, 1780, *MPHC* 9:523–26, 530, 579; Ingram, *Indians and British Outposts*, chapter 3.

53. Sinclair to Brehm, Feb. 15, 1780, *MPHC* 9:538–43, 545–46; Madame Langlade to a priest at Montreal, Jan. 16, 1780, *WHC* XVIII:403–404; Madame Langlade to Haldimand, May 22, 1780, *WHC* XI:150.

54. Armour and Widder, *Crossroads*, 122, 124–25; Sinclair to Brehm, Oct. 7, 1779, Oct. 29, 1779, *MPHC* 9:526, 530–32; "Remarks by Samuel Robertson on Board the Felicity, 1779," *WHC* XI:207.

55. Trap, "Charles Langlade," 9:13.

56. *MPHC* 9:546–47; Sinclair to Bolton, June 4, 1780, *MPHC* 19:529; Orders to Capt. Langlade, [1780], Ayer MS 809, 810; Sinclair to Haldimand, May 29, 1780, *MPHC* 9:548–49; Edmunds, *Potawatomis*, 109; Brehm to Sinclair, May 19, 1780, *MPHC* 9:555; Chevalier to Unknown, Mar. 13, 1780, Apr. 30, 1780, *MPHC* 10:380–81, 392–93; Ainsse to Sinclair, June 30, 1780, *MPHC* 10:406–407.

57. Sinclair to Haldimand, May 29, 1780, *MPHC* 9:548–49; Tanner, *Atlas*, 71; Ed-

munds, *Potawatomis*, 109; Armour and Widder, *Crossroads*, 149; Ainsse to Sinclair, June 30, 1780, *MPHC* 10:406–407.

58. Sinclair to Brehm, Feb. 15, 1780, *MPHC* 9:538–44; Sinclair to Haldimand, Feb. 17, 1780, May 29, 1780, *MPHC* 9:546–47, 548–49; Sinclair to Langlade, Michilimackinac, Langlade File 1780, SHSW; Armour and Widder, *Crossroads*, 140, 156; Sinclair to Bolton, June 4, 1780, *MPHC* 19:529–30; Sinclair to Haldimand, July 8, 1780, *MPHC* 9:558–60; John Francis McDermott, "The Myth of the 'Imbecile Governor': Captain Francisco De Leyba and the Defense of St. Louis," in John Francis McDermott, ed., *The Spanish in the Mississippi Valley, 1762–1804* (Urbana: University of Illinois Press, 1974), 314–91; Martin Navarro to José de Galvez, Aug. 18, 1780, *WHC* XVIII:405–408; White, *Middle Ground*, 398; Sinclair to De Peyster, July 30, 1780, *MPHC* 9:586; Martin Navarro to Francisco Cruzat Feb. 15, 1781, *WHC* XVIII:420; *MPHC* 9:578; Sinclair to Haldimand, July 8, 1780, *MPHC* 9:558–60; Kent, *Rendezvous*, II:574–76.

59. Sinclair to Haldimand, July 8, 1780, *MPHC* 9:558–60; Haldimand to Sinclair, Aug. 10, 1780, *MPHC* 9:568; Mason Bolton to Haldimand, Feb. 8, 1779, *MPHC* 19:371–72; Brehm to Sinclair, Apr. 17, 1780, *MPHC* 9:533–36; Haldimand to De Peyster, July 6, 1780, Aug. 10, 1780, *MPHC* 9:635–36, 638–39; Haldimand to Germain, Sept. 25, 1779, *MPHC* 9:362; Haldimand to De Peyster, Feb. 12, 1781, Oct. 8, 1781, Nov. 1, 1781, *MPHC* 10:377, 524, 534–35; Haldimand to Brig. Gen. Powell, June 24, 1781, *MPHC* 10:493.

60. Haldimand to De Peyster, Aug. 10, 1780, *MPHC* 9:638–39; Haldimand to Germain, Sept. 17, Sept. 25, 1781, 1780, *MPHC* 10:362, 431; De Peyster to Haldimand, June 8, 1780, *MPHC* 10:399–400; Mompesson to De Peyster, Sept. 20, 1780, *MPHC* 19:575; Sinclair to Haldimand, July 8, 1780, *MPHC* 9:561; Kent, *Rendezvous*, 578; Brehm to Sinclair, Quebec, Apr. 17, 1780, *MPHC* 9:533–36; Haldimand to Brig. Gen. Powell, June 24, 1781, *MPHC* 10:493.

61. Haldimand to De Peyster, Aug. 10, 1780, *MPHC* 9:638–39.

62. The Chiefs and principal warriors of the Mingoes, Hurons, Delawares, and Shawnee to Captain Lernoult at Detroit, Oct. 20, 1779, *MPHC* 10:364–65; De Peyster to Haldimand, Mar. 8, 1780, *MPHC* 10:378–79; De Peyster to Sinclair, Mar. 12, 1780, *MPHC* 9:580–81; De Peyster to Captain McKee, Nov. 2, 1779, *MPHC* 10:370–71; De Peyster to the Commander in Chief, Nov. 20, 1779, *MPHC* 10:372.

63. De Peyster to Haldimand, June 8, 1780, *MPHC* 10:399–400; Haldimand to Lord George Germain, Sept. 13, 1779, *MPHC* 10:359, 360.

64. Michael A. McDonnell, *The Politics of War: Race, Class, and Conflict in Revolutionary Virginia* (Chapel Hill: University of North Carolina Press, 2007), 435–77; De Peyster to Captains Thompson and McKee, Sept. 13, 1781, *MPHC* 10:512.

65. Raphael, *People's History*, 218–20; De Peyster to Captain McKee, Apr. 3, 1782, *MPHC* 10:565–66; De Peyster to Haldimand, May 13, 1782, *MPHC* 10:574; Haldimand[?] to De Peyster, May 31, 1782, *MPHC* 10:582.

66. Sinclair to Haldimand, June 25, 1782, June 28, 1782, *MPHC* 10:595, 595–96; De Peyster to McKee, July 27, 1782, Aug. 6, 1782, *MPHC* 10:600, 624; Indian Department Account, Sept. 16, 1782, *MPHC* 10:636; McKee to De Peyster, July 23, 1782, *MPHC* 20:32–33; Trap, "Charles Langlade," 9:21–22; De Peyster to Haldimand, Sept. 4, 1782, *MPHC* 10:634; De Peyster to Powell, Aug. 17, 1782,

MPHC 20:44–46; Powell to Haldimand, Aug. 17, 1782, *MPHC* 20:45–46; White, *Middle Ground*, 407.

67. Ray Raphael, *Founding Myths: Stories That Hide Our Patriotic Past*, rev. ed. (New York: New Press, 2014), chapter 14.

68. Haldimand to Thomas Townshend, Oct. 23, 1782, *MPHC* 10:663–64; Robert S. Allen, *His Majesty's Indian Allies: British Indian Policy in the Defence of Canada, 1774–1815* (Toronto: Dundurn Press, 1992), 54–56.

CONCLUSION: PERSISTENCE IN AN ERA OF REMOVAL

1. James H. Merrell, "Declarations of Independence: Indian-White Relations in the New Nation," in Jack P. Greene, ed., *The American Revolution: Its Character and Limits* (New York: New York University Press, 1987), 197–223; Frederick Hoxie, Ronald Hoffman, and Peter J. Albert, eds., *Native Americans and the Early Republic* (Charlottesville: University of Virginia Press, 1999).

2. "Nissowaquet," *DCB*; "Langlade," *DCB*; J. A. Girardin, "Life and Times of Rev. Gabriel Richard," *MPHC* 1:481–95; McClurken, "Ottawa Strategies," 29–31; Brian W. Dippie, *The Vanishing Americans: White Attitudes and U.S. Indian Policy* (Lawrence: University Press of Kansas, 1991); Witgen, *Infinity of Nations*, 216–22.

3. Taylor, *Divided Ground*, 116; Allen, *Indian Allies*, 57–86; Woody Holton, *Unruly Americans and the Origins of the Constitution* (New York: Hill and Wang, 2007), 137–44, 216–18.

4. De Peyster to Haldimand, June 14, 1779, *MPHC* 9:385; Memorial of the Merchants . . . , April 4, 1786, *MPHC* 11:483–84; Memos for John Johnson, *MPHC* 11:485–88; Indian Council, July 11, 1787, *MPHC* 11:493–96; Gautier to Unknown, Jan. 27, 1790, enclosed in Dorchester to Grenville, no. 56, Oct. 7, 1790, *MPHC* 12:20–21.

5. Colin G. Calloway, *The Victory with No Name: The Native American Defeat of the First American Army* (Oxford: Oxford University Press, 2015), 127.

6. Calloway, *Victory with No Name*, 129–64; Allen, *Indian Allies*, 71–84.

7. Calloway, *Victory with No Name*, 99, 106, 108.

8. Timothy D. Willig, *Restoring the Chain of Friendship: British Policy and the Indians of the Great Lakes, 1783–1815* (Lincoln: University of Nebraska Press, 2008), 47, 54; White, *Middle Ground*, 463; Captain LaMothe to Unknown, May 17, [1793], *MPHC* 12:261–62; Thomas Duggan to Joseph Chew, July 10, 1794, Aug. 22, 1794, *MPHC* 12:121–22; Guillaume la Mothe to Joseph Chew, July 19, 1794, *MPHC* 20:365; William Doyle to Charles Langlade, July 26, 1794, *WHC* XVIII:443–46; John Butler to Joseph Chew, June 14, 1794, Alexander McKee to R. G. England, July 5, 1794, July 10, 1794, Thomas Duggan to Joseph Chew, July 19, 1794, Simcoe to R. G. England, Aug. 12, 1794, Simcoe to Alexander McKee, Aug. 13, 1794, in E. A. Cruikshank, ed., *The Correspondence of Lieut. Governor John Graves Simcoe, with Allied Documents Relating to His Administration of the Government of Upper Canada*, 5 vols. (Toronto: Ontario Historical Society, 1923–1931), II:265, 305–306, 315, 367–68, 317, V:103; Trap, "Charles Langlade," 10:7–8.

9. Willig, *Chain of Friendship*, 14–15; Allen, *Indian Allies*, 55–56; Tanner, *Atlas*, 78; Robertson to Haldimand, Aug. 5, 1784, *MPHC* 11:442; Robertson to Matthews, Aug. 26, 1784, Sept. 7, 1784, *MPHC* 11:450, 453.

10. Leonard Brown to Alexander McKee, Aug. 18, 1796, *MPHC* 20:466; Major Bur-beck's Report of Michilimackinac, Sept. 1, 1796, MG 23, K9, Western Posts, National Archives of Canada; Brown to McKee, *WHC* XVIII:447–48; Susan E. Gray, "Writing Michigan History from a Transborder Perspective," *Michigan Historical Review* 34, no. 1 (Spring 2008): 11; Allen, *Indian Allies*, 88–91; Cleland, *Rites of Conquest*, 159–60.

11. Colin G. Calloway, *Crown and Calumet: British-Indian Relations, 1783–1815* (Norman: University of Oklahoma Press, 1987), 131; "Statement Concerning Trade," [July 1794?], *Simcoe Correspondence* II:312–13; Memorial of the Mer-chants . . . , April 4, 1786, *MPHC* 11:483–84; Memos for John Johnson, *MPHC* 11:485–88; Ferdinand Smyth Stuart, Memorial No. 3, 1783, 1794, Liverpool Papers, Add. Mss. 383/155–160b, BL; Memorial Indian Council, July 11, 1787, *MPHC* 11:493–96; Gautier to Unknown, Jan. 27, 1790, enclosed in Dorchester to Grenville, no. 56, dated Oct. 7, 1790, *MPHC* 12:20–21; James McGill to Herman Witsius Ryland, Feb. 7, 1797, *WHC* XVIII:453–56; Ernest Alexander Cruick-shank, "Robert Dickson, the Indian Trader," *WHC* XII:135.

12. Haldimand to Thomas Townshend, Oct. 22, 1782, Oct. 23, 1782, *MPHC* 10:662, 663–64; Thomas Duggan to Joseph Chew, July 9, 1797, *MPHC* 20:522; Capt. Drum-mond to Capt. Green, Sept. 9, 1797, *MPHC* 12:270–71; Allen, *Indian Allies*, 88–166; Willig, *Chain of Friendship*, 6–7; Witgen, *Infinity of Nations*, 216–22; Ferdinand Smyth Stuart, Memorial No. 3, 1783, 1794, Liverpool Papers, Add. Mss. 383/155–160b, BL.

13. Council Minutes, May 20, 1807–Aug. 3, 1807, Charles Robert to the Adjutant General, Aug. 22, 1812, both in vol. 2, box 2, Upper Canada Civil Control 1796–1816, RG 10, National Archives of Canada.

14. Allen, *Indian Allies*, 129–30; Tanner, *Atlas*, 108, 114, 117; Alan Taylor, *The Civil War of 1812: American Citizens, British Subjects, Irish Rebels, & Indian Allies* (New York: Alfred A. Knopf, 2011), 152–53, 164.

15. Taylor, *Civil War of 1812*, 435–38; Calloway, *Crown and Calumet*, 248–57; Allen, *Indian Allies*, 168–94; Karim M. Tiro, "The View from Piqua Agency: The War of 1812, the White River Delawares, and the Origins of Indian Removal," *Journal of the Early Republic* 35 (Spring 2015): 25–54.

16. Tiro, "View from Piqua Agency," 25–54; Bernard W. Sheehan, *Seeds of Extinction: Jeffersonian Philanthropy and the American Indian* (Chapel Hill: University of North Carolina Press, 1973); James A. McClurken, "Ottawa Adaptive Strategies to Removal," *Michigan Historical Review* 12 (Spring 1986): 29–55; Gray, "Writing Michigan History," 11; Cleland, *Rites of Conquest*, 198–230; Tanner, *Atlas*, 155–68.

17. "Nissowaquet," *DCB*; "Charles Langlade," *DCB*; McDonnell, "Indian and Métis Persistence," 149–71; Appointment of Augustin Hamelin Jr., Head Chief, May 3, 1835, Ayer MS 669; Blackbird, *History of the Ottawa*, 30; McClurken, "Augustin Hamlin, Jr.," 83.

18. John Akin Jr. to John Askin, Sept. 1, 1807, *WHC* 19:322–23; Anderson, "Flow of European Trade Goods," 385–410; Peter Mancall, *Deadly Medicine: Indians and Alcohol in Early America* (Ithaca, NY: Cornell University Press, 1995), 15–16, 163, 211. Nor is there much evidence that they were dependent on European trade goods, either (see White, *Middle Ground*, 479–85). Cf. Kent, *Rendezvous*, II:434–532, for details of the goods being traded at Michilimackinac, at least

60 percent of which were either fabric (including blankets), sewing items, or finished garments during both the French and British regimes (ibid., 513).

19. Kay, "Land of La Baye," 153, 155–58; Calloway, *Crown and Calumet*, 154; Ruth Craker, *First Protestant Mission in the Grand Traverse Region*, 2nd ed. (Leland, MI: Leelanau Enterprise, 1935), 7; Miller, *Ogimaag*, 14–15; Willig, *Chain of Friendship*, 98, 101–102; McClurken, *Gah-Baeh-Jhagwah-Buk,* 3; Blackbird, *History of the Ottawa*, 11–13, 33–35, 45–46.

20. Jedidiah Morse, *A Report to the Secretary of War of the United States, on Indian Affairs* . . . (New Haven, CT: S. Converse, 1822), Appendix, 23–26.

21. Tanner, *Atlas*, 130–33; H. Bedford-Jones, *L'Arbre Croche Mission: A Memorable Relation* (Santa Barbara, CA, 1917), 11–13; Craker, *First Protestant Mission*, 4–5; McClurken, "Adaptive Strategies," 29; McClurken, "We Wish to Be Civilized," 79–83.

22. Morse, *Report*, Appendix, 23–26.

23. "Petition of the Ottawas residing at Arbre Croche," Aug. 12, 1823, as printed in Edward Osgood Brown, "Two Missionary Priests at Mackinac," *Magazine of Western History* (Apr. 1890): 11:408–17; Keith R. Widder, *Battle for the Soul: Métis Children Encounter Evangelical Protestants at Mackinaw Mission, 1823–1837* (East Lansing: Michigan State University Press, 1999), 91, 92–93; McClurken, "We Wish to Be Civilized," 134–40; Blackbird, *History of the Ottawa*, 47–48, 50–54.

24. Rhoda R. Gilman, "Apprentice Trader: Henry H. Sibley and American Fur at Mackinac," in Brown et al., eds., *The Fur Trade Revisited*, 324; Susan Sleeper-Smith, "'[A]n Unpleasant Transaction on this Frontier': Challenging Female Autonomy and Authority at Michilimackinac," *Journal of the Early Republic* 25 (Fall 2005): 417–43.

25. Tanner, *Atlas*, 132; Kay, "Land of La Baye," 323–25; McClurken, "Adaptive Strategies," 49; McClurken, "We Wish to Be Civilized," 131–32; Bela Hubbard, Notebooks, Field Notes, Peninsula Coast Survey, Detroit to Chicago, May 19 to July 24, 1838 (Bentley History Library, University of Michigan, Ann Arbor, photocopy at Mackinac State Historic Parks Library, Mackinaw).

26. McClurken, "Adaptive Strategies," 32.

27. McClurken, "Adaptive Strategies," 35; McClurken, "We Wish to Be Civilized," 73–75, 185–86.

28. Andrew J. Blackbird, or Mac-ke-te-pe-nas-sy (hereditary chief of L'Arbre Croche, now Harbor Springs, Michigan), *The Indian Problem, From the Indian's Standpoint* (Ypsilanti, MI: Scharf Tag, Label & Box Co., 1900), 7; Gray, "Writing Michigan History," 12; Tanner, *Atlas*, 130, 146, 160, 163; Roger L. Nichols, *Indians in the United States and Canada: A Comparative History* (Lincoln: University of Nebraska Press, 1998), 164; Robert J. Surtees, "Land Cessions, 1763–1800," in *Aboriginal Ontario: Historical Perspectives on First Nations*, edited by Edward S. Rogers and Donald B. Smith (Toronto: Dundurn Press, 1994), 107–11; Craker, *First Protestant Mission*, 9; Bellfy, *Three Fires Unity*, 108–16.

29. McClurken, "Adaptive Strategies," 37–41; "Missions in North America," *Baptist Missionary Magazine* 19, no. 6 (June 1839): 124–25; "Letter of Mr. Slater, dated Ottawa Colony, Richland, June 10, 1839," *Baptist Missionary Magazine* 19, no. 9, (Sept. 1839): 225; Tanner, *Atlas*, 130, 166, 175; McClurken, "We Wish to Be Civilized," 205–206, 223–24, 323–29; Assikinack, "Legends and Traditions," 115.

30. McClurken, "Adaptive Strategies," 41–45.

31. McClurken, "Adapative Strategies," 31–32, 43–47; Gray, "Writing Michigan History," 12–13; Tanner, *Atlas*, 155–68.

32. McClurken, *Gah-Baeh-Jhagwah-Buk*, xi; Little Traverse Bay Bands of Odawa Indians, *Our Land and Culture*; Witgen, *Infinity of Nations*; Sturtevant, "Jealous Neighbors."

33. Susan Gray, *The Yankee West: Community Life on the Michigan Frontier* (Chapel Hill: University of North Carolina Press, 1996), 71–79, 90; Tanner, *Atlas*, 180; Edmund Jefferson Danziger, *Great Lakes Indian Accommodation and Resistance During the Early Reservation Years, 1850–1900* (Ann Arbor: University of Michigan Press, 2009); Bradley J. Gills, "The Anishnabeg and the Landscape of Assimilation in Michigan, 1854–1934" (PhD dissertation, Arizona State University, 2008); Adriana Greci Green, "Anishinaabe Gathering Rights and Market Arts: The Contributions of the WPA Indian Handicraft Project in Michigan," in Hosmer and Nesper, eds., *Tribal Worlds*, 219–51; Tanner, *Atlas*, 167–68, 180; Kathleen Marie Way Thomas, "'Their Habits Were Startling': The Perceptions, Strategies, and Erasing of a Mixed-Heritage Family in the Old Northwest" (PhD dissertation, University of Minnesota, 2005); Blackbird, *The Indian Problem*, 10; Gray, "Writing Michigan History," 2–6; Peterson, "Many Roads," 52–64; McClurken, "We Wish to Be Civilized," 196.

34. Sleeper-Smith, *Indian Women and French Men*, 8–9, 154, 157–58; Clifton et al., *Peoples of the Three Fires*, 2; McClurken, *Gah-Baeh-Jhagwah-Buk*, xiii; Matthew L. M. Fletcher, *The Eagle Returns: The Legal History of the Grand Traverse Band of Ottawa and Chippewa Indians* (East Lansing: Michigan State University Press, 2012); www.ltbbodawa-nsn.gov.

35. McClurken, *Gah-Baeh-Jhagwah-Buk*, xiii; Fletcher, *Eagle Returns*; Tanner, *Atlas*, 12, 182; Bellfy, *Three Fires Unity*, 131–50.

ACKNOWLEDGMENTS

I started this book in old South Wales, finished it in New South Wales, and researched and wrote substantial portions of it in South Africa, Canada, and the United States. I've left a sprawling trail of debts and I fear in enumerating them that I'll miss someone. If that includes you, please forgive me in advance.

For generous and vital financial assistance and support while I was researching and writing this book, I thank the University of Sydney and the Australian Research Council. Librarians and archivists across the world have also been generous in sharing their expertise and time, including Rena McGrogan, Anthony Green, and Nicholas Keyzer at the University of Sydney; Katherine A. Ludwig at the David Library of the American Revolution; and various staff at the British Library and National Archives in the UK, the Library and Archives of Canada, the John P. Robarts Library at the University of Toronto, the Wisconsin Historical Society, the Newberry Library, the Clements Library, and Mackinac State Historic Parks. Grateful thanks go also to Briony Neilson for her research assistance and her help in translating French sources, and to Ellen R. White for her work on the maps at the front of the book. Also to Shane Langlade for generously sharing his carefully reconstructed family genealogy with me. I especially thank Eric Hemenway of the Little Traverse Bay Bands of Odawa for welcoming me to Anishinaabewaki and sharing his time and knowledge of Charles

Langlade and the history and geography of Waganawkezee. His insights were invaluable.

Many colleagues and students here in Australia have enriched various parts of this work, but for their specific comments and suggestions on earlier drafts or more recent chapters, my thanks to Robert Aldrich, Alison Bashford, Leigh Boucher, Trevor Burnard, David Cahill, Michaela Cameron, Ann Curthoys, Desley Deacon, Andrew Fitzmaurice, Kirsty Flannery, Lisa Ford, Kate Fullagar, David Goodman, Chris Hilliard, Miranda Johnson, Marilyn Lake, Steph Mawson, Cindy McCreery, Mark McKenna, Donna Merwick, Dirk Moses, Alan Rome, Carolyn Strange, Blanca Tovias, Ian Tyrrell, Ben Vine, and Angela Woollacott. While they haven't had to read portions of this work, the extraordinary history students and teachers of the Sydney and NSW high schools our department has worked with over the past few years have inspired me to keep going. These include Chifley College, Granville Boys, Kogarah, Malek Fahd, Miller Technology, Trinity Catholic College, Auburn, and Sir Joseph Banks in Sydney, Coonabarabran, and Willyama in Broken Hill.

In Canada, the United States, and the UK, I've presented various drafts-in-progress over the years, and for their comments, suggestions, and valuable conversations I would like to thank in particular Fred Anderson, Heidi Bohaker, Drew Cayton, Gregory Dowd, Kathleen DuVal, R. David Edmunds, Adriana Greci Green, Dallett Hemphill, Eric Hinderaker, Ron Hoffman, Forrest Hylton, Jacob Lee, Karen Marrero, Elspeth Martini, Gary Nash, Simon Newman, Jon Parmenter, Joshua Piker, David L. Preston, Joshua L. Reid, Nancy L. Rhoden, Daniel Richter, Brett Rushforth, Susan Sleeper-Smith, Jennifer Spear, Jason Sprague, Ian K. Steele, Scott Manning Stevens, Andrew Sturtevant, Alan Taylor, Sinclair Thomson, Coll Thrush, and Peter Way. More recently, Colin G. Calloway, Keith Widder, Melissah Pawlikowski, and Woody Holton all read the entire manuscript and offered suggestions that improved the book and likely saved me from a few embarrassments. So too did my editors at FSG, starting with Thomas LeBien, who encouraged and supported the project from the outset. Subsequently Dan Gerstle, and more recently Alex Starr and Laird Gallagher, have worked closely on the manuscript. Laird in particular has been a saintly figure for his patience, but especially for his timely and astute interventions and advice.

Colin Calloway, Kate Fullagar, Woody Holton, and Keith Widder are among those who have not just shared their work and made important suggestions but have also provided much-needed encouragement and support at critical moments. They have also endured a great deal of whining. So too have Barbara Caine, Frances Clarke, Clare Corbould, Hannah Forsyth, Marjoleine Kars, Gabrielle Kemmis, Elliot McGarva, Cam Mackellar, Maggie Mackellar, Iain McCalman, Kirsten McKenzie, Sally Mason, Sarah Paul, Ray Raphael, Marcus Rediker, Penny Russell, Glenda Sluga, Richard Waterhouse, and Shane White. The late, great Rhys Isaac also cast a long shadow over this book. We initially bonded over lost brothers and revolutionary acts. He was the first to welcome my wife and me to Australia, and our daughter to the world. Even while he was dying, he insisted on reading my work and urged me onward with the infectious enthusiasm for which he will always be remembered.

Rhys and Colleen Isaac were also always ready to provide a home away from home on my travels, for which I am grateful. So, too, were Ray and Marie Raphael in San Francisco; Anne, Bill, and Leela Ehrhart in Philadelphia; Clare Corbould, Dugald Jellie and Alastair and Marcus in Melbourne; and Sue and Norm Loomer in Ripon, Wisconsin. And I am especially thankful for the room made for my writing (literally and figuratively) by my immediate and extended family, including Mel, Jim, Molly, and Paddy in London; Karen, Herb, David, and Emma in Christchurch, New Zealand; Flo, Jacoby, Darren, and Huey in Kimberley, South Africa; and Jody and Ali in Toronto. My mum, Pam, as well has been extraordinarily patient with me over the long life of this project and has always kept the door open—whether it was in Caledon, Ontario, or now just down the road here in Sydney—with hot coffee, warm meals, and free babysitting always on offer.

My daughter and son, Carys and Rohan, have been less patient, thankfully. They have always been quick to climb across the keyboard and spill milk on my books. And as they have grown they have reminded me that surfing, camping, and just playing can be as much fun as reading and writing. My wife, Frances, will steadfastly deny she has had anything at all to do with this book. But she has been with me from the start of this project and brought much-needed perspective on it, along with a great deal of joy outside of it. She's also been a rock through some very trying times for both of our families. It is impossible to imagine this book, and my life, without her.

Most recently, within the life span of our five-year-old son, we've lost Frances's dad, mum, and brother, Robbie. All three, along with Robbie's wife, Marian, and their two daughters, Roxanne and Kayla, warmly welcomed us on our many visits to Kimberley, South Africa, and went out of their way to find me a quiet and comfortable place to read and write during our extended stays. They also politely refrained from asking why the book was taking so long, and made sure there was tea and biscuits by day and brandy and Coke by night. It is difficult to measure their contribution to this work, and their influence over all our lives. This book is dedicated to them. They will always have a place in my heart.

INDEX

Page numbers in *italics* refer to illustrations.

A NOTE ABOUT THE AUTHOR

Michael A. McDonnell is an associate professor of history at the University of Sydney. He is the author of *The Politics of War: Race, Class, and Conflict in Revolutionary Virginia*, winner of the 2008 New South Wales Premier's History Award, and coeditor of *Remembering the Revolution: Memory, History, and Nation Making from Independence to the Civil War*. He lives in Sydney, Australia.